Translational Systems Sciences

Volume 35

Yuhsuke Koyama

History of the Japanese Video Game Industry

Springer

Yuhsuke Koyama
College of Systems Engineering and Science
Shibaura Institute of Technology
Saitama, Saitama, Japan

ISSN 2197-8832 ISSN 2197-8840 (electronic)
Translational Systems Sciences
ISBN 978-981-99-1341-1 ISBN 978-981-99-1342-8 (eBook)
https://doi.org/10.1007/978-981-99-1342-8

This Springer imprint is published by the registered company Springer Nature Singapore Pte Ltd.
The registered company address is: 152 Beach Road, #21-01/04 Gateway East, Singapore 189721, Singapore

Preface

This book is an English translation of Yusuke Koyama's *A History of the Japanese Digital Game Industry*. Each country has its own unique history of computer games. Among them, Japanese computer games were strongly influenced by the USA in the early days of the industry, but they escaped from its influence much earlier than in other countries. In addition, Japan differed significantly from the USA and Europe in its industrial development path and game culture, as evidenced by the fact that arcade games, which have declined in other countries, are still alive and well today, and that Japan has its own unique game genres, such as JRPG[1] and visual novels. This book outlines the history of computer games in Japan from the perspective of industrial history.

The English translation was based on the expanded and revised edition published in 2020, which differs in several respects.

- As a prehistory of the history of the Japanese game industry, Chapter 2 in the Japanese edition covers the period from the birth of computer games to the collapse of the US market (Crash of 1983, often referred to as Atari Shock[2] in Japan). However, since this information is not new and is well-known in English-speaking countries, it was deleted. Therefore, the chapters after Chap. 3 are one chapter different between the Japanese and English versions.
- Statistics within the last chapter were added up to the latest possible date. Minimal additions were made to the PS5 and Xbox Series X, which could not

[1]On the birth of JRPG, see Koyama "Evolution of a Genre: Dragon Quest and the JRPG", RACHAEL HUTCHINSON AND JÉRÉMIE PELLETIER-GAGNON (ed), Japanese Role-Playing Games Genre, Representation, and Liminality in the JRPG, Lexington Books, p19–38,22022.

[2]In Japan, when some major event occurs that has a significant impact on industry, it is often named XX shock. Past examples include the Nixon Shock, when the U.S. stopped exchanging gold for dollars in 1971; the Oil Shock, the oil crisis that accompanied the Fourth Middle East War in 1973; and the Lehman Shock, the financial crisis from 2007 to 2010.

be described because the situation was in flux at the time of the expanded and revised edition in Japan.
- The supplemental discussion in the expanded and revised edition was removed. The six topics discussed in the supplemental essay were cloud gaming, VR, disease recognition of gaming disorders, the root box issue, the development of e-sports, and the expansion of video game viewing and distribution.

We hope that you will read this article with an understanding of these differences.

Minuma, Saitama, Japan Yuhsuke Koyama

Contents

Chapter 1
History of the Game Industry

Abstract This chapter defines the history of the game industry and divides the history of the game industry in Japan into five periods. It also classifies the companies that are the players in the history of the game industry and describes their principles of action.

The chapter then outlines the characteristics of the three markets discussed in the first half of the book (PC, arcade, and home video game consoles) and the path of performance growth for each platform up to the 1990s.

Keywords History of Video Game Industry · Dawn · 2Dera · 3D era · Handheld era · Smartphone era

1.1 What Is the History of the Game Industry?

What do you think of when you hear the words "history of games[1]"? It may be the history of hit titles such as Space Invaders, Dragon Quest, and Final Fantasy, or home video game console such as the Famicom (Nintendo Entertainment System), Super Famicom (Super Nintendo Entertainment System), and PlayStation. It could be game companies such as Nintendo, Sega, Namco, and Konami. In any case, if the title "history" is used, it is important to present the events of the past in an organized manner from a clear perspective, rather than simply listing past events or talking about the past. The following are some of the ways to look at the history of games.

- The history of technology, which describes the development and changes in the technology used in games.
- The history of game design or game genres, which describes the birth and differentiation of game genres and their development within each genre.
- Social history, which describes the way games are accepted and consumed in society.

[1] Strictly speaking, the term "game" includes so-called "non-powered games" such as card games and board games, but in this book, unless otherwise specified, it refers to digital games.

Y. Koyama, *History of the Japanese Video Game Industry*, Translational Systems Sciences 35, https://doi.org/10.1007/978-981-99-1342-8_1

- Industrial history, which describes the development of industries related to games and the nature of competition.

This book deals with the history of the part of the *industrial history* of games in Japan. In other words, it focuses on the activities of various companies that aimed to make continuous profits and keep their business entities alive, how consumers responded to these activities, and what results they continued to produce. Game titles themselves and the fun of games will be discussed only when they relate to the core of the industry. Therefore, readers who like games may often find that "that title is not covered."

Of course, in order to describe the industrial history, it is not enough to simply follow the activities of the companies. The game industry itself was born from the accidental success of a game called PONG developed by Atari. Since then, the industry structure has undergone major changes triggered by blockbuster titles. The industry has also experienced changes in business styles and product (i.e., game) trends due to legal restrictions and social opposition. Like other industries, it has also been affected by the improvement of computer performance and the expansion of the Internet. The history of the game industry is not completely independent of the history of games from other perspectives. The relationship with game history from other perspectives is as follows:

1. When looking at games from the perspective of industrial history, the perspectives of technological history, management history, and social history are indispensable in addition to the perspective of game history.
2. From the perspective of business history, "coevolution among multiple markets," "establishment of intellectual property rights," "struggle for de facto standards," and "changes in the external environment" are important.
3. From the perspective of technological history, the transition and application of technological paradigms are important. These include the shift from electric to electronic, and electronic to computerized machines at the dawn of time, the shift from 2D to 3D, from CISC to RISC, and from machine language (assembler) to high-level language in the late 1990s, and the shift to online and the use of middleware in the twenty-first century.
4. The game industry has been viewed as a problem by society many times, and each time it has made efforts to recover its image. From the viewpoint of social history, the acceptance, tolerance, and establishment of games in society are very important. This includes "juvenile delinquency and the application of Act on Control and Improvement of Amusement Business," "the gambling machine problem," "the Saori Incident," "game addiction," and "the problem of excessive charges in social games."

Some of the contents listed here will be discussed in later chapters, but "coevolution among multiple markets" needs to be explained in this chapter as a viewpoint for looking at the entire history of the game industry. There are many studies on the game industry that focus only on the home video game industry. However, Space Invaders, which established the game industry in Japan, was an arcade game, and

RPGs (role playing games), a hot-selling genre of home console games, were originally created as games for PCs. In the early days, the home game market was a market for arcade games or PC games that were ported and sold to make another profit with the same title.

As time progressed, the home video game market became more independent and unique, but the situation where experimental titles were first released in arcades and PCs, and home video game consoles were influenced by them, continued for a long time. The mutual influence and coevolution among the three markets continued until the late 1990s, when online games and mobile phone games emerged as new markets with the spread of the Internet. Since then, the relationship between the five markets has been one of mutual influence.

1.2 Historical Classification of the Game Industry: Overview of Industry History

As is common in any industry, when an industry is launched, it is not known what the target will be, and all sorts of companies (or individuals) flock to it because they see a business opportunity. Eventually, the standard form of the industry (business model) begins to form. If we call the period until the standard form of an industry is established the dawn period, then each market has its own dawn period.

For arcades, Taito's Space Invaders appeared in 1978 (Chap. 2); for PCs, the "8-bit trinities" (NEC's PC-8801, Fujitsu's FM-7, and Sharp's X1), which enjoyed a large share of the domestic market, came out in 1982 (Chap. 3); and for home video game consoles, Nintendo's Family Computer was released in 1983 (Chap. 4).

As for online games, Pre-Internet online communication gradually spread from the latter half of the 1980s, but it did not connect well with the game business and did not take root as a business. In the end, online games could not escape the dawn of the Pre-Internet online communication era and finally took root in the Internet era (Chap. 10). As for mobile phone games, the dawn of mobile phone games started in 1999 when NTT DoCoMo launched its i-mode service and continued until 2003 when applications could be launched directly on the mobile phone OS and QVGA (320×200 pixels) or higher resolution became the standard for mobile phone LCDs (Chap. 14).

As an indication of the structure of this book, Fig. 1.1 shows the time period classification of the game industry. Each period is named after the market (platform) that had a central position at that time. The first period, the arcade era, lasted until 1983, when three markets were established. The other two markets appeared at the end of the twentieth century and in the twenty-first century. The following terms are used to symbolize each era: 2D era, 3D era, handheld era and smartphone era.

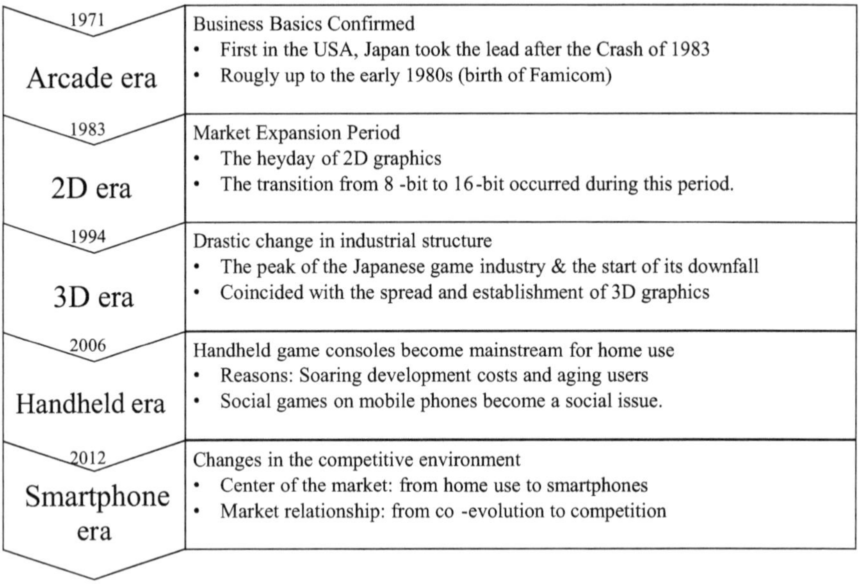

Fig. 1.1 Period classification of the game industry

As in the USA, Japan's game industry started with arcade games, but the arcade game market weakened due to issues of youth protection and gambling regulations, and the center of the market shifted to home video game consoles. After that, the industry structure remained relatively stable until the major changes in the mid-1990s. In the middle of the 2D era, the mainstream computer architecture shifted from 8- to 16-bit, but the basic structure of the business remained unchanged. In the first half of the 1990s, the next generation of technology, 3D graphics (three-dimensional graphics), gradually began to be adopted in various markets.[2] Although it is difficult to clearly define the time period, this book defines the 2D era as the period up to 1994, when PlayStation was released (Chaps 2–7).

In the mid-1990s, the game industry underwent major changes in both technology and business environment, and home video game consoles became the center of the industry more than ever. In this book, the period from 1994 onward is named the 3D era (3D graphics era) because of the way game screens are created. During this period, not only was game development made more sophisticated by the spread of 3D graphics, but also the business model of games was greatly changed by the spread of disk media (CD-ROM, DVD-ROM) (Chap. 8). This period also coincided with the spread of Internet access and the launch of the online game market. With the

[2] As for arcade games, the first 3D graphics game board appeared at the Amusement Machine Show (AM Show) in 1992. As for home video game machines, 3DO (1993 in the USA, 1994 in Japan) was released by Matsushita Electric (Panasonic) before PlayStation (1994). For PCs, it is difficult to determine the timing, but a rough estimate is around 1995, when Windows95 was introduced and DirectX technology was installed.

release of PlayStation 3 in 2006, development costs for both hardware and software soared, and the business model came to a standstill. At the same time, the average age of users increased due to the declining birthrate and aging population in Japan, and the majority of users were working adults. As a result, the "long hours in the living room" play style of home game consoles no longer fit the lifestyle of the users. The Nintendo DS and PSP, released in 2004, saved the struggling game industry. In this book, we define the period up to 2006 as the 3D era. 2006 was also the year when PlayStation 3 was released and also the year when software sales for handheld game consoles exceeded those for stationary game consoles (Chaps. 9–12).

Next was the handheld era. The handheld era was short, only a few years, when Nintendo DS and PSP were leading the market. In 2011, the Nintendo 3DS and PlayStation Vita were released, however, the shift to smartphones was just around the corner. In the following year, 2012, Puzzle & Dragons, released for smartphones, drastically changed the game market (Chaps. 13 and 14).

The period from 2012 to the present is the smartphone era. The most significant feature of this period is that the intermarket competition became severe; for PCs, Steam, an online sales platform, became widespread and completely competed with home game consoles. As for handheld devices, smartphones have overwhelmed handheld game consoles (Chap. 15).

In addition, there are different generations of home video game consoles depending on the era in which they were released and their technical level. In Japan, because home video games were a form of entertainment imported from overseas, generations of video game consoles prior to the 1983 Family Computer were released in a mixed manner (see Chap. 5). In the USA, on the other hand, there is a clear distinction. Table 1.1 shows the author's additions to the time classification and characteristics in the Encyclopedia of Video Games (2012). Each generation of game consoles was influenced by computer technology, communication technology, and the business environment.

The eighth generation PlayStation 4 and Xbox One have been released with upward compatibility for 4 K (3820 × 2160) screen output; the PlayStation 4 Pro and Xbox One S were released in 2016, and the Xbox One X in 2017. For the sake of convenience, we refer to these as 8.5th generation. Nintendo Switch released in 2017 is a type of game console that can be played both as home and handheld console, while the Switch Lite, a specialized handheld game console, was released in 2019. It is difficult to decide where to classify this as well, but for the time being, it is placed in the ninth generation. The eighth and subsequent generations are still in flux.

Table 1.1 Generation classification of home game consoles

Epocs		Generation	Main model	Characteristic
Dawn	Quite different between Japan and USA	1st 1972–1977	Magnavox Odyssey (1972) Home PONG (1975)	Hardware implementation of game with logic circuit
		2nd 1976–1984	Fairchild Channel F (1976) Atari Video Computer System (1977)	Software–Hardware separation CPU + ROM
2D era	8-bit era	3rd 1983–1995	Family Computer (1983) SG-1000(1983), MarkIII (1985)	Hardware Scrolling Sprite function
	16-bit era	4th 1987–1999	PC-Engine (1987) Megadrive (1988) Super Famicom (1990)	16 bit CPU Increase the number of simultaneous colors
3D era and after		5th 1993–2002	Saturn (1994) PlayStation (1994) Nintendo 64 (1996)	Multiple defeated console CD-ROM 3D Graphics
		6th 1998–2004	Dreamcast (1998) PlayStation 2 (2000) GameCube (2001) Xbox (2002)	Internet connection DVD playback
		7th 2005–	Xbox 360 (2005) PlayStation 3 (2006) Wii (2006)	Download sales Home server Motion controller HD screen
		8th 2012–	WiiU (2012) PlayStation 4 (2014) Xbox One (2014)	GPU computing Support for streaming game play
		8.5th 2016–	PlayStation4 Pro (2016) Xbox Ons S (2016) Xbox One X (2017)	4 K compatible
		9th 2017–	Nintendo Switch (2017) PlayStation 5 (2020) Xbox Series X/S (2020)	Ray tracing

Table 1.2 Characteristics of the market (around the late 1980s)

	Arcade (Sega System16)	Home console (Family computer)	PC (PC-9801VM)
Graphic Solution	320 × 224	256 × 240	640 × 400
Graphic Device	Dedicated CRT	TV	Dedicated CRT
Colors	4096 colors	25 in 52 colors	16 in 4096 colors
Sprite Function	Up to 128 objects in a screen Can be scaled	Up to 64 objects in a screen and 8 objects in a line	No Sprite Function
Well-played Game genre	Genre satisfied with short playtime such as action or mahjong	Compromise between arcade and PC, but close to arcade	Genre playing for a long time such as simulation, adventure, and role playing
Play Time	Extremely short (3 min per play)	Compromise between arcade and PC	Long time Using a recording device (floppy disk)
Sales Form	Coin Operation (100 yen per play)	Package Sales (About 5000 yen)	Package Sales (Up to 10,000 yen)
Platform innovation speed	Very fast	Significant innovation once in a few years	Stagnation for game technology

1.3 Markets in the 2D Era

1.3.1 Characteristics of the Three Markets

The overall characteristics of the game industry in the 2D era are described below. Table 1.2[3] summarizes the characteristics of the three markets in the latter half of the 1980s, when the differences between them were clear.

In the 1980s, computer performance was still low. It was impossible to provide a computer at a realistic price that satisfied the requirements of both the PCs, whose primary role was to perform office work and scientific and technical calculations, and the arcade board, whose most important function was to draw beautiful screens for games at high speed. Therefore, each was specialized hardware for its own use. This hardware characteristic determined the characteristics of the games produced.

The arcade game is characterized by a short playing time (3 min per play as a rough guide for the first play) due to the requirement of the business model to have players pay 100 yen for each play. Therefore, in terms of game design (product characteristics), it is necessary to be able to obtain strong satisfaction in a very short

[3]For arcades, we assume Sega's System 16 (released in 1985), a standard board using Motorola's MC68000 CPU, which was the mainstream at the time. For home console, we assume Nintendo's Family Computer (1983), and for PCs, we assume the PC-9801VM (1985), which became the de facto standard after the 8-bit trinities.

time. This principle has remained unchanged up to now. For this reason, games that require reflexes, such as action (ACT), shooting (STG), and fighting games (FTG), have developed. These genres are of the type that requires players to concentrate for a short period of time to defeat enemies or clear stages.[4]

To meet these requirements, it was important for the computer to be able to (1) draw the screen at high speed and (2) move many characters at the same time. If the screen resolution was too high, the amount of data to be processed at once would increase, so the resolution was about the same as that of analog TV monitors at the time. Instead, the barometer of performance was the number of simultaneous colors on the screen, which was important for drawing characters, and the number of sprites[5] that could be displayed on the screen at the same time. The computing performance was not so important.

PCs, on the other hand, are used for office work such as word processing, programming, and scientific and technical calculations.[6] For this reason, computing performance was important, but high-speed drawing and the number of simultaneous colors on the screen were not so important for normal use. What was important in the PC was the screen resolution, which was necessary to increase the number of characters that could be displayed on the screen. High-resolution display was achieved by using a special monitor with a higher resolution than a TV monitor. Another feature of the PC was that it was equipped with a floppy disk drive as standard to record daily work.[7]

PC games and the game market are characterized by the following three points:

1. High-resolution screen, although high-speed rendering is not possible.
2. Data can be recorded.
3. High cost and high user age.

These characteristics have led to the development of games for enthusiasts and adults, such as games that allow players to play for a long time while recording the progress of the game, games that display many characters on the screen during the game, games that allow players to appreciate high-resolution still images, and games that take advantage of high-speed computing functions and where the opponent's

[4]Later, table games such as mahjong were added to the game center for businessmen who came to take a break or to adjust their time, but the game design was the same as before: if the player did not win in the first round, the game was over.

[5]In those days, game consoles used to display small characters superimposed on the background screen that covered the entire screen. The function to do this is called the sprite function.

[6]The PCs discussed here are the image of the 8-bit trinities and NEC's PC-9801 (VM and later), which later became the mainstream of PC games. We exclude inexpensive PCs designed for games, such as MSX, and machines that focus on AV functions rather than corporate office processing, such as the X68000 (Sharp) and FM TOWNS (Fujitsu), which appeared at the end of the 2D era.

[7]At the beginning of the popularization of PCs, floppy disk drives were very expensive and were treated as peripherals, but because of their convenience, they came to be built into PCs. Instead of a floppy disk drive, an analog cassette tape is used to store data. Games for PCs were sold with the game program data recorded on cassette tapes until the early 2D era.

thinking routine is important. The game genres include role playing (RPG), adventure (ADV), and simulation (SLG). Games were sold as packages containing floppy disks (or cassette tapes) containing game data, and were quite expensive, ranging from about 8000 yen to 10,000 yen per game, reflecting the age and income of the purchaser.

In the case of home consoles, the launch titles (titles released at the same time as the console) were ports of titles that had become hits in the arcades several years earlier. Home video game consoles are equipped with sprite functions and are similar to the hardware of arcade game machines of 2–3 years ago, which were made cheaper by thoroughly cutting costs through mass production effects. As a result, it was superior to the PC in terms of rendering performance, but inferior in terms of screen resolution, computing power, and memory capacity. In the beginning, most of the games released were of the genres found in arcade games, such as action games, but RPGs and ADV were also released in response to user demand. Games were supplied in the form of ROM cartridges,[8] which were characterized by (1) ease of handling even by children, (2) high data transfer speed, and (3) inability to be easily copied. As home video game consoles were positioned as "toys for children," and the price per game was less than 4000 yen in the 1980s. However, in the 1990s, the production cost of games increased due to the increase in the size of games and the sharp rise in the price of semiconductors at that time, and some games began to be sold for more than 10,000 yen per game.[9]

1.3.2 *Characteristics of Each Market by Platform Performance*

Figure 1.2 shows the performance image of a computer in the 2D period. The horizontal axis shows the computing power and the scale of data that can be handled simultaneously, and the vertical axis shows the drawing performance. An arcade is a machine that specializes in drawing performance and does not have high computing power. On the other hand, the PC specializes in computing power. Since home video

---

[8]In many cases, other control signals also flow through the terminal for the ROM cartridge. Therefore, it is possible to connect peripheral devices through the cartridge terminal, as in the case of the Family Computer disk system. In addition, there were many cases where a dedicated chip was inserted into the game ROM cartridge to expand its functions, such as Konami's integration of a sound chip (SCC) into the ROM cartridge of the Family Computer. Since the design allows for additional hardware to be installed depending on the game, it cannot be said that the strict separation of software/hardware has been achieved for home game consoles that supplied games in the form of ROM cartridges during the 2D era.

[9]As the amount of game data increases, it is necessary to install a larger capacity ROM (or install multiple low-capacity ROMs). Since high-capacity ROMs are expensive, the manufacturing cost will increase. On the other hand, in the case of disk media, such as floppy disks and CD-ROMs, the cost of a single piece of media is quite low, so the increase in the data size of games has little impact on the manufacturing cost.

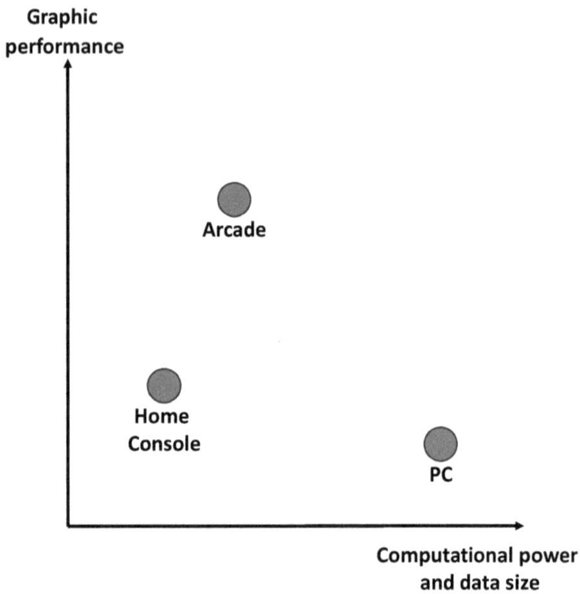

Fig. 1.2 Performance of game consoles in 2D era

game machines are following the performance of arcades for several years, they are the lowest in computing power but exceed PCs in drawing power.

Figure 1.3 shows the increase in performance of game machines during the 2D era. Since arcades do not require consumers to purchase a game machine, it is easy to introduce the most advanced technology in hardware, and they functioned as a testing ground for new technology. Therefore, boards equipped with new technology were actively released. In the case of Sega, which is engaged in both arcade and home video game business, 5 types of home video game consoles[10] and 16 types of system boards[11] were released between 1983 and 1998. Therefore, it is shown as a straight line in the graph.

The performance of home game consoles increases in a 5–7 year cycle, which is the replacement of hardware, because consumers cannot be required to replace their game machines frequently. The range of performance increase at that time is relatively large, but the performance is lower than that of arcades. In Fig. 1.3, performance was increased at three points in time: Family Computer (1983), Super

[10]The five types of hardware are SG-1000 (1983), Sega Mark III (1985), Mega Drive (1988), Sega Saturn (1994), and Dreamcast (1998). Note that hardware with minor changes such as SG-1000 II (1984, a cheaper version of SG-1000) and Master System (1987, Mark III with FM sound unit) are not counted.

[11]These are SYSTEM I (1983), SYSTEM II (1985), SYSTEM E (1986), SYSTEM 16 (1986), X-Bord (1987), SYSTEM 24 (1988), Y-Bord (1988), SYSTEM 18 (1989), C-Bord (1990), SYSTEM 32 (1991), SYSTEM MULTI 32 (1992), MODEL 1 (1992), MODEL 2 (1994), ST-V (1994), MODEL 3 (1996), and NAOMI (1998).

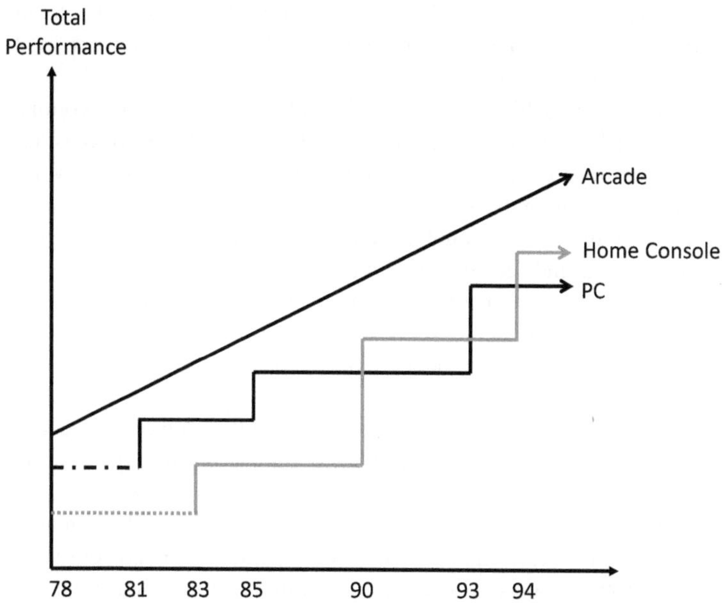

Fig. 1.3 Path of performance increase in 2D era

Famicom (1990), and PlayStation (1994), which had the highest number of sales in each generation.

As for PCs, the performance required for games was fixed with the PC-9801VM, which was released in 1985. The reason why the performance did not increase for 8 years is that (1) PCs are basically for business use and compatibility with old hardware was emphasized even when new hardware was released to run business software, (2) the increase in graphics performance for games was not emphasized in the increase in PC performance, and (3) the penetration rate of PCs in general households was low and compatibility with old machines was necessary to increase the number of games sold.

1.4 Behavioral Principles of Market Participants

Companies from various fields are entering the game industry. Therefore, there are significant differences in the motivations and behavioral principles of each company. Each company is aware of its surrounding environment and makes decisions to increase its chances of winning and survival in the competition as much as possible within its limited resources. The history of industry is an accumulation of such decisions. These decisions reflect the corporate culture or identity core of each company, and the "main principles" and "principles of action" when making decisions.

Before entering the main part of this book, I would like to describe the image that the author had of the behavioral principles of the leading players in the game industry when writing this book.

Specifically, I would like to describe the behavioral principles common to the four companies (Sega, Nintendo, Sony, and Microsoft) that have developed more than three generations of home video game consoles in the past, as well as to PC game companies, online game companies, and social game companies, and also the behavioral principles of individual developers, called "indies " or "doujin," who develop games on an individual or group basis.

This is a kind of intuition of the author, and it is not something that can be demonstrated in an academic sense. Therefore, I hesitate to include it in the first chapter, but I hope it will help readers understand the complex history of the game industry.

In the case of Sega, it was "arcades" that were at the core of their actions. Sega, which has many hit arcade games, has created game consoles with a strong awareness of arcade game portability in order to utilize its overwhelming assets in the home game market. Both the Mega Drive (Genesis) and Saturn had an arcade game board as a performance reference during development. Having arcades at the core of the Mega Drive was a success. However, the failure of the Saturn was that it was designed with the porting of arcade 2D games in mind, even though it could produce some of the world's best 3D games at the time. Although the Dreamcast did not have a base arcade board, it was designed to be highly compatible with arcade games, as evidenced by the long-lasting success of the Dreamcast-compatible NAOMI board. As the hardware evolution accompanied by the shift to 3D games shifted the focus of the game industry from arcade games to PCs and home consoles, Sega was forced to exit the hardware business.

In the case of Nintendo, the core of its activities has always been toys. To put it simply, Nintendo's game consoles and games have innovative interfaces that are fun to touch, and the content is safe for children. They are truly toys. Nintendo has been very particular about the user interface of its game consoles. In the Family Computer (NES), they adopted the cross buttons that were popular in the Game & Watch, and in the Super Famicom (SNES), they created a novel controller with four buttons on the right-hand side plus L and R buttons on the top of the controller. The Nintendo 64 adopted an analog stick for intuitive operation of the "depth" of 3D games, and the Wii adopted a TV remote control-type controller for intuitive and sensory operation. Portable game consoles also adopted touch panels for the DS and naked-eye stereoscopic vision for the 3DS. Although it failed to become popular, the Virtual Boy is a forerunner of today's VR (Virtual Reality). On the other hand, as is typical of the Mario series, Nintendo emphasizes the importance of game content that can be enjoyed by the whole family and that parents can buy for their children with peace of mind.

In the case of Sony, the core of its activities is audio-visual (AV). As symbolized by the fact that the company Sony established when it entered the game industry chose the name Sony "Computer" Entertainment instead of Sony "Game" Entertainment, Sony has a strong awareness of the need for a new type of entertainment that integrates computers and video. It is recognized that games are one of the ways to achieve this. The PlayStation 2 and PlayStation 3 were the pacesetters for the spread of DVD and Blu-Ray, respectively, and the PSP was called "the Walkman of the twenty-first century" in early advertisements, clearly demonstrating the company's commitment to AV. The launch of PlayStation VR, a peripheral device for PlayStation 4, is also easy to understand in this context.

In the case of Microsoft, the core of its actions is the "operating system (Windows)," and it is easy to understand the principle of Microsoft's actions when one considers that it is acting with the intention of making its OS the standard in all areas, not only PCs but also embedded devices, game consoles, music players, and mobile phones. From the perspective of Japanese people who are insensitive to the rigors of global-level business of ICT companies, Microsoft's actions seem somewhat imperialistic and paranoid. However, as the main role of computers has shifted from PCs to smartphones, Microsoft has been overtaken in terms of market capitalization by Apple, which even helped the company during its past financial crisis. Considering this, Microsoft's actions were not excessive. Since Sony had also dreamed of becoming a home server in every home with the PlayStation 3 and using that as a foothold to expand into consumer electronics and beyond, Microsoft's move into games was partly a defensive move.

The core of the behavior shared by PC game companies, online game companies, and social game companies is that the game business is a means to an end. A typical example of this is Enix's entry into the PC game business from the housing information magazine business. Many of the companies in this category did not start a game company or become a game company because they wanted to make games but entered the game business because they could make a profit and survive as a company. Some companies, such as Enix, Koei, and Nihon Falcom, became established in the game industry, but when the game business became difficult, other companies withdrew from the game field to avoid bankruptcy and started other businesses to survive. This is evident in the companies participating in Project EGG, a service to reprint old PC games through emulation.[12] In addition, online games that plagiarize pictures, 3D models, and sometimes even game designs from other games are created on a regular basis. In this way, there are some companies that behave in a morally problematic manner, considering games as a means to make money in a short period of time.

On the other hand, the core of the behavior of those who develop games individually or in groups of several people can be described as "game development as an end," if we use the phrase as a counterpart to the "means" mentioned earlier. Individual developers are not a homogeneous group. They range from those who develop games as a complete hobby to those who dream of making a fortune as entrepreneurs. Among those who develop games as a hobby, there are those who release their games as freeware for free, and those who distribute their games at Comiket for a very small fee. The former group (freeware) is from the so-called

[12]https://www.amusement-center.com/project/egg/

"hacker" culture, and their principles of action are different from those of the latter (Comiket) "doujin" culture, but they produce similar results in terms of supplying games at very low prices. The same is true for the birth of what is called independent (indie) companies to develop games as an ongoing business from among both groups. Among the companies that became successful from indies and became small or medium-sized companies, game development became a means to an end as mentioned earlier. However, in the case of companies that survive at the level of studios with only a few members, they stick to game development until the end and often go bankrupt or dissolve when they fail.

1.5 Summary

In this chapter, after defining what the history of the game industry is, I described the classification of the game industry into periods. The game industry is characterized by the coevolution of multiple markets with mutual influence, and after describing the overall characteristics up to the 2D era for home consoles, I described the characteristics of the behavioral principles of players on the supplier side.

In this era, arcades led the innovation in terms of performance, and PCs had a strong presence in RPGs, ADVs, and SLGs, which are game genres for adults and enthusiasts. Home video game consoles occupied a position somewhere in between. The development of each market will be gradually unraveled in later chapters.

Chapter 2
Arcade Games (1): From Elemecha to Video Games

The Birth of Space Invaders and the Establishment of the Arcade Game Industry

Abstract This chapter outlines the arcade game market from the post-World War II period to the early 1980s. During this period, arcade games have shifted from elemechanical to computer games in terms of installed machines. Computer games have also undergone a transition from undifferentiated hardware and software, in which game programs are implemented directly on the base as logic circuits, to the same format as today, in which the CPU executes programs stored in memory. In the early years of their appearance, computer games, including PONG, were not as expressive as the elemechanical machines. Space Invaders overturned this situation, followed by Galaxian and Pac-Man. This was achieved only after the hardware and software were separated, and the programs were loaded in memory and executed by the CPU, the same system used in today's computers.

Keywords Elemecha · PONG · TTL · F1(namco) · Space Invaders · CPU · Two transitions

As in other industrial fields, Japan's game industry began by learning from overseas, and then followed a development path of developing and producing its own similar products (import substitution) and then producing its own original products. This was the same in the pre-computer era of entertainment machines and in the era of computer games.

2.1 The Dawn of Japan's Entertainment Machine Industry: The Prehistory of Arcade Game Companies[1]

An entertainment machine that produces motion when a coin is inserted is now called an elemecha. Elemec has have existed since the beginning of the twentieth century, and the most famous example is the stationary automatic wooden horse, in

[1]This section draws heavily on Nakafuji (1997) and Akagi (2005).

Y. Koyama, *History of the Japanese Video Game Industry*, Translational Systems Sciences 35, https://doi.org/10.1007/978-981-99-1342-8_2

Photo 2.1 Sega Enterprises jukebox (made in 1970). The photo on the right shows only the fee-paying part. Photo: Koyama (at a bar in Shinjuku, 2005)

which a saddle carrying a person moves up and down when a coin is inserted, invented by a Japanese, Yoshikazu Endo. Endo established Nihon Gorakuki[2] (Japan Amusement Machine) Co., Ltd. and was involved in the operation of various department store rooftop amusement parks in addition to the manufacture and sale of amusement machines. Among them, Sports Land, which was established in 1931 on the roof of Matsuya Asakusa Department Store, was equipped with not only amusement facilities but also many game machines and rides. This was the forerunner of game arcades in Japan. However, with the start of World War II, the manufacture of entertainment machines was banned, and the once existing trend was over.

The entertainment machine industry after World War II started from the outflow of goods from PXs of the Occupation Forces. PX (Post eXchange) usually means a store in a US military base, but in Japan after World War II, a few large commercial facilities were confiscated as stores of the Occupation Forces, and they were also called PXs. Game machines, such as pinball machines and slot machines, and jukeboxes were sold there, and the postwar entertainment machine industry in Japan started with the sale of these machines (Photo 2.1).

In the postwar period, Service Games (1952), Rosen Enterprises (1954),[3] and Taito Trading (1953) (Later Taito), which were established in the 1950s, were

[2] The company name was later changed to Nichigo, and it continues to operate a rooftop amusement park.

[3] Service Games was dissolved and its business was taken over by Nihon Amusements Bussan (sales division) and Nihon Kikai Seisakusho (manufacturing division) in 1960, and Nihon Amusements Bussan merged with Nihon Kikai Seisakusho in 1964. Nippon Entertainment Bussan merged with Rosen Enterprises to form Sega Enterprises in 1965.

among the pioneers of the entertainment machine industry. These companies not only sold machines paid for by the Occupation Forces, but also maintained the machines in the stores where they were installed. Eventually, the machines supplied by the Occupation Forces ran out, and under the economic conditions of the time, it was difficult to import entertainment machines from the USA. Therefore, the companies started manufacturing their own machines. The main customers were department store rooftops, movie theaters, amusement parks, etc. In the 1960s, bowling alleys, which boomed during the period of rapid economic growth, were added to the list.

In addition to the construction of amusement machine corners in large facilities, single-location facilities, in which wooden horses, jukeboxes, and amusement machines are installed in restaurants and retail stores, also came to be used. The first single-location facility in Japan was opened by Taito Trading in front of Kintetsu Ueroku Station in 1960. This was 18 years before the birth of Space Invaders and 12 years before PONG. The games installed were pinball, shooting games, driving games, and other elemechas.

At the same time, Nakamura Manufacturing (later Namco) and Kansai Seiki Manufacturing were established in 1955. Both companies started their business by manufacturing amusement machines for amusement parks and playgrounds, the same as the three companies mentioned above. Kansai Seiki has produced several hit products under the brand name Casco. Among them, Mini-Drive (1959), a type of electromechanical machine in which the player drives a car along a driving course drawn on a belt-like cloth, was a big hit. However, in the 1980s, when computer games became mainstream, they could not keep up with the changing times and were left behind.

2.2 The Importation of PONG and the Emergence of Computer Games

When PONG was released in the USA in 1972, several Japanese companies imported samples of the console. Tomohiro Nishikado, a developer at Taito (renamed Taito Trading in 1972), was amazed at the technical capabilities of PONG, but the response from the sales team selling the machine was not so positive. At that time, elemechas were very heavy because they were crammed with mechanical parts and relay circuits used to calculate the number of points. The weight of the device was proof of its elaborate gimmickry. PONG, on the other hand, contained only a TTL board in which the application logic was expressed as a circuit of transistors. This lightness was disliked. PONG realizes the game program in hardware by combining TTL. Therefore, although it is an “electronic” game using semiconductors, it is not a "computer" game in the current sense of the word, where the program is loaded into the CPU.[4]

Finally, Taito released and shipped the game in 1973 under the name Elepon without any license from Atari.[5] It is estimated that nearly 100,000 units of PONG and its similar products were made worldwide, but all of them were dead copies or close to dead copies except for Midway's Winner which was licensed by Atari. During this period, the concept of intellectual property rights was not yet conscious in the industry.

After that, several computer games were released, but the next real hit was "Block Kuzushi" in 1977. Block Kuzushi is not the official title of the game, but a generic name given to a copy of Breakout released by Atari in April 1976.

At that time, the Nakamura Manufacturing had a Japanese agency contract with Atari, and Breakout was shipped in May, the month following the US launch. The market response was muted at that time. However, over the next 2 years, the popularity of the product gradually increased, and in 1977, the Scratch of Universal and the TT Block of Taito were sold. Later, by the end of 1978, companies such as Hoei Sangyo, Data East, Nihon Bussan(Nichibutsu), Leijac (later Konami), IPM (later Irem), Jatre, Shin Nihon Kikaku (later SNK), Nintendo, Sun Electronics, and Sigma released Block Kuzushi games. As a matter of fact, Block Kuzushi (Breakout imitations) laid the groundwork for the arcade game industry in Japan. However, these Block Kuzushi games did not differ in base, although they added a few variations from the original. These companies did not have the resources to create new and innovative games.

Nakamura Manufacturing, which sold the original version of Atari, asked Atari to take countermeasures, but Atari did not have the capacity to do so and there was nothing they could do. In the meantime, Taito developed a table-type chassis that could be installed in a coffee shop, Block Kuzushi further expanded the market for the arcade game machine.

When pong and Block Kuzushi were sold, this was a time when both electronic and computer games coexisted. The processing and expressive power of the computer was not yet very high, and the expressive power was higher in the case of the elemecha, which combined various devices. For example, in 1976, electronic components were used for peripheral parts such as the score display and effect sound in

[4]The Intel i4040, a 4-bit microprocessor, was released in November 1971. Although CPUs already existed at the time of the development of Pong, TTL was used in PONG to reduce the cost, and the appearance of games using CPUs can be traced back to Midway's development of the 8080 board equipped with Intel's 8-bit processor i8080. In November 1975, Gunfight, a computer game based on WesternGun (September 1975) developed by Mr. Nishikado using TTL, was released. There is a time lag of about 3 years from PONG.

[5]According to Mr. Nishikado's lecture at the Digital Game Research Association of Japan, "The PONG board had been lying under my desk for almost half a year, but when Sega started the PONG location first and it was well received, we (Taito) started it in a hurry." Eventually, both Sega's Pontron and Taito's Elepon were presented at the 12th Amusement Machine Show (AM Show) in September 1973. Other computer games were also exhibited, and the 12th AM Show was the first time that computer games other than elemecha were exhibited in Japan.

F1 released by Nakamura Manufacturing.[6] The new technology, called computer games, was not superior from the start and took over elemecha's position.

2.3 First Intellectual Property Infringement Issue: Namco F1

The game industry has been plagued by copying problems up to the present, but copying problems also occur in the analog era of elemecha. The F1 was a big hit, and Atari received permission from the Nakamura Manufacturing to launch it the month after the Japanese launch, and it became an international hit.

Soon after its launch, at the end of 1976, Ushio Sangyo made an unannounced copy of the machine as Z-Machine, and it became a controversial product when Taito, who had been unable to purchase the popular machine F1, purchased Z-machine for their directly operated game centers. F1 is a type of magic lantern machine that projects a racing course onto a screen. Z-machine copied these parts as they were. However, only the custom-made electric bulbs with right-angle bent frames[7] could be copied, and it was not possible to project the F1 course of the original (Photos 2.2 and 2.3).

In June 1977, Namco (renamed from Nakamura Manufacturing in 1977) filed a provisional injunction against Ushio Sangyo to prohibit the manufacture and sale of Z-machine, and the Tokyo District Court approved it in August. Taito, which stocked the copiers, reached a settlement with Namco in October 1977, and both jointly announced that they had reached an agreement to eliminate discontinued copiers from the industry. This was the first case in which a dispute over the copying of arcade game machines was resolved.

---

[6] In a lecture at the Japan Digital Gaming Association Conference, Shigeichi Ishimura, who later became the president of Bandai Namco Games Inc. said as follows:

"Electronic circuits are not used to control the game machine from the time you deposit money to the time you play, and then to the time the game is sold. This was achieved by a relay, which is a mechanical mechanism. The core of the game in F1 was also in such a form. Therefore, as Mr. Nishikado just mentioned, the running sound was made by an electronic circuit. The scoring part was also made by an electronic circuit. It was a very hybrid or unbalanced era."

[7] Toru Iwatani, who was working at Nakamura Manufacturing at the time, stated in a lecture at the Japan Digital Game Association Conference as follows: "The reason why we used this special bulb is that the player's view of the screen in the table is wider in the foreground and narrower in the distance, creating a sense of urgency. In short, the idea is to make it look as if the driver's point of view is lowered. However, since they could not use a custom-made lump for the copied product, it comes right in the middle of the glass, so the image seen from the front is as if it were viewed with a camera at a very high position. This means that in order to make the game more compelling, the driver's eyes have to be lowered. That's what led to the current racing game."

Photo 2.2 F1. http://www.arcade-museum.com/game_detail.php?game_id=7743

Photo 2.3 The custom-made bulb used in F1. The filament is bent (Taken from Iwatani's lecture materials)

2.4 Space Invaders and Its Social Impact

If the Breakout copier shot the industrial base of the game machine development side, it was Taito's Space Invaders (1978) that started the industrial base of the game center side. In the history of the Japanese game industry, the importance of Space invaders lies not only in its historical sales, but also in the fact that it was the first game developed in Japan based on the use of CPU. It was developed by Tomohiro Nishikado using 8080 board of Midway with which Taito had technical exchanges.

At that time, the necessary tools for game development did not exist, so the development process started with the creation of the development tools, which took about 10 months, including the 6 months required for the creation of the development tools. In terms of game design, the Space Invaders were influenced by Breakout, which they greatly expanded upon. Specifically, the game design is such that in Breakout, the area that was a square block becomes an enemy with a concrete shape and moves to the bottom of the screen while shooting bullets. In terms of computer performance, the processing performance of the 8080 board was not very high, and there was no room for performance in Japan's first CPU game, the Spaces Invaders. The background was all black, and there was no room to draw stars with dots as a direction, so the screen output was all white, and the color cellophane was placed on the screen for shipment. The drawing was done in a bitmap format, where all the changing areas, including a player's battleship, enemies, and bullets, were redrawn each time. It did not have a line buffer to change only the character parts. As the number of enemies decreased, the enemy invader's lateral movement speed increased, but this was possible because there was more room in the hardware due to the reduction in the number of replacement parts.

The Space Invaders became an unprecedented boom in history. Launched in July 1978, the Spaces Invaders was extremely popular from the very beginning. The price of the first monochrome version of the table cabinet was 460,000 yen (580,000 yen for the color version released later), but in a single day, it generated 20,000–30,000 yen. In less than a month, game center can make their investment money back, and the rest will be all cash income. It was impossible for Taito alone to fulfill the orders that kept coming in. Therefore, the company decided to break with the current industry practice of licensing game production only to foreign companies and to license production to other domestic game companies at the end of 1978.

The number of units shipped in July 1979, when the Space Invaders' boom reached its peak, was 200,000. In addition to the 100,000 units shipped from Taito, 100,000 units which contained licensed production by domestic companies that had agreed to produce and imported on consignment to Midway. It is said, however, that there were far more than 200,000 units, at least 300,000 units, and as many as 500,000 units of the product on the market. The difference is that all of them were illegal copies.

There was a great deal of opposition to the game in the field of education.

The school teachers' association of Sapporo pointed out that (1) most of the students who are enthusiastic about the games stop by the amusement facilities on their way out of school, (2) money lending and borrowing among friends occurs, and (3) recently there has been a tendency to put money on scores. They decided to prohibit all junior and senior high school students from entering the game center. Similar decisions have been made in other prefectures.

In response to this social outcry, the Japan Amusement Park Association issued the "Invader Type Game Machine Operation Restraint Statement" on June 2, 1979. The contents are as follows: (1) Do not set up games in an unsupervised area,

(2) Children under 15 years of age must be accompanied by a parent or guardian, (3) Children under 18 years of age are not allowed to enter after 11:00 p.m., and (4) no prizes should be given away based on the results of the game. The reason for the fourth was that offering drink tickets or prizes based on game scores was a violation of Item 7 of the Act on Control and Improvement of Amusement Business which was mainly for pachinko.

Following these self-regulations, the National Police Agency conducted a nationwide survey in July. As these were reported in the press, the image of Space Invaders worsened, and the number of customers in the game centers declined drastically. The end of the invader game boom is described in the white paper on police in 1980 as follows:

> Invader games became popular among young people around October 1978, and quickly created a boom throughout Japan. However, some young people who did not have money to pay for the game but wanted to play it, used coins tied with strings to play the game for free and collected them after they were thrown in, used the ignition part of electronic lighters for electric shocks that malfunctioned, and stole for money to play the game.
>
> Therefore, in July, the police conducted a nationwide survey of the situation and requested related industries to impose voluntary regulations. By the end of the year, most of the game machines, which numbered about 300,000 at their peak, had disappeared from the streets as if they had never existed.

As a result of the Space Invaders, Taito ranked 53rd among Japanese corporations in terms of income reported to the corporate sector (and seventh among non-listed corporations) in 1979, but the following year it dropped off the rankings. It was truly a 1-year boom.

2.5 Establishment of Intellectual Property Rights

Unlike elemechas, computer games can be copied by assembling electronic components to create a base system board and then mounting ROMs with coded game data on them. Since it is easy to copy without any knowledge of mechanical parts, the problem of copying games has become more serious. However, since the computer game was a very brand-new thing that had never existed before, it took a long time for the creator's rights to be established.

Atari, a pioneer in the field, had not taken adequate measures to address the piracy problem. However, in Japan, with the big hit of the Space Invaders, measures against copying became serious. First, between 1979 and 1980, a series of injunction proceedings and applications for provisional disposition were filed by major companies such as Taito, Namco, and Sega to stop the manufacture and sale of copiers and licensed products manufactured more than the contracted number, based on the Copyright Act and the Unfair Competition Prevention Act.

In 1982, a series of copy lawsuits were filed against Spaces Invaders.

In the first case (September 1982), the court ruled that "it is well known to society that the game of Space Invaders is a product of Taito, and the fact that the copier makes the same representation as the display function of the Space Invaders (i.e., the function of transforming the image of the game and its display) violates the Unfair Competition Prevention Act." However, this decision did not mention the violation of copyright. In the second decision (December 1982), the copyright was recognized as a computer program, but it was not recognized that the game itself was a work of authorship.

The first decision to protect a game as a visual or auditory work was issued in 1984.

This was a case involving an unlicenced copy of Namco's Pac-Man (1981), in which Namco sued a coffee shop that set up an unlicenced copy of the game for violating its right to show the game as a work of art.

In the decision, it was recognized that the Pac-Man had a copyrightness and that it was a work that produces visual and auditory effects similar to the effects of a movie. The defendant was ordered to pay damages for infringement of the right of reproduction of the work of art by the commercial use of the uncut copy product. Thus, even if the programs were different, infringement of copyright was recognized as long as the visual and auditory effects (effects on the eyes) were the same.

The lawsuits continued and the number of illegally copied products decreased from the arcade games in Japan.[8]

2.6 Post-Space Invaders: Galaxian and Beyond

After the big boom of the Space Invaders, it was Namco that delivered the game that was required by the game centers that were looking for a hit. Namco also started basic research to develop a computer game using a CPU at the same time as Taito, but the first computer game, Gee Bee, was not released until October 1978, after the launch of the Space Invaders. It was followed by "Bomb Bee" (July 1979), but it was overshadowed by the boom of Space Invaders. Amid all this, Galaxian (November 1979) was created with the explicit goal of creating a game that could surpass the Space Invaders.

The Z80[9] was used as CPU, and it was equipped with the[10] sprite function as a dedicated circuit to quickly replace characters in the screen. In addition, a

[8]When a big hit is released, the copy boards start to appear again. Later, during boom of the fighting game, there was a large amount of copy boards for Street Fighter II, Capcon, 1991, which was called Street Fighter II Rainbow by gamers.

[9]Later, this CPU became the standard of the 8-bit era gaming CPU, which was used for both arcade and home console.

[10]The sprite function is an extension of the technology called line-puffer, which Atari introduced in the Night Driver (1976). In Night Driver, to represent the speed of a car, the two ends of the road are expressed as squares that resemble streetlights in the dark. In order to quickly move this rectangle to the left or right for drawing, the horizontal coordinates of the place to be drawn are recorded in a memory with a horn, and the line buffer is interrupted in accordance with the timing of the running

background image display circuit was also specially designed and installed to display the flowing stars to create an atmosphere of space. With the sprite function, it was possible for multiple enemies to fly in a curvilinear arc and attack the ship, whereas in Space Invaders, enemy characters could only advance sideways in a line (descending one step when they reached the edge of the screen).

The Galaxian surpassed the level of the Space Invaders subspecies and reached a completely new level of expression. Namco also hit its sequel, Galaga (1981). This series of hits established the shooting[11]genre as one of the most popular arcades.

Following Galaxian, Namco produced hit products such as Pac-Man[12] and Rally X (both in 1980), which came to occupy a major position in the game center at that time.

In addition to Namco, there were many other products such as Sega's Monaco GP (1979), Nichibutsu's Moon Cresta (1980) and Crazy Climber (1980), Scramble (1981) of Konami Industry (Rejak), Denki Onkyo's Heiankyo Alien (1979), and Alpha Electronics' Jumputer (1981), and many other titles were released, and even in the age of post-Space Invaders, the game center was established as a form of entertainment.

2.7 Summary: Two Technological Shifts

In this chapter, I have described the Japanese arcade game industry from its prehistory to the post-industrial era. In the 35-year period from the end of World War II to around 1980, the entertainment industry at that time and the current arcade game industry experienced two major technological shifts. These are the following two:

1. Transfer from elemecha to computer.
2. Separation of the hardware and software of the game machine: From the TTL substrate that was implemented in hardware with the game program as the logic circuit, to the system that reads data from the ROM that recorded the game program and executes it on the CPU.

---

line to be drawn on the screen by the plane tube. The sprite function is a mechanism that extends the line-puffer to two dimensions so that the game-character image can be displayed at a desired location on the screen instead of in a horizontal row.

[11] It was not until the scrolling screen type of shooting games (where the background moves), rather than the fixed screen type such as Galaxian and Galaga, hit the scene that shooting was fully established as a genre. Specifically, after Xevious (Namco, 1983), a large hit of the vertical scrolling type, and Gradius (Konami, 1985), a large hit of the horizontal scrolling type. A shooting game requires a lot of processing to move many objects quickly at the same time, and it was the best way for game companies to show their technological capabilities.

[12] Pac-Man has had several sequels, but Ms. Pac-Man (1982) has not been shipped in Japan.

The first migration was not intermittent, but was gradual with large overlapping parts. In the middle stage of the migration, the older technology, elemecha, had much higher expressive power and entertainment value than computer games. Therefore, the final migration proceeded along with the second migration, the separation of hardware and software. With the method of representing the game program in a hard form on the TTL board, not only was trial and error difficult during game development, but it was also impossible to implement a more complex program in hardware. It was only when hardware and software were separated, and the expression and performance of the game were handled software-based, that games such as Space Invaders, Galaxian, and Pac-Man were created, and computer games were able to surpass the expressive power of elemecha.

The fact that the two migrations were completed in the 1980s can be seen from the specialization of the game developers employed at that time. The developer of the Space Invaders, Nishikado, was an elemecha designer and also developed the famous elemecha, Skyfighter (Taito 1973). Shigeichi Ishimura (later president of Bandai Namco Games, Inc.), who was a main member to develop Galaxian, was involved in the development of electronic components for the F1, and was also involved in the development of the CPU-equipped motherboard for Galaxian. In Nishikado's case, he was involved in electronics and computers, while in Ishimura's case, he was involved in computer hardware and software, and although the areas covered were different, it was a time when skills in multiple fields were necessary.

It was not until the 1980s that computer system developers were clearly separated into those in charge of hardware design and those in charge of software (game design and programming) at the time of hiring.

Chapter 3
PC Game (1): Establishing the 8-Bit Trinities

Abstract This chapter describes the birth of PC games in Japan and the probability of the market. Only a few years after Apple in the USA, the personal computer wave that began in Japan spawned many PC enthusiasts and a myriad of software companies. Three models with a good balance of price and performance survived in the crowded market, creating a unique game culture that differed from that of the USA and arcades.

Keywords 8-bit trinities · PC-8801 · PC-9801 · FM-7 · X1 · MSX

3.1 Birth of the Personal Computer

In the late 1970s to early 1980s, computers for individual hobbyists were called micoms.[1] The TK-80, released by NEC on August 3, 1970, is called the originator of the Japanese microcomputer. However, the TK-80 was sold as a study kit (the TK in the model number means a training kit) to master the 8080 compatible CPU manufactured by NEC and was not a computer made for individual use. The product was a semi-completed product that consisted of a motherboard with a semiconductor, a decimal keypad for direct input of mechine language programs, a LED for displaying results, and an I/O port.

The MB-6880(nickname: Basic Master) from Hitachi was released in 1978, and the PC-8001 from NEC and the MZ-80K from Sharp were released in 1979 as complete PCs with the main unit stored in a case and connected to a keypad. Table 3.1 shows the specifications of the first 8-bit PCs. The CPU is not much different from the next generation of PCs and game-dedicated machines, but the graphics function was weak. The CPU is not much different from the next generation of PCs and game-oriented machines, but the graphics function was weak. It was

[1] At that time, the mainstream of computers were mainframes, which required a large floor space, and minicomputers, which were about the size of today's supermarkets. In comparison, the microcomputers for hobbiests were much smaller and were called micom(s) for short.

Y. Koyama, *History of the Japanese Video Game Industry*, Translational Systems Sciences 35, https://doi.org/10.1007/978-981-99-1342-8_3

Table 3.1 Specifications of the first generation 8-bit PCs

Company	Hitachi	NEC	Sharp
Year	1978	1979	1979
Product Name	MB-6880	PC-8001	MZ-80K
CPU	HD46800 (1 MHz) (6800 compatible)	μPC780C (4 MHz) (Z80 compatible)	LH0080(2 MHz) (Z80 compatible)
ROM/ RAM	8 KB/4 KB	24 KB/16 KB	4 KB/20 KB
Graphics	64*48 monochrome	160*100 8 colors	80*50 Semi-graphics (Simplified graphics with special characters for graphics)
Form	Keyboard integrated	Keyboard integrated	All-in-one (Built-in 10-inch CRT)
Price	188,000 yen	168,000 yen	198,000 yen
Notes			Released as a semi-kit

Source: Compiled by Koyama from "History of Computers in Japan" by the Information Processing Society of Japan and materials from each company

extremely unsuitable for gaming, and its position was taken over by newly released machines in the 1980s.

3.2 The Early Days of the PC Game Industry

3.2.1 Shops and Magazines

In the late 1970s and 1980s, at the dawn of the widespread use of personal computers, simple programming environments in BASIC language were provided, but the number of people who were able to create and use their own programs was quite small among those who purchased personal computers.

For these people, it is natural that there will be a business that sells the completed programs. In the radio shops and wireless communication equipment shops[2] that were selling PCs at the time, programs developed by the store workers or brought in by customers hanging out in the stores were sold in the form of recorded data on a cassette tape. This is exemplified by companies such as Tsukumo Electric and Fuji Audio, both of which have stores in Akihabara. The games were sold in stores, but

[2]In the days before computers, many young people and adults who were interested in science and crafts were into electronic engineering and amateur radio. They were also interested in PCs, and stores that sold wireless naturally began to sell PCs.

they also sold them by placing a mail order advertisement in the computer magazines that the users read and sending the payment by registered mail.

Many of these PC games were sold at the level of "made in one night by a shopkeeper who knows a lot about PCs or a young man who hangs out in a store," and most of them were simple at best, or cheap and lacking in depth at worst.[3] Because of the lack of game-oriented performance (especially graphics performance), there was a clear difference when compared to arcade games such as Space Invaders (Taito), which had been released a year earlier in 1978. Even so, when there were no other options, the games sold well.[4] As the 1980s progressed, the graphics capabilities of PCs improved, and the game content became more sophisticated. As the game programs sold became more sophisticated, the production and sales of programs in shops were naturally eliminated. One of the companies that survived by focusing on software development was Hudson, a wireless communication equipment store in Sapporo.

Another source of game software in the early days was personal computer magazines. *I/O* (Kohgaku-sha, October 1976-present), *Gekkan maikon (Monthly MyCom)* (Dempa Publications, October 1977–April 1995), and other PC magazines published at the time contained lists of programs, some of which were games. PC users played with the programs published in the magazines by typing them in with their own hands. However, the published programs were long, and it was necessary to enter decimal machine language program printed over several pages. Therefore, there was a demand for cassette tapes with the programs already recorded, and these became available for sale.[5]

In the 1980s, the first issue of *Maikon BASIC Magazine (Mycom BASIC Magazine)* (Dempa Publications, July 1982–May 2003—known as *Bê-Maga*) was published, which publishes short (up to two-pages) programs in BASIC language submitted by readers. The magazine received submissions from a wide range of people, from junior high and high school students to adults, and was appreciated by junior high and high school students who could not afford to buy game software frequently and served as a model for live programming. In addition, the magazine was very popular because it included programs for minor computers for which no game software was available on the market. Some of the people who submitted excellent works were scouted by the editorial department and were in charge of transferring arcade games for sale at the Dempa Publications. In the early days of the game industry, many developers were scouted from magazines.

[3] Some enthusiasts play the old games, calling them "retro games," but even then, they are played only after the launch of Family Computer for home console or arcade games after Space Invaders, and PC games from this period are rarely played.

[4] Hudson, who was a radio store in Hokkaido at that time, put an advertisement in *Gekkan maikon (Monthly MyCom)* and started receiving 300,000 to 400,000 yen a day from all over Japan by registered mail. (Aida & Otsubo, 1997, p237)

[5] These tapes were duplicated in a music studio. In some cases, the number of copies in hit game titles was greater than the number of music tapes of hit singers at the time.

3.2.2 The Birth of Software Companies

As the spread of PCs has progressed, companies from other fields have joined the development and sales of games or have started new businesses. Although there are many companies that have already withdrawn from the game industry, the following section describes those companies that are still in the game industry.

KOEI was founded in 1978 as a sales company of dyes and industrial chemicals unrelated to games, but it also started out as a rental record store. In 1980, Yoichi Erikawa, the founder of the company and famous for his designer name Kō Shibusawa, purchased a PC, which led to the start of PC sales and business software business. In 1981, at the dawn of the company, KOEI released Kawanakajima no Kassen (The Battle of Kawanakajima) for the PC-8001, indicating its orientation toward historical simulations from that time. KOEI established its position with the hit Nobunaga no Yabou (Nobunaga's Ambition) in 1983, selling many types of machines, from hobby PCs for home use such as the PC-8801 and the FM-7 to business PCs such as the FM-16β and the IBM-JX,[6] and later to Family Computer. In 1985, he released Aoki ookami to Shiroki Mejika (The Blue Wolf and the White Stag) and Sangokushi(The Romance of the Three Kingdoms) to establish his position as a leading historical simulator.

SystemSoft (the game division was taken over by Nippon Ichi Software in January 2020) was established in 1979. Initially, the company sold games as well as utility software for PCs. The Lode Runner (1983), a transfer from Apple II, became a big hit. In 1986, the company launched Gendai Dai-Senryaku (Modern Grand Strategy) and in 1989, Tenka Touitsu (Unification of the Whole Country), which were both successful in establishing its position in the simulation game market.

When Enix was founded in 1975 by its founder Yasuhiro Fukushima, it was a completely different business and had a different name. Fukuyama turned his attention to the booming PC market and changed the business model to PC cams in 1982, at which time the company name was changed to Enix. What differentiated Enix from other PC game companies was that it did not develop games on its own but focused on the business of finding and selling excellent games as a publisher. In September 1982, Enix held the first Game Hobby program contest. Although similar attempts had been made by other companies such as PC shops and PC magazines, the prize money for the contest was as high as 1 million yen for the winner and 3 million yen in total, and many excellent programs were submitted. In the end, a total of 13 titles were commercialized by adding the best program award Morita's Battle Field (Kazuo Morita[7]), the good program award Door Door (Koichi

---

[6]Because the target age of the games released by KOEI was older, KOEI actively transferred games to PCs that were used by office workers and home business owners to manage their business affairs.

[7]He is a game programmer who specializes in thoughtful routines, and his representative work is Morita Shogi. He died in 2012.

Nakamura[8]), the best program award Marichan Kiki Ippatsu (Marichan's Clutch) (Tadashi Makimura[9]), and other prize-winning works.[10]

Nihon Falcom was established in 1981 as a PC introduction advisor company. From the very beginning, the company was involved in game development, releasing games in various fields, and experimenting in the market. After the hit Dragon Slayer in 1984, Nihon Falcom established its position in action RPG. In 1985, Xanadu shipped a total of 400,000 copies. In 1987 and the following year, with the release of Ys and Ys2, the company made a bold shift from a focus on solving difficult riddles to a focus on storytelling,[11] which had a significant impact on subsequent games, making it one of the top game companies of the time.

Square was founded in 1983 as the software development division of an electrical engineering company owned by founder Masashi Miyamoto's father. Masashi Miyamoto set up a salon in Hiyoshi, Yokohama, with the latest PCs of the time, and gathered students there. One of the students who came was Hisashi Suzuki, who had started working as an assistant at a record rental store run by KOEI, and was now helping with the PC gaming business. Square developed adventure games such as Will: Death Trap II (1985) and Alpha (1986), as well as the RPG Cruse Chaser Blasty (1986), for which the character design and animation were handled by Sunrise. The company placed emphasis on graphics from the time it was established, as evidenced by the fact that part of the screen was animated. Square was established relatively late, and after its first entry into the Family Computer market, THEXDAR (a port of a PC game released by Game Arts in 1985), it quickly migrated to home

[8]Nakamura was a bit of a celebrity among the younger generation of PC enthusiasts, having contributed to various magazines even before the Enix program was commissioned. He was a high school student when he participated in the contest and founded Chunsoft (now Spike Chunsoft) in 1984 after entering the Junior College of The University of Electro-Communications. In the early days of the company, he was closely associated with Enix and developed the first five Dragon Quest, a national RPG. His representative works are Kamaitachi no Yoru (Banshee's Last Cry) and Furai no Shiren (Shiren The Wanderer) series.

[9]He later became active as a manga and illusionist as a pen name Doronpa. Other works developed as a game designer including *Eldorado Denki* (1985, Enix), and *Gundhara* (1987, Enix).

[10]Among the prize-winning works is Yuji Horii's Lovematch Tennis. After the trilogy of adventurer games, Portpia Renzoku Satsujinjiken (Portpia Serial Murder Case), Okhotsk ni Kiyu (Disappear in Okhotsk), and Karuizawa Yukai-Annai (Karuizawa Kidnapper), Yuji Horii designed Dragon Quest, which has now become a national RPG. He is also a game designer who has created hits in a variety of fields, such as the hit board game Itadaki Street (Fortune Street).

[11]In terms of volume, compared to today's games, the games of the early 1980s are less voluminous. In an adventure game, it takes less than an hour to figure out the solution. For this reason, many games were designed to extend the playing time by forcing the player to solve extremely difficult riddles without any tips, or by setting up many traps in which the player has to play again from the beginning. A classic example of Nihon Falcom's game is Romancia (1986), which is full of unreasonable mysteries. Ys did not have extremely difficult riddles and could be completed in about 8 h by a casual player who was not too bad at action games. Although the cost per playtime was relatively higher for a game at that time, it was a big hit due to its high quality, and it was ported to many types of machines, including home game machines.

consoles. As a result, the company was only in the PC game market for a short period of time, which is a little different from other PC game companies.

3.3 Convergence of the PC Market

In the 1980s, various companies entered the business of manufacturing and selling personal computers. At that time, the PC was a very new product that had not yet established a market, and not only companies that manufactured large computers, but also companies from various fields such as home appliances, toys, and start-up companies participated in the industry. The details of the history of the Japanese PCs at that time are not relevant to the main topic of the history of the game industry, so they will be omitted. However, from the viewpoint of the history of the game industry, it is important to note that in the early 1980s, when products from various companies had run their course, the PCs sold could be grouped into three main categories.

The first is an 8-bit hobby PC. These include NEC's PC-6001[12] and PC-8801, Fujitsu's FM-7, and Sharp's MZ-2000 and X1. This is a group of PCs that individuals purchase for their own taste and entertainment. PCs other than the PC-6001 are assumed to be connected to a dedicated monitor. The screen resolution is relatively high, and computer graphics can be enjoyed, but they do not have the sprite function that is standard in game consoles.

The second is the personal computer for gaming. These include the Takara's game Pacocom which was the OEM of SORD M5, the SC-3000 from Sega, and the MSX[13] PC from various companies. Although the price of a hobby PC was lower than that of a 16-bit PC, a full set of a PC (main unit + display + data recorder) cost several times the starting salary of a new employee.[14] On the other hand, game PCs

---

[12]The PC-6001 was designed to be connected to a TV via a RCA connector, and the resolution was low accordingly, so it was positioned as an introductory PC. In addition to the PC-6001, other models such as the MZ-700 of Sharp are also applicable. They fell out of the mainstream at a relatively early stage because of its inadequate performance as both a hobby PC for enjoying programming and graphics and as a PC for gaming.

[13]MSX was a technology standard proposed by Microsoft Corporation of the USA and ASCII Corporation of Japan in 1983 and was sold not only in Japan but also by various companies around the world. In the first generation of the standard, which was later called MSX1 for distinction, compatible PCs were sold by many companies in Japan. However, at the time of the establishment of the standard, the performance was not very high, as it was not intended for use with floppy disks, and it did not spread widely.

[14]The NEC PC-8801 was released in 1981. In 1981, the per capita GDP in Japan was 2.25 million yen, and the average starting salary was 120,800 yen for a college graduate. On the other hand, the original price of the PC-8801 was 228,000 yen, which was about 1.9 times the starting salary. In addition, a display was necessary for actual use, but displays were expensive at the time. A monochrome display was about 60,000 yen, and a color display was about 200,000 yen, which was not much different from the price of the PC-8801 itself. The data recorder, which stores data on an anaglyphic cassette tape, costs about 10,000 yen, so the total purchase price is about 400,000 yen, more than three times the starting salary.

were made available as monitors for home TVs, and the price was lowered to less than 100,000 yen to make them more appealing to general households. Since games are the most common application in many households, a splicing function that allows fast re-drawing of a large number of characters on the screen is standard. Games are mainly offered in ROM cartridge format, which does not require waiting time for loading and is easy for children to handle. For this reason, a slot for ROM cartridges is provided in the main body of the PC.[15] In terms of performance, the CPU is a Z80, the graphics are equivalent to the resolution of a TV screen plus a sprite function, and the music is mostly PSG sound sources with three sounds that can be played simultaneously. Compared to a dedicated display, a TV has a lower screen resolution and fewer characters can be displayed on the screen. It was not suitable for advanced programming and business operations. For these reasons, PCs connected to televisions were naturally positioned as entry-level PCs or gaming PCs[16] and were sold at a much lower price than full-fledged PCs.

The third is the 16-bit personal computer. These include NEC's PC-9801 and Fujitsu's FM-16β. At that time, there were computers called Off-Coms that were designed to be used in offices, but 16-bit PCs had slightly lower performance than the cheapest Off-Coms and were therefore cheaper. Many 16-bit computers were used for business purposes in companies and universities. Since 16-bit PCs were mainly used for administrative work and scientific and technological calculations, their graphics were highly detailed for drawing graphs, but they were weak in quick screen switching and multi-color display, and only beep sound was used for music.[17] In the early days, 16-bit PCs were extremely expensive despite their insufficient graphics performance for gaming, so there were few individual hobbyists. In the late 1980s, when the graphics were enhanced and the price decreased, it became the center of hobbyists' for personal computers.

As a market for games, there was competition in each category of PC, with the PC-9801 being the standard for 16-bit machines and the MSX being the standard for gaming PCs. In the hobby PC market, which was the largest of the three categories, the PC-8801 occupied a central position. However, many games developed for the PC-8801 were also ported to the X1 and FM-7. In addition, there were a few cases where games developed for the X1 and FM-7 were ported to the other two

[15] The slots of the MSX PC were strictly expansion bus slots, and it was possible to use peripheral devices by plugging them into the slots. For this reason, several MSX PC games were released with semiconducting devices for function expansion, such as sound source tips and numerical calculation tips. The same phenomena have also happened with home game consoles such as Family Computer and Super Famicom.

[16] Although there is no strict definition of "entry-level" or "gaming" PC, we define it as "a PC that can be purchased for less than 100,000 yen and can be connected to a TV."

[17] A sound emitted from an electronic device for various notifications. The sound emitted when a PC starts up is the beep sound. The PC is equipped with a piezoelectric buzzer, which sounds an alarm when an error is detected during the start-up check. A beep sound is also made during the start-up of the PC when there is a notification from the system. The length and pitch of the beep sound can be adjusted to some extent, and there are games that use beep sounds to play music.

Table 3.2 Basic performance of PCs for gaming around 1983

	PC-9801	8-bit trinities	MSX
CPU	i8086 (16-bit)	Z80 or 6809 (8-bit)	Z80 (8-bit)
Screen resolution	640*400	640*200	256*192
Number of simultaneous colors	8 colors	8 colors	16 colors
Sprite function	No	No	Yes
Sound function	Beep only	PSG 3 sound	PSG 3 sound
Price	From 300,000 yen	From 200,000 yen	Under 100,000 yen
Dedicated display	Required	Required	Not required

models. Reflecting this situation, the PC-8801, X1, and FM-7 were known as the "8-bit trinity."

Table 3.2 lists the basic performance of the mainstream machines in each category in 1983, when the weakest PCs were eliminated, and the situation converged to some extent. The PC-9801 had a fine screen resolution of 640 × 400, but it was not suitable for gaming because it could not change the screen at high speed and did not have a sprite function to change characters quickly. What was emphasized was the CPU speed required for business operations. In war simulation games such as Nobunaga no Yabou (KOEI) and Gendai Dai-Senryaku (System Soft), the high CPU speed shortened the computer's thinking time, and play was more comfortable than in the PC-8801 version. The simulation game was also in tune with the tastes of the older generation, which was thought to be the majority of PC-9801 owners and established a unique position in the PC game market.

The internal architecture of the 8-bit trinities is quite different, and the FM-7 even has a different CPU. However, they were almost identical in terms of screen resolution, and the games were ported to each other to maintain homogeneity in visual appearance. The game genres released varied from action, adventure, role playing, and simulation. They occupied a central position in PC games.

The MSX is characterized by many simultaneous colors, but the resolution of the screen is low. Therefore, MSX was not very good at simulations, adventures, and role-playing games that required many characters to be displayed on the screen. On the other hand, MSX had a sprite function, so many action games were sold.

3.3.1 Market Convergence Through Competition and Selection

Check the current market conditions from the rankings in game magazines. Table 3.3 shows the top 10 from the ranking corner of a PC game called "Best Hit 21" published in the March 1985 issue of the game magazine *Beep* (SoftBank).

In 1985, as shown in Table 3.3, the market selection is still in progress. This can be read from the following two points:

Table 3.3 PC game ranking in the March 1985 issue of Beep, a game magazine

	Title	Company	Genre	Hardware
1	*Lode Runner*[a]	Sony, Soft Pro, Systemsoft	ACT	PC-6001mk2, PC-8001mk2, PC-8801, PC-9801, X1, FM-7/77. SMC-777
2	*The Fire Crystal*	BPS	RPG	PC-8801, PC-9801
3	*Yakyuu-kyou*	Hudson	ACT	PC-6001mk2, PC-8801, X1, FM-7
4	*Volguard*	dB-SOFT	ACT	PC-8801, X1, FM-7/77
5	*PLAZMA LINE*	Tecno Soft	ACT	PC-6001mk2, PC-6601, PC-8801, X1, FM-7, MZ2000/2200
6	*LEGENDS OF STARARTHUR III TERRA4001*	T&E Soft	ADV	PC-6001mk2, PC-6601SR, FM-7/77
7	*The Black Onyx*	BPS	RPG	PC-8801, PC-9801, PC-9801F, X1
8	*Professional Mahjong*	Chatnoir	TBL	PC-8801, PC-9801
9	*Chack'n Pop*	NIDECOM	ACT	PC-6001, PC-8801, FM-7/77, MZ-2000/2200, X1, MSX
10	*Tiny XEVIOUS*	DEMPA	ACT	PC-6001, PC-6001mk2, PC-6601

[a]Since the licensing process for *Lode Runner* was different, and each ported edition had a different company, there were several publishers. The last issue to appear in Beep's ranking was the November 1985 issue (No. 15). In that issue, the IBM-JX and MSX were added to the list of compatible machines. The game was also transferred to home game consoles such as Nintendo's Family Computer and Sega's SG-1000 and was also released as an arcade game by Irem

1. The medium through which the game is provided is diverse. Specifically, there are ROM-cartridges, an analog cassette tape, 5-inch floppy disks, and 8-inch floppy disks.

   At that time, floppy disk drives were expensive peripheral equipment, and there were still many individual users who did not have them. They stored the data on a cassette tape and read it with a data recorder (or a radio cassette if they did not have one). On the other hand, 8-inch floppy disks were used for the PCs used in companies. However, the volume of 8-inch floppy disks was small, and they disappeared from the business scene when 5-inch floppy disks with the same volume and even larger volume appeared on the market.

   In addition, when the successor models with a standard 5-inch floppy disk drive are released, the game with the cassette tape will disappear.[18] Except for MSX, which had characteristics close to gaming consoles and was supplied on a ROM cartridge, games were now supplied on easy-to-manage 5-inch floppy disks.

[18]The data transfer speed of the data recorders at that time was about 600–1200 bits per second, and even in relatively simple games at that time. The amount of data for games was becoming larger and casette tape was more and more difficult to use. Not only did we have to wait 15–20 min for loading at the start of the game, but we also had to wait several minutes to 10 min or more for loading during the game. In action games, every time a player cleared a stage, several minutes of waiting time were required, and it was the issue of time that weeded out the tape-delivered games.

2. There are many different types of machines that are compatible with the games that appear in the ranking. A total of 16 PC names,[19] including those that do not appear in the Top 10, appear in the ranking.

   In arcade games, where computers are replaced in each game and high-performance hardware appears one after another, the rate of hardware evolution (rate of selection) is extremely fast. On the other hand, in the case of PC games, the rate of hardware selection is extremely slow. This is because, as shown below, the interests of manufacturers selling PCs, users purchasing games, and companies developing and selling games are aligned in their actions:

   - PC manufacturers: To inherit software assets developed in the past, compatibility with previous models is emphasized in personal computers. For this reason, it has been difficult to create bold new models.
   - Users: PCs are much more expensive than home video game consoles and cannot be replaced easily.
   - Game companies: Since most games are developed on a small scale, it does not take much time for the companies to transfer them to other PCs. In addition, since the number of each type of PC in use was not that large, it was not efficient from a profit perspective to develop for a single type of PC.

Thus, in the early days when games for PCs became a business, the number of units sold for each type of machine was small, and it was common to transfer a game to multiple types of machines for sale. As the results of the PC sales competition became clearer and the winners and losers became clearer, the number of PCs on which games were sold was slowly but surely decreased.

The graph in Fig. 3.1 shows how many of the 20 top-ranked game software titles of each year[20] can be played on each PC by model name. Data was from *Yomigaeru PC-8801 Densetsu* (The Revival of the PC-8801, ASCII, 2006).[21]

[19] All the machines that appeared on the market were the PC-6001, PC-6001mk2, PC-6601, PC-6601SR, PC-8001mk2, PC-8801, PC-9801, PC-9801F from NEC, X1, MZ-1500, MZ-2000, MZ-2200 from Sharp, FM-7, FM-77 from Fujitsu, SMC-777 from Sony, and MSXs from various companies.

[20] According to *Yomigaeru PC-8801 Densetsu*, the order is calculated by adding up the number of years in the ranking of each issue of PC game magazine *LOGiN*, with 20 points for the first place and 1 point for the 20th place. However, since the first three issues of 1983, the year of the magazine's first issue, were unavailable, the calculation for 1983 was based on the first nine issues (No. 4 to No. 12). As only the top 10 were listed in the first 10 issues, there is no data for the 11th to 20th place until the tenth issue. In addition, there are some titles that have been ranked for multiple years. Since *LOGiN* was the first magazine to rank game software, there are no data prior to that time.

[21] The series is expressed as a single series including the successor models. For example, in the case of NEC's PC-6001, it includes the direct successors such as PC-6001mk2, PC-6001MK2SR, and PC-6601. The MZ series includes all PCs with the MZ-xx model number sold by Sharp but does not include the X1 series. Fujitsu's FM-7 series includes FM-8, FM-77 and their successors (FM-16β is not included).

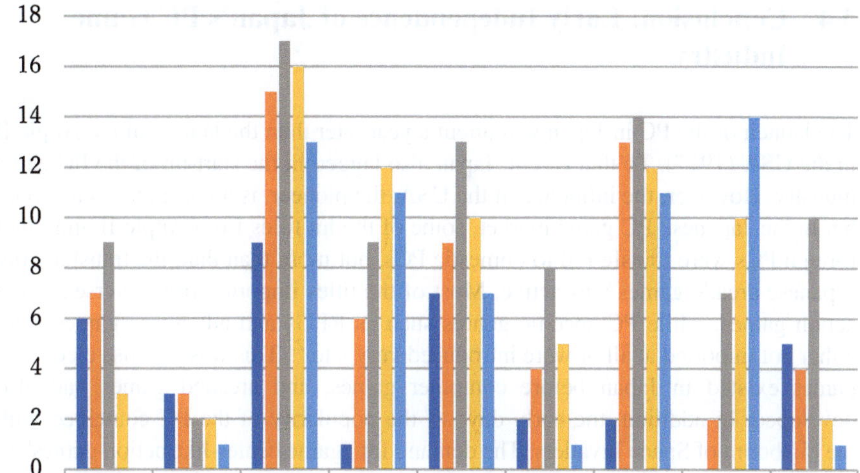

	PC-6001	PC-8001	PC-8801	PC-9801	FM-7	MZ series	X1	MSX	Other PCs
1983	6	3	9	1	7	2	2	0	5
1984	7	3	15	6	9	4	13	2	4
1985	9	2	17	9	13	8	14	7	10
1986	3	2	16	12	10	5	12	10	2
1987	0	1	13	11	7	1	11	14	1

■1983 ■1984 ■1985 ■1986 ■1987

Fig. 3.1 Number of PC game titles supported by model among the top 20 PC game titles of the year

The PC-8001 and PC-6001 series, which appeared at the dawn of the PC era, had several games that were transferred to many PC models, but the PC-6001 series disappeared from the lineup in 1986 and the PC-8001 series disappered in 1987. The MZ series appears to have a certain number of machines because it is a collection of several models. However, for each model, the highest number was five for the MZ-2200 in 1985, and MZ series disappeared after one for the MZ-2500 in 1987 and 1988. Other PCs were various, but all of them were ported games that were also sold for other models, and none of them were made exclusively.

The PC-8801 series has the largest number of ranked-in titles. The X1 series and FM-7 series, which are mostly transferred from the PC-8801, also have many titles in the lineup. At this stage, the PC-9801's originality was limited to simulation games where the CPU's thinking speed could be utilized.

3.4 Conclusion: Early Independence of Japan's PC Game Industry

The launch of the PC in Japan was about a year later than the launch of the Apple II in the USA (1977). To that extent, Japan also lagged in the start-up of the PC game industry. However, the influence of the USA, the pioneer, is not as great as it should be. In the Japanese PC game market, some of the hit titles from Apple II and other foreign PCs were transferred to domestic PCs, but more than that, the transfer from Japanese arcade games was active. Most of the titles imported from overseas were action games, while PC-specific genres such as RPGs and adventure games were either not imported at all or were introduced very late.[22] This was because electronic games existed in Japan before computer games, and arcaded games had also developed. In addition, the early days of the popularity of the PC coincided with the big boom of Space Invaders. The demand for "game center-like action games" to be played on the PC was also a major factor.

Returning to the ranking of 3-3 again, confirm the trend from the appearing title.

First prize was Lode Runner, which was the big hit title of the time. Lode Runner was released for Apple II from Brøderbund, USA, but because of being ported to numerous Japanese PCs, it became a bigger hit in Japan than in the USA.[23] The game content was an action puzzle, which gained popularity due to the ability to edit the stage oneself.

In second place is The Fire Crystal, the sequel to The Black Onyx (seventh place). The Black Onyx is the first hit RPG made in Japan, and it is a title that played a major role in the spread of RPGs in Japan.

LEGENDS OF STARARTHUR[24] (sixth place) is an adventurer game, Professional Mahjong (eighth place) is a table game, and the rest are action games. Two of the titles are from Arcades, and the other two are from overseas. The remaining three titles are originals. Although omitted for the sake of space, there are many PC-original action games ranked lower than 11th place.

---

[22] At the time, the two largest series of role-playing games in the USA were Wizardry (first released in 1981) and Ultima (first released in 1981, the ancestor Akalabeth was released in 1979). However, both series were not introduced to the Japanese market until 1985, when the Japanese PC game industry was already established (the first Ultima game was not released, but only 2 and 3). Therefore, it was not for the reason of transferring the latest hit titles from the USA, but for the reason of playing the classic masterpieces on their own PCs.

[23] There was an interview with Douglas E. Smith, a developer of Lode Runner, in the video game magazine *Beep* in the October issue of 1985 (page 29).

Interviewer: Lode Runner has sold 150,000 in the USA, and 2 million in the Japanese including for Family Computer.

Doug Smith: I do not remember the amount, but it took quite a while: -). I had got a house with four bedrooms and a pool, a motorboat and two Porsches: -).

[24] LEGENDS OF STARARTHUR is a command-driven adventuring game published by T&E soft, and the stories of *PLANET MEPHIUS* (1983), *DARK NEBULA* (1983), and *TERRA 4001* (1984) are space opera influenced by the Star Wars and King Arthur biographies.

It can be confirmed that the PC game industry in Japan has developed its own unique style of products, which are not mere transplants, while relying on America for game genres and systems, and has achieved its own development. RPGs, adventure games, which are unique to PC games, became commonplace only after they were released for sale on home consoles such as Family Computer.

Chapter 4
Console Games (1–1): Beyond the Crash—The Birth of the Family Computer

Abstract This chapter describes the establishment of the home video game console market in Japan. As in the USA, many game consoles with games implemented directly in hardware were launched in Japan in the 1970s. This was followed by a boom in portable electronic game consoles, as typified by Nintendo's Game&Watch, and then the era of game consoles connected to TVs again. Many game consoles were born, but Nintendo's Family Computer, with its outstanding performance, dominated the market.

Keywords Game&Watch · Cassette Vision · SG-1000 · Family Computer · Third-Party Controle

4.1 Early Days of Home Game Consoles in Japan

4.1.1 The Era of Hardware-Based Home Game Consoles

In the USA, Atari launched Pong in 1972, and the Home Pong was launched in 1975. In Japan, the EPOCH Corporation released a game machine called TV Tennis in 1975, which had a similar game content to the pong. At that time, the price of toys for children was 2 ~ 3000 yen, while the price of TV Tennis was much higher at 19,500 yen, but it became a hit product selling 10,000 units. Later, Tommy, Bandai, Takara, and other companies that dealt with toys such as EPOCH, entered the TV game console market. Perhaps because TV game consoles were considered attractive as peripheral equipment for TV, companies dealing with home appliances such as Matsushita Electrics, Toshiba, and Hitachi also sold game consoles that were hardware-based home game consoles. Also, Atari's Home Pong was imported by the Nakamura Manufacturing Company and the Seibu Department Store.

Among the companies challenging the newly emerged market of TV games was the toy manufacturer Nintendo. In 1977, the peak year for the boom, Nintendo released the Color TV-GAME 6 and Color TV-GAME 15. While most of the other game machines had black-and-white displays and cost 20,000 yen or more, the Color TV-GAME 6 and 15 sold 800,000 units combined, partly because they had color

Y. Koyama, *History of the Japanese Video Game Industry*, Translational Systems Sciences 35, https://doi.org/10.1007/978-981-99-1342-8_4

Table 4.1 Major hardware-based home game consoles released in Japan

Year	Name	Seller (Importer)	Price (JPY)
1975	TV Tennis	EPOCH	19,500
1976	Home Pong	Seibu Department Nakamura Manufacturing	24,800
1976	TELESupo	DAISHIN	24,800
1976	T.U.C.	TAKATOKU TOYS	22,800
1976	Champion	PACKEL	22,500
1977	TV-JACK Series	Bandai	9800–38,000
1977	Color TV-GAME6/15	Nintendo	9800/15,000
1977	National TV Game	Matsushita Electronics	24,800
1977	Hitachi Video Game	HITACHI	24,800
1977	Toshiba TV Game	TOSHIBA	9800
1977	Black jaguar 4/6	Takara	8900/14,800
1977	BeLLcon	TSUKUDA	29,800
1977–1978	TV-FUN Series	Tomy	9800-18,000
1978	TV Baseball-	EPOCH	13,400
1978	VIDEO PINBALL	Toyo Bussan	38,700
1978	RACING 112	Nintendo	18,000
1979	TV BLOCK	EPOCH	13,500
1979	Block Kuzushi	Nintendo	18,000
1980	TV VADER	EPOCH	16,500
1980	Computer TV Game	Nintendo	48,000

Source: Compiled by the author from Yamazaki, 2014a, b)

displays and were inexpensive at 9800 yen (Color TV-GAME 6) and 15,000 yen (Color TV-GAME 15), respectively (Table 4.1).

In the early days, home game machines were like arcade games in that the game was packaged in a hardware format (see Chap. 3). The first game machine in Japan, TV Tennis, could only be used to play the tennis game, but some of the game machines sold after it could be used to play other games by flipping a switch on the machine. However, because the games were implemented in a hardware format, it was not possible to add new games, and the characters for the games were all rectangular or square, and the rules for each game were simple, so the differences between the games were small. Therefore, the time required for redemption was not very long.

Later, in response to the popularity of *Block Kuzushi* and *Space Invaders* in arcade games, several companies released game machines that could play *Block Kuzushi* and *Space Invaders* like games. However, due to their high price, the fact that they could only be played in front of a TV, and the fact that they were insufficient for the transfer of arcade games and the level of fun was not high enough, the boom in TV game machines ended around 1980. In their place, the heyday of inexpensive and convenient electronic games arrived.

4.1.2 Success of Electronic Games and Game & Watch

The Japanese toy industry was aware that CPU + ROM cartridge type game consoles, the next generation of hardware format game consoles, were being sold in the USA, but they preferred to do business in a format closer to their specialty, toys. The toy companies actively developed single-function electronic games that used semiconductors and light-emitting diodes or fluorescent display tubes as display parts.

Among the many electronic games, Nintendo's Game & Watch, which was released in 1980, was a major success. Compared to electronic games, which tended to be large and toy-like, Game & Watch was designed in a way that adults would want to play and was thin and compact enough to fit into a shirt's breast pocket. In addition, using the word "watch" in the product name and implementing the clock function reduced the psychological resistance of "just buying a toy."

To implement a clock function means that the power is always on. Nintendo collaborated with Sharp to achieve a low power consumption that could run for several months on a coin battery by using the technology used in desktop calculators (such as liquid crystal display and low power consumption CMOS type LSI), which was the subject of fierce technological development competition at the time. Since the power is always on, the function of preserving the high score (highest score) can be realized. The technological level of Game & Watch was extremely high, and similar products did not appear on the market for about a year (Photo 4.1).

As in the case of hardware-assembled game machines, the "model" for electronic games was the arcade games that had come before. However, the arcades here were not limited to computer games such as Space Invaders and Pac-Man, but also included submarine games, drive games, and other pre-Computer Era games.

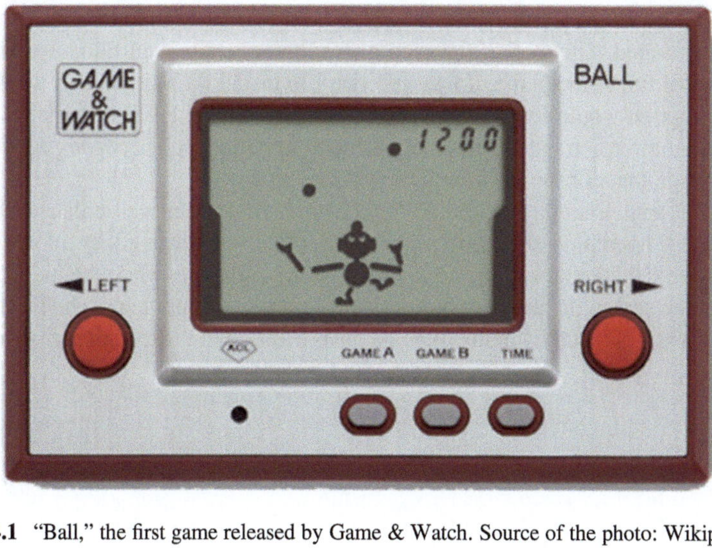

Photo 4.1 "Ball," the first game released by Game & Watch. Source of the photo: Wikipedia(JP)

There are also several electronic games that directly copy the contents of the game, and games that do not name themselves but whose source material is immediately recognizable. As the pace of technological progress in arcade games accelerates after the introduction of Galaxian, electronic games with insufficient performance will not be able to catch up, and sales of electronic games will decline accordingly. In the case of Nintendo's Game & Watch, the migration of Donkey Kong (1982), one of the biggest hits of the company's arcade games, reached a peak of 1.2 million units in Japan. By the end of 1982, sales of all electronic game machines, including game-and-watch, had plummeted. After 1983, when the first Family Computer were launched in Japan, Game & Watch was mainly sold overseas, where the popularity of home gaming machines was slow.

4.1.3 Early Days of Cartridge-Type Game Consoles in Japan

The history of cartridge-type game consoles in Japan is relatively old, with Takatoku selling the "Video Cassette Rock" in 1977. However, it did not have a CPU in the main console, but rather the circuit board of the game was mounted on the cartridge side. The first game machine with a CPU was the Fairchild Channel F, which was released in 1977 (1976 in the USA). The first game console to be released by a Japanese company was the VISICOM sold by TOSHIBA in 1978, which was equipped with the same CPU as the Studio II (released in 1977 in the USA) by RCA. However, sales were sluggish due to the high price of 54,800 JPY and the fact that the product was sold through the home electronics trade but not through the toy trade.

The problem facing cartridge-type game consoles in the late 1970s and early 1980s was cost. Without a CPU, the price was lower, but only games like existing hardware format games could be developed, and the market for such games was already saturated. The market for such games had already been filled up. To add a new level of fun to the game, it was necessary to install a CPU, but this would have meant the price would have been around 50,000 yen, making it impossible to sell. This was a time when it was extremely difficult to include the necessary functions at a price range that consumers would be willing to pay.

The Cassette Vision, released by Epoch in 1981, was a well-balanced gaming console that overcame such difficulties. The price was lowered by mounting the inexpensive CPU and the game component on the cartridge, while the main console only had the screen display function and the controller component. The reason why the CPU was not installed in the main console was due to the technical reason that it

Photo 4.2 Cassette vision (Photo credit: Wikipedia)

was difficult to extend the circuit length between the CPU and the ROM part at that time,[1] but the result was a great success (Photo 4.2).

The Cassette Vision game used an inexpensive chip that integrated the CPU and ROM because the CPU was mounted on a game cartridge.[2] Due to the nature of the chip used, the dots displayed on the screen were very coarse (54 × 62 pixels), but it was possible to display parallel quadrilateral dots by skewing the edges of the dots.

[1]An interview with Epoch's developer, Masayuki Horie, on the website Classic Video Game Station Odyssey, states the following. (http://www.ne.jp/asahi/cvs/odyssey/hyperlink/setframe_creators_horie1.html)

"It was not possible to separate the CPU and ROM at once. The LSI for the TV game itself was already a single chip, and it was difficult to separate the bus and add ROM from it with the technology available at the time.

This is a lot of bits (48 bits). So I think the speed was reasonably high. This chip can read and write orders, jump addresses, and register contents with a single command. If we try to do the same thing in ROM, the reading speed will be four times slower than that of an 8-bit ROM.

In addition, there is the drive capability of the bus, but I think it was uncertain when the ROM was installed externally. At the time, it would have cost a lot of money to install a computer and then install a separate ROM. Nowadays, the CPU has its own drive capability, so it can be connected as it is, but back then it was tough. It's just too weak. It can cause noises and malfunctions.

There is a big difference between having an electric current flowing through a single chip and pulling it out by about 10 cm. It is necessary to use the weak electricity in the LSI to achieve this."

Since ROM cartridge-type game machines with CPUs mounted on the main body were already on the market in Japan and overseas, it was not a technology that did not exist at that time. However, many of the articles on the development of game machines at that time talk about the difficulties involved in connecting the CPU to the ROM.

There is no doubt that this was a very difficult problem.

[2]The game cartridge contained NEC's D777C, a chip that had both CPU and ROM functions in one chip.

Table 4.2 Cartridge-type game machines sold in Japan by 1983 (excluding Family Computer)

Year	Name	Seller (Importer)	Price (JPY)
1977	Video Cassette Rock	TAKATOKU	9800
1978	TV-JACK add-on 5000	Bandai	19,800
1978	VISICOM	TOSHIBA	54,800
1979	Super Vision 8000	Bandai	59,800
1981	Cassette Vision	EPOCH	13,500
1982	Odyssey2	Philips North America	49,800
1982	Intellivision	Bandai	49,800
1982	CREATIVISION	CHERICO	54,000
1982	Atari 2800	Atari	24,800
1982	Dynavision	YAMAGIWA	49,800
1983	Arcadia	Bandai	19,800
1983	Kousokusen(Light-Speed Ship)	Bandai	54,800
1983	Pyuuta Jr	Tomy	19,800
1983	TV Boy	Gakken	8800
1983	PV-1000	Casio	14,800
1983	SG-1000	SEGA	15,000

Source: Compiled by the author from Yamazaki (2014a, b)

Although it was less powerful than the Atari VCS, the Cassette Vision was highly evaluated in the market and became the top share in the market before the release of the Family Computer. In 1983, a low-cost version, the Cassette Vision Jr., was released at a much lower price of 5000 JPY. It became a hit product with 450,000 units sold in the end (Table 4.2).

4.1.4 Personal Computers for Gaming

As mentioned in the previous chapter, one of the categories of personal computers was the game-use computer. In the USA, the mainstream of game-playing machines shifted from game-only machines to game-use PCs around 1982, when Atari's VCS began to lag behind in terms of performance. Commodore launched the VIC-20 (the machine name in Japan was VIC-1001), Commodore 64, and Max Machine, a low-cost version of Commodore 64 for gaming developed for Japan market but was withdrawn (Table 4.3).

All of Commodore's PCs were equipped with MOS technology's 6502 CPU, but in Japan, most of the PCs for game machines other than family computers were equipped with the Z80.

Since 1982, the price of Z80s produced in Japan in license has fallen sharply. This led to a succession of Z80-equipped PCs, not only for gaming such as the M5

Table 4.3 Game-use personal computers (excluding MSX) released in Japan by 1983

Year	Name	Seller (Importer)	Price (JPY)
1981	VIC-1001	Commodore Japan	69,800
1982	Pyuuta	Tomy	59,800
1982	Max Machine	Commodore Japan	34,800
1982	Commodore 64	Commodore Japan	99,800
1982	Game Personal Computer/ M5	Takara / SORD	59,800
1983	SC-3000	SEGA	29,800
1983	RX-78 GUNDAM	Bandai	59,800
1983	PV-2000	Casio	29,800

Source: Compiled by the author from Sasaki (2013)

(SORD), SC-3000 (SEGA), RX-78 (Bandai), and PV-2000 (Casio), but also for hobby use such as the PC-8801 (NEC) and X1 (Sharp).[3] As the price of the Z80 dropped, the price of the PC for gaming became the same as that of gaming console only a few years before. As a result, old-style gaming consoles are now completely obsolete.

In the end, the MSX won the market for gaming computers, and other companies either withdrew or joined the MSX, like Casio. Although the gaming PC lost out to the dedicated gaming consoles as a computer for gaming, it did serve to entice game-interested children into programming and game development.

4.2 Rise of the Family Computer (Famicon)

4.2.1 Development of Family Computer

Nintendo used the arcade-hit Donkey Kong (1981) as the standard for developing Family Computer (hereinafter referred to as “Famicom”). Nintendo’s goal was to create a game console at a level that would be able to replicate Donkey Kong almost exactly, for less than 10,000 yen. To lower the price, it was essential to reduce the number of semiconductor parts, and to do so, it was necessary to design a dedicated LSI. Nintendo had to scramble to find a partner who could co-develop the LSI.

The search for companies that could be commissioned to design and manufacture specialized LSIs was difficult. At the time, the personal computer market was just starting up, and all the companies were being pressed by the high demand. It was during this time that Ricoh accepted a request from Nintendo. Ricoh entered the semiconductor business at a very late stage, in 1980, and had just started operation of its first plant in 1981 and was still searching for an outside sales partner.

[3]Tommy’s Pyuuta is an exception; it is equipped with a 16-bit CPU (TMS9995) developed by Texas Instruments.

Photo 4.3 Family computer (Photo credit: Wikipedia)

The CPU license contracted by many other Japanese companies was for the Z80, but Ricoh was in the process of concluding a contract for the 6502. The 6502 was not as well known in Japan as the Z80, but it was possible to reduce the circuit area to a smaller size than the Z80. When manufacturing a chip of the same size as the Z80, it was possible to incorporate other functions, which was convenient for lowering the price. In response to Ricoh's proposal to develop a custom chip based on the 6502, Nintendo developed a chip that combined a CPU and a sound source chip.[4] In addition to the CPU, the semiconductor related to image processing is important for the computer, and the one developed for the PC was excellent in text processing but weak in image processing, so Nintendo co-developed this with Ricoh. This was called the PPU (Picture Processing Unit)[5] (Photo 4.3).

As for the controller, it was decided to use the cross-shaped controller used by Donkey Kong (1982) in Game & Watch Multiscreen[6] instead of the joystick used in

[4]Since the CPU of the arcade version of the Donkey Kong was the Z80, it was feared that the 6502 would be selected for the Family Computer. However, when Donkey Kong was transferred for the Family Computer, the performance was satisfactory.

[5]The selection of other functions to be realized in the PPU is the responsibility of the game developer. It is known that actual game designers such as Shigeru Miyamoto are involved in the selection of 54 colors.

[6]A two-panel Game & Watch that has been sold since 1982.

existing game consoles.[7] There was some debate on the number of controllers to be installed, but it was finally decided to install two, because the home game console would be installed in the living room where the TV was located at the time, and that it would be played by several people.

It was assumed that keyboards and programming functions would not be added due to the high manufacturing costs. However, due to the harsh evaluation of a game-dedicated console in the PC boom at the time, Nintendo decided to annunciate the release of the keyboard as a peripheral device later.[8]

4.2.2 *Sales of Family Computer*

Famicom, which was launched on July 15, 1983, lost the end-of-year sales in the first year because the hardware was recalled once due to a heat generation problem of the PPU. The following year, however, sales grew steadily without any impact from this, and the number of units shipped exceeded 2 million by the end of 1984. As is customary in the toy market, the durability of a hit product boom is at most 2 years, and in the case of the 1983 release of the Famicom, that was in 1985. However, it became a big boom in 1985 when several leading companies entered the market and Super Mario Bros. was launched, selling 3.74 million units a year. Nintendo withdrew from arcade games and decided to focus its management resources on home video games. The total number of popular PCs at that time was about 2.5 million, and the number of popular MSX PCs, which were launched in 1983, was about 300,000.[9] The sales volume of the Famicom was overwhelming.

In 1987, sales halved, partly because the product had spread to many households. In addition, the functional obsolescence of the Family Computer began to become apparent around this time. In 1987, NEC Home Electronics introduced the PC Engine, and the following year, Sega introduced the Mega Drive, the next generation of gaming consoles, and the market share of Family Computer dropped to about 50%.

Sales of the Famicom continued for a long time, and even after the next generation Super Famicom was introduced in 1990, sales continued. In 1993, the price was lowered to 7000 yen, the design was redesigned, and the output was changed

[7] The reason why a cross key was used was because game consoles are often placed on the floor, and there is a possibility that a child may step on the joystick on the floor and break the stick, which may cause the child to become injured. This delicacy is because Nintendo has been doing business in the toy market for a long time.

[8] The keyboard and programming environment were released as the *Family Basic* in July 1984, one year after the main product launch. *Family Basic* was developed by Hudson, and was Hudson's first foray into Family Computer.

[9] *Nikkei Business*, February 4, 1985, p. 142.

Table 4.4 Family Computer and Sega 8-bit game consoles

Model name	Family Computer	SG-1000	MARK III
Company	Nintendo	SEGA	SEGA
CPU (operating speed)	6502 (1.79Mhz)	μPD780C(Z80A compatible chip,3.55 MHz)	μPD780C(Z80A compatible chip,3.55 MHz)
Resolution	256*240	256*192	256*192
Number of simultaneous colors	25 out of 52 colors	All 16 colors simultaneously	All 64 colors simultaneously
Sprite function Number of units Size Number of colors	64 units 8*8, 16*16 4 colors	64 units 8*8 1 color	64 units 8*8 16 colors
Release date	July 15, 1983	July 15, 1983	October 20, 1985
Price	14,800 JPY	15,000 JPY	15,000 JPY

Source: Compiled by the author from Yamazaki (2014a, b)

from RF[10] to composite, and an AV-specification Family computer was released. Finally, in September 2003, when parts procurement became difficult, sales of Family Computer were terminated (sales of Super Famicom were also terminated at the same time).[11] The accumulated sales volume in Japan was 19.35 million units.

On the other hand, most of the other company's hardware was withdrawn. Epoch, which had been a leading company in the market before the emergence of Family Computer, launched a Super Cassette Vision in 1984, but sold only 300,000 units and withdrew from the home video game market in 1986. The SG-1000, which SEGA launched in 1983, did not sell well at all, partly because its performance was inferior to that of Family Computer. In 1985, SEGA launched MARK III, which was upper compatible with the SG-1000 and had higher performance than Famicom, but the total sales were only 700,000 units. The 300,000 units sold by Epoch and the 700,000 units sold by SEGA would have been sufficient figures for success in the pre-Famicom era, but the fact that the company had changed the business scheme so drastically and the cost of developing hardware and software was higher than in earlier generations meant that the success hurdle was much higher (Table 4.4 and Fig. 4.1).

[10] A method of displaying a game image on a radio wave in the same frequency band as the vacant channel of a television and connecting it to the antenna terminal of the television. RF is an abbreviation for Radio Frequency. At the time of the introduction of Family Computer, televisions equipped with a compositor terminal to connect a video deck were not yet widespread, so many home video game consoles used the RF output.

[11] Currently, mass merchandisers sell compatible hardware that can run the game cartridge for Family Computer, but these are not official licenses from Nintendo.

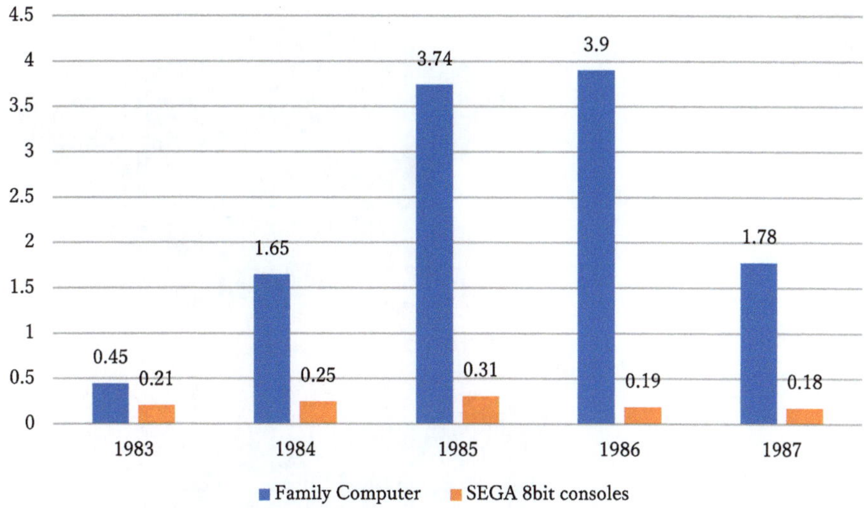

Fig. 4.1 Trends in the number of shipments of Family Computers and Sega 8-bit game consoles (million). Source of data: Family Computer: *Jouhou Media Hakusyo* (Information Media White Paper), 2000 edition. Sega 8-bit consoles (total of SG-1000 and MARK III): Compiled by Koyama based on Yanagawa and Kuwayama (1999) and Family Computer sales data (In Yanagawa and Kuwayama (1999), the trend of market share by game console is shown from 1983. In 1983 and 1987, the total of Nintendo and Sega was 100%, and the number of hardware shipped by other companies was not considered. The number for Sega is calculated from the number of units shipped for each year in the 2000 edition of the *Jouhou Media Hakusyo* and the share ratio between Nintendo and Sega in Yanagawa and Kuwayama (1999).

4.2.3 Failure of the Disk System

Disk System was a peripheral device launched by Nintendo in 1986, at the height of the boom. It contains a disk drive[12] that can be read and written on, and provides the game via disk media. The disk capacity was 64 kilobytes (512 kilobits) per side, which was larger,[13] cheaper, and shortened the time from master-up to game release compared to the games provided in ROM at the time. Not only does it take time to record the data in ROM for the number of ROMs shipped, but at the time it was difficult to find the necessary number of ROMs due to a shortage of semiconductor devices.[14] Disk System was a mechanism that made it possible to reduce the burden

[12] As floppy disks were still expensive at that time, Nintendo adopted a magnetic disk called a quick disk. Unlike floppy disks, quick disks did not have random access functions. It is a high-speed version of the data recorder, which was the main recording device used in inexpensive PCs at the time.

[13] The volume of Super Mario Bros. released in 1985 is 320 kilobytes (40 kilobits), and Dragon Quest released by Enix in 1986 is 512 kilobytes (64 kilobits).

[14] In the case of the ROM for the firmware, it took at least 3 months from the submission of the finished product (master) to its sale. In the case of disk systems, it took about 3 weeks, or about a quarter of the time.

Photo 4.4 Disk system (Source of the photo: Wikipedia)

of procuring ROMs and to respond to the gradually increasing volume of games at the same time. After purchasing a disk system with an original price of 15,000 yen, consumers could play a new game for 2600 yen (both sides) or 2500 yen (one side), or they could replace the purchased disk game with another one for 500 yen.[15] The disk writers for games were placed in toy stores throughout the city.

At first glance, the disk system seemed to be beneficial to both the consumer and the third-party game developer, but both the third-party and the toy store complained about it. The main complaint from the third party was that the revenue per game would be drastically reduced.[16] Toy stores were also dissatisfied that only 500 yen per rewrite did not contribute to sales, even though the distributor had to take up space in the sales floor (Photo 4.4).

The disk system was launched on February 11, 1986, but the sales pace was not good, and only 500,000 units were sold as of June 1986.[17] This may have been related to the fact that most of the titles released at the same time were transfers of games from existing ROM cartridges to the disk system, and the only new title was

[15] It was 500 yen per game regardless of whether it was a single- or double-sided game. If a user purchased a game disk with only one side recorded, it was possible to have the user write on the other side that was left over.

[16] According to Takahashi (1993), in the case of disk system games, a third party's income per game is about 570 yen, which is only about half the price of selling a ROM game. In the case of disk rewrites, the 500 yen is shared among game developer, Nintendo and toy stores, so the income for the game developer is much smaller.

[17] *Nikkei Business*, June 9, 1986, p. 248.

The Legend of Zelda.[18] The Legend of Zelda took advantage of the data-savable nature of the disk system to incorporate RPG elements into action games, which were still too difficult for Japanese game players, and became a major hit for disk system sales. However, the peak in the number of tales sold for the disk system was in 1987, the year after its release, and in 1988, the number of tales sold for the disk system decreased despite an increase in the number of titles sold for ROM. Although 4 million disk systems were sold at the end of the year, only 199 disk system titles were sold, including the re-release of ROM versions, compared to a total of 1053 ROM titles.

At the time of the launch of the disk system in 1986, Nintendo was planning to switch to disks as the main medium of game sales. In fact, Nintendo did not release any games in ROM format in 1986.

However, due to the following reasons, there is no longer a problem with providing games in ROM:

1. The market for mask ROMs became stable and there were no problems with supply.
2. Higher-volume game ROMs than disk appeared because of higher semiconductor integration.
3. It was possible to save game data even for ROM games by installing a battery in the ROM cartridge.

Also, users did not like games with a disk system that required loading time during the game, as it reduced the sense of immersion. Some companies, such as Konami, actively marketed titles for Disk System, but overall, Disk System business was sluggish.[19]

4.3 Massive Participations of Third-Party[20] Vendors into Famicom

Like Atari's VCS, Nintendo also had companies that wanted to develop and sell games for the PC.

---

[18] The Legend of Zelda, along with Dragon Quest, helped to popularize RPGs, which at the time were still too difficult for Japanese gamers. It is still a popular series with many titles being released, but it is more popular overseas than in Japan.

[19] Perhaps due to the failure of the Disk System, Nintendo began to emphasize the provision of games in ROM, which does not have a loading time lag during play, and even though other mainstream game consoles moved to CD-ROM in the mid-1990s, Nintendo 64 was initially provided games in ROM format only.

[20] A company that develops and sells games for another company's console is called a third party. It is customary to refer to the platform holder that sells the game console as the first party, the subsidiary of the platform holder, or the company that develops products requested by the platform holder as the second party, and other companies as the third party. In the case

In July 1984, Hudson, which had developed the BASIC language for Famicom, entered the market with NUTS & MILK, a transfer of its own PC games, and Load Runner, a transfer of hit versions of foreign PC games. A little later, Namco entered the market with its own arcade titles (Galaxian in September and Pac-Man, Xevious, and Mappy in November).[21] In 1985, Arcade game companies such as Konami, Taito, JALECO, Irem, and Capcom, and PC game companies such as Enix, Square, dB Soft, and ASCII entered the market one after another. At the same time, in 1985, Bandai, a toy company, and music content companies such as Toshiba EMI and Pony Canyon entered the market as part of efforts to diversify their businesses. In the years that followed, new companies continued to join the industry. On the other hand, in the case of SEGA, only one company Salio entered the market in Mark III.

Third parties produced and sold games under license agreements with Nintendo, and there were two types of license agreements: royalty agreements and OEM agreements.

Royalty contracts are an agreement to pay a fixed amount of fee per ROM cartridge as a royalty for the trademark of Family Computer and awarded to arcade game companies (an exception is Bandai,[22] a toy company) that had the ability to manufacture ROM cartridges on their own or find contractors to do so at a time when the contracting system was not yet in place. Compared to the OEM contract, the cost of production was lower because Nintendo's profit was not added to the manufacturing cost of the ROM cartridge, and the shape[23] of the ROM cartridge and the package of the product could be unique, making it possible to differentiate the product from other developers' game cartridges made by Nintendo.

The OEM contract is a contract in which the manufacture of ROM cartridges is entrusted to Nintendo and the entire manufacturing cost is paid in advance. An early third party, Hudson, is an OEM contract. Hudson entered the market with its own PC game Nuts & Milk and a port of the hit PC game Lode Runner, and ordered 200,000 cartridges at the time of entry. The price of the ROM cartridges was not disclosed by Nintendo, and the details of the amount paid are unknown, but even if we assume 2000 yen per cartridge, which is about half of the selling price of the ROM cartridges

---

of Famicom, it can be said that Hudson, who developed Family Basic, was the actual secondary party.

[21] According to Mizukami (2012), Namco analyzed the hardware structure of Famicom by itself and brought the completed game Galaxian to Nintendo. Since Nintendo did not have a contracting system in place and did not have the negotiation card of providing technical information, the negotiations went in Namco's favor. As a royalty fee, Nintendo insisted on 100 yen and Namco insisted on 10 yen, and the agreement was finally concluded in Namco's favor.

[22] According to Mizukami (2012), the reason why there were many entries into the Famicom market at this time was that KAGA ELECTRONICS, an electronic parts trading company, was actively selling ROM cartridges to various companies on a manufacturing contract basis.

[23] Many of the ROM cartridges manufactured by companies that had royalty agreements with Nintendo were different in shape and design from those manufactured by Nintendo, so they were easily recognizable. Some of the most distinctive game cartridges are the LED-embedded game cartridges by Irem. In addition, Namco's Super Xevious GAMP no Nazo and Dragon Buster are famous for their use of gold colored cartridges.

(4500 yen), the payment would be 400 million yen.[24] In this way, game production and manufacturing under OEM contracts are extremely risky,[25] but many companies have joined the market due to the market competitiveness of Famicom.

At that time, there was a severe shortage of semiconductors, and it was extremely difficult to procure mask ROMs for games, and in order to prevent overproduction of games, companies with OEM contracts were required to produce three games per year (later relaxed to five). On the other hand, companies with royalty contracts did not have such a restriction, and Namco sold 10 products in 1986 and 14 in 1987. The contract was unfair to the companies that signed the OEM contract. Since the royalty contract was for a period of 5 years, Nintendo switched to OEM contracts in order to maintain fairness among the companies, starting with those whose royalty contracts were about to expire, and finally completed the conversion of all the companies to OEM contracts in 1991.

In addition, Nintendo is equipping third parties with development materials. Nintendo developed a development tool that combined a programming tool (Nintendo Capture) and a graphical drawing support tool (Digitizer) originally developed for in-house use and sold them to third parties that requested them.[26] However, companies in the arcade game industry used their own development tools.[27] Family Computer had different versions depending on the modification of the internal semi conductor bug, and it was difficult to guarantee that the independently developed materials would work for all of them. As a result of the establishment of the contract with the third party, the use of general-purpose development tools was prohibited, and it became impossible to use other than the designated development tools.[28]

[24]When requesting the production of game ROM cartridges for Famicom, half of the payment was required up front and the remainder at the time of delivery. At the time of the entry into the Famicom market, Hudson was a small company selling mainly PC games, and this payment was extremely difficult for the company in terms of financial resources. In the end, Yuji Kudo, then president of the company, received a personal loan from the bank to pay for this order.

[25]Small and medium-sized developers without financial resources could not bear the cost of ROM cartridges, so they either asked large companies with financial resources to publish and sell their products, or they became subcontractors who received development fees from the large companies.

[26]The development tool was developed by an employee of a major electronics manufacturer who was a partner of Nintendo at the time, and who had developed games for Nintendo during his student days. He later established the company, Intelligent Systems, and officially joined the second party. According to Mizukami (2012), the development tool was a hardware emulation board, which was connected to Fujitsu's FM-R personal computer.

[27]In the case of Namco, development was carried out using HP 64000, which is the same material used in arcade game development. The HP 64000 was a type of hardware development material called an ICE (in-circuit emulator), and it was capable of emulating various CPUs with an emulation probe (CPU emulator in hardware). Namco was developing games using this environment to emulate the Family Computer.

[28]In the next generation console Super Famicom, Sony's NEWS workstation was used in the early days of Super Famicom, and later the emulator of Super Famicom developed by SETA was used.

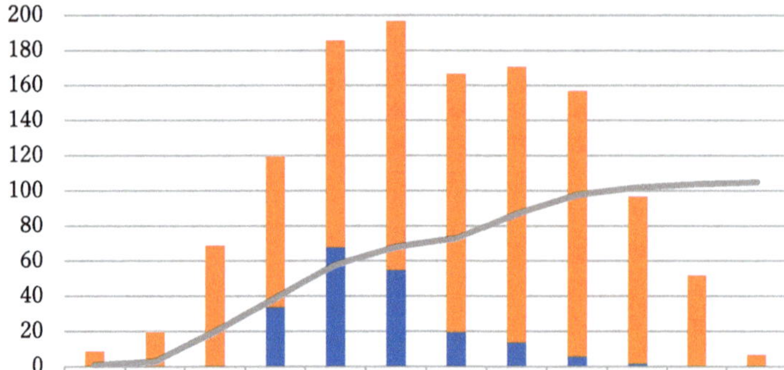

	1983	1984	1985	1986	1987	1988	1989	1990	1991	1992	1993	1994
ROM game titles	9	20	69	86	118	142	147	157	151	95	52	7
Disk game titles	0	0	0	34	68	55	20	14	6	2	0	0
number of entered companies	1	3	20	39	58	68	73	87	98	102	104	105

Disk game titles ROM game titles number of entered companies

Fig. 4.2 Game titles sold and a number of companies selling games. Source: Compiled by the author from Uemura et al. (2013)

4.3.1 Third-Party Participation and Its Impact

Figure 4.2 shows the trend of the number of companies participating in the sales of Family Computer games and the number of titles sold. Fifty-five companies participated in the three-year period from 1985 to 1987, and the period between 1985 and 1987 was a peak.

The number of companies that joined the market tripled from 1985 to 1987, when new entrants were active, and the number of titles sold tripled when ROM and disk system versions were combined. However, the market size of home video games (including consoles) between 1985 and 1987 was 411 billion yen and 437 billion yen, not much difference.[29] Since the sales of Famicom themselves have halved in the past few years, the sales of software itself have increased, but even taking this into account, the competition among individual games has become fierce. As a result of the fierce competition, the average number of units sold per game has decreased and the profit margin has also declined.

Among the companies aiming to enter the market, there were 73 companies that released less than 10 game titles and 26 companies that released only one game title. Some of the companies are exceptions because they entered the market in the late stage, but there were many companies that entered the market because of the Famicom boom but were drowned out by fierce competition.

In addition to the restrictions on (1) the number of titles that each company can sell per year, Nintendo has set the following conditions: (2) prior consultation on the

[29] The source of the data is each annual editions of the *Leisure White Paper*.

content of the game (content check), (3) a minimum production lot of 10,000 units, and (4) payment terms (half at the time of order and the remaining amount in advance at the time of receipt). In addition to controlling the content of the games, Nintendo requested that third parties take the risk when selling the games.

Although this contract has been criticized for being too large in terms of the amount of money Nintendo could obtain without any risk,[30] it became the basic type of third-party contract for game platforms in the following years.

4.4 Summary: Expanding the Diversity of Games and the Independence of Home Gaming Consoles

The biggest impact of the entry of many third parties was the increase in the variety of games released. Nintendo was a hit in arcade games such as Donkey Kong, but it did not have such a large position in arcade games. Namco, which was producing a series of hit titles for arcade at the time, joined Family Computer, and many hit titles for arcade games were transferred to Family Computer, contributing to the increase in sales of Family Computer itself. In addition, the joining of Enix led to the release of the adventurous game Portpia renzoku satsujinjiken (Portopia Serial Murder Case) and the role playing game Dragon Quest,[31] both of which had not previously been available on home game consoles, thereby broadening the range of game genres available.

Portpia renzoku satsujinjiken and Dragon Quest not only showed that adventure and role playing games, which had been considered difficult to play on home consoles, could now be played on Family Computer, but also that sales were strong. Since the release of them, the number of adventure games and role playing games has increased, and with the addition of simulation games, the three game genres originating from PC games have not only broadened but also grown to become major genres. Figure 4.3 shows the share of the three game genres among the titles released on Family Computer (RPGs include ARPGs (action RPGs) and SRPGs (simulation RPGs) in addition to regular RPGs). Since 1986, the share of the three genres has

[30] In Takahashi (1993), p. 158 states "The cost of a ROM is less than 900 yen at the time of ordering 5000 units. Nintendo orders in large quantities, so the price is probably even lower, around 700 yen. On the mask ROM, Nintendo writes the game developed by third-party and hands it over. The handover price was 1600 yen. Third party wholesales it to the primary wholesaler with the package and the game's manual. The wholesale price is 2750 yen, which is 55 percent of the retail price. If the package price is 100 yen, the third party will receive 1050 yen per package. This is only 150 yen less than Nintendo's 900 yen per package (as of June 1987)."

[31] Although Dragon Quest was the first command type RPG on Family Computer, but the first action RPG to be released on Family Computer was HYDLIDE Special (Toshiba EMI, original PC version by T&E Soft). However, the fact that non-action RPGs with command selection and a large amount of text could be played on Family Computer, and the fact that the Family Computer users (who are likely to be children) supported a game without actions, is a significant achievement.

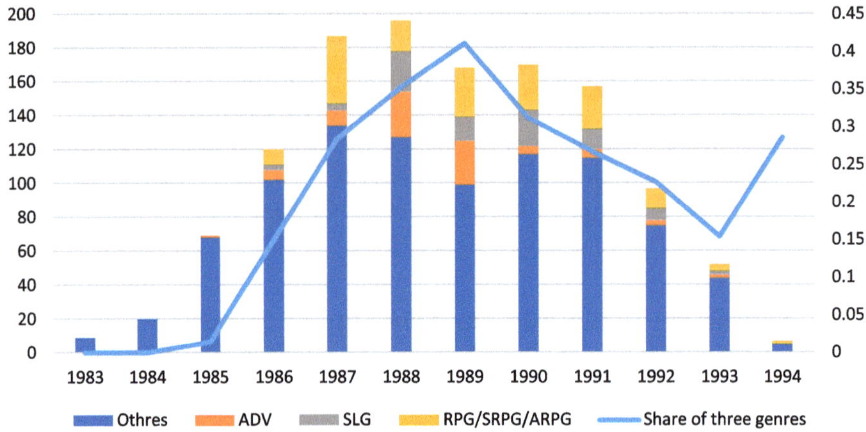

Fig. 4.3 Percentage change of the three PC game genres among the released titles (Famicom). Source of data: *Daigirin 2011* CD-ROM

been increasing, and by the peak year of 1989, it had reached more than 40%.[32] After 1990, when Super Famicom appeared on the market and the center of the market shifted, it decreased, but from 1993 to 1994, when Family Computer market almost came to an end, titles were continuously sold.

On the other hand, Sega's game consoles did not attract third parties, and it was not possible to escape from the situation where action games were the mainstream. Figure 4.4 shows the ratio of the three PC game genres among the titles sold by Sega's game consoles (SG-1000 and Mark III combined). In SEGA's 8-bit consoles, simulation games did not appear, and adventure games and role playing games were only sporadic. As a result of SEGA's failure to attract third parties, it was unable to escape from the situation where its characters were biased toward action games and the replication of arcade games, which were its forte. This greatly diminished the appeal of the game consoles.

In the beginning, most of the third-party companies used their own software assets, but they gradually shifted to original products. The games released by Nintendo were also transferred from arcade games at the beginning of the launch

[32] As for adventure games, many titles were released in 1988 and 1989, but the number of titles has rapidly decreased since then. This is related to the overwhelmingly short playing time of the games. Role playing games and simulation games take at least 20–30 hours to reach an end and require a lot of trial and error to reach the end, such as solving riddles and overcoming strong enemies. Adventure games, on the other hand, allow players to solve riddles and complete them by basically guessing the entire command. When compared to role playing games, which are similarly narrative content, adventure games have a much shorter play time. For this reason, pure text adventures without action are no longer sold, except for a few mystery adventure games or games with manga/anime characters. This situation continued until 1992, when Chun Soft released Otogirisou on Super Famicom, and the popularity of PC novel games influenced by it was returned.

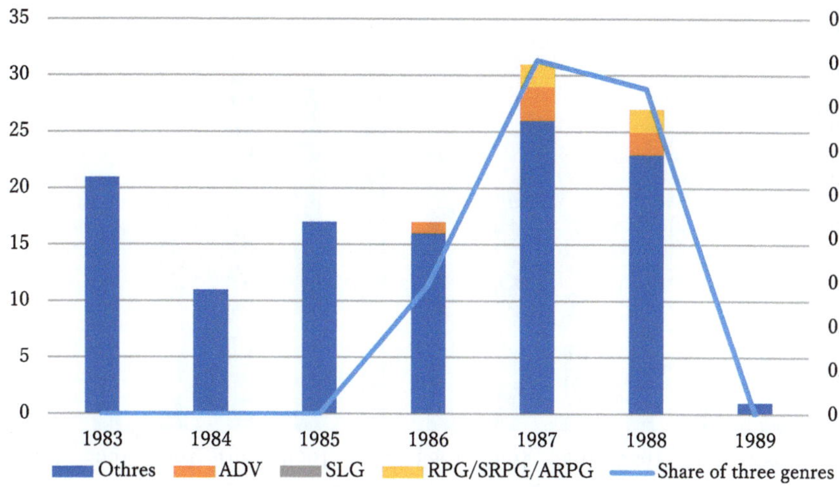

Fig. 4.4 Percentage change of the three PC game genres among the released titles (SEGA). Source of data: *SEGA HARD Daihyakka* (https://sega.jp/fb/segahard/)

of Family Computer,[33] but Nintendo had a small line-up of arcade games and quickly withdrew from arcade games, and soon became exclusively localized (Fig. 4.5).

Initially, the companies participating as third parties were from the arcade and PC game industries, but with the boom in Family Computer, many companies from the toy, publishing, music, and video (film, animation, and video production) industries also joined. The titles produced by companies in the toy and publishing industries included many games with manga and anime characters, and those produced by companies in the music and movie industries included many games with characters from the musicians and entertainers. In addition to the fact that characters could not be represented beautifully with the performance of Family Computer, many of the participating companies were technologically inept, and many of the games did not receive good reviews. With the advent of the next generation consoles, poor technology companies were weeded out, and as the performance of the computer improved, games related to manga and anime characters, which had a high affinity for computer representation, continued to be released, and more and more titles received high evaluations, but companies in the video and music industry either withdrew or concentrated on developing ordinary game titles. As a result, games by musicians and entertainers are no longer sold.

[33] The launch titles (released at the same time as the hardware) were Donkey Kong, Donkey Kong Jr, and Popeye, all of which were ported from Nintendo's own

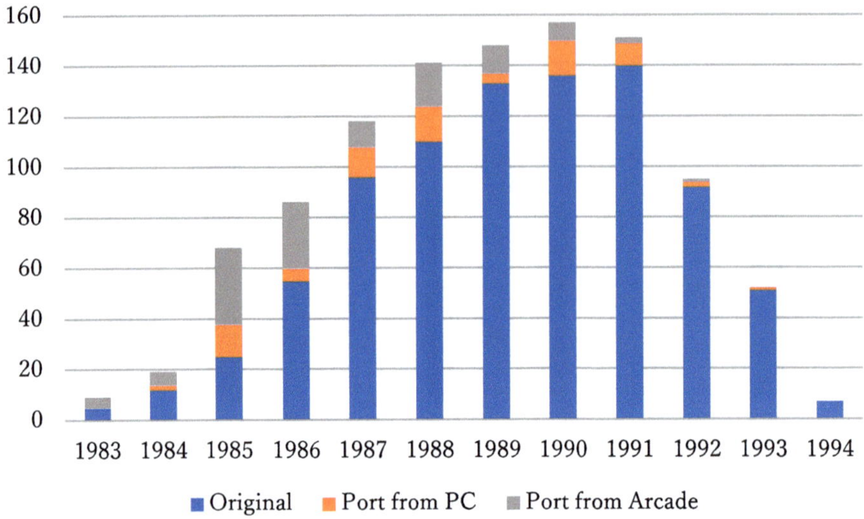

Fig. 4.5 Percentage of ported titles among Famicom game titles (ROM only). Graph: Created by the author. Source of game titles: Tokyo Metropolitan Museum of Photography exhibition “Level X” catalogue

Chapter 5
Arcade Games (2): Shock of Act on Control and Improvement of Amusement Business, Etc. and Recovery from it

Abstract This chapter describes the downturn and revival of the arcade game market. Sales of arcade games plummeted in the wake of the Act on Control and Improvement of Amusement Business and the release of the Famicom. Combined with the gambling problem caused by modified game machines, the arcade game industry was plunged into a crisis of survival. Game arcades began to improve their image with new prize machines and games that featured a large cabinet. The fighting game boom that emerged in the midst of these efforts ushered in a new era.

Keywords Act on Control and Improvement of Amusement Business · Gambling machine · Prize machine · Large cabinet games · Fighting games · Street Fighter II

5.1 Shakeout of Stores

The first statistics on stores with arcade game machines appeared in the Police White Paper in 1979. According to the results of the survey at that time, there were 69,875 stores with arcade game machines.[1] Most of them were cafés (46,356) and restaurants (15,259), and only about 10% were amusement arcades or game centers (8260). On the other hand, the number of arcade game machines installed was 283,802, of which 129,407 (2.8 machines per store on average) were installed in cafes and 37,029 (2.4 machines per store on average) were installed in restaurants, and 117,366 (average of 14.2 machines per store) for amusement and game centers.

Figure 5.1 shows the trend of the number of stores with video game machines from 1979 to 1994. The number of stores that installed game machines thinking that they could make money from the Space Invaders boom left after the boom ended, and many of them withdrew from the game business. Therefore, the number of stores with game machines gradually decreased until 1983, and then started to increase. The application of the Fuuzoku Eigyou hou (Act on Control and Improvement of Amusement Business, etc.) to game arcades stopped the trend of increase.

[1]National Police Agency Headquarters, "Iwayuru TV Game ki ni kansuru jittaityousakekka (Results of a Survey on the Actual Condition of TV Game Machines)," 1979.

Y. Koyama, *History of the Japanese Video Game Industry*, Translational Systems Sciences 35, https://doi.org/10.1007/978-981-99-1342-8_5

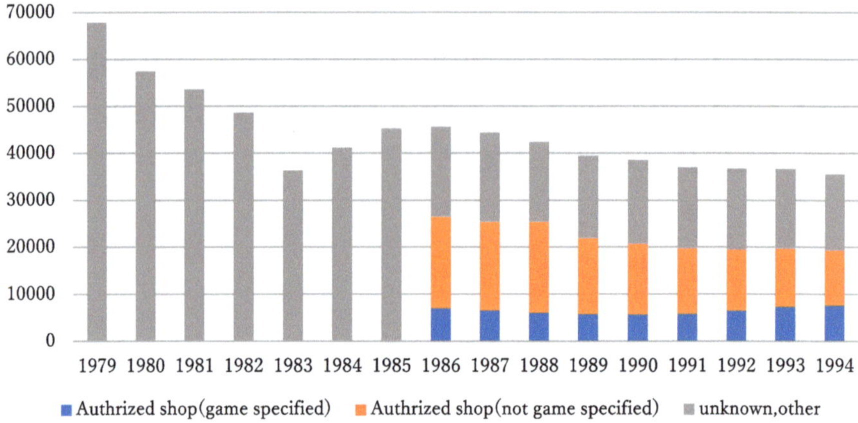

Fig. 5.1 Trends in the number of stores with arcade games. Source: Police White Paper (1980–1995)

5.2 Problem of Gambling Machines and Juvenile Delinquency

Another issue that arose during this period was gambling machines. In addition to the medal games that have been operating in the game centers since around 1971, there have been incidents of gambling machines using elemechas being imported from abroad and used since the 1970s. In the era of computer games, modified game machines were used, in which the ROM and control panel of a computer game machine manufactured in Japan were replaced with those of gambling games such as poker.

The 1983 White Paper on Police stated, "In 1979, the mainstream of amusement machines installed in game centers and other facilities were those with technological intervention,[2] such as invader games, but in the latter half of 1981, amusement machines without technological intervention, such as poker games, began to be installed, and this trend spread rapidly throughout the country. This led to a rapid increase in the number of such machines nationwide. As a result, the number of gambling crimes using such machines increased rapidly, and in 1982, 1870 cases and 10,353 people were arrested for gambling crimes, 3.8 times the number of cases

[2]The legal definition of gambling is "a dispute over the gain or loss of a property interest based on an accidental win or loss. Therefore, two points are important in determining whether arcade machines are legally considered as gambling: (1) the outcome of game play does not depend on the skill of the player (i.e., non-existence of technical intervention), and (2) there is no refund of the property value of the outcome. Many of the medal game machines commonly found in game centers are models where the outcome of play is determined solely by luck and there is no room for technical intervention. Therefore, although medal games technically fall under the category of gambling, they are operated on the premise that they do not constitute gambling because they are refunded with medals that can be used only for the machines in the game center.

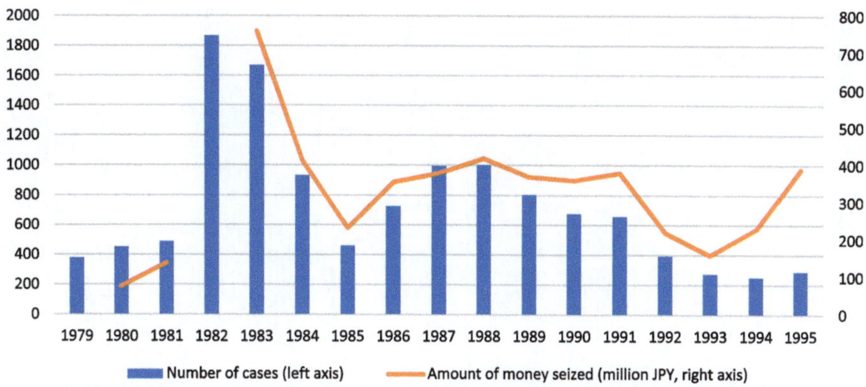

Fig. 5.2 Trends in arrests for gaming gambling offenses. Source: The White Paper on Police, 1980–1995 edition; where no data are available, values are not given in the White Paper

and 4.1 times the number of people compared to the previous year." As noted in this report, the problem peaked in 1982, when some stores operated gambling during the daytime using modified gaming machines. Since gambling was an important source of funds for the gangs, the police actively raided actual stores and seized gambling machines and deposits (Fig. 5.2). However, there were incidents in which police officers received bribes from operators in return for leaking information on gambling machine seizures, and this became a major social problem.

In addition, since the Space Invaders boom, there has been continuous social criticism that game centers are a breeding ground for juvenile delinquency. The National Police Agency has long been concerned about this issue. The name "game center" first appeared in the police white paper in 1978, merely to introduce a case of "a game center being used as a hangout for juvenile delinquents," but from the following year onward it was treated in the same way as snack bars, discos, and late-night cafe. The police viewed game centers as "a factor that encourages juvenile delinquency and hinders healthy development"(National Police Agency, 1981).

When the police surveyed the hangouts of delinquent youths (places where youths hang out, smoke, drink, engage in immoral activities, etc.), game centers were the third most common place in 1983 after snack bars or cafes, and apartments, and the most common place in 1984. There was no time to wait for any legal restrictions to be imposed on gaming centers (Photo 5.1) (Table 5.1).

5.3 Decline in Sales Due to Application of Fuuzoku Eigyou Hou and the Introduction of Family Computer

Although there were protests from the industry, the Fuuzoku Eigyou hou was finally passed by the Diet in 1984 and went into effect the following year. As a result, game centers were classified as "Type 8 Business" under the law, which regulated the

Photo 5.1 A game center in National Police Agency 1984. Source: http://www.npa.go.jp/hakusyo/s59/s590300.html

Table 5.1 Ranking of hangouts for young people

	First	Second	Third
1983	Snack bar or Café 22.4%	Apartment 15.1%	Game Center 14.8%
1984	Game Center 18.3%	Snack bar or Café 18.1%	Apartment 11.5%

Source: National Police Agency, 1984, 1985

hours of operation, the noise they could emit, and the areas they could operate in. Hours of operation were limited to 0:00 midnight, and no one under the age of 18 years was prohibited to enter the store after 10:00 p.m.

In addition to the Entertainment Establishments Control Law, the Family Computer (Famicom), which was launched in 1983, also caused problems for the game centers. The price of Famicom was 14,800 yen and the game software was 3800 yen[3] and considering that a game software could be played for a long time once purchased, 100 yen per game play was quite expensive.[4] Famicom was designed to

[3] At the time of the Famicom launch, the price of a single game was 3800 yen, but later, 4500–5500 yen became the mainstream price.

[4] Arcade games have been priced at 100 yen per play since Speed Race was released by Taito in 1974 (as pointed out by Yasushi Takeda in a private email). At that time, the price of playing arcade games in the USA was cheaper than in Japan because in the USA was 25 cents (one quarter) per play. Considering that $1 = 360 yen at the time, this price was quite expensive considering the

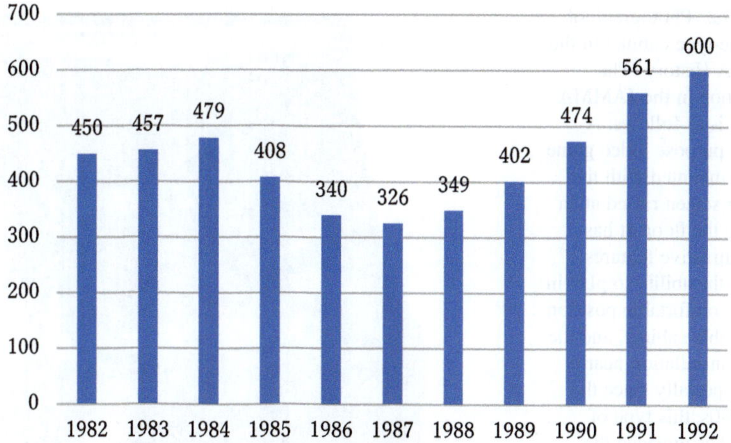

Fig. 5.3 Trends in coin-operation sales (billion yen). Source: Japan Productivity Center 1993 edition

work with most of the arcade games at the time of development. Not only Nintendo's Donkey Kong, which was considered the benchmark for performance at the time of its development, but also Taito's Space Invaders (1979) and Namco's Galaxian and Pac-Man (both 1981) were transferred at almost the same level. As a result, it became possible to play high-quality games without going to a game center.

The combination of these problems resulted in a decrease in the number of sales of game center operations (sales due to the investment of coins in game machines). Figure 5.3 shows the trend in sales of operation by year. Sales increased slightly in 1983 and 1984, when the popularity of the Famicom (launched on July 15, 1983) was still in its infancy. Sales declined from 1985, when the sales of Famicom boomed, to 326 billion yen in 1987, about one-third of the peak in 1984 (479 billion yen).

The arcade game industry was forced to work hard to restore the image and the number of customers.

5.4 Recovering from a Bad Image and Turning it around with a New Approach

In response to the two crises of bad public image and the departure of the game center due to the release of Family Computer, the game center took the following two approaches:

---

difference in prices and incomes between Japan and the USA. However, considering that the companies developing arcade games in the USA eventually almost disappeared, it ultimately supported the profitability of arcade games in Japan and contributed to the development of the industry.

Photo 5.2 Photograph of the mule-type cabinet in the JAMMA History (The description in the JAMMA History is as follows: A general-purpose video game cabinet mounted with the monitor screen raised at an angle to the floor. It has many attractive features, such as the ability to play in a more comfortable position than a table cabinet, and the ease of installation near a wall. Especially since the mid-1980s, this type of cabinet has replaced the standard for general-purpose video game cabinets).

5.4.1 Making Game Centers Safe

After the Space Invaders hit, game centers often adopted store layouts that crammed as many games as possible into a small space to increase revenue. Therefore, managers would cram in a tabletop cabinet with very little space. The lights were turned down as much as possible so that the light would not reflect on the glass top of the tabletop cabinet, and the atmosphere was dim. The combination of the dimness of the store and the sound from the game machines made it difficult to notice any extortion going on in the game center.

Midi-type cabinets, in which the monitor is set at an angle to the floor and the player can sit on a chair for comfortable gameplay, were first introduced by TEHKAN in 1981 as mule-type cabinets. As a result of the widespread use of midi-type cabinets after Fuuzoku Eigyo hou, the lighting in many arcades became brighter and the atmosphere became healthier (Photo 5.2).

5.4.2 *Differentiation from Home Video Games*

If they can only play games at the same level as home video games, consumers will not bother to visit arcades. Therefore, to maintain the ability to attract customers, game companies actively introduced and developed new technologies for arcade games.

In game centers, when the income of old games deteriorated, they were replaced with new games, and the system boards inside the cabinets were frequently changed to new ones. Taking Sega, which was active in both arcade and home video games, as an example, the number of system boards for arcade games released in the 16 years between 1983 and 1998 was 14,[5] excluding minor changes. During the same period, five home video game consoles[6] were released, excluding minor changes. FM sound chips, 16-bit/32-bit CPUs, dedicated 3D-CG hardware, etc. were all introduced in arcade games and later expanded to home video games and PC games.

The reason for the aggressive adoption of new technology was that arcade games did not require game players, the ultimate consumers, to replace their game hardware, and they could play games equipped with the latest technology by paying 100 yen. As a result, arcades succeeded in differentiating themselves from home video games as a place where games using new technologies and expressions could be played on a large screen.

5.4.3 *Turning Game Centers into Leisure Lands*

The trend of making games more wholesome and differentiating them from home video games eventually resulted in the "conversion of game arcades into a leisure land." Products were created with not only male adults and middle and high school students, but also female customers and families.

In 1985, UFO Catcher (Sega), a crane game machine, was introduced. The machine works by inserting coins, moving the magic hand once vertically and once horizontally, and successfully picking up the prize at the bottom to get the prize. As a result of trial and error, stuffed animals could be placed inside the machine as prizes,[7] which greatly contributed to attracting female customers.

---

[5]The system boards released from 1983 to 1998 are SYSTEM I (1983), SYSTEM II (1985), SYSTEM E (1986), SYSTEM 16 (1986), X-board (1987), SYSTEM 24 (1988), SYSTEM 18 (1989), C-board (1990), SYSTEM 32 (1991), MODEL 1 (1992), ST-V (1994), MODEL 2 (1994), MODEL 3 (1996), and NAOMI (1998).

[6]Five home video game consoles were released between 1983 and 1998: SG-1000 (1983), Sega Mark III (1985), Mega Drive (1988), Saturn (1994), and Dreamcast (1998).

[7]When UFO catchers were first introduced, the maximum amount of prizes was set at 200 yen by law. Therefore, capsule toys (so-called Gashapon or Gacha) were used as prizes. Later, as the

Photo 5.3 Crane game machine (Photo: NEW UFO CATCHER, 1987). Source: Wikipedia

Print Club (Purikura) (1995, Atlus) is one of the first arcade game machines developed for women. Print Club created the "photo sticker machine" genre, and although the huge boom has since died down, it is still one of the staple devices in game centers (Photo 5.3).

In addition, several games with large-sized chassis were created as games that could not be experienced on home video game consoles. Sega's Hang On (1985) had a chassis in the shape of a motorcycle, with a monitor in front of the handlebars. It had a novel control system in which the player tilted the motorcycle when turning a corner in actual play. Sega called the games in the large chassis "Taikan Games (cenesthesic games)," and introduced them in rapid succession: Space Harrier (1985), Enduro Racer (1986), Outrun (1986), and After Burner (1987). These games were characterized using a mechanical system such as a hydraulic system to tilt the seat in response to the player's actions, creating an experience like that of a small amusement park attraction.

As a result of these various efforts and innovations, the number of customers and sales of game centers returned to an upward trend (Photo 5.4).

---

maximum amount of prizes was raised, the variety of prizes increased, and now they have become the mainstay of game center sales. As for 2022, the upper limit is 1000 yen.

Photo 5.4 Arcade games in a large cabinet. Street Fighter (Capcom) in the back, Outrun (Sega) in the center, and DARIUS (Taito) in the foreground. Source: Wikipedia

5.5 The Advent of the Fighting Game Boom

In 1990, arcade operation sales recovered to the level before Fuzoku Eigyo hou, and expanded even more rapidly. This was due to the explosive success of Capcom's Street Fighter II (1991), a fighting game.[8]

As the name suggests, Street Fighter II is a sequel to Street Fighter (1987, hereafter referred to as Street Fighter I). Street Fighter I is a fighting game just like Street Fighter II, with the same weak, medium, and strong punches and kicks used to fight the enemy. The difference is that Street Fighter I was designed along the lines of the cenesthesic games that were popular at the time, requiring players to hit pressure-sensor buttons mounted on a special chassis at different strengths. Street Fighter I was shipped to Japan and the USA and was a hit in both markets. However, while the large buttons with pressure sensors were fine for the US market, not

[8] Fighting games themselves existed long before *Street Fighter*. The first pre-*Street Fighter* fighting game was Brøderbund's *KARATEKA* (1984) for the Apple II PC, and Nintendo's *Urban Champion* (1984) for Family Computer. In the arcades, there are *Karate-Do* (1984) by Data East and *Yie Ar Kung-Fu* (1985) by Konami. However, these games were considered by users to be a type of action game. With the huge success of *Street Fighter II*, fighting games became a standard genre and many titles were released.

everyone in Japan was strong enough to punch and kick hard enough, so a type with six buttons (strong, medium, and weak buttons for each punch and kick) in a midi-type chassis was released. By freeing the player from having to hit the buttons so hard, it allowed for finer control and a wider range of game play. This was so well received that it became the basis for future fighting games.

Street Fighter II was first released as a six-button midi cabinet and became a huge hit immediately after its release. When the game was first released, two players could play against each other on a single cabinet, but soon the telecommunication battle cabinet became popular. At first glance, it may seem like a waste of space, but they were very efficient in terms of management. In single-player matches, the player plays two out of three matches with each character. In two-player matches, the player plays against the other player in a two-out-of-three game, with the loser having the game over, but the winner can continue playing alone. It was also possible to "brawl in" when someone was playing alone and playing against them. The loser of the match would always lose one credit. During the boom, there was a lot of brawling and fighting going on, so it was important to create an environment where people could play comfortably and throw in 100-yen coins.

To make Street Fighter II a long-lasting hit, the company released Street Fighter II', an improved and rebalanced version, and Street Fighter II' TURBO (both 1992), which increased the overall speed of the game.[9] Both were released in 1992. Super Street Fighter II (1993), with additional characters, and its improved version, Super Street Fighter II X (1994), were also released in succession. Street Fighter II was also ported to home video game consoles. Among them, the Super Famicom version of Street Fighter II (1992) became a huge hit, selling 6.5 million copies worldwide, and tournaments using the home version of Street Fighter II were held in many places. The 1993 national tournament was held at the Ryogoku Kokugikan.

The huge success of Street Fighter II pushed fighting games into the standard genre, and fighting games were released one after another by various companies. Several companies produced moderate hits, but it was SNK's THE KING OF FIGHTERS series that eventually became the standard title alongside Street Fighter II. THE KING OF FIGHTERS '94 (1994, KOF94) was a game that ran on SNK's MVS platform, and featured a two-player battle system with three players per team. The game features a variety of characters from SNK's past games, including the company's hit fighting games Garou Densetsu (FATAL FURY) (1991) and Ryuuko no ken (Art of Fighting) (1992), as well as characters from SNK's previous games Ikari (1986) and Psycho Soldier (1987). KOF '94 was a hit and became a

[9] In a fighting game, players are greatly demotivated when there are extreme strengths, weaknesses, or disadvantages of the controllable characters, or when there are situations where the opponent can't resist and is beaten unilaterally (so called "*hame waza*(cheap techniques)"). In fighting games, it often takes a long time (6 months or more) to adjust the balance of play after development. However, after adjusting the game balance to compensate for undiscovered *hame waza* and disadvantages caused by tactics often used by actual players, sequel titles with new characters are often released.

long-lasting title, with new titles released every year, including KOF '95 the following year and KOF '96 the year after that.[10]

As a result, fighting games have contributed greatly to attracting people back to game centers, and this is due to the following two points:

1. Because the main attraction of fighting games is the competition with humans, it is necessary to visit a game center in order to play against other players (advantage from the game content).
2. The number of characters appearing on the screen is small, so at first glance it looks easy to develop, but the image data for the many moves performed by the characters must be stored in memory and drawn quickly in response to the player's operation. As a result, hardware requiring specifications for ROM and RAM are high, making porting difficult.[11]

As with cenesthesic games, fighting games were a hit because of the unique appeal of arcade games, which was not found in home video games.

5.6 Summary: Out of the Crisis and Further Development

This chapter described the crisis that hit the arcade game industry after Space Invaders and its escape and re-expansion from the crisis. The arcade game industry faced a crisis of social recognition due to Fuzoku Eigyo hou. The problem of social credibility had already existed since the birth of Space Invaders, but it was a crisis that was met by neglecting to address it. If Fuzoku Eigyo hou crisis was a crisis of being deemed "unnecessary" by society, the crisis by the launch of Family Computer was a crisis of being deemed "unnecessary" by individual users because games equivalent to those in arcades could now be played at home.

Ultimately, these crises were overcome by a healthy atmosphere and vigorous innovation. In the process, it became possible to attract female customers, making it easier for many people to enter game centers. In addition, the huge success of Street Fighter II and later fighting games brought them back to life completely. From now until the mid-1990s, the heyday of arcade games will last for a while.

[10] Although there were some troubles along the way, such as SNK's bankruptcy (2000), one title was released per year until THE KING OF FIGHTERS 2003 was released in 2003. After that, there was a gap between releases. The current latest title is THE KING OF FIGHTERS XV, released in 2022, but it is for home consoles and PC.

[11] Street Fighter II, which was ported to the Super Famicom, was very good, but some parts of the presentation and techniques were omitted. Other fighting games were also ported to various game hardware of the time, but none of them were completely ported, as the characters were reduced in size and some techniques were omitted. The exception to this was the NEOGEO (SNK) game console, which used the same system board as the arcade game system, allowing the exact same fighting games to be played at home, but the price of the game ROMs was over 30,000 yen each, so they were not widely available.

Chapter 6
PC Games (2) Establishment and Stagnation of the PC-9801 Long-Term Regime

Abstract This chapter describes the changes that occurred in the PC gaming market from the late 1980s to the early 1990s. During this period, computers were becoming more powerful, and PCs for personal hobbyists were also shifting to 16-bit. In particular, the PC-9801VM released by NEC in 1985 became the de facto standard and lasted until the mid-1990s. This stalled technological innovation. This chapter also discusses the piracy problem and R18 games as social issues that arose with PC games.

Keywords PC-9801VM · MSX2 · X68000 · Indie games · Illegal copy · R18 games

In the world of personal computers, compatibility with the past is important in principle, but there are times when a major innovation occurs that causes past software assets to be neglected. This happened in the late 1980s. With the advent of 16-bit computers, the PC game market was dominated by the PC-9801 series, which already took center stage in offices. At the same time, it was also the beginning of a long period of stagnation.

In addition, there are two major problems with PC games that continue to this day. One is the problem of illegal copying and the other is the problem of restrictions on the expression of adult games. Both problems have existed since the dawn of PC games, but they have suddenly become apparent due to the expansion of the market scale and the improvement of the PC's expressive power. In this chapter, we will discuss this point as well.

6.1 Replacement of the 8-Bit Trinity

In the latter half of the 1980s, the three 8-bit families had successors: the PC-8801mk2SR (NEC), the FM-77AV (Fujitsu), and the X1 turbo (Sharp). As the demand for business use was met by office computers and 16-bit computers with lower prices, 8-bit computers specialized in hobby use. Specifically, the graphics and audio functions were enhanced to increase the number of colors that could be

Y. Koyama, *History of the Japanese Video Game Industry*, Translational Systems Sciences 35, https://doi.org/10.1007/978-981-99-1342-8_6

Table 6.1 Three 8-bit Trinity (second generation)

Manufacturer	NEC	Sharp	Fujitsu
Year of release	1985	1984	1985
Product name	PC-8801mk2SR	X1 turbo	FM-77AV
CPU	μPC780C (Z80 compatible) (4 MHz)	Z80A (4 MHz)	6809(MBL68B09E) × 2 (2 MHz × 2)
RAM	64 KB	76 KB	128 KB
VRAM	48 KB + 4 KB	96 KB	96 KB
Graphics	640 × 400 1 color	640 × 400 8colors	640 × 200 8colors/ 4096colors
Sound	FM 3 sounds PSG 3 sounds	FM 3 sounds PSG 3 sounds	FM 3 sounds PSG 3 sounds
Price[a]	258,000 yen (model 30)	278,000yen (model30)	158,000 yen(AV-2)
Remarks		Equipped with kanji ROM	

[a]The price is for the top-of-the-line model

displayed and moved on the screen, and FM sound chips were installed as sound sources. Floppy disk drives were also included as a standard feature (Table 6.1).

Each year, compatible successors were introduced for each model, and performance gradually increased as prices decreased, but games continued to be developed for the above three models. The only exceptions to this were the PC-8801FA and MA, released in 1987, for which the sound board (released as Sound Board II as a peripheral for past models) became the de facto standard sound source.

Although there were differences in performance between them, the PC-8801mk2SR, which had the lowest performance, was practically the sole winner. In the game market, games for the FM-77AV, then the X1 turbo, were no longer released, and finally there were almost no games for 8-bit hobby PCs other than the PC-8801mk2SR.

6.2 The Spread of the MSX2 and the Demise of the MSX

The MSX released in 1983 had a single-color sprite, a fixed number of 16 colors, and a standard RAM of 16 KB, making it a low-performance PC and game machine. The number of units sold also fell far short of expectations.

Under these circumstances, the MSX2 standard was announced in 1985, which greatly improved the graphics capabilities of the MSX2 while maintaining the basic performance of the CPU and other components. The screen resolution was slightly inferior to that of 8-bit hobby PCs, which cost about twice as much, but considering a

Table 6.2 Main specifications of MSX and MSX2

	MSX	MSX2
Year	1983	1985
CPU	Z80A (3.57 Hz)	Z80A (3.57 Hz)
Screen resolution	256 × 192	256 × 212 (Screen 5)
Number of simultaneous colors	Fixed 16 colors	16 colors / 512 colors in (Screen 5)
Sprite function	Yes (single color)	Yes (4 colors)
Sound function	PSG 3 sounds	PSG 3 sounds
Price	Less than 100,000 yen	50,000-60,000 yen or less
Dedicated display	Not required	Not required
Remarks		3.5-inch floppy disk drive

MSX2 is the specification of Matsushita Electric's FS-A1F (1987)

Table 6.3 MSX standard and companies that released compatible models (in Japan)

	Year	Companies
MSX1	1983	Casio, Canon, Sanyo Electric, Sanyo Electric Special Equipment, General, Sony, Toshiba, Japan Musical Instruments, JVC, Pioneer, Hitachi, Fujitsu, Matsushita Electric
MSX2	1985	Mitsubishi Electric, Canon, Sanyo Electric, Sony, Toshiba, JVC, Hitachi, Matsushita Electric, Mitsubishi electric
MSX2+	1988	Sanyo Electric, Sony, Matsushita Electric
MSX turboR	1990	Matsushita Electric

large number of simultaneous colors, the expressive power of still images was almost the same (Table 6.2).

In addition to the ROM cartridge slot (general-purpose expansion slot), which was a feature as a PC for games, the popular models were equipped with floppy disk drive. On the system side, it also ran an operating system (MSX-DOS), making it a full-fledged personal computer.

However, in the fall of 1986, the FS-A1 was released by Matsushita Electric for 29,800 yen and the HB-F1 by Sony for 32,800 yen. These two models were not equipped with floppy disk drive, but their successors, the FS-A1F and HB-F1XD, which were released the following year, were equipped with floppy disk drive and were inexpensive at 54,800 yen, which accelerated their popularity.

Later, the MSX2+ (1988) was released with further enhanced functions, but it was not a big hit as the 8-bit personal computer market was nearing its end. The only companies that developed and released hardware were Matsushita Electric (now Panasonic), its group company Sanyo Electric, and Sony.

In 1990, a 16-bit version of the MSX turboR (1990) was released, but this time it was only Matsushita Electric. 16-bit performance was improved, but the price of the machine also increased to over 100,000 yen. The MSX standard came to an end here, partly because by this time it was quite inexpensive and could not be differentiated from the PC-9801 (and its compatible machines) (Table 6.3).

6.3 The Appearance of the PC-9801VM and its de Facto Standardization

1985 was also a turning point for 16-bit PCs, with the release of the PC-9801VM. PC-9801VM featured a new graphics chip that greatly enhanced graphics functions, and, although it was an option on the PC-9801VM, it enabled the simultaneous display of 16 out of 4096 colors using analog RGB, which later became the de facto standard (Table 6.4).

Numerous models of the PC-9801 series are released every year, and although the inclusion of FM sound sources and the transition from 5-inch to 3.5-inch floppy disks occur, the "PC-9801VM and later" becomes the de facto standard for basic architecture in games. In addition, the 8-bit hobby PC stalled after completing its mission in time, and PC-9801VM also became the de facto standard architecture.

The PC-9801 series saw a gradual increase in performance and decrease in price with each year's release of successive models, and the PC-9801 rose to the status of a hobby PC. The next standard architecture for games on 16-bit PCs was the PC-9821 series in 1992, but it took a few more years for the architecture to shift, as the PC itself needed to become popular for game companies to develop and sell games for the PC-9821 series.

6.4 AV-Enhanced Hobby PCs

In the latter half of the 1980s, hobby PCs also evolved in terms of audiovisual functions and became much more like dedicated game machines. It was positioned as the 16-bit successor (FM TOWNS was 32-bit) to the 8-bit trinity, and its multimedia functions were greatly enhanced. The PC-8801VA (NEC) and X68000 (Sharp) were released in 1987, and the FM TOWNS (Fujitsu) in 1989.

The PC-8801VA was an ambitious model that was equipped with the V30, a 16-bit CPU developed by NEC, and sprite functions while maintaining some compatibility with the PC-8801mk2SR and later to a certain extent, but it was

Table 6.4 Specifications of PC-9801VM

Manufacturer	NEC
Year	1985
Product name	PC-9801VM
CPU	V30 (10 MHz)
RAM	384 KB
HDD	None (VM0) / 20 MB (VM2)
Graphics	640 × 400 8 colors/ 640 × 400 16 colors / 4096 colors (option)
Sound source	None
Price	295,000 yen(VM0) / 830,000 yen(VM2)

insufficiently compatible with both the PC-9801VM(or later) series and PC-8801mk2SR(or later) and was not blessed with compatible game software.

The FM TOWNS was a PC with a rather advanced design, including a 32-bit Intel 80386 CPU and the first CD-ROM in Japan. It was designed as a pure 32-bit PC, and its basic performance was high because it allowed development without worrying about compatibility with past 16-bit machines. However, the lack of a sprite function was a weak point for gaming applications.

As the name implies, the X68000 used Motorola's MC68000 CPU, which is used in many arcade games, as its CPU, and it also had a sprite function. Due to the nature of the hardware, it was suitable for porting arcade games, and many games were ported to it. In addition, the user community was very active because the hardware specifications were open to the public. In 1993, the X68030, the successor to the MC68000 and equipped with the 32-bit CPU 68030, was released. It was used for the longest time among the PC8801VA, FM TOWNS, and X68000.[1]

6.5 Convergence to the PC-9801

When the PC-8801mk2SR was first introduced, many games were released, but as the price of the PC-9801, a 16-bit PC, came down, it gradually lost momentum and handed over its position as a hobby PC to the PC-9801. As for the rest of the PCs, especially those of Sharp and Fujitsu, their presence was greatly diminished because of the failure of the generational change.

This is confirmed by the same data as in Chap. 3. Figure 6.1 shows the number of supported hardware in the top 20 game software titles of each year listed in *Yomigaeru PC-8801 Densetsu (Reviving the PC-8801 Legend)* (ASCII, 2006). Compared to the 1983–1987 period shown in Chap. 3, the number of hardware models appearing in the ranking has decreased significantly. Sixteen of the top 20 titles were compatible with PC-88 series (almost all of which were compatible with mk2SR or later) in 1988, but the number of titles has decreased year by year to 3 in 1992. In 1992, the number of titles was 3. The PC-98 series (almost all of which were compatible with VM or later) replaced the PC-98 series and became the de facto standard around 1990, while the MSX continued to do well in the 1990s due to the relatively low price of the MSX2 console, but only one title was ranked in 1992. In 1992, only one title was ranked.

[1]The X68000 was the best PC for learning the 68,000 CPU operation, and there were examples of it being used in the twenty-first century in technical schools that teach game development.

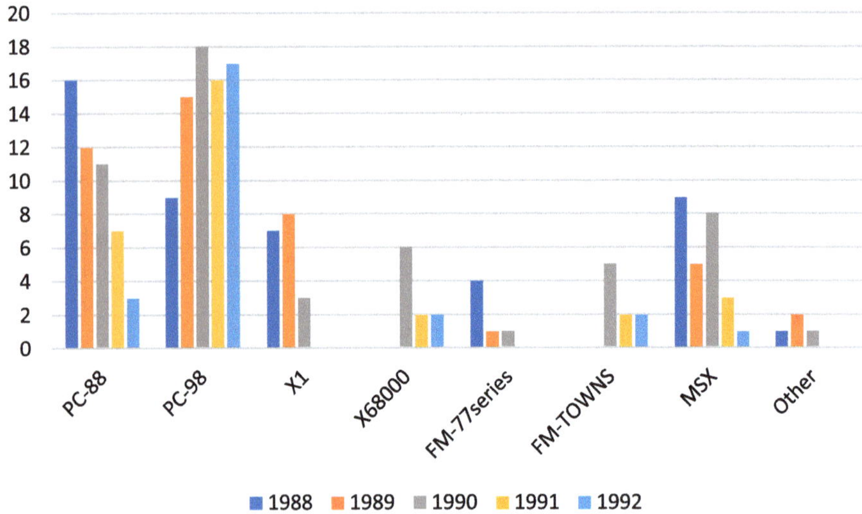

Fig. 6.1 Number of titles released for the corresponding model among the top 20 titles of the year

6.6 Self-Production of PC Games

The movement for users who have purchased PCs to create and publish games has existed since the early days of PCs. In the winter of 1983, the University of Electro-Communications SF-Z Society (Science Fiction Study Group) released the game Nico Nico Girl Puzzle for the PC-8801, and the following year in 1984, Teikoku Soft, a circle of SF-Z Society members, released Ningyo no Namida (Mermaid's Tears) for the PC-8801, which is considered to be the first software to be labeled as doujin software. After that, the number of doujin game groups exhibiting at the Comic Market continued to increase, and in 1989, the number exceeded 200.

Other than the Comic Market, there was a monthly exhibition called Pasoket held once a month from 1988 in various parts of Japan. Roughly, several hundred games were sold each time, equivalent to a quarter to a third of the sales at the Comic Market (Photo 6.1).

Many of these game creators were young, in their teens and twenties, and had taught themselves to master machine language (or assembler language that expressed it in primitive instructions) that could directly codify the hardware to make the games run faster. Because of the close proximity of the creators and purchasers, and the high level of interaction, there was quite a bit of technical exchange at Pasoket.

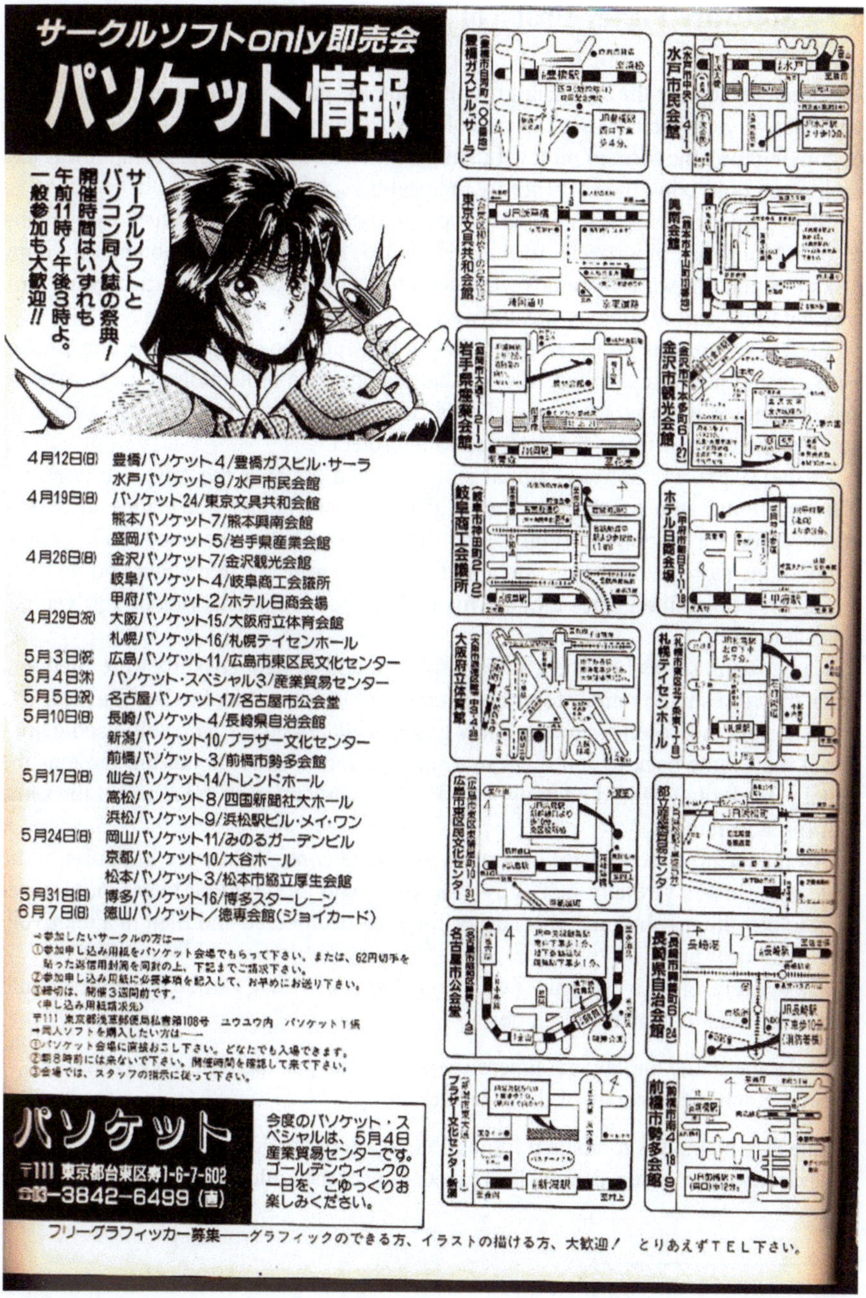

Photo 6.1 Advertisement for Pasoket in a PC game magazine (*Technopolis*, May 1992)

6.7 Software Piracy Problem

The main reason for the sluggish growth of the PC game market was the fact that it was relatively easy to copy. In the case of movies, animation, and music, the problem of copying took the form of piracy, but in the case of PC games, the problem was that each user could copy the software by themselves.

Most game software is technically copy-protected in some way, such as by being recorded on a disk in a special format.[2] However, for software distributed on floppy disks, special software to remove the copy protection was sold as a backup tool, which could be used to copy the software.

Each software was protected in a different way, and the companies selling backup tools created programs (called "filers") that matched the protection of each software and distributed them at a low cost. Users could copy games by combining the filer that matched the software they wanted to unprotect.

In the 1980s, PC software rental stores existed all over the city, and such PC software rental stores were lined with games. Users rented out games for a few hundred yen for a couple of nights or 500–1000 yen for a week and made copies. Many of the stores would give you a filet of the software for free when you rented it out. Users copied the games they borrowed back to blank disks (about 100 yen per disk) at home.

Game rental stores became a social problem, and several lawsuits were filed, but when they did so, the rental stores changed their business model to become used PC game dealers only on the surface. They guaranteed customers who sold used games that if they came back to sell them in a short period of time (about the same as the rental period), they would be bought back at the same price as the rental at the same cost (pseudo rental).

No matter how technically ingenious the game companies were in applying the protection, it was virtually ineffective for users who thought that they would never want to pay the regular price, because it could be deciphered and filed in a relatively short period of time.

There were effectively only two countermeasures that game companies could take other than to protect the game:

1. Make the game unplayable unless users have the package and accessories.
2. Strengthen the contents of the package.

The first method is to make it impossible to enjoy the game without the package, for example, the game cannot be played unless the unlock code written on the

[2]This protection is the biggest problem when archiving past games. Since the actual machines become inoperable over time, the games are archived on the premise that they will run on an emulator environment, which is a virtual version of the operating environment of the time on the current PC. To run on the emulator, the data on the disk must be sucked out and converted into an image, but if there is any protection on the disk, the image cannot be sucked out, so it must be removed by hacking. This is to recreate what the backup tool companies did back then.

designated page of the manual is correctly entered when the game is started, which is called manual protection. Another example is that there are parts of the game where the game cannot be played without the accessories.[3] This method was not well received by users because it was troublesome to play the game and some users lost the manuals and accessories.

The second method is to increase the satisfaction level of users buying the package, thereby stimulating their desire to collect it. For example, the manual should be a beautiful, full-color book that also serves as a setting material collection, and the package should include a world map or newspaper to stimulate the user's imagination about the game world.

The problem of copying games is so serious that it is believed that several times, sometimes more than 10 times, the number of games sold have been illegally played. The impact on the market is immeasurable. The problem was still manageable when games were supplied on floppy disks, which could be copy-protected with technical ingenuity, but from the mid-1990s onward, when the supply media shifted to CD-ROMs, which were difficult to protect, the problem was over.

As time went on, computer performance increased, and even though development became more time consuming (i.e., costs increased), business could no longer be conducted in a situation where most of the games released were copied. It is safe to say that this is one of the reasons why PC games, except for adult games, have become all online games that user accounts and passwords for authentication online and prepaid cards such as Web money or credit cards for payment.

6.8 Adult Games and Regulations

Since the PC is a hardware suitable for producing high-resolution single pictures, adult games have existed since the dawn of PC games as "games for viewing pictures." In the early days before the PC package game market was established, major game companies that are now active in home video games were experimentally selling adult games.[4] Once the PC game market was established and they were able to produce hit games for the public, these major companies quickly withdrew from the market. After that, adult games were released under different brands by companies specializing in adult games and medium-sized companies.

In 1986, the game "177" (developed by Macadamia Software, released by Davey Software), which was based on Article 177 of the Penal Code (rape), was discussed

[3]When you need to make a phone call during the game, the phone number is only written in the newspaper that comes with the game, the map of the game world is only included in the package and you cannot find your way without it, and you need the deciphering chart written in the manual to solve the cipher, etc.

[4]The Strawberry Porn series for Koei Microcomputer Systems (Night Life (1982), Danchizuma no Yuwaku (Temptation of the Apartment Complex Wife) (1983), Oranda zuma ha denki unagi no yume wo miruka? (Does the Dutch Wife Dream of Electric Eels?) (1984), Enix's Lolita Syndrome (1983), Nihon Falcom's Joshidaise private (Female College Student Private) (1983), etc.

in the Diet and became a problem.[5] However, it did not lead to direct regulation, but only to guidance through an industry group.

This was followed by the arrest of the perpetrator of the serial kidnapping and murder of a young girl in 1989, which led to a tighter social scrutiny of sexual expression in the media. Movements to ban as harmful spread throughout Japan, and local governments began to designate more and more horror and adult videos and manga as harmful in their ordinances for the sound development of youth. However, PC games have been left completely unregulated.[6]

In 1991, a junior high school student shoplifted a copy of the PC adult software Saori-Bishoujo-tachi no Yakata-(Saori-the house of beautiful girls-) (Fairytale[7]) in Kyoto, which led to the arrest of the president and employees of the company that sold the software for the purpose of selling obscene pictures.[8] In 1992, Miyazaki Prefecture designated three games as harmful under its Youth Development Ordinance. When Gainax's Dennou Gakuen Scenario I (computer high school scenario I) released in 1990 was designated as harmful, Gainax filed an administrative lawsuit against the governor of Miyazaki Prefecture, demanding that the designation be revoked. The lawsuit eventually went all the way to the Supreme Court (the first trial was held in 1994, and the second trial was dismissed in 1995), but the case was dismissed in 1999, and Gainax lost the case.

In the face of this growing social criticism, there was a need for the industry to promote self-regulation.[9] In 1992, the Japan Personal Computer Software Association (called PASOKYO in Japan) began to produce stickers for adult games to be

[5] At the House of Representatives Accounts Committee in 1986. It was taken up by Shozo Kusakawa, a member of the Komei Party. The details can be read at

http://kokkai.ndl.go.jp/SENTAKU/syugiin/107/0410/10710210410001a.html

[6] With the improvement of drawing know-how of PC game companies, the drawing of pictures has become more detailed. However, there were some games in which the genitals were not mosaicked, or in which the mosaic was removed by certain hidden commands.

[7] At the time, Fairytale had released several games under the "X-rated" brand, all of which were designated as harmful.

[8] For reference, quote a newspaper article from that time. The names of the suspects have been changed from their real names to alphabet.

Asahi Shimbun, evening edition, November 25, 1991: "Trader arrested for selling obscene computer game software."

On November 25, the Kyoto Prefectural Police Juvenile Division arrested Kirara, a software distributor in Takadanobaba 1-chome, Shinjuku-ku, Tokyo, Just, a software distributor in Miyasaka 3-chome, Setagaya-ku, Tokyo, and an electronics store in Shimogyo-ku, Kyoto, for selling obscene computer software. A total of four locations were raided on suspicion of possession with intent to sell obscene documents. The suspects, H, 27, head of the delivery office of Kirara, and S, 35, president of Just, were arrested on the same charges and software and other items were seized. There are a number of video games on the market that feature naked women or sex scenes, and some magazines specializing in them have appeared, making them popular among junior and senior high school students.

[9] Industrial policy in Japan is not based on direct regulation by laws or ministerial ordinances, but rather on indirect regulation by having industry groups established to self-regulate and monitor the industry groups. The game industry is following this custom.

Photo 6.2 A sample of stickers for adult games published in a game magazine (*Technopolis*, May 1992 issue)

attached to packages and sell them for 300–400 yen per 100 copies. At the same time, the major PC game distributors agreed that they would (1) not handle adult software without the stickers and (2) obtain a guarantee from the manufacturers that the software was not obscene. As a result, products without sticker could no longer be distributed. Through the efforts of the PASOKYO, the Computer Software Ethics Organization (called SOFURIN in Japan) was finally established in December 1992, with 44 game companies and 3 distributors joining (Photo 6.2).

6.9 Maturity and Stagnation of the PC Game Market

During the 1980s and the first half of the 1990s, there was little progress in terms of the diffusion of personal computers into households. The graph in Fig. 6.2 shows the trend of PC penetration rate from 1987 to 1993. The number of households itself increased between 1987 and 1993 (from 38 million to 41.2 million households, according to the National Survey of Living Essentials), so the number of PCs in households itself increased, but it did not show any further growth.

In addition to the sluggish penetration rate, the copying problem caused the market size to grow sluggishly at a relatively early stage. Figure 6.3 shows the transition of the market scale of PC games, which expanded to 19.48 billion yen in 1990, but has been stagnant since then. The year 1990 marked the release of the Super Famicom by Nintendo and the transition from the 8-bit to the 16-bit home video game consoles. At the time, home video game consoles had greatly improved screen display functions and had established a method for storing game data in the form of battery backup RAM. In the latter half of the 16-bit era, CD-ROMs were also installed, and the only inferiorities to PCs were the low screen resolution due to the use of TVs for screen display and the strict restrictions on expression. In 1990, the

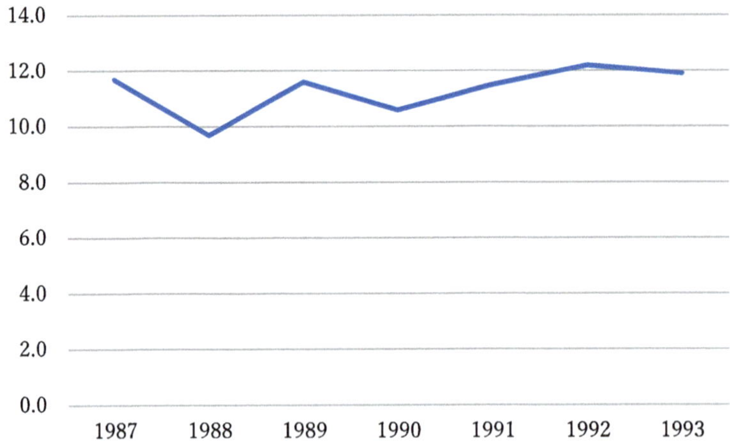

Fig. 6.2 Trends in household penetration of personal computers (%). Source: Consumer Confidence Survey, Cabinet Office

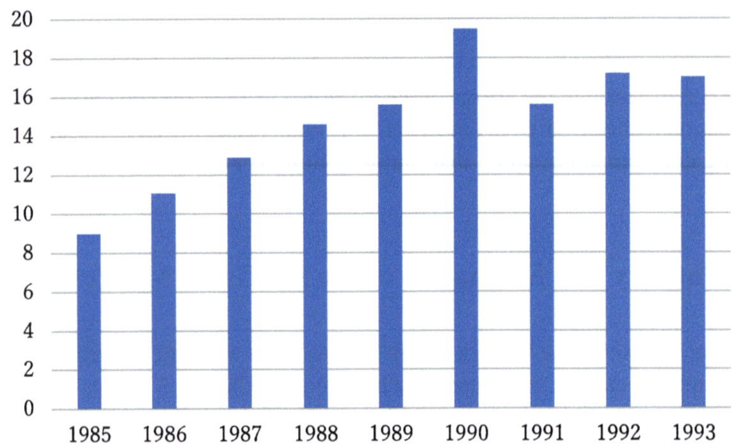

Fig. 6.3 PC game market size transition. (Unit: billions of yen, adult software is not included.) Source: Japan Personal Computer Software Association, *Survey Research Report on Understanding the Market Characteristics of PC Software*

market size was 270.5 billion yen, which was 13.9 times larger than that of PC games, and the PC game market had begun to stagnate from 1990.

The PC game market was small and had little room for growth. Even the biggest hit in the PC game market, *Xanadu* (Nihon Falcom, 1985), sold 400,000 copies.[10]

[10] Since there were no clear statistics for PC games at the time, it was not clear what the best-selling game title was. Among them, Xanadu was declared the best-selling PC game title in Japan by Nihon Falcom on its web page. Other than that, T&E Software's Hydlide is said to have sold one million copies ported to various PCs and one million copies ported to Famicom.

The unit price of PC game packages was higher than that of home video games, but even so, sales from a single title were in the hundreds of millions of yen. This was the limit of growth for the company.

In the end, companies whose main business was PC games were forced to either enter the home video game market for further development or withdraw from the PC game market. However, not many of the companies that entered the home video game market were successful.

Chapter 7
Console Games (1-2) Famicom and its Successors

Abstract This chapter discusses the social impact of Nintendo's Family Computer and the competition for the successor to the Family Computer. The Family Computer was the first home video game console to become the de facto standard in Japan, and its installed base attracted attention from many industries. A service that allowed users to trade stocks using the Family Computer as a communications terminal was also offered, but it was not a great success. As home video game consoles became a popular pastime, there was a flurry of activity aimed at replacing the Family Computer, but the competition was ultimately won by Nintendo's Super Famicom.

Keywords Super Famicom · Famicom trade · Megadrive · PC Engine · Neo Geo · Game magazine · Strategy book

7.1 Disk System as a New Media Terminal

The Disk System had another purpose: to turn Famicom into a home information terminal. As Famicom was placed in the living room, companies in various fields approached Nintendo about related businesses using Famicom. At that time, the Nippon Telegraph and Telephone Public Corporation (NTT) was promoting a new media, which included text broadcasting and captain systems,[1] and the arrival of a futuristic lifestyle. Famicom attracted attention as a strong candidate for such a device. Before various companies started their own business, Nintendo took the lead in developing the disk system as a unified standard,[2] and the idea was to connect the disk system and keyboard to Famicom and use it as a communication terminal.

[1]The service is a forerunner of today's Internet, which allows users to connect their information terminals to an information center via analog telephone lines and access information stored in the center, such as newspapers, shopping, and game downloads. The service was terminated in 2002. It was a novel system, but it did not become popular.

[2]The disk system had an interface for connecting a communication terminal, but no peripheral device (communication adapter) was eventually released.

Y. Koyama, *History of the Japanese Video Game Industry*, Translational Systems Sciences 35, https://doi.org/10.1007/978-981-99-1342-8_7

As an experiment in the communications business, Nintendo released Golf Japan Course and Golf US Course (released on blue disks instead of yellow disks to distinguish them from regular games) for the Disk System in 1987. In these games, users registered their scores at a communication terminal called disk fax, which was set up nationwide, and a nationwide tournament was held. The top 10,000 players received the limited-edition game software Punch-Out, and the tournament was held on a large scale. Nintendo was bullish that about one million people, half of the two million disk systems sold as of January 1987, would participate in the tournament, but the results were disappointing: sales of the first game, Golf Japan Course, were about 700,000 copies, and about 130,000 people participated in the tournament.[3]

In 1988, several securities companies launched trading systems using Famicom one after another. Among them, the most large scale was Famicom Trade, an online trading system developed by Nomura Securities in collaboration with Nintendo. The service was launched in November, 6 months after the signing of the contract with Nintendo, with more than 100 staff members. Later, the company launched not only stock trading but also home banking services, but the number of users remained at 200,000 even at the peak.

Since the home video game console is the only computer that sits in the living room, there have been repeated attempts since Famicom to create a new business using the home video game console as a home server.[4]

7.2 Social Repercussions of the Famicom

7.2.1 Establishment of the Game Magazine and Strategy Book Business

With the Famicom boom, the number of people who play games expanded, and a variety of games were released, creating a demand for information on the contents and release dates of games. At the same time, the increase in the number of game players also meant that more and more people were unable to play the games they had purchased until the end,[5] and there was a demand for information on game strategies.

At the time of the Famicom boom, doujin and player community activities already existed for PC games and arcade games, and by involving these people as

[3] Even so, the number of participants in the network experiment was outstanding for its time.

[4] After the spread of the Internet connection, the attempts were shifted to STB (Set Top Box), but all failed.

[5] Here, "until the end" means "until a player sees the ending or the final stage." In addition, many action games from the dawn of time to the early days of the Famicom simply repeated a set stage, and even if a player cleared the final stage, he would only return to a specific stage and there would be no ending.

writers, *Mycom BASIC Magazine* began to publish game strategy articles in *Super Soft Magazine*[6] as a supplement from the November 1983 issue. In addition, *LOGiN*, which started as a separate volume of the PC magazine *Monthly ASCII*, became an independent PC game information magazine from the April 1983 issue, and *Beep*, a general game information magazine, was released from the January 1984 issue. The groundwork had already been laid for the release of Famicom dedicated game magazines.

Amid this situation, Tokuma Shoten, which had released *Technopolis* as a PC game magazine, launched *Family Computer Magazine* (hereinafter referred to as *Famimaga*) in July 1985 with a circulation of 120,000. *Famimaga* made a conscious effort to create a magazine that was easy to understand, even for lower elementary school students, by using ruby for kanji characters. As a result, sales increased dramatically, reaching 430,000 copies for the January issue the following year. Seeing the success of *Famimaga*, ASCII launched *Famicom Tsushin* (now *Famitsu*) as a separate issue of *LOGiN*, Kadokawa Shoten launched *Marukatsu Famicom*, and JICC Publishing Bureau launched *Famicom Hisshou Hon* in 1986, establishing Famicom magazines as a standard genre.

It was also during this period that strategy books for specific games, which had appeared in the form of player community magazines for arcade games, took root as a business.[7] *Super Mario Bros. Kanzen Kouryakuhon (Super Mario Bros. Complete Strategy Book)*, released by Tokuma Shoten in 1985, was the best-selling book in Japan for two consecutive years (1985 and 1986), achieving record sales. In addition to *Super Mario Bros. Kanzen Kouryakuhon*, two other books were ranked in the top 20 of the best-selling book category in 1985 (three books in total) and four books in 1986 (five books in total).

In addition to game magazines, there were many other magazines that paid attention to the popularity of Famicom and ran special features and serialized articles. Among them, the children's manga magazine *CoroCoro Comic* partnered with Hudson to run an active event. Looking for a publisher or magazine to collaborate with on a campaign for released game titles, Hudson participated in the "CoroCoro Manga Festival" event held on March 31 and April 1, 1985, and the event was so successful that it was suddenly decided to hold a nationwide caravan during the summer vacation. It was also around this time that Mr. Toshiyuki Takahashi, one of Hudson's public relations staff, became Takahashi Meijin (Grandmaster Takahashi), traveling around the country on caravans and actively appearing on TV programs.

The publication of strategy articles in game magazines and the release of game strategy books have an advertising effect in terms of exposing game information, but on the other hand, there is also the possibility that people who are thinking of buying

[6]The magazine was integrated into the magazine as *Super Soft Corner* from the January 1985 issue due to the number of cases where only *Super Soft Magazine* was taken out at bookstores.

[7]At the earliest stage, a strategy book for the arcade game Space Invaders has already been commercially published (*Invader kouryakuhou korede anatamo 10000ten player(Invader Strategy—Now You're a 10,000 Point Player)*, Herald Enterprises, 1979).

the game may lose interest because they know what is coming next (the so-called "spoiler" problem). Spoilers can be fatal for ADVs and RPGs, which give the game a narrative and make the player look forward to the future.

In February 1986, Nintendo requested publishers to establish certain rules regarding publishing games released by the company after The Legend of Zelda. In exchange for Nintendo providing information about the games, the publishers were asked to (1) collect a certain amount of royalties from strategy books, (2) set a date for the release of strategy books, and (3) set no royalties for magazines, but impose greater restrictions on the content.[8] In 1987, Enix took a provisional injunction against the publication of a strategy article for *Dragon Quest II* in the game magazine *High Score*, which mistakenly included the last enemy from the previous *Dragon Quest*, and the publication was suspended.[9] Considering this, it became customary for game magazines to censor articles by game companies in advance, known as "maker checks" (Photo 7.1).

7.2.2 The Famicom Boom and its Impact on Elementary School Students

The Famicom and other video game consoles rapidly became popular among elementary school children, replacing the electronic games that had been available until then. Figure 7.1 is one of the results of a survey conducted on elementary school students in September 1987, almost four full years after the release of the Famicom. Only 0.5% of boys and 2.4% of girls answered that they had no experience of playing video games, while about 80% of boys and more than 50% of girls answered "I have played countless times," meaning that they play video games regularly.

Most children who play TV games have a video game console at home. Figure 7.2 shows the ownership of video game consoles among elementary school children in Tokyo; more than three-fourths of boys and more than half of girls owned and played video game consoles as of November 1986. Although many elementary school children own game consoles, it is clear that the majority of them are Famicom, judging from the actual number of video game consoles sold. Figure 7.3 shows the time when fourth to sixth graders in Tokyo purchased (or had their parents purchase for them) Famicom. Although the percentage of boys who purchased Famicom earlier is higher than that of girls, it can be seen that all of them purchased Famicom between 1983, the year of its release, and 1984, the following year.

[8] '86 nen shuppan gyoukai no omo na ugoki(Main Movements in the Publishing Industry in '86) in *Shuppan shihyo nempo(Annual Report of Publishing Indicators)* (1987), p. 43.

[9] "Dragon Quest II jiken karishobun kettei(Provisional Disposition Decision in the Dragon Quest II Case.)" http://www.isc.meiji.ac.jp/~sumwel_h/doc/juris/tdcd-s62-2-24.htm

Photo 7.1 *Super Mario Bros. Kanzen Kouryakuhon* (personal collection of the author)

Just as with Space Invaders, the Famicom was subjected to a lot of criticism. One of the most controversial was the release of the Dragon Quest III game software. Dragon Quest was released on the Famicom in 1986 (I), 1987 (II), 1988 (III), and 1989 (IV), with one title released each year, and its popularity grew with each sequel. Particularly for Dragon Quest III, the release date of February 10, 1988, was a weekday (Wednesday), which led to a number of incidents, such as students being arrested for standing in line at a retail store before it opened or being robbed by other people on their way home after purchasing the game. According to news reports at the time, the number of cases reached 392 nationwide. In response to this incident, Enix changed the release date of the Dragon Quest series to Sundays and national holidays when schools are closed (including Saturdays after the school week became a two-day holiday). This practice continues to this day.[10]

[10]The release date of game software is often set on Thursday to Friday before a holiday so that the software can be played after purchase, and the shipment date is often 2 days before the release date (Tuesday to Wednesday) so that the software always arrives on the release date. For this reason, it was not uncommon for some retailers to have games lined up in their stores 1 or 2 days before the

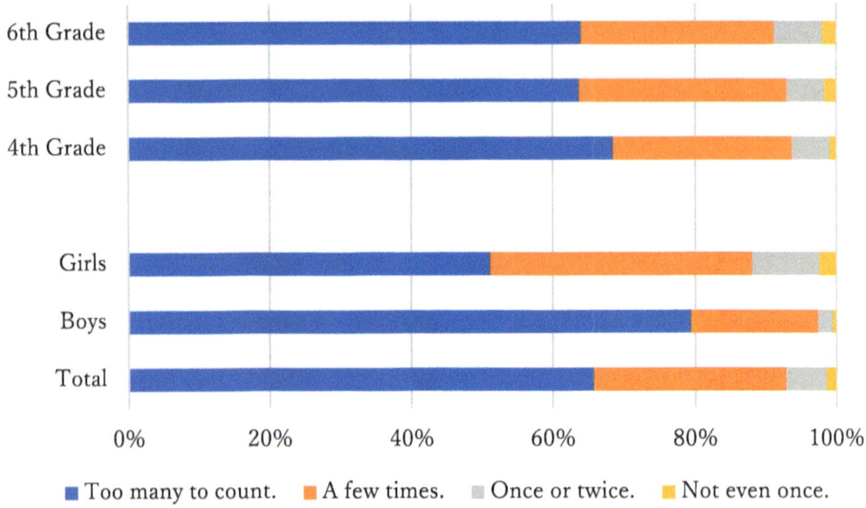

Fig. 7.1 Tokyo elementary school children's experiences of playing video games (4th–6th graders in Tokyo, September 1987). Source: Fukaya and Fukaya (1989)

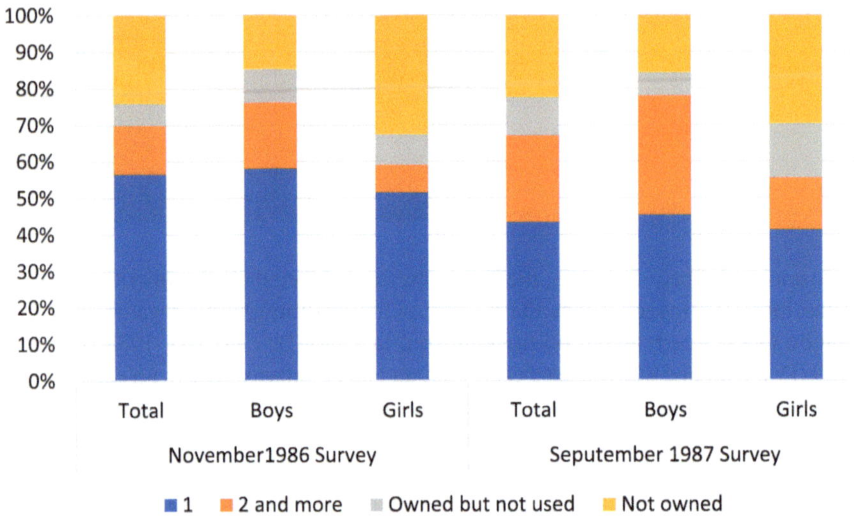

Fig. 7.2 Ownership of video game consoles by Tokyo elementary school students (4th–6th graders in Tokyo). Source: Fukaya and Fukaya (1989)

official release date listed in magazines, and for consumers to purchase them. In the case of Dragon Quest, the game was released on a holiday, which meant that it had to be shipped separately from the normal delivery schedule, placing a heavy burden on the distributors and retailers. Enix decided to do this as part of its social responsibility as the publisher of a "national game." The company also strongly urged retailers not to sell the products to consumers without permission (not to let them pre-purchase) until the authorized time even if the products arrived before the release date.

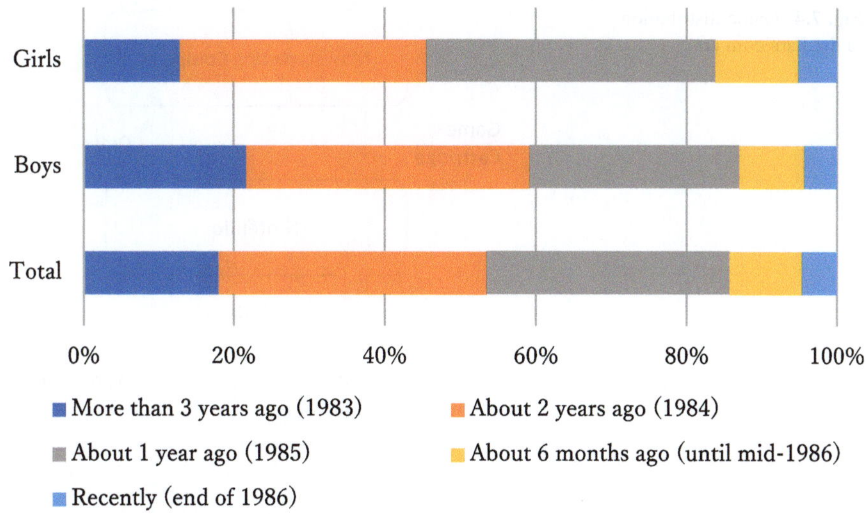

Fig. 7.3 Time of purchase of Famicom by Tokyo elementary school students (Survey year: 1987, 4th–6th graders in Tokyo). Source: Fukaya and Fukaya (1989)

7.2.3 Copying Problem of Famicom Software

As with arcade games and PC games, problems related to piracy have also occurred with home video games. In 1986, an elementary school student found Tecmo's game Solomon's Key in a store before its release date, contacted Tecmo, and the pirate was arrested.[11]

As for illegal copying of games after they were released, a machine that copies game data from commercially available game ROM cartridges to raw ROM cartridges was released, and by using the machine and blank ROM cartridges, it was possible to copy games. Advertisements for the copying machines appeared in major game magazines, and it can be said that their existence was widely known.[12]

In addition, there were machines that illegally copied games and blank discs that were not legitimately sold on the disc system. Furthermore, adult games that had not been approved by Nintendo were also being sold.

[11] Nihon Keizai Shimbun, morning edition, July 30, 1986. It was an incident in which a sample sent to a sales company was copied.

[12] The author, who was in elementary school at the time, knew of the existence of machines that could copy ROMs as a matter of course. However, I had never heard of anyone around me who had bought such a machine and copied games with it. At that time, elementary school students were in the position of having their parents buy games for them, and it was hard to imagine that their parents would approve the purchase of this kind of illegal machine (to begin with, the machine itself cost the equivalent of two video games and was not something that could be easily purchased). In the absence of data, I can only speculate, but it is likely that the number of elementary school students using the machines was low.

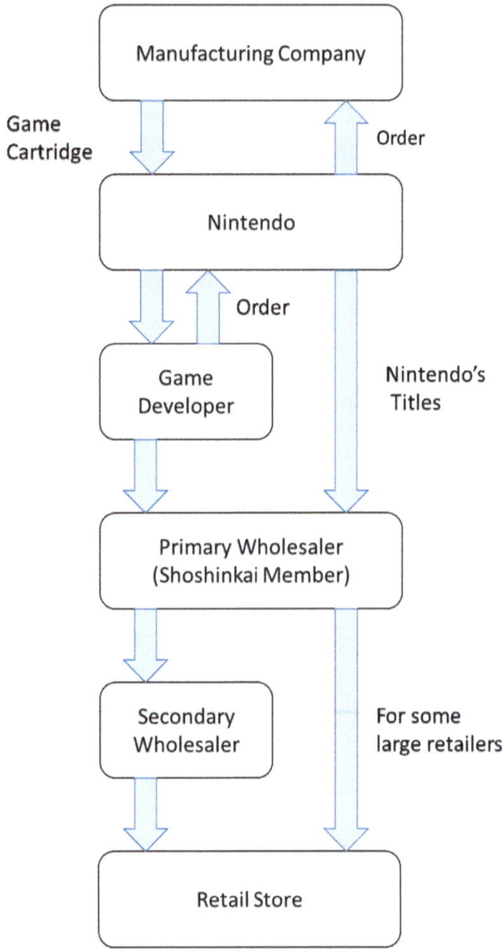

Fig. 7.4 Game distribution in the Famicom era

Nintendo took these copying problems very seriously, and for the NES (Nintendo Entertainment System) released in the USA, a security chip was built into the console so that games that did not pass the security check at startup could not be played.

7.2.4 Problems Faced by Game Distribution and the Home Video Game Business

At that time, home video game consoles and game software used the toy distribution system. As shown in Fig. 7.4, Nintendo received orders for games from game companies (except for some companies) in bulk as a production consignment and delivered the games to each company after manufacturing. All the delivered games were wholesaled to primary wholesalers and shipped to large retailers through primary wholesalers and to small retailers through secondary wholesalers. The distribution of games was controlled by the Shoshinkai, a group of distributors and retailers who had accounts with Nintendo.

This system was fine when the number of game titles released in 1984–1985 was small, but as the number of game titles released increased, the distribution inventory of unsold titles became a serious problem for both wholesalers and retailers. As a result, unfair transactions were rampant in the shipment and sale of popular titles demanded by retailers and consumers. Unfair transactions include "Push-in," in which wholesalers require retailers to stock old titles that have become bad inventory along with popular titles, and "Tying," in which retailers will not allow consumers to purchase popular titles unless they also purchase old titles that have become bad inventory at the same time.

Such unfair trade was rampant because of the difficulty in overcoming the problem of uncertainty of demand faced by the entertainment business in a broad sense, including home video games.

There is a time lag of 3–6 months between the completion (mastering) and release of a home video game. This is because (1) it takes time to manufacture ROMs, and (2) Nintendo is a fabless[13] company with no factories of its own, which limits the monthly production volume of ROM cassettes that can be secured for OEM production.

In those days, the production volume of games was determined by the following process:

1. Retailers place orders with the primary wholesaler.
2. Primary wholesalers collect the orders from each retailer and place an order with Nintendo.
3. Nintendo and the game companies decide the production volume based on the number of orders.

The amount of information that retailers can refer to when deciding the number of orders is very small. In such a situation of high uncertainty, there are many titles that do not sell as well as initially expected and become bad inventory, or on the contrary, sell out in a flash and cause opportunity loss.[14] Push-in and tying are phenomena that have been caused by wholesalers and retailers to reduce bad inventory as much as possible.

[13] Nintendo has a factory in Uji, Kyoto Prefecture, but it is for card games such as Hanafuda, not for video games.

[14] If the popularity of a released game is very high, it is possible to reproduce additional game ROMs. However, even in this case, there is a time lag of several months between production and delivery. In an environment where new titles are released one after another every month, commercial opportunities are often already lost by the time additional production is finished. Commercial opportunities in the toy market in a broad sense, including games, are extremely short.

Another change that occurred on the retail side was the appearance of game specialty stores which sold not only new game packages but also secondhand ones. The first stores selling used games appeared in 1986. Since then, game specialty stores have continued to grow, and several major chains have emerged in Yamaguchi, Hiroshima, Okayama, and other areas, reaching the level of an industry in 1989. The origin of the secondhand game business was a store called VISCO in Hiroshima, and its affiliates started operating in various areas, and the chain branched out. Secondary wholesalers with low-profit margins and rental video stores that focused on used games as another way to attract customers also entered the market.

The reason why the number of stores selling used games had increased was because of their profit margins. The gross profit margin of new games is very low at around 10%.[15] On the other hand, the gross profit margin of used games is extremely high, ranging from 35% to 40% for chain stores and 50% to 60% for individual stores.[16] Although game specialty stores also deal in new games, their purpose is to attract customers and to purchase used games from customers who have sold new games. Supported by the high-profit margin, the number of game specialty stores increased. At their peak, there were more than 6000 stores, and they could be seen on every street corner.

Game specialty stores were significant because (1) they made people feel more familiar with video games by being located here and there on street corners, and (2) they increased the number of games available to middle and high school students with little pocket money by supplying used games at low prices.

7.3 On the Post-Famicom Era

By 1986, 3 years after the release of the Famicom, the post-Famicom movement had begun in the market. The Nintendo's Family Computer was the platform that had won the de facto standard, and as long as Famicom continued to be the standard, many games could be sold, and profits could be expected. Therefore, there is no incentive fot Nintendo to actively shift from the current hardware to the next hardware. On the other hand, Sega, which lost the battle with the SG-1000 and Mark III, and other game companies that were aiming to make a leap forward by

[15] The purchase price of a retail store is usually 70%–75% of the suggested retail price (so-called "list price"). The first few days after the release date of a new game are the biggest business opportunity, and competition among stores is fierce. As a result, retailers often sell at a discount of 10%–20% of the list price, resulting in a fairly low gross profit margin.

[16] The difference in the profit margin between individual stores and chain stores is the share of the chain headquarters. In the case of chain stores, the used games they buy are purchased by the chain headquarters. Conversely, stores that have difficulty purchasing used games can purchase them from the chain headquarters. Since there is a distribution margin for this, the profit margin is lower than that of individual stores.

developing their own game hardware like Sega, were aiming for a rematch by making the Famicom obsolete at an early stage and shifting to the next-generation platform.

In addition, the generation of home video game consoles changes every 5–7 years, and since the technological innovations in the computer industry during that period are reflected all at once, the architecture often changed significantly. The expressive power of games, such as graphic solution, became more sophisticated, and the capacity of recording media increased, enabling the development of larger games. At the same time, game companies were faced with increasing costs associated with adapting to new technologies and developing games on a larger scale.

In the future, the game industry will see the launch of next-generation hardware amidst the various speculations of the winners, losers, and newcomers of the previous generation.

7.3.1 PC Engine: Lost of the "Core Concept" Strategy

7.3.1.1 Stray Strategy of the PC Engine

The first game console to appear in the next generation of the Famicom was the PC Engine, a hardware system designed entirely by Hudson, including the new CPU, and manufactured by NEC. The HuC6280, the original CPU, was an 8-bit CPU[17] with four times the operating speed of the Famicom's 6502 CPU with extended instructions. In addition, the number of simultaneous colors on the screen and the sprite function was considerably enhanced, and the beauty of the screen was second to none compared to the later 16-bit machines such as Sega's Mega Drive and Nintendo's Super Famicom. When the console was first released, games were provided in the form of Hu-Cards, which were thin IC cards[18] (Photo 7.2).

[17]The HuC6280 has a 16-bit bus for exchanging data, but the CPU's internal processing is 8-bit. Therefore, it is not strictly correct to call the PC Engine, Mega Drive, and Super Nintendo generation "the generation of 16-bit machines."

[18]The My Card for the Sega SG-1000 was the first to offer games in a similar card format. The card-type game media was compact and convenient, but the capacity limit was severe. Sega eventually gave up on providing games via My Card and moved to ROM cartridges (called gold cartridges) that used high-capacity rom chip(1 mega-bit ROM). The PC Engine also shifted to CD-ROMs due to insufficient capacity, as described later.

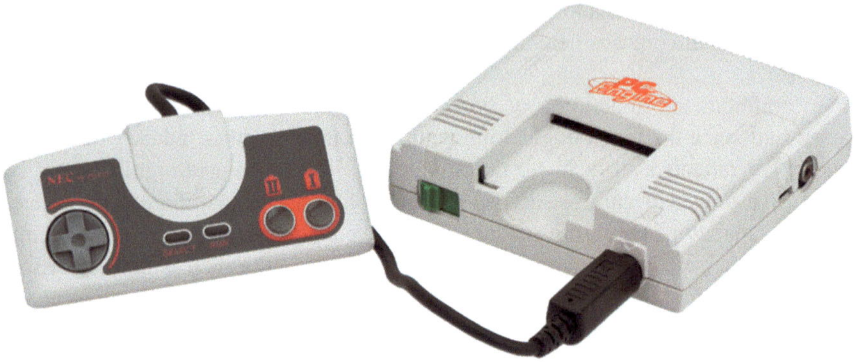

Photo 7.2 PC Engine (Source of the image: Wikipedia)

The performance of the console was so high that it was able to port Wonder Boy Monster Land[19] (Sega, August 1987) and *R-TYPE*[20] (Irem, July 1987), both of which were released as arcade games in the same year as the console's release, with almost no difference. The difference in performance was overwhelming when compared to Famicom, which was still in use.

When the PC Engine was first released, it had a "core concept" and was planned to be connected to a variety of peripherals and other PCs to do various things other than playing games. However, interconnection with the PC was canceled because the speed of the PC Engine was overwhelmingly too fast for the time, and it lacked balance. Almost no other peripherals were released. The only success was the CD-ROM used in games.

At the end of 1989, the sales strategy was renewed and the lineup was increased to three models. These were the PC Engine Core Graphics (24,800 yen), which had a minor change in RF output to composite output, the PC Engine Shuttle (18,800 yen), which eliminated the expansion bus used to connect peripherals necessary for the Core concept, and the PC Engine Super Graphics (39,800 yen), which was an upwardly compatible machine with two graphics chips and enhanced graphics functions. The Shuttle was designed for users who specialized only in games, while the Core Graphics and Super Graphics were designed to continue the Core

[19]Perhaps to appeal to children, the game was released as Bikkuri-man World, with the characters from the Wonder Boy Monster Land game replaced by the popular Bikkuri-man characters of the time. Bikkuri-man is a sticker enclosed in Lotte's chocolate confectionery, Bikkuri-man Chocolate. Each sticker depicted one character, with a brief explanation on the back. Reading through the different explanations for each character, you could learn the story of the battle between the devil and the angel.

[20]Since the capacity of the Hu-Card at the time the PC Engine was released did not allow for all the stages, the first 4 stages were released as R-TYPE I in March 1988, and the last 5–8 stages were released as R-TYPE II in June 1988. The PC Engine screen resolution was shorter than the actual arcade screen, but the game was ported with some scrolling up and down to shrink the graphics and not ruin the atmosphere.

concept. However, in the end, only five exclusive software titles were released for the Super Graphix, and sales of the Shuttle, which could not be connected to a CD-ROM as a peripheral device due to the elimination of the expansion bus, were also sluggish. After that, the PC Engine GT (Hu-Card only, 44,800 yen, 1990), which turned the PC Engine into a portable game machine with an LCD and TV tuner, and the PC Engine LT (99,800 yen, 1991, LT means "LapTop" but without battery), which had a 4-inch LCD monitor and looked like a notebook PC, were introduced.[21]

7.3.1.2 Success as the world's First CD-ROM Game Console

What is notable about the PC Engine is that it was the first home video game machine to release and establish CD-ROM (product name CD-ROM^2) as a peripheral device. The CD-ROM system consisted of a CD-ROM drive, an interface unit with a composite output terminal (early PC Engines only had an RF terminal for connection to a TV) and a battery backup ROM, and a system card (a Hu-Card with a ROM in which the startup OS was written and 64 KB (512 kilobits) of RAM to read data from the CD-ROM).

The CD-ROM system was a very expensive peripheral device, costing 57,300 yen, and sales did not increase much when it was first released, but sales increased due to the strong sales of major RPG titles such as *Tengai Makyo* and *Ys I and II* (both by Hudson), which were released the year after the launch of the console (1989). The weight of games released gradually shifted from Hu-Cards to CD-ROMs. CD-ROM games were vulnerable to frequent data loading due to the low RAM capacity of the system card, but in 1991 the Super CD-ROM^2, a new peripheral device that quadrupled the RAM capacity to 256 KB (2 Megabits), and the PC Engine DUO, a game hardware integrated with the new CD-ROM system, were released. In 1994, the Super CD-ROM2 system became the de facto standard for games, as existing CD-ROM users only needed to purchase a RAM card called the Super System Card. In 1994, an arcade card with eight times more data (2 MB (16 megabits)) was released, but it did not become a big hit as the next-generation models were already available in the market.

Figure 7.5 shows the number of PC Engine titles sold by media. In 1988–1989, when CD-ROM^2 was released and was still in the process of spreading, Hu-Cards were the main media, but in 1990, the percentage of titles released on CD-ROM began to increase, and in 1992, after the release of Super CD-ROM^2, almost all games were released on CD-ROM. The PC Engine started with Hu-Card, went through a transition period to CD-ROM^2, and was effectively upgraded with Super CD-ROM^2.

[21] In addition to the PC Engine Duo described below, the PC-KD863G, a monitor with a built-in PC Engine, and the X1 Twin, a Sharp X1 PC with a built-in PC Engine (Each X1 and PC Engine has completely different circuitry in a casing), were also released.

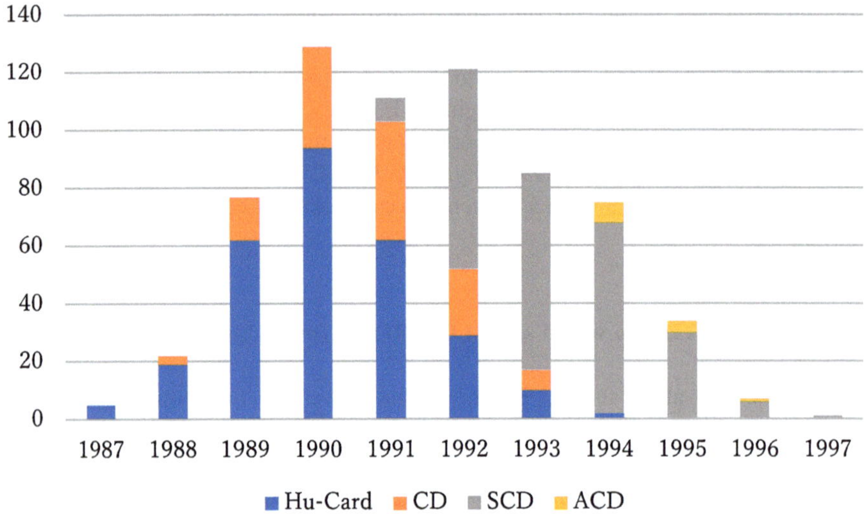

Fig. 7.5 Number of PC Engine titles sold by media (Although omitted from the graph, only one game title for Super CD-ROM² was released in 1999, when it had finished its role as a game console) CD: CD-ROM, SCD: Super CD-ROM, ACD: Arcade Card. Source of data: CD-ROM accompanying *Daigirin 2011*

7.3.1.3 The PC Engine as Bishōjo Game Console

The adoption of CD-ROM as a game media brought revolutionary changes in game production, such as a larger game scale, the use of voice in games, the use of live BGM using CD-DA, and the enhancement of in-game presentation (single pictures using the entire screen, animated scenes,[22] etc.). In particular, the hardware characteristics of "the ability to add voice to the characters in the game" and "the ability to use many single-picture still images" made the existence of the heroine in the game stand out more.

Among them, games of the "many cute girls" type, which are now called "bishōjo games," were first officially ported to home consoles on the PC Engine. Starting with the porting of the adult RPG Dragon Knight 2 (1991) by Elf, which had been a hit on the PC, in 1992 after cutting and changing the adult scenes, several bishōjo games were ported and released. The introduction of these bishojo games had a great impact on the game industry in the following years.

---

[22] Since video playback was not possible with the performance of the PC Engine, animation scenes were created using sprites and background screen redrawing. Also, due to the limitations of the screen redrawing capability, games at that time did not draw pictures on the entire screen for animation scenes with a lot of movement but limited them to the center of the screen. It was not until the next generation of consoles that movie scenes could be played as video files.

7.3.1.4 PC Engine Summary

The PC Engine was supplied with games mainly by Hudson, the hardware designer, and NEC, the hardware distributor, but it was also blessed with third parties. Of the 668 titles released for the PC Engine,[23] 123 were released by Hudson, 88 by NEC Avenue (later NEC Interchannel) and NEC Home Electronics, and the remaining 400 or more by third parties. Arcade game companies, which lost their significant position when their contracts with Nintendo were renewed,[24] also entered the market, but they were not the ones who released many games for the new medium of CD-ROM.

After NEC (70 games) and Hudson (59 games), the next companies to release games for CD-ROM were Telenet Japan (38 games), which originated from PC games, and Naxat (31 games) and Victor Entertainment (25 games), which newly entered the market after the NES. The PC Engine was supported by such companies.

In the end, 7.5 million units of the PC Engine and 1.92 million units of CD-ROM^2 and its successors were shipped. The CD-ROM of the Mega Drive, which will be discussed later, did not become very popular, selling only about 400,000 units, and the Super Famicom did not release a CD-ROM, so CD-ROM games in this generation were the sole domain of the PC Engine, which became the unique hardware of the PC Engine. In the end, the PC Engine surpassed Sega's Mega Drive because it was the first game console in the world to use CD-ROM.

7.3.2 *Mega Drive: Bright and Dark in Overseas and Japan*

The Mega Drive was released by Sega in 1988 as a successor to the SG-1000 and Mark III 8-bit machines. It was based on the System 16, an arcade game board that was in operation at the time and aimed to produce high-performance games by using the 68,000 16-bit CPU. In addition, it was also equipped with a Z80 sub-CPU for sound processing, so it was possible to play Mark III/Master System[25] games with the purchase of a peripheral device (mega adapter), although it did not support FM sound sources. In addition, while the PC Engine had a cross-key and two-button configuration similar to that of Famicom, the Mega Drive's controller had three buttons to accommodate the increasing complexity of games (Photo 7.3).

---

[23]The number of registrations to the CD-ROM accompanying the 2011 edition of Daigirin.

[24]After the renewal of the contract with Nintendo, Namco aggressively sold games on the PC Engine. The number of titles released reached 25. However, all of the titles were offered on Hu-Card, and Namco withdrew from PC Engine game sales by 1992, when Super CD-ROM^2 games became the mainstream.

[25]Unlike other countries, the Master System in Japan is equipped with the FM sound source unit, which was released as a peripheral device for the Mark III, as standard equipment, and has a completely new design.

Photo 7.3 Mega Drive (Photo credit: Wikipedia)

At the same time as the console, Space Harrier II and Super Thunder Blade, which were arranged versions of popular arcade games, were released, and during the same year, Jyuohki(Altered Beast), a port of an arcade game, was released. In this way, the Mega Drive emphasized that it was a high-performance hardware that was strong in action games, but the hardware specs of popular Sega arcade games that users wanted ported were much higher than that and porting them was quite difficult. In terms of porting arcade games, the high performance of the Mega Drive was half-hearted,[26] but the MC68000 CPU was also used in the X68000 (Sharp) in Japan, which had the advantage of increasing the number of PC game companies entering the market.

However, the Mega Drive did not improve the action bias in game genres; unlike the 8-bit era, the Mega Drive was blessed with third-party companies, and the ratio of RPGs, ADVs, and SLGs, which are genres derived from PC games, improved to a level slightly lower than other consoles, but the lack of RPG titles, the best-selling genre, did not improve. Although some PC game companies entered the market, they did not contribute to the improvement of the genre bias, as most of the games for X68000 were action games.

The strategy for peripherals and expansion devices can hardly be called successful. Following the success of the CD-ROM in the PC Engine, a CD-ROM (Sega CD) was also released as a peripheral for the Mega Drive, but due to its late release and the lack of sufficient software, sales were limited to about 400,000 units. The

[26]The arcade version of Space Harrier was designed to use two 68,000 CPUs, making it difficult to port to the Mega Drive. Therefore, it was not ported as-is, but released as a sequel.

Teradrive (1991), a combined machine with the IBM-PC, and the Super 32X (1994), a performance expansion unit, were released during the transition to the next-generation machines, but their sales were also very small.

The final sales volume of the Mega Drive in Japan was only 3.58 million units, less than half of the PC Engine, and the number of titles released was 555, less than the PC Engine. Although the Mega Drive was defeated in Japan, it was released overseas as Sega Genesis and became a huge hit with a total of 30 million units.[27]

7.3.3 NEO GEO: High-End and Unique Strategy of Arcade Game Compatibility

SNK's NEO GEO, which became famous for its catchphrase "100 Mega Shock,[28]" was a hardware system that adopted a unique line of development, using arcade game platforms as home game consoles. SNK developed the MVS (multi video system) as a game system for arcades, and the AES (Advanced Entertainment System) for home use. Usually, the term NEO GEO refers to the AES.

The MVS had a game cartridge terminal, and by inserting a game cartridge into the terminal, the player could switch between up to six different games. The system was suitable not only for small-scale game centers where the number of machines is limited, but also for toy stores and candy shops in the city that want to attract children.[29]

The AES had a memory card slot (similar to the PCMCIA slot for PCs) that allowed users to exchange information such as high scores through the memory card. The price of the AES was 58,000 yen when it was released (later lowered to 48,800 yen), but the price of the game ROM cartridges was also very expensive[30] at around 30,000 yen per cartridge. The reason for this was that the games on the NEO GEO were originally designed for arcades, and the ROM cartridges for the NEO GEO were ten times larger than the ROM cartridges for other game consoles, or more,[31] and used a large amount of mask ROM.

[27] Sega of America offered game titles with a "cool" and "edgy" image to the older generation with the catchphrase "Genesis does what Nintendon't." Sonic the Hedgehog, released in 1991, became the killer application and drove hardware sales. Sonic the Hedgehog 2, released the following year, was a huge hit, selling over 6 million copies.

[28] The catchphrase "100 Mega Shock" is well known, but 100 mega refers not to the size of the game data, but to the bandwidth of the bus that exchanges the data.

[29] SNK also leases MVSs, and this framework allowed store owners in the city who were unable to maintain their enclosures to set up their own MVSs.

[30] It was expensive for a home game, but unbelievably cheap for an arcade game. This cheapness was one of the reasons why MVS became popular.

[31] At that time, ROM versions of games for home game consoles were at most 16 megabits, and regular games were 4–8 megabits, but NEO GEO games were over 40 megabits even in the first low capacity games, and later 100 megabits or more was the standard.

NEO GEO is a very expensive system, so when it was first released in 1990, it was only available for rent at video rental stores and not for sale. However, due to the popularity of the games released, the demand for the console increased, and in 1991, the console went on sale. It became a huge hit, thanks in part to the popularity of fighting games such as Garou Densetsu (FATAL FURY), Ryuko no ken (Art of Fighting), and THE KING OF FIGHTERS.

In 1994, the NEO GEO CD was released with CD-ROM as the game media, but it was shunned by users due to the extremely long data loading time[32] from the CD-ROM. In 1996, NEO GEO CD-Z was released with a double-speed CD-ROM drive instead of a constant-speed drive, but the long loading time did not improve much, and it was not a hit either. Eventually, the CD-ROM version of the NEO GEO was discontinued earlier than the ROM version.

As THE KING OF FIGHTERS became a series and titles were released continuously, the ROM version of the NEO GEO continued to be produced until 2004, eventually selling one million units.

7.3.4 Super Famicom: A New Model that Created New Fun

7.3.4.1 Specifications of Super Famicom

The Super Famicom,[33] the successor to the Famicom, was released by Nintendo in 1990. It was the last game console of its generation. At the beginning of the development of the Super Famicom, Nintendo was aiming to create hardware that was upwardly compatible with the previous generation Famicom,[34] which had an overwhelming market share, but gave up due to technical specifications and manufacturing costs.[35]

In the same way that the Famicom established the new game of video games in society, the Super Famicom pursued a new level of fun in games. Due to its late release, it is natural that the Super Famicom had higher performance than other hardware of the same generation (Table 7.1), but the hardware support for sprites and screen enlargement/reduction/rotation allowed for expressions that were impossible

[32] In the case of the NEO GEO's hit fighting games, a large amount of image data was required to represent the various movements of the large characters. As a result, some games took more than a minute to load each time you went from one stage to the next.

[33] Super Famicom is the official name, not an abbreviation or common name for Super Family Computer.

[34] This is evident from the fact that the Super Famicom uses the 65816 as its CPU, which is upwardly compatible with the 6502 used in the Famicom.

[35] Even after Nintendo gave up on supporting both systems with a single Super Famicom due to technical specifications and other problems, they were still considering selling Famicom compatible adapter that would allow screen input and output to be done on the Super Famicom side, and a prototype that was announced at a press conference was published in a magazine. In the end, the compatibility adapter was not released, and the configuration became simple.

Table 7.1 Basic specification of the three game machines

Model name	PC Engine	Mega drive	Super Famicom
Company	NEC Home Electronics	Sega	Nintendo
CPU(Operating speed)	HuC6280 (7.16 MHz)	MC68000 (7.67 MHz) Z80A sub-CPU	65,816 Custom CPU (3.58Mhz)
Screen resolution	320*224 512*256	256*244 320*244	256*224 512*224
Number of colors at the same time s	32 colors in 512 colors	64 colors in 512 colors	256 colors in 32,768 colors
Sprite function Number of pieces / Size / Color	64 16*16–32*64 16colors	80 8*8–32*32 16colors	128 8*8–64*64 16colors
Release date	Oct. 30, 1987	Oct. 29, 1988	Nov. 21, 1990
Price	24,800 yen	21,000 yen	25,000 yen
Remarks			Enlargement, reduction, and rotation functions

to achieve with other game consoles. These functions were also used in F-ZERO and Super Mario World which were released at the same time as the console, letting users know that they could play games that could not be played on other hardware. In addition, Super Famicom had an overwhelmingly improved controller. Four buttons, A, B, X, and Y were placed on the right side of the controller, and the L and R buttons were placed on the top of the controller.[36]

7.3.4.2 Market Domination

In 1991, the year after Super Famicom was introduced to the market, the cumulative number of consoles sold was almost the same as that of the PC Engine, and after that, far greater than that of the other two. While the PC Engine and Mega Drive peaked in sales in 1990, Super Famicom, which was released in 1990, peaked in sales in 1993 and sold an overwhelmingly large number of units. In the end, Nintendo sold more hardware than the PC Engine and Mega Drive combined (Fig. 7.6).

[36] In the early days of the Famicom, most games were simple, and two buttons were sufficient, but in later, the start button and select button, which were not originally intended to be used during games, were increasingly used for operations such as calling up the menu screen and changing equipment during games. To prevent accidental pressing of the start and select buttons, they are smaller than the A and B buttons and are placed in a position where they are difficult to press. It was easy to make mistakes when trying to press them while playing. With Super Famicom, the controller was equipped with a large number of buttons, which made it possible to assign dedicated buttons to those operations, greatly improving the playability of the game. The L and R buttons were also used in combination with the screen rotation function.

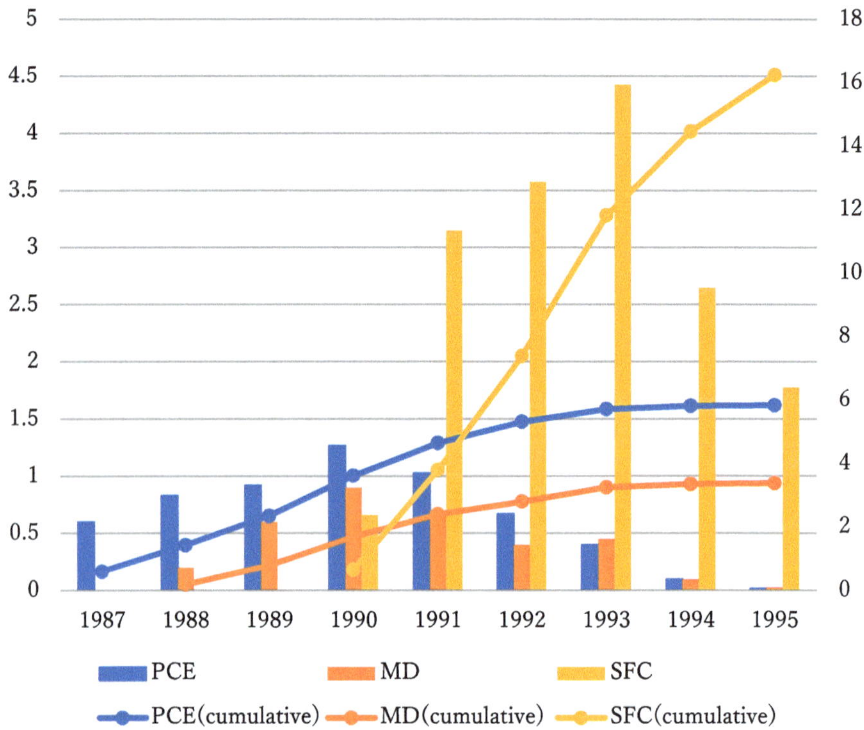

Fig. 7.6 Sales of the three game consoles (Unit: million)

In the competition between the Famicom and Sega consoles (SG-1000 and SEGA Mark III), the presence or absence of third parties led to differences in the variety of game genres sold, which in turn led to the appeal of the hardware.

In this hardware competition, all hardware camps were well aware of this fact and added various game titles of different genres to their lineup, including arcade game ports and PC-based genres such as ADV and RPG. Figure 7.7 shows the percentage of PC genres (ADV/RPG/SLG) among the titles of the three hardware platforms. Unlike the competition of the previous generation, Nintendo's Super Famicom is the lowest. However, Super Famicom had the largest number of game titles in absolute terms, since more game titles were released than other hardware due to its strong hardware sales. In particular, the number of RPG titles, the best-selling titles of all time, was overwhelming. Popular RPG series such as Dragon Quest and Final Fantasy were also released on the Super Famicom. In addition, when compared to Hudson (PC Engine) and Sega (Mega Drive), Nintendo itself released many titles that greatly drove the hardware. Super Mario World (1990 (launch title), 3.55 million), Super Mario Kart (1992, 3.83 million), Super Donkey Kong (1994, 3 million), and so on. This contributed to the sales of console and the longevity of game console.

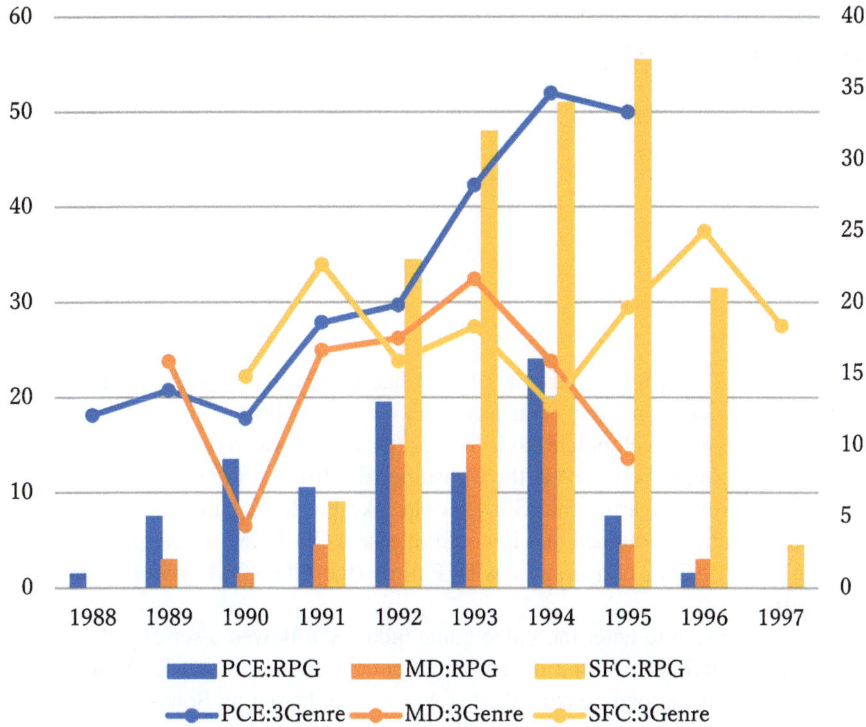

Fig. 7.7 Number of RPG releases by platform (right axis) and RPG/ADV/SLG ratio (left axis: %)

7.3.5 Game Price Hike and Cancellation of CD-ROM Announcement: A Milestone for Next-Generation Consoles

Super Famicom was sailing smoothly as a game console, but as the amount of data increased with the sophistication and complexity of the games, the number of ROM chips installed increased, which increased the manufacturing cost and the price of game titles soared.

Table 7.2 shows the ROMs installed in Dragon Quest series, a popular RPG series, and their prices. Dragon Quest I to III were the standard prices for game titles released on the Famicom at that time, but Dragon Quest IV, released in 1990, the last year of the Famicom (i.e., the year the Super Famicom was released), cost 8500 yen due to the increase in data volume. Dragon Quest V released on the Super Famicom was priced at 9600 yen, and Dragon Quest VI released after the launch of PlayStation exceeded 10,000 yen (Table 7.2).

On the other hand, with the release of CD-ROM as peripherals for the PC Engine and Mega Drive, titles with large capacities were developed for CD-ROM, so the rising price of games was not a major problem.

Table 7.2 ROM capacity and price of successive generations of Dragon Quest

Dragon Quest	Console	Year	Capacity(bit)	Price
I	FC	1986	512 K	5500yen
II	FC	1987	1 M	5500 yen
III	FC	1988	2 M	5900 yen
IV	FC	1990	4 M	8500 yen
V	SFC	1992	12 M	9600 yen
VI	SFC	1996	32 M	11,400 yen
VII (reference)	PS	2000	CD-ROM 2disks	7800 yen
VIII(reference)	PS2	2004	DVD-ROM 1disk	9240 yen

Nintendo did not ignore this situation. It had jointly developed a CD-ROM as a peripheral device with Sony, and leaked information about it to check NEC and Sega. In the joint development with Sony, a prototype was developed, and a press release was about to be issued at the Consumer Electronics Show (CES) in Chicago in 1991. However, fearing that Sony would take the lead, Nintendo canceled the press release and announced that it would release a CD-ROM adapter for the Super Famicom in 1992 in cooperation with Philips (the CD-ROM adapter was never released).

Sony's decision to enter the video game industry followed a series of twists and turns. "Play Station" was the development code name for a CD-ROM-integrated Super Famicom compatible console that was to be released by Sony.

Chapter 8
Drastic Changes in 1994: Technological and Business Revolutions

Abstract This chapter does not focus on a specific market, but rather on changes in the environment surrounding the game industry since the mid-1990s. The Japanese video game industry underwent major changes from around 1994. It was not merely the launch of a new generation of home video game consoles. It was a major transformation that included changes in the technological paradigm and the economic environment surrounding the game industry.

Keywords Hardware abstraction · 2D Graphics · 3D Graphics · Disk media · Multimedia boom · Stock listing · Price discrimination strategy

The Japanese game industry underwent a major change around 1994. It was not just the release of a new generation of home video game consoles. It was a major revolution that included changes in the technological paradigm and the economic environment surrounding games.

8.1 Changes in Technology

8.1.1 Hardware Abstraction and Development Advancement

Since the late 1990s, the design paradigm has changed dramatically. To use a metaphorical expression, the paradigm has shifted from "a craft created by a few craftsmen" to "an industrial product created by a large team of people." Also, after this period, games began to run on operating systems (OS).

From the establishment of the game industry until the early 1990s, games continued to be controlled directly by their executable programs. Games, unlike other software, use hardware performance (especially drawing performance) to the utmost limit. For this reason, the execution engine of the program was written in

Y. Koyama, *History of the Japanese Video Game Industry*, Translational Systems Sciences 35, https://doi.org/10.1007/978-981-99-1342-8_8

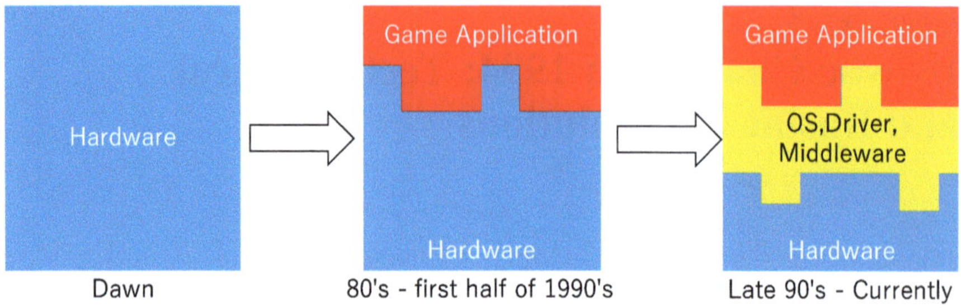

Fig. 8.1 Classification of the game industry in terms of the development of modularity

assembler language[1] according to the requirements of each game. The usual method in other software industries, where hardware is abstracted by the OS, hardware control is performed by various libraries, and only the core part of the application is built, has been used since the late 1990s,[2] when direct control became difficult due to the increasing performance and complexity of hardware. Subsequently, the libraries used as various functions of games evolved into middleware, game engines, and integrated development environments, and a number of companies began to develop and provide game development environments themselves.

Figure 8.1 shows the changes in the technological paradigm of the game industry in three stages from the viewpoint of the development of "modularization." In the early days before the establishment of the game industry, the performance of integrated circuits was still insufficient and expensive, and the first games were built with dedicated logic circuits (DTL or TTL circuits). The current form of computer games, in which the CPU executes games written in ROM or RAM, was established from the late 1970s to the early 1980s.[3] In game consoles after this era, game applications do not directly control the hardware. The hardware is abstracted

[1] A translation of instructions (machine language) that directly control a computer into a form that is easily understood by humans. It is fast in operation, but difficult to understand because the program is written at the level of direct control of the CPU.

[2] One of the reasons why the game industry started using libraries in their programs was because Sony forced them to be used in PlayStation (Asakura 1998). Another reason is that the assemblers for the various RISC processors that began to be used around this time were too complex, making it difficult to write optimal programs. In the case of compiling programs using high-level languages (mainly C), the method of combining with existing libraries is highly efficient.

[3] In many cases, other control signals also flow through the terminals for ROM cartridges of game consoles, and peripherals can be connected through the cartridge terminals, as in the Family Computer Disk System. In addition, Konami incorporated a sound source chip (SCC) in the late stages of the Family Computer, and Nintendo incorporated a numerical calculation processor (Super FX chip) in the ROM cartridge for the Super Famicom title "Star Fox" (1993). In this way, there were many examples of functional expansion by inserting a dedicated chip into a game ROM cartridge. Therefore, it cannot be said that a strict separation of software and hardware was made for home video game consoles in this period. The strict separation of software/hardware was not achieved until 1994, when PlayStation and Saturn were released, when games were provided on disk media.

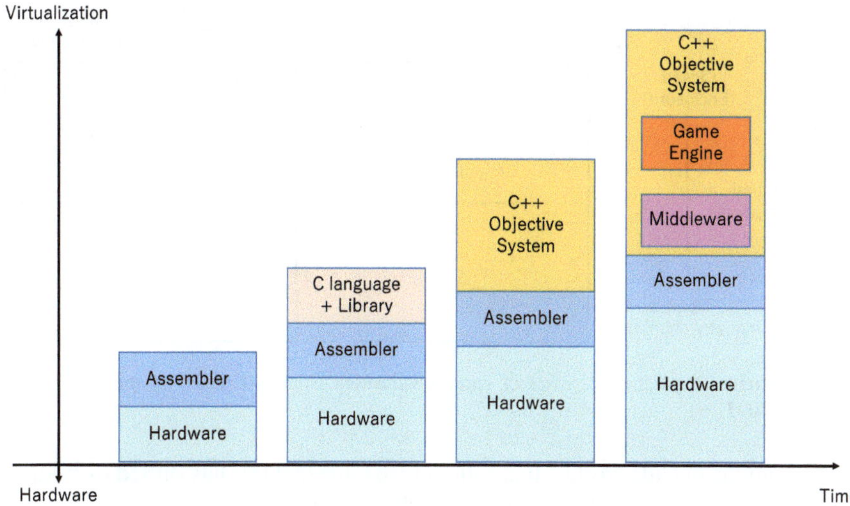

Fig. 8.2 Program environment used in game consoles. Source: "Research and Study on the Application of Advanced Technology in Digital Content Creation," 2010 edition

by the OS and drivers provided by the hardware companies, and the game application performs the required processing by communicating with the OS and drivers. It is now prohibited by hardware companies for game applications to directly control hardware.

As the generation of home consoles has progressed, so has the trend toward more sophisticated development. The increasing performance and complexity of the hardware meant that it was possible to achieve the desired look and feel without having to use the full potential of the hardware, but at the same time it became impossible to create a system that could control every single CPU clock for every single game. Eventually, the OS and drivers to control the hardware were supplied by the hardware companies. In addition, for the parts of processing that are highly specialized but common to each game, such as 3D physics, graphics, and sound, companies began to purchase libraries developed by specialized companies as middleware, in addition to their own libraries (Fig. 8.2).

From this period, game development shifted from an artisanal and elaborate programming style to a style that focuses on the core of the game while saving development resources by using available libraries and middleware. Figure 8.3 classifies the architectural characteristics of various industries by the degree of interdependence of component design (horizontal axis) and the interconnection of technologies across companies (vertical axis). The horizontal axis indicates whether the product design is integral or modular, and the vertical axis indicates whether the technical specifications are private and developed within the same company or group of companies (closed) or whether the technical specifications are open and developed by each company using the results of other companies that are open. In the 1980s, game development was done in-house, and even the developers were kept

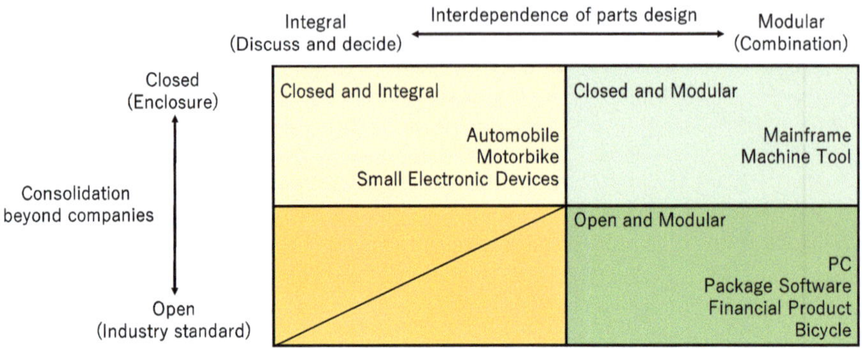

Fig. 8.3 Architectural characteristics of various industries. Source: Created by the author from Fujimoto (2003)

secret from the outside world.[4] It is natural to assume that this has shifted to modular development under closed conditions at each hardware company.[5]

8.1.2 Continuous Improvement and Price Reduction of Game Consoles

Hardware abstraction had another effect as well: it contributed to lowering the cost of game hardware. Up until the 2D era, the hardware specifications of previous home video game hardware remained largely unchanged from the time the console was released until the end of its life. If there were changes, they were in the form of minor adjustments to the shape and material of the controller or the elimination of unused expansion buses.

Sony aggressively made changes in this area. As technology developed, Sony reduced the cost of hardware by combining functions that were previously performed by multiple semiconductors into a single semiconductor, or by replacing them with memory with equivalent or better performance and passed some of the savings on to users in the form of lower hardware prices. Table 8.1 shows the transition of the PlayStation model number and price, from 39,800 yen at the end of 1994 to 19,800 yen a year and a half later. The SCPH-100, which was released after the launch of PlayStation 2 and was nicknamed PS-ONE, ended up costing less than 10,000 yen.[6]

[4]Many games have a staff roll at the ending, but in the 1980s many games used aliases or nicknames in the staff roll for fear that companies would rip off the developers.

[5]To introduce development equipment, game development companies are required to sign a non-disclosure agreement (NDA). As a result, the technical specifications of game consoles are not openly disclosed.

[6]The strategy of reducing the price of hardware was also used for the PC Engine and Mega Drive, but the content was almost the same and the frequency was low. It was also a way of boosting the sales of machines that were not the top models of their generation.

Table 8.1 Model number and price of PlayStation

Date	Model number	Price(yen)
December 3, 1994	SCPH-1000	39,800
July 21, 1995	SCPH-3000	29,800
March 28, 1996	SCPH-3500	24,800
June 22, 1996	SCPH-5000	19,800
November 13, 1997	SCPH-7000	18,000
December 1, 1998	SCPH-7500	15,000
May 28, 1999	SCPH-9000	15,000
July 7, 2000	SCPH-100	15,000
September 12, 2001		9800
May 16, 2002		Open Price

The strategy of targeting new customers by aggressively redesigning and repeatedly lowering the price of the top models of that generation was actively used in subsequent hardware. This strategy was used to attract new customers by lowering the price of Sony's game console (PlayStation), which was more expensive than previous game hardware. This was made possible by the abstraction of the hardware from the game, and the technical specification that did not allow the game software to directly control the hardware. However, in the early games, when the libraries provided were not yet complete and the drivers themselves were not yet mature, some of the more technically advanced game developers used direct hardware control in their programs. Some of these games did not work on game consoles with different model numbers.

8.1.3 Graphics Shift to 3D

8.1.3.1 Changes in the Spec Table

This generation of hardware marked a major change in the specifications of game machines. The reason is that, in principle, 2D graphics were used to depict the screen on earlier machines, but this has changed to 3D graphics.

Figure 8.4 shows the basic mechanism of the graphics of a game machine in the 2D era. The sprite layer is a mechanism for drawing fast-moving characters on top of multiple virtual screens, such as the background of the game, the part displaying the score, and the part drawing objects in the actual game. The player who plays the game sees all these layers superimposed.[7]

Because of this format, the number of sprites that could be displayed at the same time, the number of virtual screens, and so on were shown in the specification list in the days of 2D graphics. In addition, the screen resolution and the number of

[7] In a game where the screen moves, a virtual screen for the destination screen may be prepared. In addition, there may be multiple sprite layers for easy management.

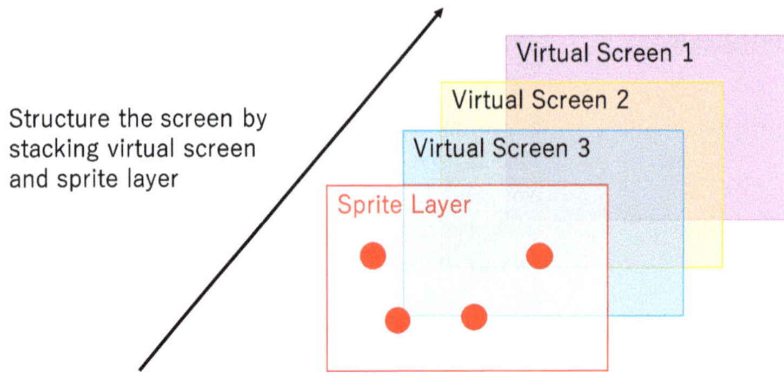

Fig. 8.4 How 2D graphics works

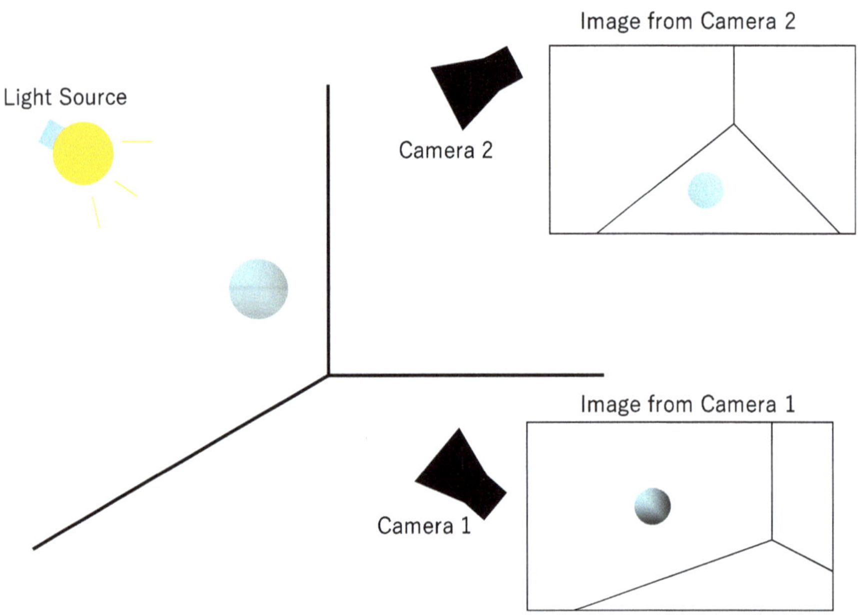

Fig. 8.5 How 3D graphics works

simultaneous colors were also important factors because the rendering performance of games was still insufficient.

On the other hand, the basic mechanism of 3D graphics is shown in Fig. 8.5. In the virtual space, there is a light source and a camera, and each object (character or object on the screen) is displayed on the screen that the player sees because of calculating its position in the space and the way the light hits it. The characters in the game move from moment to moment, and the image is generated and displayed at each screen display timing (usually 60 times per second). In addition, in the normal video generation process, various effects are added, such as adding textures (graphical data that expresses the surface texture) to objects and applying haze to the entire screen.

In 2D graphics, if the same character has different orientations and sizes, it is necessary to create all variations of the character, but the load on the hardware is small. On the other hand, in 3D graphics, the entire image is calculated and generated, so it is possible to express different sizes and orientations with a single object data,[8] and the load on the hardware is very large although the load on the creation is small. In the 2D graphics era, 3D space was represented by pseudo-expressions such as changing the scrolling speed of each virtual screen or using raster scrolling to represent the depth of the screen. Therefore, game expressions that were impossible before are now possible.

From this era of game consoles, 16-bit (65,536 colors) and 24-bit (16,777,216 colors) colors became standard, effectively eliminating the simultaneous color expression constraint. The resolution also exceeded the TV resolution of the time, so it was no longer a constraint until the advent of high-resolution TVs for digital broadcasting. In its place, a measure of 3D graphics computing power became the focus of attention as an indicator of performance. In 1994, the number of polygons per second[9] was used in the PlayStation/Saturn era, and now the number of computable vertices per second is used.

8.1.3.2 Convergence of Hardware Performance

Due to the advanced nature of 3D graphics, Namco and Sega were the only game companies that were able to produce 3D graphics-based platforms for arcade games when the PlayStation/Saturn were released in 1994. Later, several companies developed system boards for 3D graphics, but the sophistication of the technology made it difficult to keep up with the continuous increase in performance, as well as the cost of production. Arcade game system boards were replaced by home console-compatible boards and PC-compatible boards, which were mass produced at a lower cost, and proprietary system boards disappeared. As a result, arcade games lost their technical superiority to both PC and home video games.

Figure 8.6 shows a conceptual diagram of the evolution of the performance of home, arcade, and PC hardware. As shown in Chap. 1, during the 2D era, arcades were able to be upwardly compatible with home consoles, while PCs were inferior in terms of drawing performance except for screen resolution but were superior in terms of the size of data they could handle and their ability to calculate complex logic. In the latter half of the 1990s, the difference between home consoles and arcade games disappeared, and the graphical performance of PCs increased rapidly

---

[8] In practice, using only precise objects (with many polygons) is computationally and memory intensive, so in games, relatively coarse objects (with a small number of polygons) are often created for distant views and used together.

[9] In 3D graphics, the surface of an object is represented as a collection of polygons.

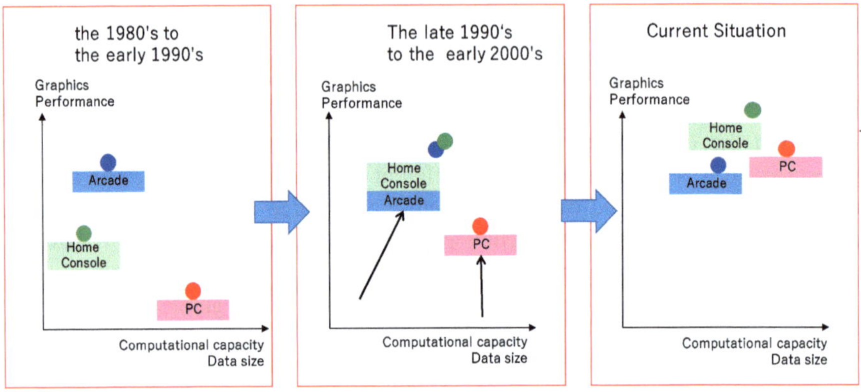

Fig. 8.6 Convergence of game machine performance

Table 8.2 Disk media and data capacity installed in game consoles (The difference in CD-ROM capacity between the PC Engine and PlayStation / Saturn is because the capacity of CD-ROM of PC Engine was small due to sector related to error control)

1988	PC Engine	CD-ROM	540 MB
1994	PlayStation Saturn	CD-ROM	640 MB
1998	Dreamcast	GD-ROM	1 GB
2000	PlayStation 2	DVD-ROM	4.8 GB
2006	PlayStation 3	BD-ROM	50 GB
2014	PlayStation 4	BD-ROM	50 GB

with the transition from PC-9801 to Windows. Nowadays, arcade games have been overtaken by PCs, which have a high rate of technological innovation, and their performance has become inferior to that of home consoles due to the time lag in the release of compatible platforms.

8.1.4 Diffusion of Disk Media

8.1.4.1 Characteristics of Disk Media

CD-ROM games were also available on the previous generation of consoles, the PC Engine and the Mega Drive, and were a near de facto standard on the PC Engine, with the PC Engine DUO being released as a minor change to the PC Engine, but as a peripheral.

After the release of the PlayStation and Sega Saturn in 1994, the provision of games on disk media became the de facto standard, with a few exceptions such as the Nintendo 64. Since then, the capacity of the disks installed has increased with each successive generation (Table 8.2).

Compared to the mask ROMs, which were semiconductor memory, loading data on disk media was far slower. This meant that when loading data in a game, the player had to wait for a "loading" message to appear on the screen. This waiting time could be reduced to a certain extent by programmatic improvements (loading less data at a time and more frequently, placing the data to be loaded closer to each other on the disk, loading in the background during play so that the player is not aware of the time taken) and by using faster disk drives. This can be reduced to a certain extent, but never completely. Nintendo disliked the waiting time and insisted on supplying games in masked ROMs for the Nintendo 64, the next hardware after the Super Famicom, but users preferred to play games on disk media. In effect, users thought that the advantages of disk media far outweighed the immediacy of ROM. The advantages of disk media compared to semiconductor (mask ROM) game delivery were as follows:

1. Overwhelmingly low production costs
   In the Super Famicom era, the cost of mask ROMs drove up the selling price of games, and it was not uncommon for the price of a single game to exceed 10,000 yen. With disk media, the unit cost of pressing a single disk is less than 100 yen, and the price can be lowered by the reduction in cost. In fact, the average unit price of a game dropped from just under 10,000 yen to around 6000 yen when we moved from the Super Nintendo era to the PlayStation era.
2. Shorter lead time from completion of development (mastering) to release
   In the days of mask ROMs, mastering had to be done at least 2 months before the game's release date. After disk media was introduced, the lead time was shortened to 3 weeks before the game release date.
   This reduction in lead time had an impact on the ordering behavior of retailers. To determine the number of games to be packaged, the hardware companies that were contracted to produce the games collected orders from retailers, but in the case of mask ROMs it was difficult to produce additional copies quickly (repeat production) and orders had to be placed at a stage when the game had not yet gained a good reputation. As a result, large quantities were repeatedly produced, including for the game developers' stock, and large quantities remained unsold. After the introduction of disk media, orders were placed closer to 1 month before the release date, which meant that advance reviews could be checked, and meant that retailers could respond more quickly to repeat orders, reducing their inventory risk.[10]
3. Far greater capacity
   At the time, even the largest masked ROM games had a capacity of only 32 Mb (32 megabits = 4 megabytes). It was possible to increase the capacity of a game by installing more than one ROM in a game cartridge, but this often meant

[10] As many game titles account for the majority of sales in the first few days after release, stocking up on repeat production does not necessarily mean that the game will sell if sufficient stock is not available on the day of release. This means that the risk of ordering more and having it remain unsold is never eliminated.

cutting out some of the game content, as higher production costs meant higher selling prices. This was when CD-ROM, a medium with a capacity of over 600 MB, was introduced.

The increase in capacity by several hundred times has necessitated the development of games with a different scale and image to existing games. One of the major turning points in game expression was the shift to multimedia content. For example, music was replaced by live sound from CDs instead of built-in sound sources, and movie scenes appeared in event scenes.

It should be noted, however, that the features of low cost and high capacity of disk media are only relative to the historical background at the time of their respective development and release. Since the semiconductor integration technology is advancing rapidly, the disk system of the Family Computer (512 kilobits = 64 KB on one side, 1 megabit = 128 KB on both sides) and the ROM cassette (up to 8 megabits = 1 MB) or the UMD of the PSP (1 GB) were an overwhelmingly large capacity at the time of the specification of the game console. However, after a while, the memory may become larger. When this happens, the low capacity and long loading times can become a weakness.

8.2 Changes in the Economic Environment

8.2.1 The Advent of the Multimedia Boom and the Focus on Games

Since the beginning of the 1990s, the term "multimedia" has suddenly become popular. The term "multimedia" refers to media that combine multiple media (such as music and video) into a single content. In the days when the performance of computers and the capacity of recording media were still low, and when most media were analogue, text information was handled separately as books, music information as cassette tapes, and images as video tapes. With the advent of CD-ROMs as a high-capacity storage medium and the improvement of computer performance, it became possible to digitize all information and handle it centrally. It was a huge business opportunity. From today's point of view, the topic is far ahead of its time. However, it was even said that a market of over 100 trillion yen would be generated in the future.[11]

Games were the first interactive entertainment that integrated visuals and music, and the previous generation of game consoles (PC Engine and Mega Drive) had already commercialized CD-ROMs as peripherals. In addition, game consoles have

[11]Here are two titles of books released in 1994. *The Impact of Multimedia: A 123 Trillion Yen Business Opportunity!* and *Multimedia in a nutshell: Creating a huge market of 100 trillion yen.*

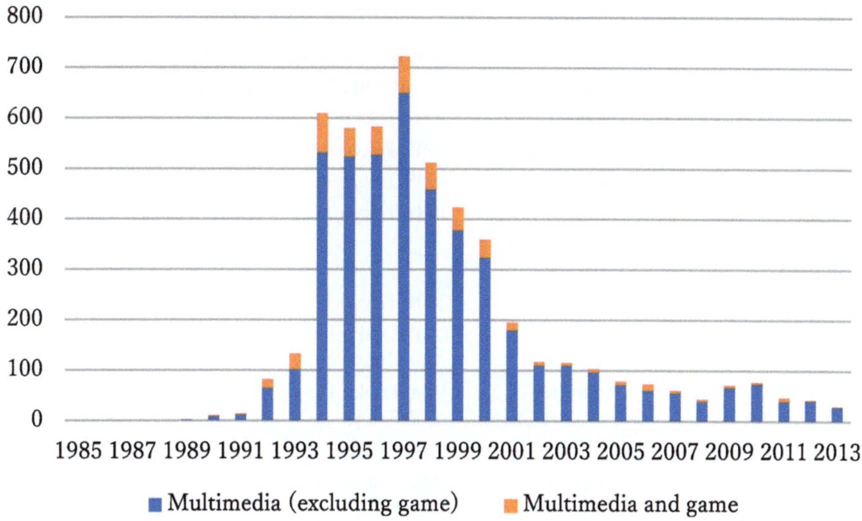

Fig. 8.7 "Multimedia"-related articles (Asahi Shimbun)

been used in 10 million households in the past. As a result, it attracted a great deal of attention as a highly feasible multimedia field that would blossom first.

Figure 8.7 shows the number of hits obtained by searching the Asahi Shimbun article database for "multimedia" and "multimedia & games." The number of articles related to multimedia rose sharply in 1994 and reached its peak in 1997, when more than 700 articles, equivalent to about two articles per day, were published. In the twenty-first century, the number of hits decreased significantly. At its peak, the number of articles about games in multimedia-related articles was about 10%.

In the midst of this multimedia boom, Philips launched the CD-i (i means interactive) and Matsushita Electric (now Panasonic) launched the 3DO multimedia machine, but they were not very powerful and were withdrawn early.

8.2.2 Pioneering the Video Standards Race

Due to the digitization of video data, the high video processing capability of game consoles can be directly used as a function of audiovisual equipment. Therefore, the overwhelming number of game consoles in households has been used to promote new video standards.[12]

[12]The first generation of PlayStation consoles released in Asia had video CD playback capability, although this was not available on the models released in Japan. This also contributed to the spread of Video CDs in Asia.

Table 8.3 Major game development companies listed on the stock market

Name	First listing	Listing in the First Section of the Stock Exchange
Nintendo	1963(Osaka 2)	1970(Osaka 1), 1983(Tokyo 1)
Sega	1988(Tokyo 2)	1990(Tokyo 1)
Namco	1988(Tokyo 2)	1991(Tokyo 1)
Bandai	1986(Tokyo 2)	1988(Tokyo 1)
Konami	1984 (Osaka new 2)	1988(Tokyo 1)
JALECO	1988(J)	
TECMO	1992(J)	2001(Tokyo 1)
TOSE	1999(Osaka 2)	2001(Osaka 1) 2001(Tokyo 1)
CAPCOM	1990(OTC) 1993(Osaka 2)	1999(Osaka 1) 2000(Tokyo 1)
KOEI		1997(Tokyo 1)
TAITO	1993(Tokyo 2)	2003(Tokyo 1)
ENIX	1991(OTC)	1999(Tokyo 1)
SQUARE	1994(OTC)	2000(Tokyo 1)
BANPRESTO	2000(Tokyo 2)	2003(Tokyo 1)
ATLUS	1997(J)	
Nihon Falcom	2003(M)	
Yuke's	2001(H)	
Hudson	2000(J)	
Marvelous Entertainment	2002(J) 2005(Tokyo 2)	2012(Tokyo 1)

Market for major and quasi-major companies: Tokyo 1, 2: Tokyo Stock Exchange 1st (2nd)section; Osaka 1,2: Osaka Stock Exchange 1st (2nd)section
Market for start-up companies: J: JASDAQ; M: Mothers (Tokyo Stock Exchange); H: Nippon New Market Hercules(Osaka Stock Exchange); Osaka new 2: Osaka Stock Exchange new 2nd section; OTC: Over the Counter

The PlayStation 2, which was released in 2000 with DVD playback capability, immediately became the "most sold DVD-playing hardware" on the day it was released and had a significant impact on the spread of DVD into the home.

The PlayStation 3, released in 2006, had Blu-Ray playback capability. At the time, Blu-ray was amid a competition with the HDDVD camp for the next generation video disk standard, but due to the popularity of the PlayStation 3, HDDVD was completely withdrawn in 2008, 2 years after its first product launch in 2006.

8.2.3 Stock Market Listing Boom

One of the reasons for the increased social attention is the increase in the number of listed companies. Table 8.3 shows when the major game development companies went public. Toy-related companies such as Nintendo and Bandai with large sales, and major arcade game developers such as Sega, Namco, and Konami were already listed in the First Section in 1994. PC game companies such as Square, Enix, Koei, and Nihon Falcom were not so large and their shares were either listed on the OTC market or unlisted. However, the situation changed when the listing standards were relaxed, and many medium-sized game development companies went public. Table 8.3 shows that a number of companies have gone public since the late 1990s.

Listing has enabled game developers to raise bloated development funds on their own. However, they are now responsible for explaining to shareholders the current development progress, the profit forecast for the current fiscal year, and the management strategy, etc., and the profit status of each fiscal year and even each quarter is closely monitored. On the other hand, the sophistication and complexity of game development has increased the development period to 2 or 3 years, requiring game companies to take a longer-term perspective than ever before.

8.2.4 Changes in the Distribution Structure of Games

In the case of home video games, the distribution route of the products was from toy wholesalers to retailers. In particular, games released on Nintendo console were mostly distributed through wholesalers who belonged to a fellowship of primary wholesalers[13] called Shoshinkai.[14]

In the days when Shoshinkai was the main distributor, games were supplied in masked ROM cassettes, which took 2 months to manufacture. In order to receive orders from wholesalers, game developers promoted their products to wholesalers 6 months to 3 months before the release date, and then collected orders from wholesalers and sent them to Nintendo. In this system, orders were placed before the product promotion to consumers, which usually started 1 month before the release date, and the sample ROMs of the games themselves were rarely completed. Wholesalers had to place expensive orders without knowing the content of the game or the response of consumers. As a result, popular titles were often out of stock, and unpopular titles were often stocked in large quantities. If additional orders were placed after the release of a title, it would take 2 months to complete the product, during which time the popularity of the title would fade, making additional production impossible unless the title was very popular or a classic. In order to dispose of bad stocks, some wholesalers purchased unpopular titles from secondary wholesalers and sold them at cost price or lower, and some wholesalers would not allow popular game titles to be purchased unless they were bundled with other unpopular titles, which was a big problem. In addition, Nintendo's relationship with toy

[13] A wholesaler who deals directly with a manufacturer to purchase goods. A wholesaler who purchases from a primary wholesaler is called a secondary wholesaler.

[14] According to Wada (2003), 97% of the total sales, excluding the sales of our own titles via Nintendo's sales division, were distributed via primary wholesalers affiliated with Shoshinkai.

distributors began before the company entered the game industry, and the Shoshinkai distribution system was not easy for other game companies to use.

When they were first released, games were truly "children's toys," and it was natural that they were handled by toy distributors. However, as the market for games expanded, it became profitable enough to build a distribution network for games rather than the existing toy distribution. With the launch of the PlayStation and Saturn in 1994, both Sony and Sega decided to move away from toy distribution, which mainly dealt with Nintendo products, and set up their own distribution networks. Sega's distribution system was influenced by the multimedia boom of the time, and used a variety of distribution routes, including those of its own distribution subsidiaries, consumer electronics (Hitachi[15]), and music shops (Toshiba-EMI), in addition to existing toy wholesaler routes. However, SEGA did not have its own CD pressing plant and relied on external orders, so the system of prospective production did not change much. SCE (Sony Computer Entertainment), on the other hand, made full use of the distribution network and CD pressing plant of SME (Sony Music Entertainment), one of its parent companies, and set up an integrated production and distribution system within the group. As a result, orders can now be placed up to 10 days in advance of the release date, and repeat production can be handled quickly, enabling detailed inventory management.

Later, in 1996, DigiCube, a wholly owned subsidiary of Square, started to distribute games at convenience stores,[16] and major game manufacturers started to sell games directly to retailers. Small and medium-sized game companies that did not develop and sell enough titles to have their own distribution network outsourced the distribution of their titles to one of the major game manufacturers' distribution networks, thus completing the model for game distribution that continues to this day.

However, for existing retailers, the composition of the profits supported by secondhand games remained unchanged. Secondhand games generate no income at all for the companies that actually develop the games. The number of used copies of blockbuster titles sold as secondhand games exceeded 1 million in some cases, which was a major frustration for game retailers. CESA (Computer Entertainment Supplier's Association, established in 1996) held a press conference on January 14, 1998, and announced that it would join with the ACCS (Association for Copyright Clearance of Computer Software) and the JPSA (Japan Personal Computer Software Association) to launch a campaign against illegal secondhand

[15] Saturn is equipped with two Hitachi SH-2 RISC CPUs. Because of this, the Saturn was also sold through Hitachi's consumer electronics distribution.

[16] DigiCube grew rapidly, thanks to measures such as selling the first copies of Final Fantasy 7 almost exclusively through DigiCube distribution. However, due to various reasons such as fixed price sales, lack of supply of Nintendo's game titles because of the bad relationship between Square and Nintendo, and the cost of kiosk terminals in convenience stores, DigiCube was petitioned for bankruptcy and dissolved in 2003. However, even after the bankruptcy of DigiCube, the distribution of games in convenience stores has been continuing and popular titles are still available in convenience stores. In recent years, web money for online games, prepaid cards for smartphone games, and cards for Nintendo's download sales are also available at convenience stores.

software. In the same year, 1998, SCE received an exclusion recommendation from the Fair-Trade Commission for restricting shipments to retailers selling used software. In response, the Association of Retailers of TV-Game Software (ARTS), a group of retailers specializing in video game software, took a stance of outright opposition and a court case ensued. The case went all the way to the Supreme Court, but in 2002 the ARTS won the case, and the sale of secondhand games was fully permitted.

8.2.5 The Emergence and Intensification of Price Discrimination Strategies

It was also around this time that the sale of low-priced versions became common. These were games that had already been released but were re-released sometime after their original release date at a lower, more affordable price, such as 2980 yen or 1980 yen. They are aimed at users who would not have bought the game at the original price, but would have bought it for 1980 yen, thus increasing sales from the same content. Such a strategy is called a price discrimination strategy.

From the point of view of the company selling the game, the most profitable way is to get each user to pay up to the maximum they can pay. However, since the retail price of a game is usually fixed, the company cannot accept more money than the retail price, even if some users are willing to pay more. Price discrimination partially makes this possible. Specifically, price discrimination refers to the strategy of dividing customers into several segments (groups) and selling at different prices for each segment in order to maximize sales.[17]

The following is an explanation of the price discrimination strategy in the game industry.

8.2.5.1 Price Discrimination Strategy in Packaged Games

First, consider the demand function for home video game software. With a few exceptions,[18] only one game per person (or one game per family) is purchased in

[17] There are several types of price discrimination strategies, for details, see the textbook on industrial organization in economics. In this book, we will focus on the game industry.

[18] In the case of bishōjo games, the strategy is to have the game developer provide materials such as images of the game characters, and to produce “goods limited to each shop” such as telephone cards and posters at the shop’s expense, and to present them to purchasers. When the sales of the shops are large and they can use their bargaining power against the game companies, they sometimes use newly drawn images or create original soundtracks or drama CDs. Some avid gamers will buy games from multiple shops to obtain each retailer’s exclusive goods, and then sell the remaining games to secondhand shops. The phenomenon of “buying multiple games for limited-edition goods” is a demand for games for reasons other than their original purpose and is excluded.

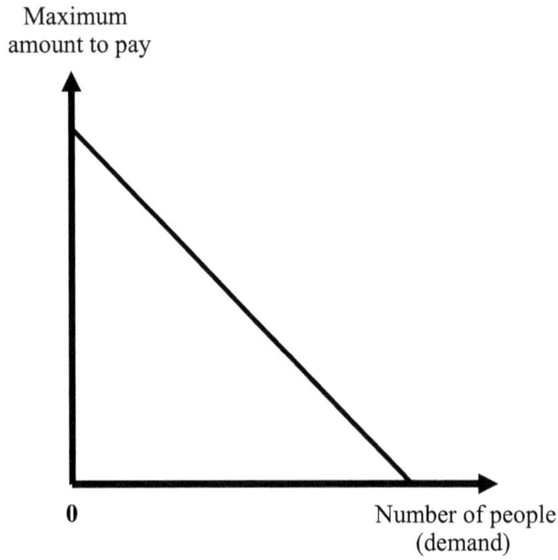

Fig. 8.8 Demand function for home console games

principle. In addition, each game has its own originality, and even if the price of a game rises, it does not flow to other games at once. For example, even if the price of Dragon Quest rises, the demand for Final Fantasy does not flow because it is the same RPG. Instead, each consumer has a maximum amount that s/he can pay for a game, and they will not buy a game if the price is higher than that. Based on these conditions, the demand function for household games is shown in Fig. 8.8.[19] The horizontal axis is the number of consumers, and the vertical axis is the maximum amount that each consumer is willing to pay. Overall, the consumers are arranged in order of the maximum amount that they are willing to pay from the origin.

Since the price of a game is the same, the sales of the game company will be the same as the rectangle inscribed in the triangle bounded by the demand function and the axes of the graph.[20] However, the upper and right parts of the demand function remain unrecoverable. The upper part is the part where the customer would have bought the product even if the price had been set higher, and the right part is the part where the customer would have bought the product if the price had been set lower (Fig. 8.9). Price discrimination strategy is a method to recover a part of the lost sales in this part.

Figure 8.10 shows the price discrimination strategies used in home video games. The first strategy is to increase sales by releasing additional downloadable contents such as costumes of game characters and additional game scenarios after the release

[19] To put it simply, the characteristics of games that I have described so far show that a rightward falling demand curve can be drawn for each individual title. If you are not interested in the details, you can ignore them.

[20] Sales = price * quantity sold. As the vertical axis is the price per package sold and the horizontal axis is the number of packages sold at that price (number of people), the sales are equal to the area of the rectangle.

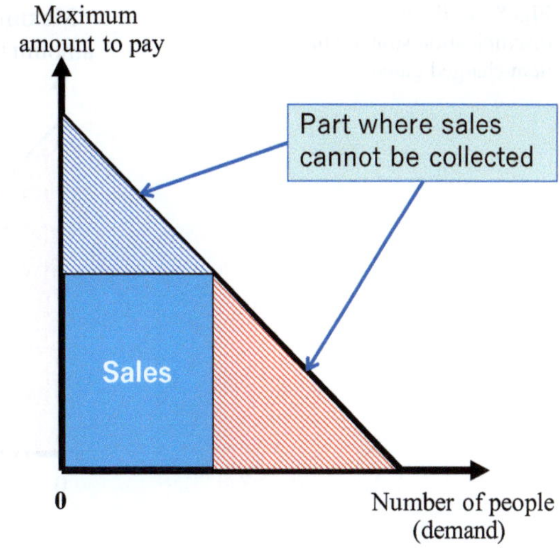

Fig. 8.9 Sales and missing parts of game software

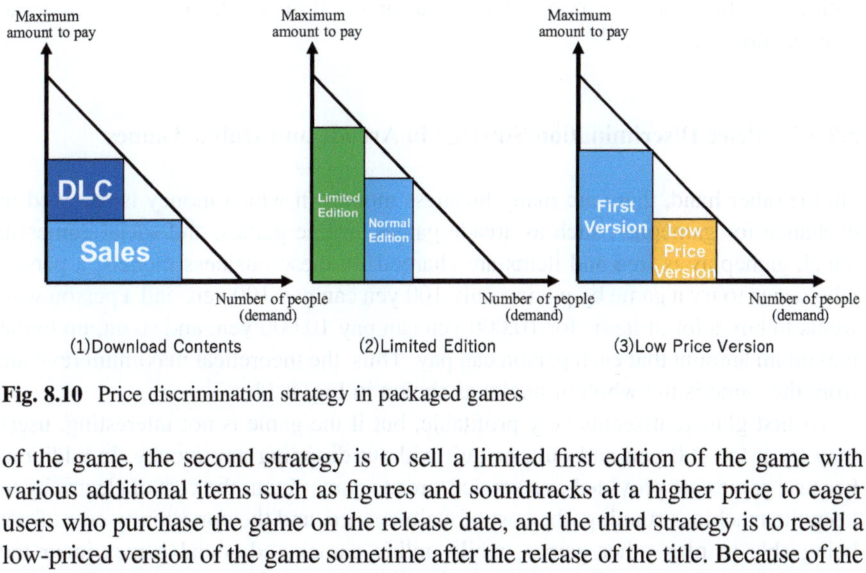

Fig. 8.10 Price discrimination strategy in packaged games

of the game, the second strategy is to sell a limited first edition of the game with various additional items such as figures and soundtracks at a higher price to eager users who purchase the game on the release date, and the third strategy is to resell a low-priced version of the game sometime after the release of the title. Because of the overwhelming results in favor of the distribution side in the secondhand game trial, the sales behavior of releasing a low-priced version of a game when its secondhand price is close to 1980 yen, which is the price range of a low-priced version, has been observed.

The first type of downloadable content was popularized by Xbox360's THE iDOLM@STER (Namco Bandai Games, 2007). The second, limited edition, has been used in a variety of products such as books and music CDs. Now that tie-ups

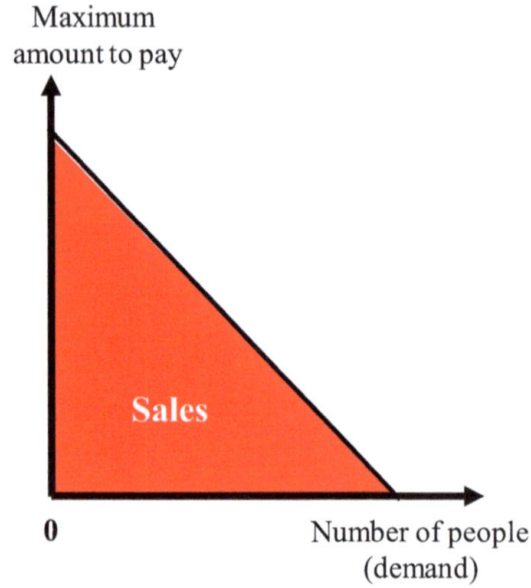

Fig. 8.11 Price discrimination strategy in item-charged games

with anime have become popular, there are many limited editions that include an original anime episode.[21]

8.2.5.2 Price Discrimination Strategy in Arcade and Online Games

On the other hand, there are many business models in which money is received in exchange for gameplay, such as arcade games, online games, and social games in which gameplay is free and items are charged. In these business models, a person who wants to try a game by paying only 100 yen can pay 100 yen, and a person who wants to buy a lot of items for 10,000 yen can pay 10,000 yen, and so on, up to the maximum amount that each person can pay. Thus, the theoretical maximum revenue from the game is the whole triangle, as shown in Fig. 8.11.

At first glance, it seems very profitable, but if the game is not interesting, users may try it for 100 yen and quit, or quit without dropping any money. In addition, because games are provided as a service, arcade games incur the cost of electricity to keep the machines running, the cost of maintenance, and the opportunity cost of not being able to play other games, while online games and social games incur the ongoing cost of maintaining and managing game servers. There are many other risks associated with service-type games than with packaged games.

In addition, in order for users to pay up to the maximum amount they are allowed to pay for a game, it is necessary to have a mechanism that allows them to pay that

[21] If one additional episode is produced on the production line that is already in operation for the anime broadcast, the cost of producing one anime episode as a bonus for the game will be about 10 million yen. Therefore, if we assume that 20,000–30,000 copies of the limited edition, which is about 3000 yen more than the standard edition, will be sold, the cost of producing the animation will be fully recovered.

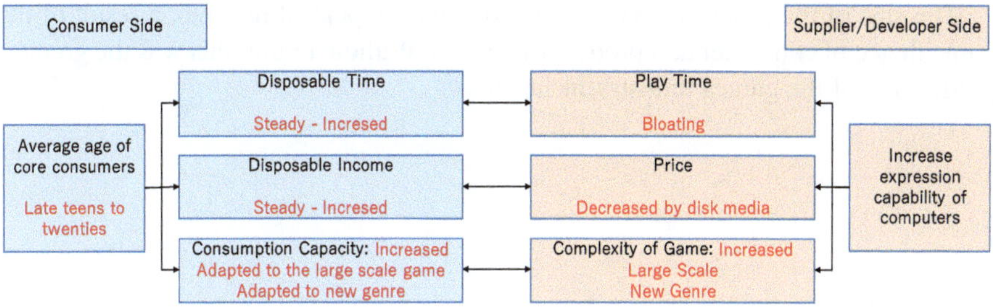

Fig. 8.12 Consumer—Supplier relations in the latter half of the 1990s

much during the game. Compared to arcade games, where users are charged per game, online games and social games, where gameplay itself is free and the revenue source is item-based, require a mechanism for continuous spending within the game. In the case of selling character costumes and equipment (avatar sales), which users can use continuously after the sale, new development costs are required continuously, and losses are incurred if sales are lower than expected. For this reason, in games where items are charged for, equipment such as character weapons are often regarded as consumption items like recovery items, with a set validity time and number of times they can be used.

Another method is to sell not the item itself but a lottery (gacha) in which the item appears, so that the player is charged repeatedly to obtain a rare item with a low appearance rate. Gacha is very profitable, but it has become a social problem because of the high expenditure on games.

8.3 Summary: The Golden Age of Japanese Video Games

In summarizing this chapter, the situation of producers and consumers is shown in Fig. 8.12. A little more than 10 years have passed since the release of the Nintendo Family Computer in 1983, and the primary school students of that time are now university students or working adults. There are still many people who have not quit playing games, and they play a central role in consumption with the younger generation. They are students or young workers, and of course most of them are single. They have a lot of disposable time and disposable income to spend on games. They are also flexible enough to adapt to the new game expressions associated with 3D.

On the other hand, from the point of view of the game supplier, the introduction of disk media has increased the capacity of games, which has increased the time it takes to play a single game, but consumers have had enough time to respond to this increase. Likewise, the shift to disk media has lowered the price per game, which has greatly increased the number of games sold. It was a win-win situation for both parties.

The size of the Japanese market for video games peaked in 1996, a result of the coincidence of consumer and producer interests. Without doubt, this was the greatest golden age of the games industry in Japan.

Chapter 9
Arcade Games (3) The Impact of Virtua Fighter and Ridge Racer: The Last Splendor of Arcade Games

Abstract This chapter describes the transformation of the arcade game market in the 1990s. The biggest change that occurred around this time was the emergence of the printed sticker machine, which drastically changed the revenue model of game arcades. In addition, the first 3D games in Japan came from arcades, where the hardware was in a state of flux. Virtua Fighter and Ridge Racer were the symbols of the new era. However, after this period, the center of innovation in the game industry shifted to PCs and home video game consoles. In arcade games, the number of compatible platforms increased and the status of arcade games declined.

Keywords Purikura(Print Club) · Virtua Fighter · Ridge Racer · Compatible board

9.1 Birth of the Print Sticker Machine[1]

In 1995, a machine was born that changed the face of game centers for the better. It was Print Club developed by Atlus and released by Sega. Print Club was a machine that allowed users to take photos in a booth and have them printed out on a sheet in 16 segments. It was expensive at 300 yen per session, but it became very popular, especially among high school girls. Lines formed at the game center, and records were set for the number of times the machine was used, including 300 times a day and over 7000 times a month.[2] The machine was expensive at 1.2 million yen per unit, but orders came in from shopping centers as well as game centers, and by the end of 1996, 8000 units had been sold. Its successor, Print Club 2, became a hit, selling 24,000 units by the end of 1998.

Due to the simple structure of the print sticker machine, more than 20 companies have released similar models. With the development and release of the successor model by Atlus, the print sticker machine has become one of the standard genres in

[1] Print sticker machines are commonly referred to as "purikura," but since "print club" and "purikura" are registered trademarks, they are referred to as print sticker machines in the industry.

[2] Asahi Shimbun, September 15, 1996.

Y. Koyama, *History of the Japanese Video Game Industry*, Translational Systems Sciences 35, https://doi.org/10.1007/978-981-99-1342-8_9

game centers. The technological development of the print sticker machine was very active, with the adoption of high-performance single-lens reflex cameras, color-changing functions such as black-and-white or sepia, doodling on images, whitening function to whiten the skin tone of the person, automatic image correction function to increase the size of the eyes, and full-body photography function. Competition was so fierce that Atlus itself eventually withdrew from sticker printing machines (and even from arcade games).

In response to the success of print sticker machines, My Stamp (developed jointly by Capcom and Matsushita Electric in 1997) and Stamp Club (developed jointly by Data East and Sega in 1997) were introduced to print stickers with portraits created from photo images. However, they failed to gain much support, and only models with a simple photo and decoration function survived.

With the advent of print sticker machines, the appearance of game centers changed drastically. Print sticker machines and prize machines, such as UFO Catcher, were placed near the entrance to attract customers, while arcade game machines, which are played by regular customers and enthusiasts, were placed at the back of the store. In the case of stores located on multiple floors of a building, the number of stores with print sticker machines and prize machines on the first floor and video games on the second and subsequent floors has increased. Now that cell phones are equipped with photo functions, these machines do not have the momentum they had when they were first released, but their position as a standard in game arcades remains unchanged.

9.2 Popularity of 3D Games and Music Games

The next mainstay of game centers that introduced new functions was 3D graphics using polygons and music games. Namco was far ahead of the curve in 3D graphics, releasing the racing game Winning Run in 1989 using the System 21 system board developed by Namco. System 21 did not yet have a texture mapping function, resulting in a flat, bare polygon image, but System 22, the next system board, supported texture mapping and increased the realism of the expression. Ridge Racer was released in 1993 and became a huge hit. Sega also released V.R. Virtua Racing in 1992, a racing game using the system board MODEL 1, which was jointly developed with General Electric. At that time, Namco and Sega were practically the only two companies in Japan that could develop arcade games using 3D graphics.[3]

[3]Both developed racing games as games using 3D graphics because racing games are one of the game genres that can most easily show the differences between 3D graphics and 2D graphics in their characteristics. In 2D graphics racing games, as the car moves forward, the display screen switches between straight ahead and curves according to the course, but this system does not allow for curves that are more than 90 degrees, such as hairpin curves, and the only way to cover them up is to display the curve scene for a long time. It also could not represent anything out of specification, such as a car turning completely sideways, driving in the opposite direction of the course, or falling

The era was set in motion when Sega released Virtua Fighter, the world's first 3D fighting game, at the end of 1993. At the time, the computing power of 3D graphics was not high, and unlike the relatively simple shape of formula cars, the limit was two characters with complex shapes and movements, such as humans. Even with these two characters, the straight lines of the polygons became apparent (making the game look crispy), and the appearance of the game was very different from existing fighting games with beautiful 2D graphics. It took a while for players to understand the game, but the battles in a realistic playing field with depth as well as left and right (or front and back, if you were in the game character's position) became popular and a big hit.

A music game is a game in which the player performs actions such as pressing buttons and stepping to the rhythm of a song. Konami released *beatmania* in 1997 and it became a hit,[4] followed by Dance Dance Revolution (1998) and Pop'n Music (1998), establishing music games as a genre. Konami branded beatmania and promoted the series along the lines of a music simulation. GuitarFreaks (1999) and DrumMania (1999) were released following beatmania, in which the player plays the keyboard, and sessions are possible by combining them. Konami's music games took the music simulation in terms of operation, while their music took dance music and club music, which were flourishing at the time. On the other hand, Sega's Samba de Amigo (1999) and Shakatto Tambourine! (1999) and Namco's Taiko no Tatsujin (2001) differentiated themselves from Konami's music games by adopting a format that was popular with the public in terms of both operation and music.

Konami placed great importance on the music game market acquired by beatmania and applied for and obtained several patents. Konami filed a lawsuit against Jaleco in 1999, claiming that VJ released by Jaleco infringed on the patents it had earned. It then filed a provisional injunction application against Namco, which had installed VJ in its own game centers, demanding that the VJ be removed. In response, both Jaleco and Namco sued Konami for infringing on their patents for games in other genres, and a legal battle ensued for a while, but it was finally settled in 2000.

Music games are intuitive and easy to play, which makes it easy to attract new players, and even if the gameplay remains the same, changing the music creates new fun and keeps the customers coming back. For this reason, once a game becomes a hit, many of them become a series and continue to be played for a long time while changing the music. The beatmania series and the Taiko no Tatsujin series continue to release sequels to this day.

---

out of a multi-level intersection. With 3D graphics, the course is created virtually in the computer, so not only can these things be expressed completely, but it is also easy to change viewpoints, such as the cockpit view or the view from behind the car, and to replay the collision or the goal. In terms of realism, games with 3D graphics were a world apart from 2D games.

[4]The idea of the same type of music game was preceded by PaRappa the Rapper (SCE, 1996), which was released on PlayStation.

9.3 The Spread of Compatible Boards and the Decline in the Status of Video Games

With the end of the twentieth century came the demise of video game arcades as places where the most advanced games could be played. This was due to the following two factors.

The first is a change in the business environment. Home video game consoles, which had a business model of "Horizontal thinking of dead technology[5]"and mass production of established inexpensive technology to make it even cheaper, began to develop their own specialized semiconductors with cutting-edge technology, attracted by the success of their business. The number of PCs sold worldwide increased with the success of Windows 95 and the spread of Internet access, and the competition for higher-performance graphics chips intensified. 3D chip vendors focused on games to show the performance of their chips in an easy-to-understand way. Both sides began to invest in cutting-edge technology, and the performance of PCs increased continuously with each new chip, while that of home consoles jumped up every few years.

Secondly, the companies that had the technology to develop hardware (system boards) for 3D graphics were limited to a few major companies. There were no companies other than Namco and Sega in Japan that were able to create system boards for 3D games prior to PlayStation (December 3, 1994). Taito and Konami announced 3D system boards in 1995, but their performance was not as high as that of home game consoles. Some companies did not have the capability to develop 3D system boards, and Sony sold system boards based on the PlayStation to those companies.

Under such circumstances, the number of compatible boards increased due to the improvement of the game development environment. A compatible board is a system board that is hardware compatible with home game consoles and PCs. Compatible circuit boards themselves have existed for a long time, but they were mainly used for inexpensively manufactured boards for games that did not require high performance. Sega developed the Saturn compatible board ST-V, and the PlayStation compatible board was used by Namco, Capcom, and Konami. Taito developed the Type-X Windows compatible board. Finally, Sega released the Dreamcast-based NAOMI board (1998), which was a big hit, and the trend of adopting compatible boards became definitive.

The fact that compatible boards have become common means that the performance advantage over home video games that was maintained since the introduction of the Famicom has been lost. In fact, there are many titles that were developed on NAOMI boards or PlayStation 2 compatible boards and were ported to home

[5]"Horizontal thinking of dead technology" is a phrase of the late Gunpei Yokoi (1941–1997), known as the developer of Game & Watch, Game Boy and WonderSwan. The idea is to develop products by making good use of technologies that are already widely available and can be used inexpensively.

consoles with almost the same content (or with additional content) about a year after they were released in arcades.

In conjunction with the retreat of existing video games, a system was born to connect game centers to the network and allow real-time competition. With the spread of the network, game companies were able to not only sell out the chassis and boards to game centers, but also receive continuous network connection fees. Today, except for Internet-connected games, music games, and sensory games in large cabinets, regular video games are a genre that is played by only a few people in game centers.

Since the Dreamcast (Sega, 1998), network connectivity has been standardized for home video game consoles, but the Internet connection rate for home video game consoles for the average player was low, so the unique added value of Internet-connected games at game arcades was maintained. The exception to this was fighting games, where core fighting game players flocked to Microsoft's platform and began to actively compete via the Internet. In fighting games, it is no fun to play against an opponent who is either too strong or too weak. With the spread of the Internet, it became possible to play against players of equal ability via the Internet using matching servers, and the Internet became the primary battleground for fighting games.

One of the most popular genres of arcade games with Internet access is mahjong. Mahjong has been around since before the Internet, but the ability to play against other players via the Internet and to save the results of play on a magnetic card has added new value to the genre. In addition, the ability to update software via the network made it possible to hold events such as limited-time rankings to attract customers. Some of the games have been ported to home consoles, but most players play them in game arcades, partly because of the fun of the events.

Along with network connectivity, another factor that has influenced the next generation is the popularity of trading card battle style games. In trading card games, players receive a card for each game they play, and use that card to compete against other players.[6] To progress in the game, players need to build their own decks by sequentially replacing the cards with stronger ones. A card is given to the player at the end of the game, which strongly encourages the player to become a repeat player of the game. WORLD CLUB Champion Football (WCCF) (SEGA, 2002)[7] and MUSHIKING the King of Beetle (SEGA, 2003) were the pioneers of this type of game for the public and for children, respectively, and became a hit due to their different gameplay and collectability from existing analog trading card games.

[6]Only the first time a player plays the game, he or she may need to purchase a starter pack. After that, the game is enhanced by cards that a player receives with each game play, but it is possible to purchase specific cards at trading card stores. Cards with strong effects are priced at a premium and can cost several thousand yen each.

[7]However, in the early days of WCCF, only direct matches were available, and network matches did not yet exist. It wasn't until the version released in 2009 that network play became possible, as it is today.

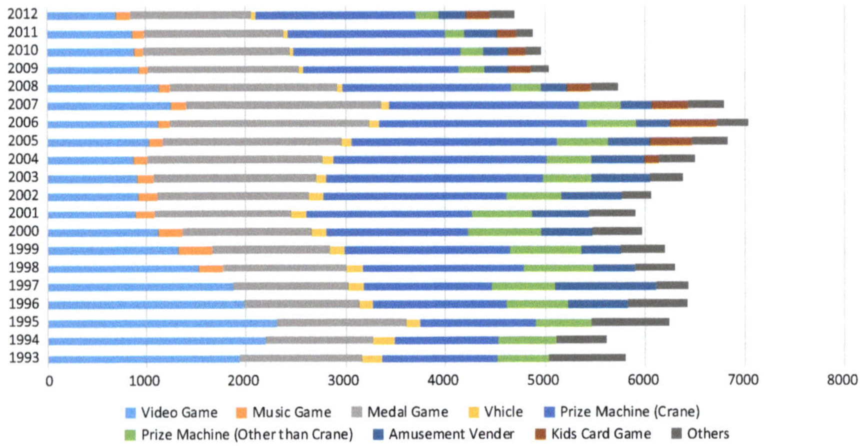

Fig. 9.1 Operation income trend (billion yen). Source: *Amusement Sangyou kai no Jittai houkokusyo (Actual State Report of the Amusement Industry)* each yearly edition

9.4 Decline in the Status of Video Games and the Increase in the Size of Game Centers

There is no doubt that the business model of "getting people to come to a game center and put in 100 yen to play" has fundamentally collapsed, at least for video games. What made up for it were the machines that offered prizes such as UFO Catcher and medal games.

Figure 9.1 shows the ratio of arcade operation sales for each year. Video games were overtaken by crane games in 1998 and by medal games in 2000. In 2012, the latest data available, prize offering machines and medal games accounted for nearly two-thirds of the total. Video game sales, including card vendors for trading card games, kids' cards, and music games, account for less than 30% of total sales.

Since prize machines and medal game machines require a large floor space for installation, it is difficult to install them in small-scale game centers. In addition, medal games and kids' card games are in high demand among families. Small game centers in urban areas that have been operating mainly with conventional video games have difficulty installing many medal game machines and prize offering machines due to the small floor space. In addition, the burden of network connections (construction of LANs and installation of servers) and communication fees became a burden, and the number of game centers gradually decreased. On the other hand, the number of roadside stores in the suburbs and stores in shopping malls increased, but the number of game arcades is on the decline. The number of game machines installed per store increased because of the upgrading of stores to larger ones (Fig. 9.2).

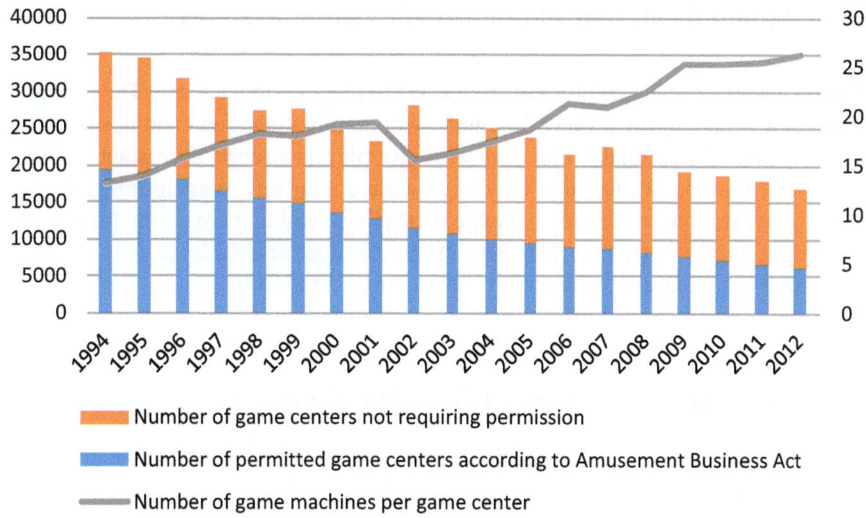

Fig. 9.2 Number of game centers and number of game machines per game center. Source: *Police White Paper* each year version. Since 2002, the number of game centers that do not require permission by Act on Control and Improvement of Amusement Business, etc., it is quoted from *Amusement Sangyou kai no Jittai houkokusyo (Actual State Report of the Amusement Industry)* each yearly edition

9.5 Summary: Stalling of Arcades and a Milestone for Online Games

As discussed in this chapter, the arcade game industry lost its position and rapidly stalled as home video game consoles became more sophisticated.

In addition to the arguments, we have discussed so far, the stalling of arcade games is also because arcade games have continued to evolve toward the enthusiast segment, which has a high cost per customer. Arcade games are played by both the public, who do not usually visit arcades, and enthusiasts, who play enthusiastically. As shown in the section on the evolution of game systems in the appendix, arcade game systems have evolved from "attracting many people to play" to "attracting the same players to play many times" and from "attracting repeated visits to game arcades" to "increasing the amount of money spent per customer per visit to game arcades."

As a result, the know-how developed in arcade games has been passed on to social games.

9.6 Appendix: Evolution of Arcade Game Systems

Arcade games are designed for novice players to play for about 3 min. The 3-minute limit itself is an empirical rule advocated by operators in the field and has no basis. However, it is the optimal length of time to give players a sense of satisfaction to the extent that they do not feel that they have wasted their time playing the game and want to invest more money to challenge themselves, and to increase the turnover of customers as much as possible. The system design of arcade games has been developed based on this guideline of 3 min per credit (=100 yen).

9.6.1 Classic Arcade Game (Twentieth Century)

9.6.1.1 Simple Remaining Characters System

Pinball, which was the main game machine in game arcades before computer games, had a system of three balls for one credit (starting with two balls remaining) and extending (increasing the number of balls remaining) at a certain score. In other words, the game started with two characters remaining, and if you made a mistake, you lost one character, and if you made a mistake when the remaining character was zero, the game was over.

In the remaining character system, the better players get more playtime. The players with the longest playtime are basically the ones who have invested many credits to improve. It is not so much a problem if the playing time is tolerable, but it was not uncommon for players to improve to the point where they could play for several hours on one credit. In addition, Depending on the stage configuration of the game, so-called permanent patterns may be constructed which enable the player if to extend the playing time by repeating the permanent pattern, where the player would get an extend item, make a mistake on purpose, and then be sent back to the stage where he could get the extend again.

Thus, the simple remaining character system gradually disappeared, as the profitability of games often suffered greatly due to longer playtimes.

9.6.1.2 Remaining Characters + Ending System

As a successor to the simple remaining character system, a model has emerged that strengthens the narrative and forces the player to finish the game by showing the ending after clearing the final stage. It often takes about an hour to clear all stages.

Avoid revenue risk by setting a maximum playtime limit and encourage players to continue (i.e., add one credit) out of a desire to see more.[8]

---

[8]One of the earliest games to have an ending was The Tower of Druaga (Namco, 1984). Masanobu Endo, the developer of The Tower of Druaga, stated that the reason why he decided to make it a

9.6.1.3 Player VS Player and Winner-Take-all System

The successor to the remaining character system in fighting games, this system has been used since Street Fighter II (Capcom, 1991). In single-player battles, the system is an eclectic mix of the previous two, with two strikes on each side and an ending, but in versus battles, the system is "game over for the loser, but the winner can continue playing." In addition to being able to collect credits from the loser, the winner was able to make a record of "defeating X number of players," which made the players more enthusiastic.

9.6.1.4 Time Extend System

A system that was originally used in racing games and is now mainstream in music games. There is a minimum score for each stage, and the playing time is extended when the stage is cleared (time is added for races, and one song is added for music games). However, even the maximum extension is limited to the finish line or the final song (usually the third song). The maximum playtime is about 10 min, which is shorter than the ending system. There are also courses (songs) that are easy to extend, and by choosing them, players can almost certainly play the maximum amount of time for one credit.

9.6.1.5 Continued Play with Password or Magnetic Card

A format in which the play history is recorded so that the next play can start from the continuation. One of the first games to use password-based continue play was The Return of ISHTAR (Namco, 1986). When the game was over, the password was displayed, and the next time the game was played, the player could resume the game from the current location (room) with a grown player character (Gil and Ki: both characters grow with experience gained from defeating enemies). This type of game, in which game data can be saved and played again, was first introduced in DERBY OWNERS CLUB (Sega, 1999).

---

game with an ending was that "a VHS tape was sent to Namco's head office showing a full recording of Xevious (1983, also created by Masanobu Endo) being played endlessly with one credit in triple mode." However, in The Tower of Druaga, there was a phenomenon called ZAP on the 59th floor and the 60th floor of the last floor, and if you tried to clear the floor without meeting the clearing conditions, you would be sent back to the previous floor. This is not a perfect countermeasure, as it is possible to use this to extend the playing time endlessly.

9.6.2 Modern Arcade Games (Twenty-First Century)

After the widespread use of Internet connections, game arcades all over the country are connected by networks. Game companies are no longer limited to selling arcade game machines but can also earn connection fees from game centers.

9.6.2.1 Network Battle

An expansion of the winner-tale-all system of fighting games. The opponents are players from other game centers across the country who are connected via the Internet. Mahjong Fighting Club (Konami, 2002) and Yonin uchi Mahjong MJ (Sega, 2002) were the pioneers. The difference between this game and the previous ones is that the player is given a data card with his/her ID recorded on it, which is combined with the server data to enable national ranking. The player's goal is to improve his or her rank. The same system was used in the quiz game Quiz Magic Academy (Konami, 2003).

9.6.2.2 Trading Card Game

A card game in which players collect cards, build decks, and play against each other. The digitalization of the battling part of the game made it possible to create complex rules and sophisticated effects that were impossible in noncomputerized trading card games. The forerunner was WORLD CLUB Champion Football (Sega, 2002). In this game, cards are laid out on a field that resembles a soccer field, and the formation of the soccer team itself. The complexity of the rules and expressions of computer games, which was difficult to achieve with existing analog games, became possible, expanding the horizons of fun. Players also have the advantage of being able to play against opponents who are similar in ability, as opponents for trading card games are matched from game centers across the country.

9.6.2.3 Action Point (Stamina) System

This method was originally used in cell phone games with no basic fee or item charge system. Players are given action points and each time they perform an event (mainly a battle), they consume a few points. The points are recovered one by one over time but can also be recovered with charged items. The game was first released for smartphones and later released in arcades, Puyo Puyo! Quest (2013, SEGA), the first time this system was used.

Chapter 10
PC Games (3) Retreat of Domestic PC Game Manufacturers and Emergence of Online Games

Abstract This chapter discusses the radical changes in the Japanese PC market with the advent of Windows 95 and the impact of online gaming. Along with this shift, the machines used for PC games also shifted, but only after many game developers and players had already shifted to home consoles, and the Japanese PC game market was dominated by adult games that could not be shifted to home consoles. In addition, Japanese companies were unable to establish a significant presence in online games, which emerged around the same time, and the market was lost to foreign companies.

Keywords Windows 95 · PC-9821 · Adult games · Novel games · MMORPG · Hangame · Browser games

10.1 The Advent of Windows 95 and the Demise of PC-9801

Windows 95 was released by Microsoft in November 1995. The PC penetration rate in general households had been flat at about 10%, but with the release of Windows 95, the PC penetration rate in households skyrocketed. Until the early 1990s, the PC penetration rate had been flat at 10%, and only a small number of enthusiasts were using PCs, except for those who used them for work. However, with the advent of Windows 95 and the rapid spread of Internet access, the PC rapidly became a household item, and even an individual item. As a result, the number of units shipped increased more than sixfold from about 2 million a year (Figs. 10.1 and 10.2).

As the popularity of PCs expanded, the power structure of the PC changed. At the time, NEC's PC-9801 series (and its multimedia-compatible PC-9821 series) held the majority share of the Japanese PC market and was the de facto standard. Outside of Japan, the IBM-PC/AT architecture was the de facto standard, but the Japanese language barrier could not be broken for a long time. Windows 95 broke that barrier.

IBM thought that one of the reasons for the lack of popularity of PC/AT compatible machines was the weakness of Japanese language support, and announced DOS/V, an OS with software support for the Japanese language by having kanji fonts as data, in 1990. However, with the performance of PCs at the time, it was not possible to break the stronghold of the PC-9801, which had kanji

Y. Koyama, *History of the Japanese Video Game Industry*, Translational Systems Sciences 35, https://doi.org/10.1007/978-981-99-1342-8_10

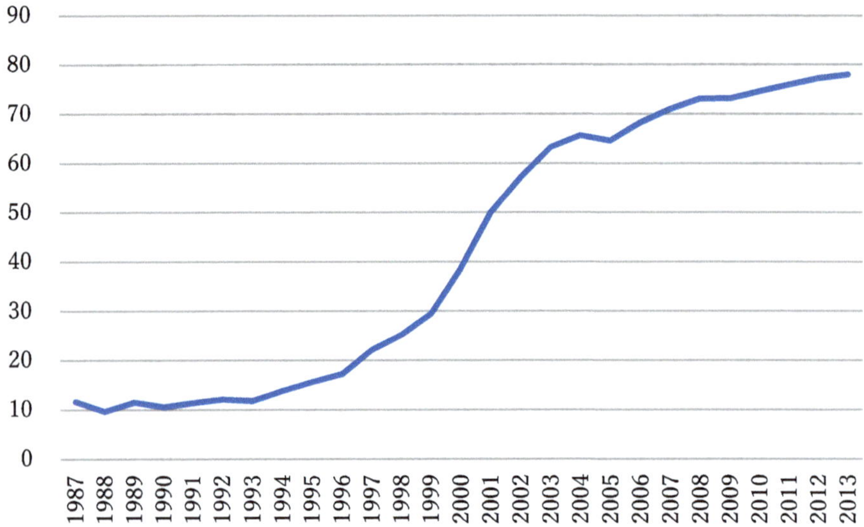

Fig. 10.1 PC penetration rate (%, created by the author from the Cabinet Office consumption trend survey)

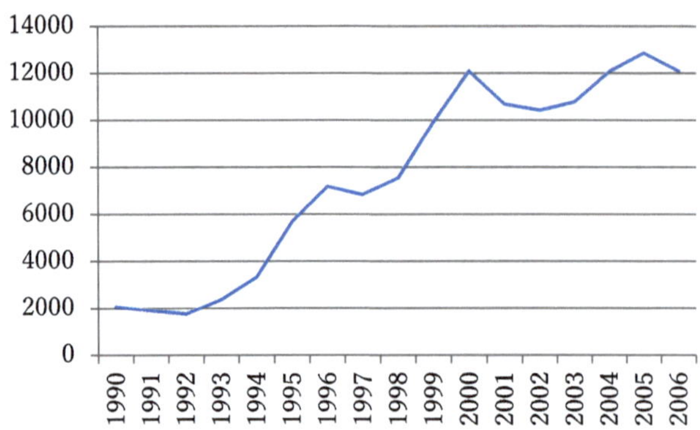

Fig. 10.2 Number of PC shipments (thousand units, created by the author from JEITA (Japan Electronics and Information Technology Industries Association) website)

data in kanji ROM and used dedicated text VRAM to speed up processing. In the end, to overcome the barrier of Japan's originality, it was necessary to introduce Windows, which processed all the data by software and did not need dedicated text VRAM, as well as to increase the hardware performance to a level where Japanese processing was not inconvenient even without text VRAM. This was achieved around the time Windows 95 was released, and with the rapid spread of PCs along with the Internet boom, the PC-9801 was overtaken.

IBM-PC-compatible machines spread to homes and offices with overwhelming speed. NEC released the PC-9821 (from 1992), which supported 640 x 480 dots (conventional PC-98 was 640 x 400 dots) and 256 colors used in Windows but was unable to break the trend. NEC released an IBM-PC-compatible machine in 1998, and after 2000, no new PC-9801 products were released, and orders ceased in 2003.

However, the PC-9801 would retain the leading role in PC gaming for some time to come. The architecture of the PC-9801VM, released in 1985, was the de facto standard for the PC game market. The PC-9801VM was a mid-1980s model with no sprite function and only 16 simultaneous colors. The reason why this architecture was able to maintain its position for 10 years was because of the business model peculiar to business PCs, which emphasizes compatibility so that proprietary business software can be used without modification. In addition, the fact that the basic architecture did not change for 10 years allowed game development companies to accumulate development know-how and to fully exploit the performance.

10.2 Failure of Platform Migration and Decline of PC Games

For PC games, the transition from PC-9801 to IBM-compatible (Windows), which occurred in the late 1990s, was delayed by the de facto standard. Since the OS absorbs the hardware differences in normal applications, many of them can run on both the PC-9801 and Windows on IBM-compatible machines, and the transition to the Windows environment was relatively quick.

On the other hand, the operating system used for games on both the IBM-PC and PC-9801 was MS-DOS for a long time, not Windows. The reason for this lies in the architectural structure of the Windows operating system. Windows is a multitasking OS that allows users to work while switching between multiple applications. In a multitasking OS, it is not possible to run only one application at a time, because the OS is controlled by interrupts while the application is running to switch the operation of each application. In addition, all interaction with the hardware is done through the API (Application User Interface) of the OS (Windows), and the hardware is abstracted. This is because the overhead (extra processing cost to perform a certain operation) incurred by interrupts and hardware control via the OS is large, making it difficult to use for games that require high-speed rendering. MS-DOS, on the other hand, is a single-task OS that uses the full functionality of the hardware only for certain applications and does not generate interrupt operations. In addition, the OS controlled only a small portion of the hardware, and the application could directly control the hardware. When Windows 95 was released, there were many cases where a game running on MS-DOS on a PC more than a generation old was much faster and more comfortable than a game running on Windows on a PC with the latest specs at the time. Microsoft understood this situation, and in the Windows 3.1 era, they introduced WinG, and in the Windows 95 era, they introduced DirectX, a technical extension to make it easier to use PCs for games. However, at the time of the release of DirectX, the performance was insufficient, and the development was difficult due to the lack of documentation.[1]

In addition, since the number of PCs in use is comparable to that of home video game consoles, major companies selling home video games entered the PC game market for Windows 95, which seemed to be a promising market, after DirectX became popular. However, because Windows users were not in the habit of playing games on their PCs and because all the games were ported titles from home consoles, the PC did not perform well in the game market. Windows 95 versions of such titles as Virtua Fighter and Sakura Taisen (Sakura Wars) from Sega, Tokimeki Memorial and Gradius Deluxe Pack from Konami, and Biohazard (Resident Evil) from Capcom were released, but no sequel titles were released. In the twenty-first century, there have been a few experimental releases of RPG titles that seemed to be designed for the PC, but basically no titles were developed specifically for the PC, and there have been no regular releases.

On the other hand, companies specializing in PC games were not able to adapt to development with DirectX and continued to develop and sell new games for the PC-9801 even after the release of Windows 95. It was not until around 1998 that they were finally able to migrate to Windows. However, the PC game market for Windows 95 (and its successor OS, Windows 98) was almost non-existent. As a result, many game companies that had been developing mainly for the PC were forced to shift their focus to home video game consoles or to other industries such as embedded software development for business use. The last company to develop and sell games for the PC was Nihon Falcom, but after the poor sales of Zwei 2 released in 2008, the company decided to enter the home video game market. The new game Ys 7 was released in 2009 on the PSP instead of the PC. Since then, there has been no major game company that has continuously developed and sold non-R18 PC games.

10.3 Adultization of the Packaged Game Market for PCs

Things changed dramatically in 1994 with the generational shift in home video game consoles. The PlayStation and Saturn surpassed the PC-9801 in the number of simultaneous colors, and their resolutions were not inferior. In terms of overall expressiveness, they were far superior. They also surpassed the PC-9801 in terms of data capacity, thanks to the use of CD-ROM as the game media. The overwhelming difference in the price of the console also made the PC almost unattractive as a game platform.

As a result, it was the adult (R18) games, which could only be released on the PC due to expression problems, that increased their relative position among PC games. Figure 10.3 shows the sales figures of the top 100 entertainment software titles

[1]According to several developers, it was not until the release of DirectX 3.0 in 1996 that development became possible to some extent.

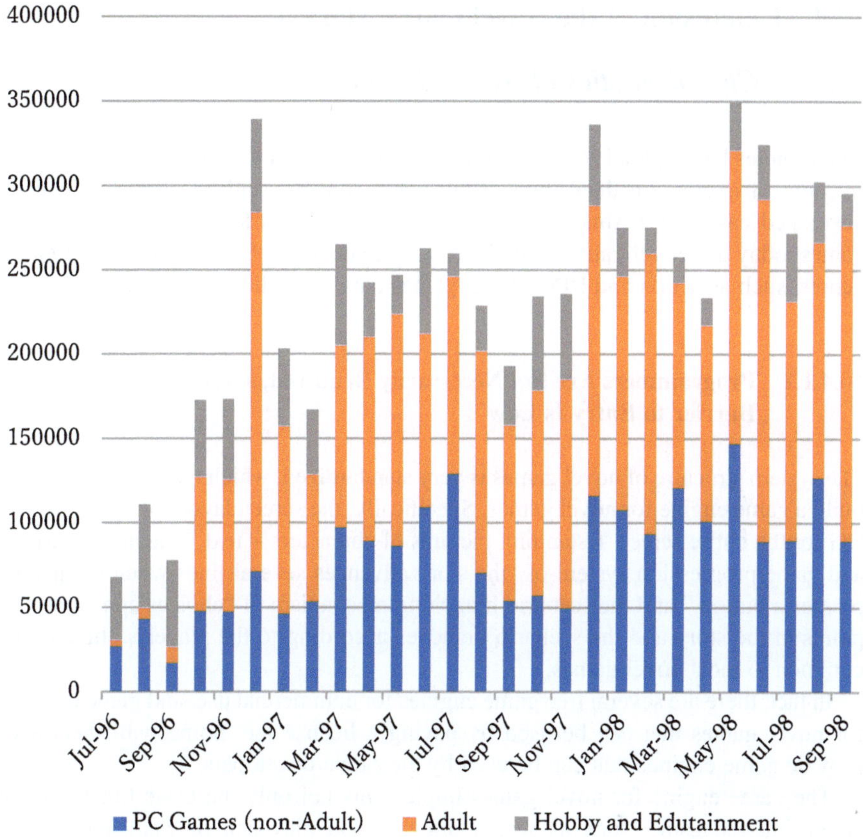

Fig. 10.3 Trends in sales of entertainment software top 100 titles (July 1996–September 1998, "Adult" includes multimedia works such as some photo books). Source: Author created from each issue of *Digital Media Insider*

published in the trade magazines (GAGA Communications, *Digital Media Insider*, July 1996 to September 1998). The number of PC games for non-adult has more than tripled (from 27,000 to 90,000), but the growth of adult titles (from 4000 to 187,000) has been remarkable.

After that, the market for packaged games for non-adult PC market continued to shrink, with only a few companies releasing the occasional game. On the other hand, novel games, which can be easily developed by a small number of people and on a low budget, have become popular in the adult game market, and many new companies have entered the market.

10.4 Expansion of the Novel Game Market

10.4.1 Characteristics of Novel Games

Adult games have spread so widely on the PC because they have a higher degree of freedom of expression than home video game consoles and because they can be developed easily by a small number of people and on a low budget. Most adult games today are novel games, which are easy to develop. Compared to other game genres, such as action and RPG, novel games have the following characteristics.

10.4.1.1 Programmers Are Not Necessarily Required, and the Technical Barrier to Entry Is Low

The system structure of novel games is very standardized, which makes it possible to build a game engine for novel games. Specifically, the screen layout of "background CG for the entire screen + standing pictures of characters + text," the user interface and game progression system of "the story advances several lines when the player presses a button," and the scenario branching mechanism of "choices appear at key points in the story and the scenario branches according to the player's choice" are common to most novel games.

In fact, there are several free game engines for commercial use, and game engines for novel games that can be used by paying a license fee. Some publishers also provide game engines that can be used by their own developers.

The game engine for novel games implements not only the basic functions for advancing the game, such as screen drawing and playback of character voices, background music, and sound effects, but also various other functions such as flag[2] management and loading and saving of play data. Various effects, such as playing voice files of dialogues, changing facial expressions of standing pictures, and inserting effects such as darkening the screen, are realized by inserting control tags in the scenario file. Since the various effects can be realized by simply inserting tags, the person in charge of the scenario often inserts control tags into the scenario and performs the effects on the screen.[3] Therefore, it is possible to develop a game without a programmer.

---

[2] A flag is a programing term that refers to a condition for branching. In novel games, the story often diverges into a happy ending if a certain condition is met, but a bad ending if the condition is not met. This condition is a flag.

[3] Since the person in charge of the scenario is also in charge of the direction, the person in charge of the scenario takes on the three roles of director, scriptwriter, and director as in other content. The burden on the scenario writer is very heavy.

10.4.1.2 Small Number of Developers and Low Cost

The most significant feature of novel games from a business perspective is that they can be developed in an overwhelmingly short period of time and at low cost. The development period is often less than a year to a year and a half, and the budget is around 20–30 million yen.

The reason why novel games can be developed in such a short period of time and at such low cost is that (a) the unit cost per person per month is quite low, which is unique to the industry, (b) the cost of communication and coordination is low because only 5–6 people are deeply involved in the development, and (c) some of the tasks that are essential in other game genres do not exist.

Regarding a), man-months, the cost of developing a home video game is 70,000–800,000 yen per man-month, while the cost of developing a PC novel game is about 500,000 yen[4] per man-month, which is quite low. The cost of development equipment is lower than for the development of home video games, but it is also since the average income is lower[5] due to the severe market environment where many titles are crowded into a narrow market size.

The reason for (b) is that only a few members of the development team belong to the developer (in the smallest case, one director and one producer), and the work for pictures and music is often outsourced to contractors. In addition, due to the nature of the titles we develop, the characteristics and appeal of the products depend largely on the artist's personality and the characteristics of the pictures. For these reasons, it is difficult to prepare substitutes. Inevitably, development will be small, and at the same time, it will be difficult to shorten the time required to create scenarios and pictures.[6]

As for (c), novel games do not require level design (difficulty adjustment work), which exists in almost all other genres of games. For titles that require delicate

[4]For reference, the median engineer fee at Japanese IT vendor companies that develop systems is 900,000 yen per month for companies with less than 1000 employees, and 1.2 million yen per month for companies with 1000 or more employees (Oiwa 2013). For companies developing home video games, the median fee is slightly lower than that of medium-sized vendors with less than 1000 employees, and for PC novel games it is even lower, about the same as that of second- and third-tier subcontractors of vendors.

[5]Fujihara (2013) is one of the few career surveys on home video game companies, and most of the cases do not reach the average annual salary (about 3.35 million yen) for people in their 20 s mentioned in the survey.

[6]This is not to say that shortening the work period is completely impossible. In the case of scenarios, there are cases where the scenario supervisor oversees the creation of the overall plot, and the post-branch scenarios (individual scenarios) are created by multiple people including the scenario supervisor. In this case, the time required for writing can be shortened, but careful coordination is required to avoid discrepancies in the images of the characters in the scenarios. In the case of pictures, it is sometimes possible to solve this problem by adding animators to the staff who can quickly draw pictures that capture the characteristics of the original artist (however, this is not possible if the original artist's pictures are too unique). However, since these methods simultaneously complicate the development process and increase costs, they can only be used by PC game companies that can expect a certain number of hits.

adjustment work, such as fighting games, level design can take nearly a year, but this part of the development time and cost is unnecessary. Also, due to the characteristics of games, what is done in debugging is limited to checking flag management, proofreading text, and checking for deviations in direction. Compared to games of other genres where various factors are taken into consideration to check for bugs, the amount of work involved in debugging is extremely small.[7]

10.4.2 Establishment of the Novel Game Market

Novel games first appeared in PC games in the late 1980s, a relatively long time ago. The first novel game was *DOME* released by System-Sacom in 1988, which was a game adaptation of the novel Dome Shumatsu heno Jokyoku (Dome: Prelude to the End) by Shizuko Natsuki. The game was called "Novelware" and was released on several PCs, including the PC-8801, PC-9801, and MSX, reflecting the state of the PC game industry at the time. Seven novellwares were created by 1991, but although they were the pioneers of novel games, they have no direct relationship with current novel games, as the UI (user interface) uses multi-window, which is different from the current one.

The ancestors that directly influenced today's novel games are Otogirisō (1992) and Kamaitachi no Yoru (Banshee's Last Cry) (1994), both developed by Chunsoft for the Super Famicom. Both of these games were based on a UI in which the text of the story was superimposed on a faintly drawn image of the entire screen and are the direct ancestors of modern novel games. The story of Otogirisō is a horror, and the story of Kamaitachi no Yoru is a mystery with a touch of suspense, matching the nature of novel games where the outcome of the story changes depending on the actions of the protagonist (player).

Under the influence of Otogirisō and Kamaitachi no Yoru, two novel games were born as R18 PC games for MS-DOS for PC-9801 and MS Windows for IBM-PC, Shizuku and Kizuato, released by Leaf in 1996. Both titles are psychological mysteries with R18 elements added to the story genre. Based on these past works, Leaf's third work, To Heart (1997), became a hit and became a standard novel game of the school type, which is the majority of novel games today.

At the same time, Tactics released two novel games, Moon (1997), a psycho-thriller, and One ~ Kagayaku Kisetsu he(One ~ to the Shining Season~) (1998), a school story. The market was completely established with the huge hit Kanon (2000) by Key, which was established independently by the team that developed the two games. After that, a number of doujin circles (game developing groups) emerged who had played Leaf and Key's works and felt that they wanted to create their own

[7] Since many PC game development companies are small companies, there are many cases where even the debugging process, which is less difficult than in other genres, is inadequate.

games, and a number of these circles became incorporated, which led to the expansion and establishment of novel games.

To Heart and Kanon made novel games the standard genre of "romance" games, but before that, the mainstream of R18 games was nurturing simulation or dating simulation games.[8] Nurturing simulation is a type of game in which the player acts as a parent or teacher and enjoys the process of guiding a girl. Examples include Sotsugyou(Graduation) (PC-9801VM, 1992) by Japan Home Video and Princess Maker (PC-9801VM, 1991) by Gainax. Dating simulation is a type of game in which the player becomes a student and enjoys the process of getting to know women of the same age, such as Elf's Doukyusei(Classmate) (PC-9801VM, 1992) and Konami's Tokimeki Memorial (PC Engine, 1994). In both genres, the player spends a certain period of time in the game world and experiences various events that occur as a result of the daily choices he or she makes.

Dating simulation games and romance novel games are the same in that the player experiences a variety of things as a story. However, compared to novel games, nurturing and dating simulation games have a very large number of choices to be made in the game, and the difference is tens to hundreds of times greater. In addition, the system of generating various events (minor and major events) through the accumulation of daily choices is quite complicated in terms of flag management. Therefore, while the gameplay of triggering the flags of events with characters through trial and error is considerably higher than that of novel games, the cost of development and the skills required for development are high (i.e., the barrier to entry is high). In addition, due to the game system, even if a player plays until the last day of the game, he or she may not be able to reach the desired ending, and it is also difficult to find a strategy on how to play the game to achieve the goal. For these reasons, some users who place more importance on the narrative aspect of the game than the gameplay tend to dislike simulation games because they cannot concentrate on the story while playing.

This demand from players to concentrate on the narrative and the motivation of producers to develop games that are inexpensive and technologically simple coincided, and novel games came to dominate the market.

10.5 The Emergence and Stagnation of PC Online Games

In this book, "online games in a broad sense" is defined as "games that are played on a PC or a device with an Internet connection function and that continuously communicate with a server during gameplay." Devices other than PCs include home game consoles, mobile phones, and smartphones. When online games are used in a narrower sense, they are defined as "games developed for PCs and home

[8]It is categorized as a kind of "simulation" game genre because it involves a lot of trial and error during the game in order to have various experiences.

game consoles that continuously communicate with servers during gameplay," and do not include games for mobile phones and smartphones. This chapter mainly discusses online games in a narrow sense.

10.5.1 Online Games in their Infancy

The history of games that allow multiple players to play at the same time via a communication environment began in the 1970s, when there were no home PCs and computers that existed only in universities and research institutes. The Multi User Dungeon (MUD), created in 1978 at the University of Essex in the UK, allowed multiple players to explore a text-only world online, and ran on a DEC PDP-1.[9]

In the 1980s, with the spread of home PCs, pre-Internet online PC communication services started not only overseas but also in Japan. Since data transmission speed and performance were still insufficient, BBS (Bulletin Board System) was the most popular entertainment service in PC communication. In this context, text-based MUDs were also being played.

As for communication services using home video game consoles, Sega released the Mega Modem for the Mega Drive in 1990, and Sunsoft, which developed the communication software, released TEL-TEL Mahjong and TEL-TEL Stadium. However, the number of users has remained at less than 10,000, partly due to the slow communication speed of 1200 bps and the lack of game software. Sega also launched Game Toshokan (Game Library), a service that allowed users to download original games for a fixed monthly fee of 800 yen, but the service was discontinued in February 1993. In addition, XBand, a telecommunication service over telephone lines launched by Catapult Entertainment in the USA at the end of 1994, made its way to Japan and started its service for the Super Famicom and Sega Saturn in 1996, but the service was terminated in 1999.

10.5.2 Starting with PC Games: Diablo and Ultima Online

Online gaming, as we know it today, began during the period of rapid expansion of the Internet population with Windows 95.

[9] As for the game content, it is an extension of text adventure games, called interactive fiction. A text adventure game is an adventure game where you explore a world described only in text. The world is described only in text such as "You're in front of a trig point. What do you do?", "There is a coffin in front of you," etc. The game is played by entering commands such as "go left," "take memo," and "attach cross." Early titles include Colossal Cave Adventure (1975) from which the name "adventure game" was derived and Zork (1977). It is interesting to note that in the early days, adventure games and role-playing games had the same root.

In 1997, MORPG (Multiplayer Online RPG) and MMORPG (Massive Multiplayer Online RPG: Massive Online RPG) were introduced to the market. MORPG refers to an action RPG that can be played by multiple players via LAN or the Internet. Diablo, one of the first of these genres, was released by Blizzard and became a worldwide hit, selling over three million copies. A MMORPG is an RPG in which thousands of players log on to the same game server and play together. It was Ultima Online,[10] developed by Origin Systems and published by Electronic Arts in 1997, that popularized the genre.

In the twenty-first century, as computer games have spread to not only developed countries but also emerging countries, MMORPGs have gained a large popularity. These games are developed on Windows for IBM-PC using a network. On the other hand, the Japanese game industry has been dominated by home video games, and PC games have been at the margins of the industry. Furthermore, PC games have long been confined to the PC-9801 architecture and do not use networks. In the shadow of the success of the home console game market, Japan lagged behind in this growing market.

10.5.3 Japanese Online Games

PC online games in Japan started with MORPGs and simulation games that can be an extension of existing games, rather than MMORPGs that require development know-hows and are large in scale.

In the field of simulation games, Koei launched Nobunaga no Yabou Internet (Nobunaga's Ambition Internet) in 1998, which allows users to play their own popular historical simulation games on the Internet. In addition, Bandai launched Gundam Network Operation in 2002. These two titles were long-lived, with Nobunaga no Yabou Internet running until 2013 with a paid matching service for opponents, and Gundam Network Operation running until 2014 with version 2 and 3 updates.

As for MORPGs, Koei released Apsaras, Japan's first MORPG, in 2000, but it was relatively short lived, with service ending in early 2003. In 2000, Sega released Phantasy Star Online for the Dreamcast as a network-enabled RPG with an offline mode for single-player gameplay and continued the service until the end of 2010 while shifting the platform to PC.

In the area of MMORPGs, home video game consoles have become the driving force. Final Fantasy XI and Nobunaga's Ambition Online were released for the PlayStation 2 in 2002 and 2003, respectively. After that, market entry peaked at one point in 2005–2006, with a series of service launches and development

[10] Due to conflicting management policies, Richard Garriott, the main developer at the beginning of the service and the founder of the Ultima series, left the management, but Ultima Online is still in service as of February 2022, making it a long-lasting title.

announcements from major Japanese companies. However, the delay in entering the market, which has a long life once it becomes a hit, was fatal, and with the exception of Square Enix and Koei, all other companies' games have become failures and have all been withdrawn.

Ultimately, the games developed by Korean companies held a large share of the market in MMORPGs. Among the titles that became hits in the early days were Lineage (NC Soft, operated in Japan by NC Japan), which was launched in 2001, and Ragnarök Online, developed by Gravity, which was launched in Korea in August 2002 and in Japan in December 2002.[11] The difference is that Lineage has 3D graphics and Ragnarök Online has 2D graphics (3D space and pixel-based characters), but the service is still ongoing. MMORPG titles have been announced continuously, but only a few Japanese titles have been released by Square Enix and Koei Tecmo Games, and the rest are all from overseas companies.[12]

In addition, FPS (First-Person Shooter) and RTS (Real-Time Strategy), which are popular genres of online games, are not very popular in Japan, and sports games have been the sole domain of foreign games ever since they were introduced because there is no culture of online competition in Japan.

10.5.4 Differences in Business Models between Packaged Games and Online Games

Why did Japan fail to capture the market for MORPGs and MMORPGs? There are several possible reasons, but the most obvious one is that Japan had already achieved great success in the home video game market, and therefore lacked the know-how in both technology and game design to create games for the non-home video game market.

The business model of online games is a fee-for-service business model that collects money through continuous play, rather than a package-sale business model like existing home video games. The major differences from package sales are as follows:

1. Timing of market entry is of great significance

---

[11]The service in Japan is operated by GungHo Online Entertainment. *Ragnarök Online* became the title that supported the backbone of GungHo in its early days, accounting for over 99% of the company's sales at one point. In addition, the majority of Gravity's shares are now owned by Gungho.

[12]Examples of failures by major companies include Namco's Tales of Eternia Online (service started in March 2006, ended in March 2007) and Konami's *Tokimeki Memorial Online* (service started in March 2006, ended in July 2007). Another game that was only announced but not launched was Tecmo's Bastard Online (announced in July 2005 as scheduled for release in 2006, development was halted in December 2009).

As mentioned in the previous section, a hit online game has a long life. This means that once a game becomes a hit and develops a fixed customer base, it can be expected to generate large profits in the long run because the customers will continue to play the game. However, entering the market late increases the possibility of failure because the potential customers have already been taken by other games.

2. End of product development is the start

   Unlike package sales, the end of product development is not really the end. The end of product development means the start of service, and from then on, the continuous development and implementation of additional elements and the implementation of various events are required to increase the login rate and retention rate of users. In other words, game companies need to continue to entertain their players. For this reason, the development team needs to continue to exist even after the service is launched, and costs will always be incurred.

3. High-cost structure

   The MMORPG game world is vast, and it takes a lot of money to create it. Therefore, in addition to the development costs of the game itself, there are costs associated with the establishment and maintenance of the network, such as the installation and maintenance of servers and line usage fees. According to an example of the revenue structure of a PC MMORPG in the "CESA Game White Paper 2006," the cost of game development and the construction of the network environment is estimated to be 1 billion yen, which is much higher than that of home video games. In addition, it is necessary to continuously advertise and promote the game in order to attract new players, and these costs are also incurred on an ongoing basis.

Online games, especially MMORPGs, can be profitable in the long term once they become a hit, and the accumulated profits are large.[13] However, it is also a high-risk, high-return market where most games lose money and are discontinued after a short period of time. With a few exceptions, Japanese companies were late to enter the market and failed to produce results. The packaged game business was also still doing well, although the profit margin was gradually declining. The market for online games was still small, and many Japanese companies entered the market and quickly withdrew when they found it unfeasible.

[13]Taking Final Fantasy XI as an example, as of 2012, 10 years after the service was launched, the cumulative profit has reached 40 billion yen, making it the top Final Fantasy of all time.
http://www.hd.square-enix.com/jpn/ir/policy/message2012_2.html

10.5.5 The Rise of Browser Games and their Transformation into Charging Platforms

MMORPGs quickly became the mainstay of online gaming, but the threshold for people to try them was high, as they required the installation of game applications on their PCs and a lot of time to play. In this environment, a type of game that can be easily and quickly played by people with low PC skills appeared a little later than the early online games.

Casual games are a general term for games that can be played easily with simple operations and in a short time, and in a broad sense include puzzle games such as Minesweeper and FreeCell that are installed as standard in Windows.

Casual games are a general term for games that can be played easily with simple operations and in a short time, and in a broad sense include puzzle games such as Minesweeper and FreeCell that are installed as standard in Windows. As an extension of these games, browser game sites that allow users to play games such as cards, puzzles, and mahjong casually using a standard PC web browser have appeared and gained popularity.

Hangame, one of the leading sites for playing casual games in a browser, was established in Korea in 2000 and started its service in Japan in November 2000. Some games, such as Hanafuda and billiards, could be played for free, while others required a monthly fee, which could be paid with points earned by viewing advertisements. Hangame also had an online community feature that allowed users to interact with other players when they were not playing, and their avatar was displayed on their community page as their alter ego character. Avatars can be decorated with hairstyles, clothes, accessories, etc. Avatar accessories can be obtained through gameplay achievements or purchased for a fee. Sales of avatar accessories became a major source of income for Hangame, and the company grew rapidly.

Most browser games were played by downloading the macromedia flash (which was later acquired by Adobe Systems and became Adobe Flash) plug-in from the browser. When browser games first appeared, most of them were casual games due to the lack of functions that Flash could handle and the problems of PC performance and communication bandwidth. Later, it became possible to run hundreds of megabytes of Flash applications in the browser, and games of various genres such as action, RPG, and strategy simulations began to be played in the browser. Adobe announced its plan to discontinue offering Flash in 2017, ending it in 2020. As a result, most browser games today are in HTML5 format.

In addition, websites that offer browser games are not limited to specialized sites like Hangame. Web portal sites such as Yahoo Japan sometimes installed browser games on their websites in order to enhance the contents of their sites and increase user access, and Hangame also provided services to such websites. Later, various websites began to allow users to access and pay for various payment services with a single account on the website, and games were positioned as one of these services. Today, browser games are one of the online gaming services that include everything from casual games to MMORPGs.

10.5.6 Business Model Changes

In the early days of online gaming, from the late 1990s to the early 2000s, online games were sold as installation packages. The installation package included the right to play the online game for free for a certain period of time (30–90 days), and the player had to purchase it to play the game. If the player wanted to play the game after the free play period, he or she had to pay a monthly fee of about 1000–1500 yen to continue playing. This was a remnant of the fact that most games played at home were sold in packages, and also because broadband Internet service was not widespread at the time, making it difficult for people to download hundreds of megabytes of game applications.

In the mid- to late-2000s, due in part to the rapid spread of broadband Internet access services, the majority of games became available for free application download (Fig. 10.4). Games downloaded for free come with a right to play for about a month, and players pay a monthly fee if they want to continue playing beyond that. The background to the spread of free downloads of game applications is also related to the intensifying competition in MMORPGs. As competition intensified and the number of users expected per game decreased compared to the early days, the free download system became essential to avoid the risk of the initial cost of producing and selling packages and to increase the number of players. Even today, some games are sold in packages for installation. Most of them are games that have a large number of users, have been in service for a long time, and have generated stable revenue. In many cases, they sell additional packages that greatly expand the game from the initial service.

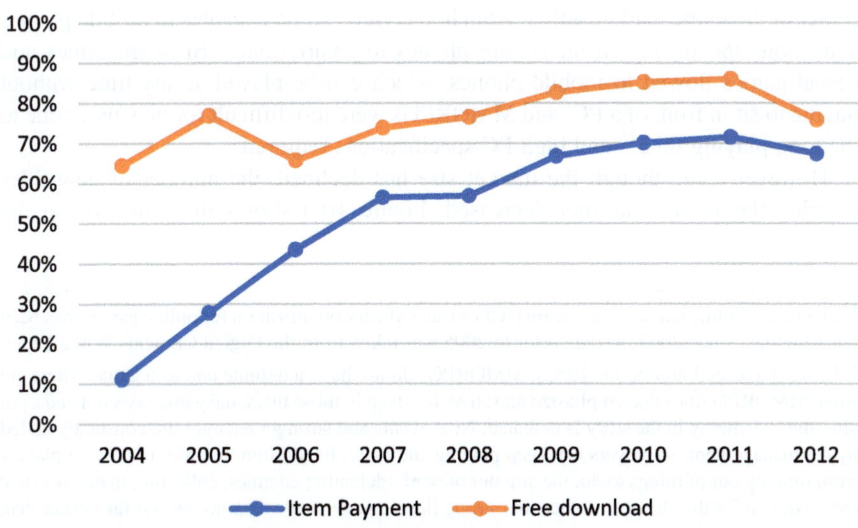

Fig. 10.4 Payment form of online game (including non-PC). Source: *JOGA (Japan Online Game Association) Online Game Market Research Report 2013*

Table 10.1 Average monthly sales per online game player (Yen)

	2004	2005	2006	2007
Average sales per capita of fixed payment games	1437	1338	1554	1223
Average sales per player of item/avatar payment games	4278	4438	4385	4676

Source: Online Game Forum, *Online Game Shijou Touke Houkokusyo(Online Game Market Statistics Report) 2007*

Next came games where not only the game application was free to download, but the basic gameplay was also free. This is an item-based business model in which the basic gameplay is completely free, but money is collected by paying for accessories that decorate the character and consumable items that give an advantage in gameplay. Compared to the fixed-price model, the per-customer cost of the item-based model was more than three times higher (Table 10.1). Therefore, it had the advantage of being able to increase sales even if the number of users did not grow. Item-based payment rapidly became popular.

10.5.7 Severe Competition and Sluggish Market Growth

Online games have attracted attention as a new market, but the market has been stagnant. Figure 10.5 shows the trend of the PC online game market.[14] The market scale expanded rapidly after 2003. However, the market size peaked in 2011 at 111.1 billion yen, which is the total of package sales and management service sales and has been declining ever since.

The reason for the decline after peaking in 2011 is that users flowed away as the center of the game market shifted from home video game consoles to mobile phones and, more specifically, from feature phones to smartphones. Browser games and casual games flowed to mobile phones, which can be played at any time without having to sit in front of a PC, and MMORPGs were too difficult for new users due to the long-playing time[15] and high PC specifications required.

However, even though the market size has declined, the number of new titles entering the market has not decreased. Figure 10.6 shows the transition in the

[14]The Japan Online Game Association (JOGA), an industry organization for online games, has been releasing data since 2005, so data prior to 2005 was taken from the Digital Contents White Paper.

[15]Unlike packaged non-online RPGs, MMORPGs do not have a definite end as a game. There are some MMORPG titles that emphasize narrative, but even in those titles, the game does not end even after the last enemy in the story is defeated. New events and stronger enemies are constantly added by the management, so players can keep playing endlessly. In addition, in order to prevent players from running out of things to do, the amount of work (defeating enemies, collecting material items, etc.) required for the character to become strong (level up, get new weapons, etc.) is far greater than in non-online package games. As a result, the extreme amount of time some heavy users spend playing (in many cases, thousands of hours) has become a social problem as *Netoge Haijin(Net Game Junkies)*.

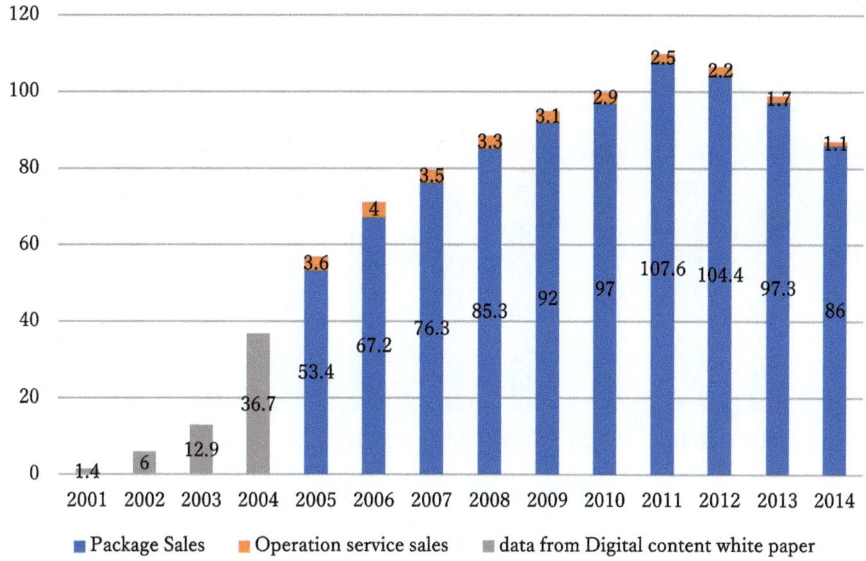

Fig. 10.5 Market Scale of PC Online Games (Billion Yen). Source: *JOGA Online Game Market Research Report Yearly edition (2005–2014). Digital Content White Paper (2001–2004)*

number of service titles of PC online games. The total number of titles gradually increased in 2006–2008, 2009–2011, and 2012–2014, but among them, about a quarter of titles are terminated every year. Online games are a business model that earns revenue by having players continue to play, and the oldest titles that have been established are the stronger. While there are a number of titles that have been in service for more than 10 years, there are also games that end after less than 1 year of service.

10.6 PC Game Summary: Falling out of Three Major Markets

In this chapter, we discussed the PC game market from the time of the appearance of Windows 95 to the present. The PC game market had already begun to shrink in size as of Chap. 7 (PC Games (2)), and with the fall of the PC-9801, the PC game market has almost disappeared except for the R18 game market. That R18 game market has also been decreasing in market size in recent years.

Since the advent of Windows 95 and the spread of Internet access, the mainstream of non-R18 PC games has been online games. The market scale of online games is about 100 billion yen, expanding to about 2–30% of the home game software market, but the market scale has been declining since 2011. PC online games in

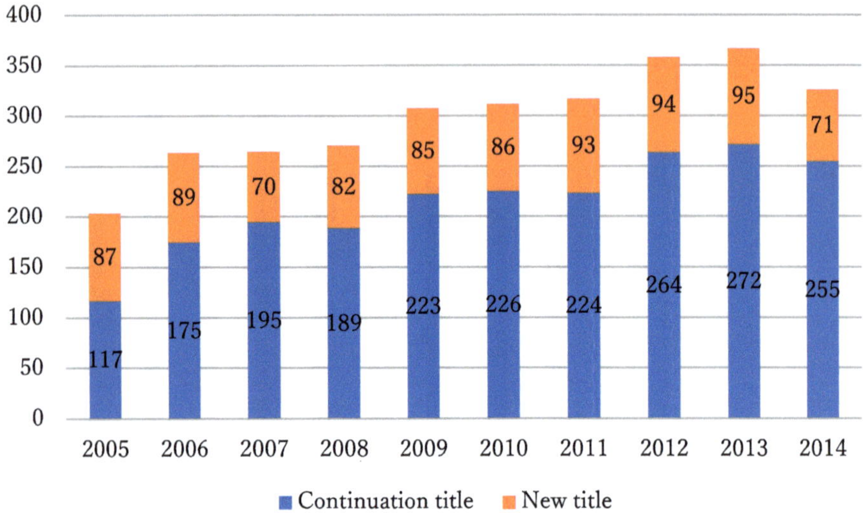

Fig. 10.6 Number of service titles in PC online games. Source: *JOGA Online Game Market Research Report 2015*

Japan were significant in two ways: they established casual games (along with the Nintendo DS), and they provided many players with the experience of playing with other players via a network. The market for these games has shifted to mobile phones (especially smartphones), which have improved performance and can be played anywhere.

Chapter 11
Console Games (2) The Age of the Three Major Hardware Platforms

Abstract This chapter provides an overview of the home video game console market in the 1990s. This period was the height of the multimedia boom, and various companies of all stripes entered the video game console market, but failed. The reasons for their failure vary, but the main reasons were that they were driven by the false image of the multimedia market and that their performance as game consoles was inadequate. The one that finally succeeded in this environment was Sony's PlayStation, which was a major turning point in the history of the video game industry.

Keywords Multimedia · Pipin@ · 3DO · PC-FX · Virtual Boy · Saturn · Nintendo 64 · PlayStation

11.1 Hardware that Disappeared with the Times

During the generation change period of game hardware, various types of hardware are born to target the next-generation market. Among them, the hardware change-over period in the early 1990s saw the birth of a variety of game hardware. Some hardware could not adapt to the changing times, while others were too far ahead of their time and disappeared.

11.1.1 Pitfall of PC Compatibility: Towns Marty and Pippin@

At the time, two types of low-cost hardware were released, which were cost-cutting versions of personal computers that were used exclusively for games. They were FM TOWNS Marty and Pipin@.

Y. Koyama, *History of the Japanese Video Game Industry*, Translational Systems Sciences 35, https://doi.org/10.1007/978-981-99-1342-8_11

11.1.1.1 Old Leather Bag:FM Towns Marty

Fujitsu had released the FM TOWNS, a multimedia personal computer equipped with a CD-ROM. FM TOWNS Marty was a home game console that could be connected to a television, eliminating the keyboard from the FM TOWNS. To show its characteristics as a multimedia terminal, the corresponding software was not called a game, but a "program." The genre of the program was called "channel," and there were five channels: Educational Time, Educational Special, Super Study, Home Variety, and Game Flash. The main selling point was that it was compatible with FM TOWNS, allowing users to play games released for FM TOWNS in the past, and at the time of Marty's release, a total of 250 titles were available from past assets.

FM TOWNS Marty was released in February 1993, and the goal was to sell 200,000 units in 1 year, but sales were sluggish at 45,000 units by December. FM TOWNS Marty was an FM TOWNS compatible machine, and in terms of performance, it was a machine of the past.[1] FM TOWNS Marty had no problem playing back multimedia content, mainly still images and sound, from CD-ROMs, but it lacked performance when it came to running complex and heavy processing games. Compared to the dedicated game consoles, the base FM TOWNS did not have the sprite function, the basic specification of the 2D graphics era, nor the polygon drawing function, the basic specification of the 3D graphics era. Despite its mediocre performance as a game console, it was very expensive, priced at 98,000 yen (more than 100,000 yen when the consumption tax was added). In 1994, the following year, FM TOWNS Marty Model 2 was released at a lower price of 66,000 yen, but it was also unsuccessful (Photo 11.1).

11.1.1.2 Unsuccessful STB: Pippin@

With the release of Windows 95 in 1995 (August in the USA, November in Japan) and the ease of connecting to the Internet, there was an Internet boom. In the midst of this trend, PiPin@ (PiPin Atmark), released in 1996, was a hardware product jointly developed by Apple and Bandai.

At that time, the majority of PCs in Japan were desktop models, not laptops, and the price of the main unit, excluding the monitor, was well over 100,000 yen. For this reason, various companies released STBs (Set Top Box) that could be connected to a TV for those who wanted to use the Internet but did not know what to do with an expensive PC. Among these STBs, the PiPin@ was unique in that it could be used

[1] The successor to the FM TOWNS (FM TOWNS II), which was on the market at the time of the release of the TOWNS Marty, was equipped with an Intel 486SX compatible CPU, but the CPU installed in the Marty was the same Intel 386SX compatible CPU as the original FM TOWNS, and its performance was at the level of 4 years earlier.

Photo 11.1 FM TOWNS Marty (Photo credit: Wikipedia)

with Mac applications and could also be connected to Mac keyboards and mice as peripherals.

Pipin@ was introduced to the market with a good response, as 104,000 applications (20% of which were from women) were received for the free monitoring campaign that was advertised in newspapers in January 1996, but the sales volume was sluggish. The reason for this was that Pipin@ was a new genre of product, an Internet terminal, so existing toy stores only had catalogs and very little inventory, and focused on direct sales via the Internet or by phone. As a result, potential consumers were unable to see/touch the actual products and thus were probably hesitant to purchase high-priced products. In the end, sales of PiPin@ were sluggish, with only 42,000 units sold overseas combined, resulting in an inventory of 50,000 units (Photo 11.2).

At the time of its launch, Bandai had expected sales of 270 billion yen and a profit of 10 billion yen at the end of March 1997, but poor sales of PiPin@ resulted in sales of 200 billion yen and a loss of 9 billion yen. In 1998, the company liquidated the subsidiary in charge of the PiPin@ business and recorded an extraordinary loss of 27 billion yen. The deterioration in business performance also led to the cancellation of merger negotiations with Sega, which were underway at the time.

Photo 11.2 PiPin@ (Photo credit: Wikipedia)

11.1.2 Hardware that Made Mistakes in Predicting Market Trends: PC-FX and 3DO

The first half of the 1990s was a major turning point in the technological paradigm for the game industry, from 2D to 3D graphics. System boards equipped with 3D graphics were in operation for arcade games, and the companies that developed the hardware fully understood that this wave would one day come to home video game consoles. However, at this stage, some companies have decided that it is too early for home game consoles due to the level of technology and cost. On the other hand, there were companies that decided to design their hardware too early, and because of the rapid increase in the performance of 3D graphics chips, the game consoles they had developed fell short in performance. The former was the PC-FX and the latter was the 3DO.

11.1.2.1 PC-FX that Misread the Performance Increase Curve

PC-FX, the successor to the PC Engine released by NEC, failed because it misread the fact that the era was shifting to 3D graphics. PC-FX could play back full-color movies, a great improvement over the popular PC Engine. However, even though it was released on December 23, 1994, at the same time as PlayStation and Saturn, it was not equipped with any 3D graphics functions. In addition, there was no significant improvement in the performance of 2D graphics from PC Engine, so it was not at the level of a next-generation console.

As a natural result, sales were sluggish. In 1995, the company developed a strategy to appeal to animation fans by using original image characters and

Photo 11.3 PC-FX (Photo credit: Wikipedia)

exhibiting at the Comic Market, a doujinshi sales event, but it was not successful. In 1995, a compatibility board PC-FXGA[2] was released to enable PC-FX games to be played on PCs, and various other efforts were taken, but without success. The final sales volume was 111,000 units, a dismal failure (Photo 11.3).

11.1.2.2 Hardware that Came Too Early: 3DO

The 3DO (3DO Interactive Multiplayer) was the hardware developed by Trip Hawkins, the founder of Electronic Arts (EA), who founded the 3DO company.

[2]First, a PC-FXGA board for the C-bus, an expansion bus for the PC-9801, was put on the market, followed by an FX board specifically for the 98CanBe. After that, PC-FXGA board with ISA bus was released for DOS/V machines. The PC-FXGA was different from the 98CanBe board in that it had a chip for 3D graphics. When playing games, the RGB monitor for the PC could not be used, and the only way was to connect the composite terminal on the PC-FXGA to the TV, which was not very convenient.

The 3DO used a 32-bit RISC (12.5 MHz) CPU and two coprocessors (numerical processors) running at double the speed (25 MHz), which could display still images at VGA (640 x 480) and 24-bit (16 million colors), which was extremely high performance for its time. In addition, the licensing fee for games was set at $3 per game, compared to the $9 to $12 per game charged by Sega and Nintendo, the mainstream companies at the time, to encourage third parties to enter the market.

3DO itself adopted a business model of licensing without production, and although there were many companies that showed interest, only Matsushita Electric (now Panasonic), Sanyo Electric, and Goldstar (now LG) of Korea eventually produced the device.[3] Among them, this section will discuss Matsushita Electric, which promoted 3DO as a project under the direct control of the president, was the first to launch the product, and temporarily took over the technical legacy after the failure of 3DO.

The first company to manufacture and sell the console was Matsushita Electric, but due to 3DO company's own policy, it was marketed as a multimedia player rather than a game console. In the USA, the 3DO was released in November 1993 for $699. In Japan, the price was set at 79,800 yen, which was very high, but it was later changed to 54,800 yen[4] and released as "3DO REAL" in March 1994.

Although the 3DO emphasized multimedia, video playback capability was still difficult to achieve with the performance of computers at the time. It was necessary to purchase a separate video CD[5] adapter (MPEG1 decoder) to play back video CD images, which had the same resolution as the analog VHS videos that were mainstream at the time. Furthermore, the number of game releases was insufficient for the North American launch in 1993. The price was too high compared to the game consoles of the time, and sales of the hardware continued to be sluggish.

Matsushita expected to sell 600,000–700,000 units in Japan and 1 million units worldwide in the first year and planned to sell 1 million units in the second year and 2 million units in the third year in the Japanese market. However, sales in the USA were sluggish. Sales in Japan were similarly sluggish, and as of October 1994, the total sales of the console in Japan and the USA were only 250,000 units. At the end of 1994, Sega released the Saturn, and Sony released the PlayStation, making the competitive environment even more difficult. In November 1994, the company launched "3DO REAL II," which was priced at 44,800 yen, to compete with those consoles, but as of March 1995, it had shipped only about 350,000 units in Japan and 200,000 units overseas. In July 1995, the price of 3DO REAL II was lowered to 29,800 yen by making it an open price, but it hardly became popular. In July 1995,

---

[3] Other than that, Creative, a PC peripheral company, has released a card called "3DO Blaster" that allows you to play 3DO games.

[4] In the USA, the price was reduced to $499 in May 1994.

[5] This is a standard that makes it possible to play video on CD-ROM. In the case of NTSC signals, the screen resolution is 352×240 pixels, which is about the same quality as VHS video. In Japan and the USA, where VCRs were already widespread, Video CD was hardly popular, but in Southeast Asia, it was quite popular.

Photo 11.4 3DO (Photo credit: Wikipedia)

3DO REAL II was released at an open price of 29,800 yen, but it did not gain much popularity. 3DO hardware sales were finally halted in 1996.

With the failure of the 3DO business, various licenses related to 3DO and the rights to M2 Technology, which was being developed as a next-generation technology, were sold by 3DO to Matsushita Electric. The total amount is said to be 100 million dollars. 3DO made a fresh start as a software company but went bankrupt in 2005. Matsushita Electric had been developing the successor to the 3DO, the M2, and had even completed a prototype. However, the company repeatedly postponed the launch of the device, and finally decided to discontinue the launch in 1997 in light of the market environment where competing devices had an overwhelming market share, and withdrew from the game console market[6] (Photo 11.4).

11.1.3 Lack of Performance and the False Market Images

So far, we have summarized the failures of the four game consoles.[7] The reasons for the failures are different, but the following four points are common to all of them (Tables 11.1 and 11.2).

[6]Even after that, Matsushita did not give up on the game market. In October 2010, the company announced that it was developing a portable game console, The Jungle, and even tested it, but stopped selling it in 2011.

[7]Other game consoles that were not accepted in the market exist but will be omitted because they do not make a significant difference to the structure of the discussion. The omitted game machines include Laser Active (Pioneer, 1993) and Jaguar (Atari, US market launch 1993, Japanese market launch 1994).

Table 11.1 Performance of each game console

	FM TOWNS Marty	PC-FX	3DO	PiPin@
Company	Fujitsu	NEC	Matsushita Electronics(Panasonic)	Bandai
Year	1993	1994	1994 (1993 in the USA)	1996
Price	98,000 yen	49,800 yen	54,800 yen	68,000 yen
CPU	386SX (16Mhz)	V810 (21.475 MHz)	ARM60 (12.5 MHz)	PowerPC603 (66 MHz)
Screen resolution (number of simultaneous colors)	640*480 (max 32,768 colors)	320*240 (max 16 M colors)	640*480 (max 16 M colors)	640*480 (max 32,768 colors)
RAM	2 MB	2 MB	2 MB	4 MB
Drives	CD-ROM FDD	CD-ROM	CD-ROM	CD-ROM
Remarks	FM TOWNS Compatible			Mac OS 7.5 Compatible, Built-in 14.4 kbps modem

Table 11.2 Failure items for each game machine

	Swept away by false images	High price	Lack of 3D performance	Non-toy distribution
FM TOWNS Marty	✓	✓	✓	✓
PC-FX		✓	✓	
3DO	✓	✓	*	✓
Pipin@	✓	✓	*	✓

*Very weak but existed

1. It was driven by the "multimedia market" (the Internet market in Pipin@), a false image that did not yet exist at the time and did not fully emphasize its appeal as a game machine.
2. The price was very high when viewed as a game machine that would be used most often.
3. It lacked performance as a game machine. It lacked the 3D graphics performance that was the trend in games at the time.
4. The company tried to distribute the product in a way other than through game and toy distribution, which would attract the attention of game users, who were the most important customers of the company. Therefore, there were significantly fewer opportunities for consumers to learn about the existence of the products.

As discussed in Chap. 9, in the first half of the 1990s, multimedia was the focus of much attention, and it was believed that in addition to the games that were already ahead of the curve, an enormous market would arise outside of games, such as education, culture, and entertainment. In addition, in the late 1990s, the same kind of talk was taking place simply by replacing multimedia with the Internet. However, the multimedia market (the Internet market) did not grow explosively in a short period of time. If the multimedia market (Internet market) does not exist, we have no choice but to consider it as a mere game machine. However, as a game machine, it was critically underperforming and overpriced. Moreover, there were few opportunities to see demonstrations or touch the actual machine, and as a result, it disappeared without many people even knowing it existed.

11.1.4 Failed Hardware from Gaming Giants

Except for NEC's PC-FX, the hardware listed so far was the product of a company that had never been in the home video game console business. Therefore, there were a few points that were clearly out of place in the game console business. However, even companies that have established themselves above a certain level in the home video game console business and should understand what the console business is all about have produced hardware that has failed. One was a failure to extend the life of successful previous generation hardware, and the other was a failure to boldly challenge the 3D trend from a completely different approach.

11.1.4.1 Sega: The Failure of the Super 32X

When Sega of Japan was preparing the Saturn as the successor to the MegaDrive, Sega of the USA had other things in mind. Since the Genesis (the US version of the MegaDrive) had a larger market share than the MegaDrive in Japan and had an advantageous position in the market, Sega decided to sell peripherals that would expand the Genesis' functions in order to maintain its position. The Super 32X (US name: Sega 32X) was a hardware project led by Sega of the USA.

The Super 32X was an expansion unit that plugged into the Mega Drive's cartridge slot and was equipped with two Hitachi SH-2 32-bit RISC processors (the same as the Saturn). By using the Mega Drive's screen output and input mechanism from the controller, the price was kept low at 16,000 yen ($159 in the USA). The company also planned to develop and release games using the CD-ROM drive (Mega CD in Japan, Sega CD in the USA), which was also available as a peripheral device. However, despite the complex hardware configuration of four CPUs of different speeds and generations (Z80, MC68000, two SH-2s, and one additional MC68000 when the Mega CD was installed), the performance was far inferior to that of the Saturn, which was designed completely from scratch. Moreover, it was already reported that the Saturn would be released as a successor model, so there was no need to go out of the way to purchase hardware with inferior performance.

The Super 32X was released on November 21, 1994, in the USA. In Japan, it was released on December 3, 1994, the same day as the PlayStation. Saturn's release date was May 11, 1995, in the USA, a half year later, but in Japan, it was already released on November 22, 1994. In an environment where attractive hardware had already appeared or would soon be released, hardware did not sell well and software development and release were not stimulated. In the end, only 18 games were released in Japan, and only 35 titles were released overseas. Hardware sales in the USA totaled only 665,000 units. Sales in Japan are not known, but they are much lower[8] than those in the USA.

11.1.4.2 Nintendo: Premature Hardware Virtual Boy

The Virtual Boy, which Nintendo released in 1995, was developed not by the Development Division II, the division that develops home video game consoles, but by the Development Division I led by Gunpei Yokoi.[9] Yokoi had developed numerous toys before Nintendo became a video game company and was also responsible for the development of the Game Boy (see Chap. 14), a portable video game console. As a result, the hardware was designed from a completely different philosophy than existing stationary game consoles.

The system was shaped like a pair of binoculars, and the game was played by looking through the scope and was designed to make the player feel as if he or she were looking at a 3D image by displaying different images for the left eye and the right eye, taking parallax[10] into consideration. The resolution of the LCD was 384 × 224 pixels, and the images were displayed in four monochromatic shades of red. This was an application of virtual reality to games, and the bizarre hardware form was a head-mounted display (HMD) with a game console integrated into it. To

[8] According to Ueda (1995), at the end of March 1995, shipments of Super32X were 50,000 units in Japan, 800,000 units in the USA, and 200,000 units in Europe.

[9] Gunpei Yokoi (1941–1997). Joined Nintendo in 1965. Developed toys such as Ultra Hand (1967), Love Tester (1969), Kousenju(Light Gun) SP, and Ten Billion (1980). Later, he developed the Game & Watch, the controller for the Family Computer, and the Game Boy. Yokoi had a strong sense of crisis over the situation where games were becoming more complex as the performance of game consoles increased, creating many people who could not keep up. This awareness of the problem led to the Nintendo DS and Wii. Yokoi left Nintendo in 1996 and established Koto Co., Ltd. but died in a traffic accident in 1997. The Wonder Swan (1999), released by Bandai, was conceptualized by Yokoi and developed by Koto. GUNPEY, a launch title for Wonder Swan, is a puzzle game supervised by Yokoi and is effectively his last work.

[10] Parallax is "the difference in the results of observation that occurs when an object of observation is observed from two different points." In this case, it refers to the slight difference between the images seen by the left eye and the right eye. Humans perceive images as having depth by processing the parallax between the left and right eyes in the brain, while Virtual Boy expresses a 3D effect by producing images with parallax.

Photo 11.5 Virtual Boy (Source: Wikipedia)

keep prices low and the display expressive, the images were monochromatic, and the main unit was fixed to a desk for the player to look into.

Due to the nature of the hardware, the game screen was not visible to anyone other than the player playing the game, making it difficult to convey the power and fun of the game machine, which was a problem in terms of advertising. Although it was possible to output images to a large screen for advertising purposes, this not only obscured the stereoscopic effect but also resulted in the excessive use of a plain, red-on-black screen.

In addition, due to the Product Liability Act enacted in 1994, the year before the product went on sale, it became necessary to add a statement to the instruction manual that "a short break of 5–10 minutes is required every 30 minutes" in consideration of the health of the eyes. These descriptions also caused parents, the actual purchasers, to become concerned that the product might not be good for their children's eye health during their growth spurt (Photo 11.5).

Table 11.3 Super 32X and Virtual Boy

	Super 32X	Virtual Boy
Company	Sega	Nintendo
Year	1994	1995
Price	16,800JPY	15,000JPY
CPU	SH2*2(23 MHz)	V810(20 MHz)
Resolution (simultaneous Colors)	320*24 (32,768 Colors)	384*224 (monochromatic)
RAM	2Mbit	1Mbyte
Drives	None	None
Remarks	Mega Drive expansion adapter	

As a result, the Virtual Boy was a business failure, although it did have some enthusiasts. Sales fell far short of Nintendo's expectations, and despite the hardware being released in July 1995, the business was discontinued by the Christmas sales season of that year. It ended up selling only 150,000 units in Japan and 1.26 million units worldwide. The number of game titles released was 19 (Table 11.3).

11.2 Three Great Hardware Age

From this point on, home video game consoles were in a state of competition among Sony, Nintendo, and Sega (and Microsoft after Sega withdrew from the market). The following describes the era of Sega's Saturn (abbreviated as SS in the graph), Sony's PlayStation (abbreviated as PS in the graph), and Nintendo's Nintendo 64 (abbreviated as N64 in the graph), in order of release.

11.2.1 Hardware Development

11.2.1.1 Most Powerful 2D Graphics Hardware: Saturn

At the time, Sega was the leader in 3D graphics, along with Namco, but in developing the Saturn, the successor to the Mega Drive, the design was to strike a balance between 2D and 3D graphics, taking into consideration the porting of many 2D graphics games. The three key development requirements were (1) 3D-CG using polygons, (2) the ability to port arcade games, and (3) the ability to play full-motion video.

Many members who developed the System 32 arcade game board were involved in the development of the Saturn, and their expertise was utilized in its design. The sprite function not only made it possible to flip, enlarge, and shrink sprites, but also to rotate and twist them by treating them as textures in the 3D graphics. Graphics for background images could also be scaled up or down. The Saturn was equipped with the best 2D graphics functions of the time. In addition to its base as a 2D graphics game machine, it was also used in the arcade game boards MODEL1 (used in Virtua Racing (1992) and Virtua Fighter (1993)) and MODEL2 (used in Daytona USA and Virtua Fighter 2 (both used in Virtua Racing (1992) and Virtua Fighter (1993)) were also incorporated into the architecture to enable 3D graphics expression.

The choice of CPU was based on several candidates, including NEC's V810 (used in PC-FX) and Motorola's MC68040 (not used in any game machines), and the result was Hitachi's SH-2[11] processor. During the development process, the lack of computing performance[12] became a problem, and it was decided to increase the number of SH-2 processors to two.[13]

The final hardware configuration was quite complex, with two SH2 CPUs, a Motorola MC68000 sub-CPU for sound, a VDP1 video processor for sprite and polygon operations, a VDP2 video processor for scrolling, and an SH1 for CD-ROM control. The complex configuration became a major burden in the price competition that followed.

11.2.1.2 3D Specialized Hardware: PlayStation

A key player in the development of PlayStation was Ken Kutaragi, then president of SCE. In 1984, Kutaragi saw the System G, a real-time effector, at Sony's Information Processing Laboratory, and was strongly impressed. The System G was a system that could perform effects such as image enlargement, reduction, and explosions on live action images in real time and was used in popular TV programs. System G used about 20,000 ICs and LSIs. One of the images that came to mind when developing PlayStation was to downsize and reduce the cost of this system so that it could be marketed as a home-use game console.

[11] It was shortly after mass production shipments of the SH-1 RISC processor had begun that Hitachi began development of the SH-2, an improved version of the SH-1, in response to Sega's decision to adopt the processor and request for performance improvements. The adoption of the SH-2 by Saturn led to the SH-2 gaining the world's second largest share of the RISC processor market for a period.

[12] According to a retrospective of SH processor development, Sega began claiming lack of performance around the time it was announced that Nintendo's new model (called the "Ultra 64" at the time) would include a chip jointly developed with Silicon Graphics. At the time, Sega paid little attention to Sony, a newcomer to the game industry, and regarded Nintendo as its rival. The fact that they called Saturn "64-bit class (with two 32-bit SH-2 CPUs)" in a TV commercial at the time of its release suggests that they were very conscious of Nintendo.

[13] Originally, SH-2 was not planned to be equipped with a multiprocessor function. A request to incorporate multiprocessor functionality into the SH-2 under development at the time for experimental terminals in the laboratory resulted in the successful implementation of a simple multiprocessor function.

The goals for PlayStation hardware performance during actual development were set to achieve the following three goals at a level where images could be output on a home TV and at the size and price of a home video game console.

1. 3D performance comparable to the world's best graphics workstations.
2. 2D performance comparable to the industry's best arcade game machines.
3. CPU computing performance is comparable to the most advanced workstations and personal computers.

The price of games on CD-ROM was set at approximately 5000 yen, half the price of ROM cartridges at the time, and the target price of the machine was set at 39,800 yen so that the purchase of two game software titles at the same time when purchasing the machine would bring the price within 50,000 yen.

PlayStation has adopted a simple, 3D-specific architecture to reduce manufacturing costs. Instead of using a sprite layer and multiple BG layers, which is common in existing 2D graphics game consoles, PlayStation adopted an architecture in which the sprite layer and BG layers are represented by a group of objects (textured polygons) that are parallel to the screen and have no depth. By including 2D as part of the 3D rendering process,[14] the company was able to reduce costs by eliminating the need for a dedicated chip for 2D graphics, as was the case with the Saturn.

In addition, the company promoted the development of SOC (System On Chip), in which multiple functions are implemented on a single LSI. On the same chip as the CPU core, the chip also contains cache memory, a coprocessor for 3D operations, image processing functions such as a decoder for video compression, and peripheral device controller and memory controller functions that are equivalent to the chipset in today's PCs. Multiple functions are also integrated into other chips. As a result of this consolidation, the number of chips in the System G was reduced from 20,000 to only a dozen in the PlayStation.

11.2.1.3 Difficult Hardware: Nintendo 64

Nintendo launched the previous generation Super Famicom in 1990, the year of its last launch. Therefore, around 1994, when the Saturn and PlayStation were released, the Super Famicom was still in its heyday, and there was no need to rush to develop and release new hardware. In response to the 3DCG features of the new generation of hardware, the company released "Super Donkey Kong[15] "with characters drawn in

[14] All parts of the BG layer on a normal 2D screen are considered sprites, and the Z value (a parameter indicating height and depth) in normal 3D graphics is used to prioritize the drawing of overlapping sprites, making them functionally equivalent to existing 2D graphics. This was possible because the object rendering performance of PlayStation was far superior to that of previous generations.

[15] Super Donkey Kong was a game developed by the British company Rare. Rare created a game with the best graphics of its time using a technique they called ACM (Advanced Computer

3DCG style at the end of 1994, right around the time when the new generation of hardware was released, to show that "the Super Famicom is fun enough." In 1995, the company continued to extend the life of Super Famicom by selling games with coupons that allowed users to purchase Super Famicom for 4000 yen less, while at the same time developing the next-generation hardware.

Virtual Boy, which was released in such an environment, was a complete dud, and this led to a great deal of attention being paid to Nintendo's next-generation hardware. Nintendo's new hardware, codenamed Ultra 64 in the press, was developed in partnership (1993) with Silicon Graphics, a company that sold graphics workstations with the highest performance at the time, including those used in CG for movies.

As the name suggests, the Ultra 64 CPU is a 64-bit MIPS R4300 Custom, and instead of preparing hardware for 2D and hardware for 3D, it uses a microcode architecture for the RCP (Reality[16] Co-Processor) graphics chip. The architecture of the RCP (Reality Co-Processor) is micro-coded,[17] which allows the graphics chip to be used for both 2D and 3D, thereby reducing manufacturing costs. For memory, the Rambus DRAM (RD-RAM), which was rarely used at the time, was adopted because of placing great importance on the speed of data transfer during games. In addition, the game hardware was designed to be stress free during game play, so the adoption of CD-ROMs was forsaken in favor of ROM cassettes only. Instead, a rewritable disk drive[18] was planned to be released as a peripheral device.

Modeling). This method involved designing characters using 3D computer graphics on the high-performance computers of the time, then creating 2D graphics dots from animations of the characters in motion and using them as characters in the game. Super Donkey Kong, which was developed using ACM, had superior graphics to games (such as Star Fox) that used an auxiliary chip (Super FX chip) for 3DCG in the ROM cartridge, and had a significant impact on subsequent Super Nintendo games.

[16]The joint development project between Nintendo and Silicon Graphics was called Project Reality. This is why the chip was named Reality.

[17]When software gives instructions to a computer (CPU), the instructions must be in the form of an instruction set that the CPU can understand (instruction set architecture). In the microcode method, instructions in accordance with the instruction set architecture are further divided into simpler instructions, microcode, and executed in the CPU. The instructions can be divided into several different microcode groups, and it is possible to program which instructions of the instruction set architecture are to be executed as which microcode group. The microcode system in the Nintendo 64 allows the RCP to be used for both high-performance 2D graphics chips capable of displaying large numbers of sprites superimposed on each other, and for 3D graphics chips, which is its intended use.

[18]This drive was eventually released as the 64DD in 1999, one year before the PlayStation 2 was released. As a result, (1) titles originally developed for the 64DD were released on ROM cartridges and (2) social attention had shifted to the next generation of the three hardware platforms. The 64DD was already outdated from the time of its launch. In addition, Nintendo established a joint venture company (RandnetDD) with Recruit Co., Ltd. and launched Randnet in February 2000, a network connection service for players to interact with each other and download and play games using Nintendo 64 and 64DD as Internet terminals. However, the company withdrew from the service after only 1 year, until the end of February of the following year, as it attracted only 15,000 members instead of its initial goal of 100,000.

Table 11.4 Performance comparison of three hardware

	PlayStation	Saturn	Nintendo 64
Company	SCE	SEGA	Nintendo
Year	1994	1994	1996
Price	39,800 yen	44,800 yen	25,000 yen
CPU	R3000A (33.87 MHz)	SH2*2 (28.6 MHz)	R4300Custom Chip (93.75Mhz)
Resolution (simultaneous Colors)	256*224-640*480 (32-bit Colors)	320*224 and others (32-bit Colors)	256*224-640*480 (32-bit Colors)
RAAM	3 MB	5.25 MB	4.5 MB
Drives	CD-ROM	CD-ROM	None

Nintendo 64 was a high-performance hardware that outperformed the Saturn and PlayStation, but its price of 25,000 yen was lower than both hardware by thoroughly adopting a System On Chip (SOC) and not using a CD-ROM. However, development was delayed significantly, and Nintendo 64 was released in 1996, a year and a half later than the Saturn and PlayStation.

11.2.1.4 Performance of Each Hardware

Table 11.4 shows the performance of the three hardware systems. Screen resolution and the number of simultaneous colors, which were important indicators for 2D game consoles in the past, have reached the upper limit of analog TV and human resolution. In addition, the sprite function is no longer a differentiator, as it has achieved overwhelmingly high performance or can be substituted at a sufficient level by other functions. The performance competition for game consoles in the future will center on the computing performance of CPU and GPU.

For the next two generations, home video game consoles were no longer "derivatives from arcade games" or "horizontal use of dead technologies." They entered an era of great competition, in which they took the lead in R&D themselves, invested in cutting-edge technology without reserve, and aggressively attacked each other without fear of hardware reverse spread (i.e., production costs exceeding sales prices).

11.2.2 Competition Among Three Major Hardware

Cross check the competition between PlayStation, Saturn, and Nintendo 64. Figure 11.1 shows the sales figures for each hardware. In 1994, the year of its launch, sales exceeded PlayStation's, probably due to Saturn's slightly earlier launch. The

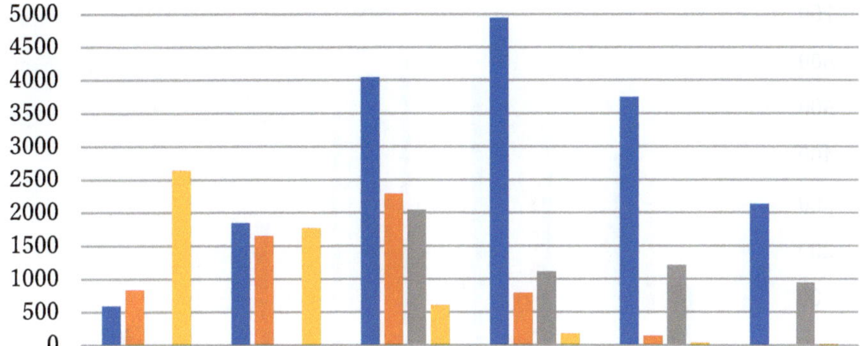

	1994	1995	1996	1997	1998	1999
PS	600	1850	4050	4950	3750	2140
SS	840	1660	2300	800	150	0
N64	0	0	2040	1110	1210	940
SFC	2650	1780	620	190	50	30

Fig. 11.1 Trends in console sales volume (thousand units)

following year, PlayStation won by a narrow margin, but from 1994 to 1995, it is fair to say that the two were almost neck-and-neck.[19] The number of game titles released in 1994 and 1995 was also close, with a total of 149 (PlayStation) and 152 (Saturn). However, when looking at the total for these 2 years, the best-selling hardware was Super Famicom. Super Famicom successfully compensated for the slow development of the Nintendo 64, partly because the console had reached maturity and many game titles had been released, and partly because sales expansion and life extension measures, such as games with discount coupons for the console, had been successful.

The situation moved dramatically in 1996, when the company was about to switch from Super Famicom to the Nintendo 64, and PlayStation's dominance became decisive. PlayStation sold 4.05 million units in 1 year, thanks in part to a price cut in June 1996. On the other hand, the Saturn also saw its sales increase from the previous year, thanks in part to a price cut in March, but only 2.3 million units were sold. The number of titles released was 414(PlayStation) and 320(Saturn), but the difference was even greater. On the other hand, Nintendo's hardware sales were also sluggish due to a lack of key game titles, even though hardware sales had switched from Super Famicom to the Nintendo 64. Ultimately, PlayStation became the winner of this generation, and the video game industry changed drastically (Fig. 11.2).

The competition between the three consoles—PlayStation, Saturn, and Nintendo 64—was fierce and unprecedented in the history of the game industry. In particular,

[19] Sony ran a campaign called "*Ikuze 100 man dai* (Let's Go Million Units)" in 1995 to promote the 1 million units sold, by which time the Saturn had already sold more than 1 million units.

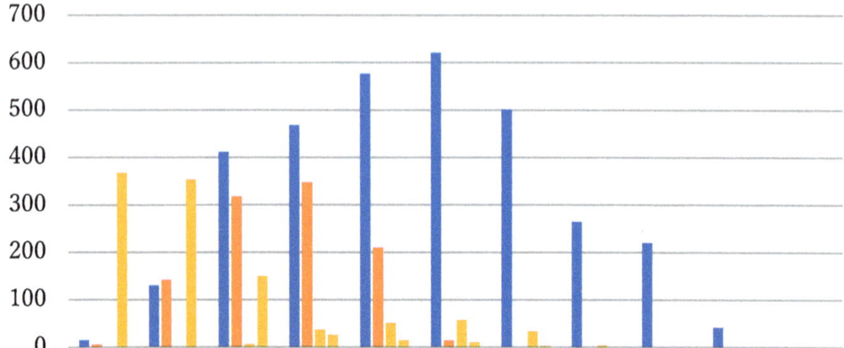

	1994	1995	1996	1997	1998	1999	2000	2001	2002	2003	2004
PS	17	132	414	470	578	623	503	266	222	43	2
SS	8	144	320	350	212	16	1				
N64			9	40	54	60	36	6			
SFC	370	356	152	29	17	13	5				

Fig. 11.2 Number of released titles on each console

the PlayStation and Saturn were almost neck-and-neck until 1995, but in 1996, the race tilted in the PlayStation's favor, and the final margin of victory was huge. Some of the reasons for this are as follows:

1. The repeat business model put forward by PlayStation was reasonably successful.

   While on the Saturn side, older titles were not being lot up and reproduced, and the competition was always fought with only the most recently released titles, PlayStation was able to fight with a complete set of past software assets. This trend became even clearer in July 1996, when the company began releasing low-priced versions of hit titles such as "PlayStation the Best[20]."
2. Sony, the new challenger, was the easiest in terms of "game development difficulty" and the most generous in terms of "third-party follow-up."

   In reverse order of the number of game titles released, the Nintendo 64, Saturn, and PlayStation were the most difficult to develop, in that order. Sony was the first to enter the games market. Moreover, it had designed hardware specializing in 3D graphics, which had never been done before, and it put a lot of effort into improving its development environment. Not only did it actively provide libraries for developers, but it also provided a standard operating system.[21] The Saturn, on

[20] Sega also began to introduce lower-priced versions under the name Satakore, which is abbreviation of Saturn Collection, but there was a delay of about a year with the first Satakore release in April 1997. This difference was significant in the face of fierce competition.

[21] This also meant hardware abstraction, which also served to reduce compatibility issues when new machines were launched.

Table 11.5 Number of titles launched in the first 3 years of the three hardware categories and in-house ratios

	Number of titles released in 3 years	Number of in-house developed titles launched during the 3-year period	In-house ratio
PlayStation	563	35	6.2%
Saturn	472	90	19.1%
Nintendo 64	103	18	17.5%

the other hand, had a complex architecture with two CPUs (three if you include the MC68000 for sound), but no OS and insufficient libraries.[22] Developers had to start by analyzing the hardware. This situation was the same for first-party Sega, which was able to overcome this situation due to its high technological capabilities, but it was much tougher for third parties. Nintendo also announced that it would carefully select third parties with the Nintendo 64, shaking off companies that lacked technical capabilities.

Table 11.5 shows the percentage of titles released by the company (SCE, Sega, and Nintendo) in the first 3 years of hardware launch (1994–1996 for PlayStation and Saturn, 1996–1998 for Nintendo 64), before the competition between the hardware was yet to be determined.[23] Even discounting the fact that Sony's game development capabilities were low and it relied heavily on third parties, a large difference can be seen.

3. Sega could not withstand the price competition for game consoles.

Originally, home video game hardware was "purchased by consumers as a means to sell video game software," and to prioritize popularization at the time of release, prices are often below or at best just below the manufacturing cost. Successful hardware in the market may become profitable by lowering the manufacturing cost due to the effect of mass production. PlayStation not only aggressively used the effect of mass production as a source of price reduction, but also further lowered the manufacturing cost by changing the hardware design. During the period from 1994 to 1996, when PlayStation and Saturn were in a fierce sales battle, both aggressively lowered the price of their consoles. Table 11.6 shows the price trends of the three hardware platforms, including the N64.[24]

---

[22] Eventually, the Saturn was also provided with a library developed by Sega's AM2 Lab.

[23] When the results of the hardware sales competition become clear, companies continue to enter the market on winning hardware, while companies continue to exit on losing hardware. When the proportion of in-house titles is examined over the entire period in which game titles were released, the results are excessively harsh on losing hardware. For this reason, results up to the third year, when the hardware winners and losers are not yet visible, were compared.

[24] At the time of its launch, the Saturn was priced 5000 yen higher than the PlayStation at 44,800 yen, but stores often sold it at about the same price as the PlayStation, with the price reduced by 5000 yen. Therefore, it is safe to assume that the prices of the two were competitive for a long time.

Table 11.6 Price trends of three hardware

		PS	SS	N64
1994	At the start of sales	39,800	44,800	
1995	July	29,800	34,800	
	November	29,800	29,800	
1996	March	24,800	20,000	
	June	19,800	↓	25,000
1997	March	↓	↓	16,000
	November	18,000	↓	↓
1998	July	↓	↓	14,000
	December	15,000	15,000	14,000

With a few exceptions, the price and internal specifications of game consoles have often remained unchanged.[25] The few exceptions that did exist were price reductions during the maturity period when the hardware had reached a point of widespread use, and this generation is the first time that the price of a market-leading game console has been lowered. In July 1995, less than a year after the launch of the hardware, Sony lowered the price of the console by 10,000 yen to 29,800 yen, and Sega followed suit. Since then, the two companies have been engaged in a fierce price-cutting competition. The price competition was overwhelmingly unfavorable to Sega. PlayStation not only had a simple design that made it easy to reduce manufacturing costs but also aggressively introduced a new design (i.e., a new model number), thereby lowering manufacturing costs. On the other hand, Saturn had many CPUs and other chips due to its design. In addition, multiple chip suppliers were involved, making it difficult to reduce manufacturing costs by integrating functions into a single chip, and there was little room for price reductions. As a result, Sega was dragged into a price war with PlayStation, and the hardware's reverse spread (a loss incurred for each unit sold) grew, sapping the company's strength.

On the other hand, the Nintendo 64 had a sophisticated design with a small number of chips and took a long time before the hardware was released, so there was no or negligible reverse spread with the hardware production cost. Therefore, although Nintendo lost in the race for the number of hardware units sold, this had no impact on the company's business.[26]

[25] An exception in past game hardware is the Core Graphics II, a game console from NEC that reduced the price of the PC Engine from 24,800 yen to 19,800 yen. However, the internal architecture is the same.

[26] The Nintendo 64 sold more than 20 million units in the USA and was able to secure revenue there. In this sense, it was saved by the US market, just like the previous generation Sega(Mega Drive).

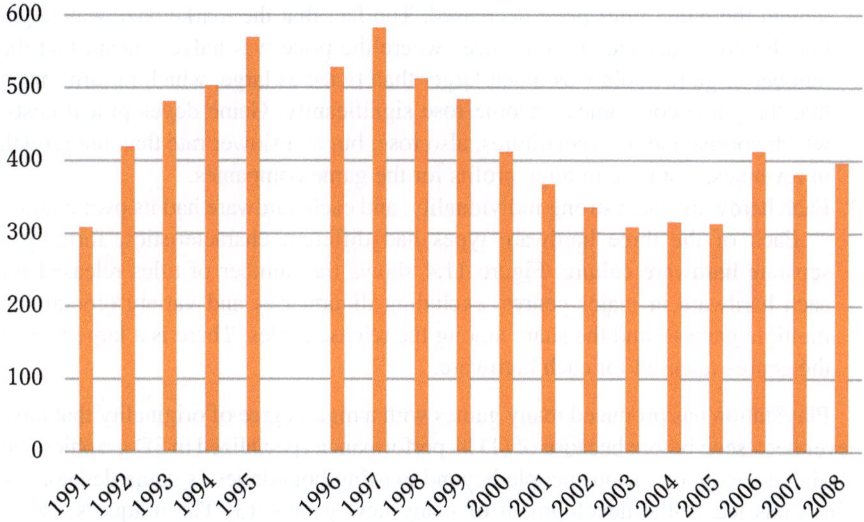

Fig. 11.3 Size of the home video game software market (billion yen). Source: Toy journal each year edition (before break), CESA game white paper year edition

11.3 Summary: The Heyday of Home Video Games

Looking back in history, this period was the largest market size for home video games. The market size reached nearly 600 billion yen, almost three times that of 2020, around 1995–1998, when PlayStation, Saturn, and Nintendo 64 were competing with each other. The reasons why the home video game market has expanded so much are as follows (Fig. 11.3):

1. Game prices have dropped significantly.

   In the previous generation when games were supplied on ROM cartridges, prices soared as a direct result of the increasing scale and capacity of games. By the end of the Super Famicom, many games were priced over 10,000 yen. However, with the introduction of CD-ROMs for the PlayStation and Saturn, the price dropped to 5800–6800 yen.[27] There is no doubt that the halving the price without a drop in the quality of the games has increased demand.

2. Profits of game companies rose significantly.

   Since the production cost of CD-ROM titles was remarkably low, the game company's share per game remained almost the same at about 2000 yen,[28] even

---

[27] Since the Nintendo 64 was supplied on ROM cartridges, the price did not drop as much as the PlayStation or Saturn, but the launch title, Super Mario 64, cost 9800 yen, and Nintendo made every effort to keep the game price under 10,000 yen.

[28] In Yata (1996), the game company's share for a Super Famicom game priced at 10,000 yen per copy is about 20% as far as the figure is read (p. 32). Yamashita (1998) also estimates the game company's share at 1792 yen for a Nintendo ROM cassette game with a list price of 9800 yen in the

though the game sales price decreased. The fact that the market size was larger than before under the circumstances where the price was halved meant that the number of games sold was much larger than twice as large, which in turn meant that the game companies' income rose significantly. Game development costs, which correspond to expenditures, also rose, but at a slower rate than the growth in revenues, resulting in huge profits for the game companies.

3. Each hardware had a strong individuality, and each hardware had its own culture.

   Each of the three hardware types had different characteristics, forming a separate hardware culture. Figure 11.4 shows the number of titles released for each hardware in major genres, excluding dictionaries and variety (containing multiple games), and the share among the released titles. There is a large bias in the genres released for each hardware.

PlayStation has produced many games with a high degree of originality that have never been seen before because of (1) its performance specialized in 3D graphics and (2) the inclusion of various people beyond existing boundaries as game developers, which has led to the development of many new games. (3) The unique sense of advertisement appealed to light gamers who had not played games before. A typical example of this is the existence of MACT (music action game), which became a well-established genre with the huge hit PaRappa the Rapper[29](1996).

Saturn was originally developed as a 2D graphics game console and was equipped with very advanced sprite functions. In addition to the large amount of memory originally installed, the memory capacity could be increased by installing an expansion RAM cartridge in the expansion slot. This made the hardware suitable for shooting games in which many sprites are moved simultaneously and fighting games in which the memory must hold data on the various movements of large characters. This led to the large ratio of STG and FTG games. In addition, the screening process for games was more relaxed[30] than that of Sony and Nintendo, and many bishoujo (beautiful girl) games were released. This led to a large percentage of ADV games.

The Nintendo 64 had the following characteristics: (1) it was supplied with games on ROM cartridges, which made it weak in terms of capacity; (2) most purchasers were children, such as elementary school students; and (3) it was a latecomer, which gave it a performance advantage over the other two game consoles. Therefore, many

---

Super Famicom era. In the case of PlayStation/Sega Saturn CD-ROM software, Yata's (1996) figure indicates that the game company's share is about 35–40% (P63 and P65).

[29] Para Pappa Rappa is a title created mainly by musician Masaya Matsuura. The game was a hit because of the adorable characters designed by Rodney Alan Greenblatt and the simple game design of pressing buttons to the rhythm of rap music. A sequel, Um Jammer Lammy (1999), was also released.

[30] Saturn was the only home video game console that allowed the release of X-rated games (so-called "adult games"), but this was banned in 1996. However, even after the X-rated game was banned, checks on game expression were still relatively lenient.

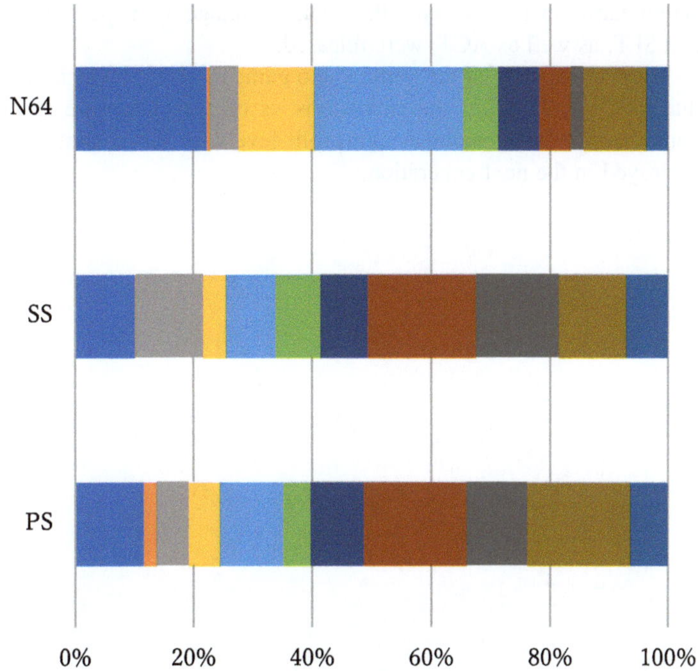

	PS	SS	N64
ACT	342	92	42
MACT	64	1	1
STG	160	103	9
RCG	157	35	24
SPT	313	75	47
FTG	137	68	11
RPG/SRPG/ARPG	263	72	13
SLG	508	164	10
ADV	298	126	4
TBL/CARD	514	102	20
PZL	191	65	7

Fig. 11.4 Game genre released by platform (The genres are as follows. ACT: Action, MACT: Music Action, STG: Shump (Shooting), RCG: Race, SPT: Sports, FTG: Fighting, RPG/SRPG/ARPG: Role Playing, Simulation Role Playing and Action Role Playing, SLG: Simulation, ADV: Adventure, TBL/CARD: Table game and Card game, PZL: Puzzle). Source: Created by the author from CD-ROM data of *Dai Girin*

action games in a broad sense that took advantage of 3D performance, such as RCG and SPT, as well as ACT, were released.

Thus, the heyday of the home video game market, in which the release of games that took advantage of the characteristics of each hardware stimulated the video game market and generated high-profit levels for video game companies, will be destroyed in the next generation.

Chapter 12
Console Games (3) Japan's Declining Position

Abstract This chapter provides an overview of the home video game console market from the late 1990s through the 2010s. The home video game console market saw the exit of Sega after the failure of the Dreamcast in 1998, but the entry of Microsoft led to continued competition among the three companies. Sony's PlayStation 2, released in 2000, was a further success, with its proprietary CPU and GPU greatly increasing performance. However, in the process of competition, the development cost of CPUs and GPUs used in game consoles skyrocketed, and the cost of manufacturing game consoles exceeded the selling price of the consoles. Sony's PlayStation 3, released in 2006, suffered from backward and sluggish sales of the console, and the company lost enough money to erase all the profits it had built up in the previous two generations of consoles. In addition, during this period, the market size expanded in North America and Europe, and the influence of the Japanese video game industry declined significantly.

Keywords Technology driver · Negative spread · Dreamcast · Xbox · PlayStation 2 · PlayStation 3 · Large-scale development · Galapagosization of the Japanese market

The rules of competition in the game industry have changed drastically since the age of the three major hardware platforms described in the previous chapter. Simply put, the participation fee or competition premium has become larger and larger. At the same time, the overseas game market expanded, and Japan's relative position declined.

Y. Koyama, *History of the Japanese Video Game Industry*, Translational Systems Sciences 35, https://doi.org/10.1007/978-981-99-1342-8_12

12.1 About Post-PlayStation

12.1.1 Dreamcast and Sega's Exit from the Hardware Business

Typically, the product life of a home video game console is 5 years or longer. With the Saturn's defeat clear, Sega's successor, the Dreamcast, was released on November 27, 1998, only 4 years after the Saturn's launch. The Dreamcast took advantage of the Saturn's complex hardware configuration and lack of an operating system, which made game development more difficult. Unlike the Saturn, which had multiple CPUs and multiple graphics chips, the Dreamcast had a simple hardware configuration with only one CPU (SH-4) and one graphics chip (PowerVR2). It also included a special version of Microsoft's Windows CE[1] operating system (known as Dragon), which enabled game developers to use DirectX for development.[2]

In anticipation of the growing number of Internet users at the time, the Dreamcast came bundled with the Dream Passport Web browser. The Dreamcast was also equipped with a 33.6 Kbps modem,[3] allowing users to play competitive games over an Internet connection. Users of existing providers could use their access points for Internet access, and users who had not previously used an Internet connection service could easily connect to the Internet through the newly established Sega provider (renamed isao.net in 2000) for the Dreamcast.

Because of bold advertising,[4] Dreamcast attracted a great deal of attention at the time of its launch. However, the production yield of the graphics chips manufactured

---

[1] WindowsCE (later renamed Windows Embedded and now renamed Windows 10 IoT) is an OS developed by Microsoft for embedded devices. It is intended for PDAs, car navigation systems, and other computer-based devices, but has also been used in the gaming field in Dreamcast and arcade game boards. There is no OS package, and the OS is shipped embedded in devices.

[2] While the size of the standard version of Windows CE at the time was several tens of megabytes, the custom OS for Dreamcast was slimmed down to 1.2 megabytes, including DirectX. However, according to what the author (Koyama) has interviewed from developers at the time, Dragon did not have a hardware emulation layer (HEL), and the details of hardware control (especially 3D processing) were left to individual game companies. The OS and libraries separately prepared by the Sega CS Lab had all of these features, and many companies used the OS prepared by Sega.

[3] Commercial ADSL service (broadband Internet access service) started in Japan from the end of 1999–2000, and its full-scale spread began in 2001. Prior to that, home Internet access was provided via modems by calling access points set up in each prefecture. In 1998, when Dreamcast was launched, a V.90 modem with a downlink speed of 56,000 bps (33,600 bps uplink) was available, but it was still too expensive, so a V.34 modem (33,600 bps both uplink and downlink) was adopted, one generation earlier. The modem adapter was detachable from the main unit and could be replaced with another communication adapter. In fact, as high-speed Internet access services became more widespread, a "broadband adapter" that could connect to a LAN at 10Base-T was available but only through mail-order sales.

[4] Dreamcast had a very distinctive advertising campaign. Akimoto Yasushi, a well-known composer and producer of female idol groups, was appointed as the advertising manager to create a series of advertisements. In newspaper advertisements, each newspaper carried a front-page advertisement with the shocking copy "Will Sega stay down?", followed the next day by a front-page

at NEC's plant did not improve, and the company was unable to prepare the planned number of units on the launch date, and reservations for the console, which began on 2 October, were closed within 2 days. In the end, only 150,000 units were available on the launch date, and they did not sell well enough for the year-end sales season. In the first year (1998), only 900,000 units were shipped.

The following year, 1999, the yield problem was resolved and the hardware shortage was resolved, but sales did not increase with the announcement by Sony that the PlayStation 2 would be released. Delays in the development of leading titles also hurt the hardware's spread. Sega held a production presentation of Shenmue at six venues across Japan between end-December 1998 and January 1999, immediately after the launch of Dreamcast, which attracted approximately 30,000 people. It was expected to be a killer title that would help popularize the Dreamcast, but development was delayed and the game was not released until the end of 1999. The development cost was also extremely high at 7 billion yen, which also contributed to Sega's poor performance. In addition to Shenmue, Phantasy Star Online, the first successful online RPG for home video game consoles, was launched at the end of 2000, while Sakura Wars 3, a sequel to the hit series, was released in 2001, after the trend of hardware competition had already been decided.

In 2000, Isao Okawa, chairman of CSK, Sega's parent company, was appointed president as a management lever, and a 100 billion yen third-party capital increase was carried out, but to no avail. Finally, in 2001, Sega decided to discontinue production of the Dreamcast and withdraw from the home video game hardware market. The extraordinary loss of 80 billion yen incurred at that time was made up by Okawa through a special transfer of 85 billion yen in personal assets. Final sales of the Dreamcast in Japan were around 2.5 million units. Sega's business continued to deteriorate even after its withdrawal from home hardware, and the company was eventually acquired by Sammy in 2003.

Although the Dreamcast was a failure as a home console business, its arcade-compatible platform, NAOMI (New Arcade Operation Machine Idea), became a hit with many gaming companies and was in use for over a decade.

advertisement "X Day Nov, to strike back, Dreamcast." For the TV commercials, a series of commercials were created featuring the then managing director Yukawa, who was an actual board member. The commercials were self-deprecating, with a child actor saying "SEGA is so lame," but they too ended with the story that the company was fighting back with the development of Dreamcast. These advertisements greatly raised the profile of Dreamcast, which in turn led to a shortage of products at launch.

12.1.2 Struggling Hardware: GameCube

The GameCube, the successor to the Nintendo 64, was Nintendo's first console to use disk media.[5] The GameCube was designed with ease of development in mind, reflecting the high degree of difficulty in developing games for the Nintendo 64 and the lack of third-party participation. The hardware design was as simple as possible, with a PowerPC750-based Gekko CPU and a graphics chip, Flipper,[6] which integrated input/output processing functions and high-speed 1 T (one-transistor)-SRAM. In relation to the ease of game development, performance is not indicated in terms of peak performance, but in terms of effective performance (6–12 million polygons/second), which can be demonstrated without difficulty when running games. It also had the ability to connect to the GameBoy Advance, which was released the year before the GameCube, but not much software was compatible with it.

The GameCube was launched on September 14, 2001, after one launch delay, but sales were slow, partly because the PlayStation 2 had been launched the previous year. Sales in Japan exceeded those of the Dreamcast, but ultimately stood at 4.04 million units. The GameCube was considered reasonably well, selling 12.94 million units in North America, but it was a far cry from the PlayStation 2's overwhelming sales figures. Although the number of third-party entries itself increased compared to the Nintendo 64, the number of games released was not large due to poor sales of the console. However, thanks to the thoroughly simple and low-cost design, the losses were not so large.

Nintendo fell behind in the standalone console competition, but thanks to its dominant market share and sales of handheld consoles, it did not suffer the losses that Sega fell into, and continued to compete in the next generation and beyond.

12.1.3 Xbox a Complete Failure in Japan

Microsoft entered the home video game market to replace Sega,[7] which withdrew from the home video game hardware market. The Xbox, launched by Microsoft in 2002, was marketed as a console that could use on a home console, driven by the popularity of DirectX for software development on PCs. With seamless development

[5]The disk media used was not the DVD-ROM that already existed at the time, but a proprietary 8-inch disk developed by Matsushita. With a capacity of 1.5 GB, it was larger than the Dreamcast GD-ROM, but about one-third the size of a DVD. Matsushita also released the hardware, named Q, which was compatible with the GameCube and could also play DVDs, but sales were sluggish.

[6]NEC was responsible for manufacturing the Flipper, for which NEC invested 80 billion yen.

[7]Isao Okawa (deceased), then president of Sega, visited Bill Gates, then chairman of Microsoft, to negotiate Xbox compatibility with the Dreamcast. An internet connection function did not exist in the Xbox concept at the time, and the negotiations broke down when Okawa strongly insisted on an internet connection function (see Toru Furukawa, then president of Microsoft Japan, tweeting: https://twitter.com/SamFURUKAWA/status/7612161941).

with PCs in mind, while other home video game consoles used RISC architecture CPUs that excelled in multimedia processing, the Xbox used Intel's Celeron, the same as a PC. Other specifications were also almost identical to those of PCs. The Xbox was also equipped with a 100 MBps Ethernet port for network connectivity, as PC games from overseas at the time that were played by connecting multiple PCs over a LAN were a big hit.

It was launched in the USA on November 15, 2001, and sold 1 million units by the end of the year, but failed miserably in Japan, with 540,000 units shipped during the entire period. Reasons for the lack of acceptance in the Japanese market include:

1. The majority of game titles released were foreign titles (so-called "Western games").
2. The console, AC adaptor, and controller were too large for Japanese housing conditions.
3. The pre-launch advertisements touted the console as "a console for core gamers," but the PR strategy was mismatched, with the launch countdown event being held in Shibuya, the fashion district, rather than in Akihabara, the city of computers and games.

Konami and Capcom had announced that they would supply software to the Xbox before the console was launched in Japan, but due to sluggish hardware sales, only a handful of titles were supplied. Although the results were disastrous, the Xbox Live online service, which started in 2003 ahead of its competitors, was highly regarded in Japan by core gamers who were keen to play FPS and other games.

12.1.4 Successor with Renewed Architecture: PlayStation 2

The winner of the post-PlayStation competition was the PlayStation 2 (hereafter abbreviated as PS2 in graphs and elsewhere). The PlayStation 2 featured an EE (Emotion Engine) and GS (Graphic Synthesizer), developed jointly with Toshiba, for the CPU and graphics chip.[8] Although the architecture was completely redesigned, compatibility with PlayStation was maintained by using PlayStation chips for the I/O processor. DVD,[9] which was still in the process of becoming

[8] SCE invested a total of 255 billion yen between 1999 and 2000 to manufacture EE and GS (http://www.scei.co.jp/corporate/release/pdf/000601.pdf). In addition, in 2003, Sony announced that the Sony Group would invest 200 billion yen over 3 years to manufacture semiconductors that combine EE and GS into a single chip. (http://www.sony.co.jp/SonyInfo/News/Press_Archive/200304/03-0421/).

[9] The world's first DVD (Digital Video Disk, later called Digital Versatile Disk because of its various uses) player was released by Matsushita Electric (Panasonic) in November 1996.

The penetration rate in Japan was only 21.9 out of 100 households in 2002, the first year that optical disk players (excluding PCs and game consoles) were included in the Cabinet Office's Survey of Consumption Trends.

popular at the time, was adopted as the game media, and DVD playback functions were included as standard.

Prior to the launch of PlayStation 2, an e-commerce site, PlayStation.com, was established and started operation on February 18, 2000. On the opening day, Playstation.com started accepting PlayStation 2 reservations, and the site was extremely popular even before the launch, with the servers being down. PlayStation 2 went on sale on March 4, 2000, and in the 3 days following the launch, almost 1 million units were sold, including 380,000 units sold online via PlayStation.com and 600,000 units sold at retail stores. This is 10 times more than the previous generation PlayStation launch. In addition, shipments exceeded 2 million units at the end of May.

The architecture of the PlayStation 2 was significantly changed from that of the PlayStation. At the time of the hardware launch, game development was delayed due to the lack of the necessary libraries, resulting in a lack of game titles at the beginning of the hardware launch.[10] Eleven launch titles were available on March 4, but only one title was released in May, and only 32 titles were available by June. Despite this, hardware sales remained strong because of compatibility with the previous generation PlayStation and its DVD playback capabilities. Although shipments of DVD players during the year 2000 more than doubled from the previous year, they still amounted to only 840,000 units.[11] The PlayStation 2 surpassed this number within 3 days of its release. This was because PlayStation 2 was by far the least expensive DVD player on the market. DVD players at the time cost around 50,000 yen[12] even during the popularization period, while PlayStation 2 was priced at only 39,800 yen. This was since game consoles and consumer electronics are produced in very different quantities (two digits in terms of annual production volume), and game consoles have strong economies of scale.

The Internet connection, which was standard on the Dreamcast, was supported by the PlayStation BB Unit peripheral device. The BB Unit was a peripheral device equipped with a hard disk and an Ethernet adapter, and it was possible to speed up game loading by installing Internet-ready games on the hard disk. However, because of the cost of maintaining the servers to which users connect, only a small number of Internet-ready games were released, and many of the Internet-ready games that were released were out of service within a relatively short period of time, about 1 year after their release. On the other hand, MMORPGs with a fixed monthly subscription fee, which have a long product life once successful, have been in service for a long

[10] At the time of the launch of PlayStation 2, SCE did not provide graphics drivers and other libraries ("Hiroshige Goto's Weekly Overseas News," May 10, 2000, http://pc.watch.impress.co.jp/.../20000510/kaigai01.htm).

[11] From the Japan Electronics and Information Technology Industries Association's statistics on domestic shipments of consumer electronic equipment.

http://www.jeita.or.jp/japanese/stat/shipment/pdf/minsei2000.pdf

[12] For example, the RV40, the least expensive of the DVD players released by Matsushita on March 10, 2000, cost 49,800 yen. Note that Matsushita was aiming for a monthly production of 5000 units together with two portable DVD players (Nikkei Sangyo Shimbun, January 19, 2000).

period of time with expansion packs released from time to time. Nobunaga no Yabou ONLINE (Nobunaga's Ambition ONLINE) was launched in June 2003 and remained in service until December 2014, after the release of the PlayStation 4, two hardware generations later. Final Fantasy XI was launched in May 2002 as a de facto launch service for the PlayStation BB service, an Internet connection and an online service for the PlayStation 2 and remained in service until March 2016. Although some games were used for a long period of time, the PlayStation BB service was never successful because broadband connection services in Japan were still in its infancy and games were not available for download. Due to the lack of demand, later production PlayStation 2 models omitted the ability to connect to the BB Unit. It would not be until the next generation that Internet connectivity would become commonplace for console video game consoles.

Another device that converted the PlayStation 2 into a consumer electronics device was the PSX. DVD recorders, which record TV programs onto recordable DVDs, had been on the market since 2000, but were priced at over 200,000 yen. As the price of HDDs declined, DVD players began to be equipped with HDDs as well, and by 2003, the price of a DVD-only DVD player for popular models was around 80,000–100,000 yen, while a high-end model with both an HDD and DVD was priced at around 200,000 yen. However, the PSX is equipped with both an HDD and DVD recorder for the low price of 79,800 yen.[13] This was made possible by sharing most of the basic components with the PlayStation 2. Sales of the PSX were not as strong as Sony had hoped, but the second-generation model, the DESR-5100, released the following September 2004, brought the price down to the 40,000 yen range and became a regular at the top of sales rankings. In 2005, however, production was announced to be discontinued, and the PSX development team was absorbed into the Sugo-roku DVD recorder development team within Sony. Although the PSX business ended in 2005, the XMB (cross-media bar) user interface, first used on the PSX, was carried over to the PSP and PlayStation 3. The idea of a game console that could record games was also carried over to the PlayStation 3.

PlayStation 2 steadily expanded its market share to become the overwhelming champion of this generation, shipping 10 million units in Japan in 2002 and 100 million units worldwide in 2005.

12.2 PlayStation 3, Xbox 360, and Wii ... The Beginning of the End of the Era of Home Video Game Consoles

The next generation of PlayStation 2 consoles continued to advance in terms of advanced functionality, and the amount invested in these consoles jumped even higher. As the PlayStation 3 and Xbox 360 continued to advance in functionality,

---

[13]The price of the DESR-5000, released in December 2003. The strage capacity of the HDD in the DESR-5000 was 160 GB, while the DESR-7000 with a 250 GB HDD was priced at 99800 yen.

Nintendo's Wii aimed to reset the course of the game industry once and for all. The three-way battle ended in a painless draw with the Wii as the short-term winner, but no winner in the long run.

Characteristics of this generation and later include the fact that game consoles are permanently connected to the Internet and that the OS that starts up when the console is turned on now has various menus, such as online game sales and video playback. In addition, the OS itself can now be updated and functions can be updated and added even after the game console is sold. This means that costs in the form of ongoing system development and provision of online services are required even after the game console is released. As platform providers, game console sales companies are now required to have comprehensive capabilities that include not only the mere design and production of game consoles and first-party game development capabilities, but also the ability to develop systems and provide online services.

12.2.1 Failure of PlayStation 3

PlayStation 3 has a more advanced architecture than PlayStation2, with the Cell (Cell Broadband Engine) CPU, which was jointly developed with IBM and Toshiba. The Cell is a heterogeneous multi-core (asymmetric multi-core[14]) design that combines one general-purpose core called the PPE (PowerPC Processor Element) and eight cores specialized for multimedia processing called the SPE (Synergistic Processor Element).[15] The Cell was a strategic product of Sony, IBM, and Toshiba, and was planned to be used in a variety of applications, starting with game consoles, including servers and digital consumer electronics. Sony invested aggressively to generate profits not only from game consoles, game software sales, and game software license fees, but also from the semiconductors used in game consoles. Sony invested approximately 200 billion yen from 2003 to 2006 to produce the Cell, totaling 500 billion yen.

In addition to CPU performance, the PS3's performance was outstanding[16]: it was capable of full HD graphics, which was still in its infancy at the time, and was equipped with an HDMI port for connection to full HD-capable TVs. In addition,

[14]By the time the PS3 was released in 2006, the increase in CPU operating frequency was sluggish, and companies were trying to improve processing power by parallel processing through the use of multiple cores in the CPU. However, CPUs for PCs and servers used homogeneous multi-cores with multiple identical cores, and heterogeneous multi-cores such as Cell were rare; Cell's performance was overwhelming at the time, and IBM's supercomputer (Roadrunner), which is equipped with an enhanced version of the Cell CPU was ranked the best supercomputer in the world in June 2008.

[15]In PS3, only 7 out of 8 PPEs can actually be used, in order to improve the CPU yield rate, so that even if one of the 8 PPEs is defective, the system can still operate (designed with PPE redundancy).

[16]The first model was also capable of playing back SACD (Super Audio CD), although its successor was not equipped with this feature.

Blu-ray disks with capacities of up to 50 GB were adopted as the disk media, as next-generation DVDs were a strong contender.

It also has enhanced functions as a home server. Wired LAN (1000BASE-T support) and wireless LAN (IEEE 802.11b/g) are standard for network connectivity, and system software updates enable additional functions and enhanced security, and games can be downloaded and purchased from the PlayStation Store service.[17] An HDD was officially installed, which not only enabled games to be installed and read faster during playback, but also made it possible to store games purchased via download, music CDs, and video data. The standard browser and e-mail software, which enabled minimal browsing and e-mailing, the PlayStation Store service offered video content on a pay-per-view (PPV) basis. The PS3 had all the functions of a home server in the living room, except for the ability to record TV programs.[18] As a game console, it was fully compatible with PS1 titles through software emulation, and with PS2 titles through the inclusion of an EE + GS chip in the console.

Since the PlayStation 3 had a considerably high spec, its price was expected to be considerably higher than existing game consoles. On May 8, 2006, the release date (November 11) and price of PlayStation 3 were announced at E3 in the USA. There will be two models: a low-priced model without HDMI and wireless LAN connectivity and with 20 GB HDD capacity will be priced at 62,790 yen including tax, while a model with HDMI and wireless LAN connectivity and 60GB HDD will be openly priced. This price far exceeded the expectations of many users. In response to the outcry from users, the price was revised at the Tokyo Game Show on September 22 to 49,980 yen including tax (North American price: $499) for the 20 GB version with an HDMI port, and to an open price (North American price: $599) for the 60 GB version even before the console was released. The PlayStation 3, which had a very high manufacturing cost, suffered from a long-term inverse spread between selling price and cost as a result of this price cut.

PlayStation 3 was launched on November 11, 2006, but shipments in Japan were limited to 100,000 units due to the delay in mass production of semiconductor lasers for Blu-ray drives. The delayed start directly affected the company's sales, and shipments in 2006, its first year, were only 610,000 units. It was clear that part of the reason for the poor sales was the high price, so in 2007, a new model with 40 GB

[17] Because the games supplied on Blu-Ray disks are too large, only PSP titles, Game Archives (past PlayStation 1 and PC Engine titles), and download-only games were available when the PS3 was first released.

[18] The TV program recording function was realized with the peripheral TORNE (2010), which was well received for its simplicity of operation and comfortable interface that took advantage of the high performance of the PS3, and achieved sales of 1 million units, which was unprecedented for a peripheral device. The TORNE for PS3 was a tuner box that connected to the PS3 system via USB + software for the PS3. Later, in 2012, nasne, a network recorder and media storage device, was released, and TORNE became the software used to schedule recordings and view recorded videos on nasne. In 2015, Android and iOS versions for smartphones were also released. Nasne was discontinued in 2019, but the business was sold and released by Buffalo in 2021.

HDD capacity, not compatible with PS2 and SACD (Super Audio CD), and a reduced price of 39,800 yen was introduced. However, although sales increased to 890,000 units in 2007 and 1,040,000 units in 2008, these figures could hardly be called a success. The PS3's popularity accelerated in 2009 with the launch of the newly designed PS3 (second-generation PS3), which was priced at 29800 yen ($299 in the USA). The second-generation PS3 was now competing almost equally with the Wii, which had seen its sales decline, but was still struggling to stay afloat.[19]

The expansion of Cell applications also fell into a vicious cycle: sales of PlayStation 3 did not increase, depreciation of equipment did not proceed, chip prices remained high, and Cell did not become widely used. Furthermore, the market for non-game consoles was very small and disappointing, to begin with. Toshiba did not release a Cell-based TV (Cell Regza) until 2009, and by then it was already too late. Finally, SCE sold its plant for Cell, which had cost 200 billion yen, to Toshiba for 100 billion yen.

The PS3's final sales in Japan exceeded 10 million units in 2014, and while it was by no means a hard-selling hardware, it was the hardware that drained all the massive profit accumulation generated by PlayStation 1 and 2 due to the long period of backward sales after its launch.

12.2.2 Xbox360 Failed to Consolidate its Position in Japan

Unlike the Xbox, which had a hardware configuration that was almost identical to that of a PC, the Xbox360 uses a customized PowerPC CPU, which is also used in other game consoles. Although the PowerPC and the x86 architecture used in PCs are completely different, Microsoft XNA, a game development environment and runtime environment, absorbed the hardware differences. Games developed using XNA ran on both the PC and Xbox360 with no or minimal modifications. This allowed the console to increase its cost-performance ratio while maintaining the advantage of easy porting of games for the PC. The graphics chip was made by ATI and supported full HD. Not all games for the previous generation of Xbox could be played through software emulation.

The Xbox360 was also involved in the next-generation DVD standardization battle, and Microsoft was on the HD DVD side. Given the fact that the HD DVD standard was not established in time for the launch of the console and that HD DVD was at a disadvantage, the HD DVD drive became an optional device, and the console was launched with DVD as the disk drive.[20] This resulted in a serious problem of insufficient media capacity for games with huge amounts of data.

---

[19] According to the iSuppli report, the cost of the second-generation PS3 is $336.27, which means that there is still about $30 of reverse cost.

[20] Ultimately, HD DVD lost out to Blu-Ray by an overwhelming margin in terms of widespread adoption and was withdrawn in 2008, just 2 years after the first HD DVD player was released in

Other notable peripherals included the Kinect, which provided an intuitive interface similar to the Wii's controller, but used a camera and microphone set into the TV screen to recognize the operator's face, voice, and movements for in-game control. The Kinect was very powerful, but like other game consoles, it did not have a lot of games to apply it to.[21]

As a result of improved PR strategies and software lineups, Xbox 360 sales in Japan improved from the dismal performance of the previous generation consoles, but total shipments remained sluggish at 1.6 million units. The titles released were characterized by a lineup of novel games due to their high affinity with the PC, and shump games due to their affinity with Windows-based arcade boards.

12.2.3 *Innovation and Stagnation: Wii*

Nintendo's Wii was a hardware that boldly changed the direction of innovation and resources. As with the Nintendo DS released the previous year (2005), Nintendo refused to regard the massive scale of development and the bloat and complexity of game content that had followed the advent of computer games as a development of games, and instead aimed to provide "new fun brought about by a new interface" with the Wii.

The CPU is the Broadway, an improved version of the GameCube's Gecko, and while performance is certainly improved, it is modest when compared to the performance gains of the other two hardware of the same generation. Graphics performance was also limited to SD (720 x 480 pixels) while the other two hardware systems support full HD (1920 × 1080 pixels). In terms of performance, the increase is not so large, it could be called "GameCube 1.5." The increase in semiconductor technology after the GameCube was used to reduce heat generation and chip size to enable hardware to operate 24 h a day. The game media was the same size as CDs and DVDs, 12 cm disk media (and 8 cm media to maintain compatibility with the GameCube), but it was adopted as a proprietary standard and did not include CD/DVD playback functionality. To reduce the price, no HDD was installed in the console, and game data was stored in the internal flash memory (512 MB) and an SD card (which could be installed in the console[22]).

2006. If the Xbox360 had included HD DVD, enthusiasts would have had to hunt around for a workable drive after its release, as they did with Dreamcast's GD-ROM.

[21] Kinect has been analyzed by users since its initial release, and drivers for Windows were distributed by volunteers. This led to many cases where Kinect was connected to PCs and used for various applications, and in response, Microsoft developed an SDK for Windows, which was released in 2011 as a beta version and in 2012 as the official version. Although Kinect was not very successful as an interface for games, its technical capabilities have allowed it to be used in a larger range of applications.

[22] The internal memory is also used by the Wii system, so users do not have access to all 512 MB. Also, when the system was first released, games that were to be launched required data to be stored

The Wii is not hardware with cutting-edge technology for core users. However, it had characteristics as a first game console that light users could easily purchase and play, and as a second game console that core users could not ignore. Specifically, they are as follows:

- The compact size of the console and its vertical placement make it easy to place even on the edge of a TV rack.
- At 25,000 yen, it is far less expensive than other game consoles of the same generation.
- It can be connected to the Internet to view news and weather forecasts at any time.
- Virtual Console service that allows users to download games from past consoles at low prices and play them using hardware emulation.
- The TV metaphor was used extensively to match the TV remote control-shaped controller, and games on disk media, news and weather forecasts, and virtual console games were all referred to as "channels."

Also noteworthy is its controller, the Wii Controller. The front of the controller, similar in shape to a TV remote control, had only a cross button, an A button, and a B button, and one button was mounted where it could be pressed when the user held it as if operating a TV remote control. By holding the controller in the hand, the user could intuitively perform operations such as swinging a racket in a sports game or turning a steering wheel in a racing game. However, there were not many games that made full use of the interface, except for multiplayer party games, and gradually the lack of performance compared to other game consoles (especially the lack of HD graphics support) became a serious problem.

Although the Wii was a huge hit both in Japan and overseas, hardware sales peaked in 2007, the year after the console's launch in Japan, and in 2008 in the rest of the world, and began to decline. In 2010, when other hardware prices dropped, sales declined to about the same level as the PS3, and by 2011, sales had reversed course. After 2011, hardware and software sales plummeted while the market for other hardware remained flat, and the market was almost over. Since the screen resolution was SD, the Wii was a hardware that had a short period of time to reap profits after its popularization.

12.2.4 Hardware Summary

Since each hardware has been discussed, Fig. 12.1 confirms the trends in hardware sales from 1998 to 2010, which are discussed in this chapter. The top hardware sales

in the system's internal memory, and storage on SD cards was only a supplementary method. However, download sales through the Virtual Console were stronger than expected, and many more users wanted to store more games, so the system was updated so that games on the SD card could also be launched.

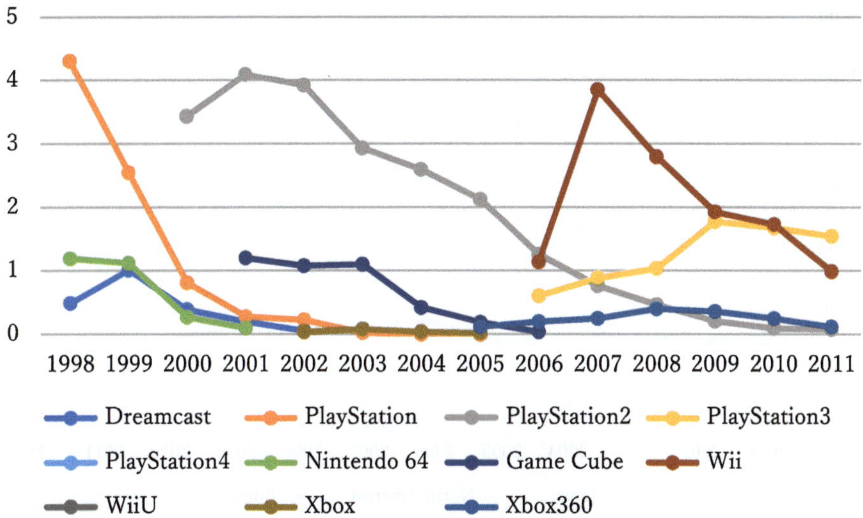

Fig. 12.1 Trends in console sales volume (Million Units). Source: "CESA Games White Paper" Yearly Edition (The sales volume of the PlayStation in 1998 is different, as shown in Fig. 12.1 (hard sales trend) in this chapter because the source of data (= the way of dividing the year) is different.)

were replaced by PlayStation 1 (1994), PlayStation 2 (2000), and Wii (2006), in that order. While PS1 and 2 maintained high hardware sales for more than 3 years, Wii hardware sales declined sharply after the year following the hardware launch at the top. In contrast, PS3 sales have increased year after year, replacing the Wii's sales decline. In 2011, the PS3 also surpassed the Wii in terms of software shipments.

The reason for the PS3's larger market size, despite the Wii's much higher cumulative hardware sales, is that the Wii was sold to a relatively lightweight segment in terms of game consumption, such as families, while the PS3 was sold to people who play games frequently. The Wii gained consumer support with its novel interface and new games using the new interface, but the "novelty" did not last, and the PS3, which outperformed the Wii in terms of basic computer performance, turned the tables in terms of hardware sales.

12.3 Growing Market Size in the World and Stagnation in Japan

12.3.1 Relative Decline of the Japanese Market

One of the most significant changes during this period was the expansion of the market size on a global scale. At the beginning of the twenty-first century, Japan, North America, and Europe were called the three largest markets, and there was not much difference in the size of the three markets. Japan's market peaked between

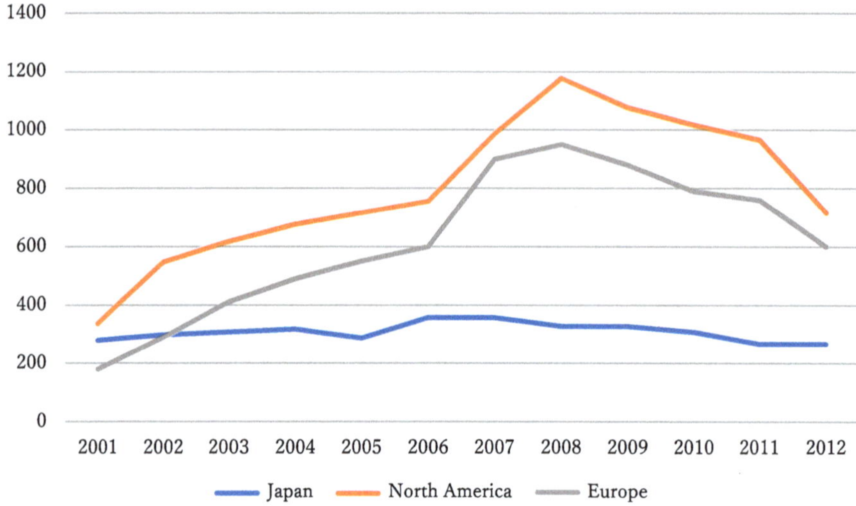

Fig. 12.2 Size of home video game software market in three major markets (Unit: billions of yen). Source: Famitsu Game White Paper

1996 and 1997, and then declined to its current level in 1998. Japan had already matured as a market, peaking in 1996–1997, with a market size of about 300 billion yen, while the North American and European markets expanded rapidly in the twenty-first century. Both markets peaked in 2008, before the impact of the financial crisis (around September 2008), but at the peak, the Japanese market share had declined to 13% (Fig. 12.2).

As both markets rise rapidly, the influence of Japanese companies declines. Table 12.3 shows the number of game titles developed in Japan out of the top 100 titles sold in the North American market. Nintendo has around 20 titles in the list, but only about 10 titles are ranked by other companies. This trend is no different in the European market.

Table 12.1 shows the sales of major Japanese and foreign companies. Nintendo is exceptional, but other video game companies are inferior in terms of home video game sales compared to foreign video game specialists such as Electronic Arts and Ubi. The degree of market growth and the size of the business affect the amount of risk that can be borne and the resulting sales, but the failure to increase sales at rapidly growing Western companies has left Japanese companies behind their Western counterparts in terms of business scale.[23]

The reason why Japanese games other than Nintendo do not sell well in the US market is that "hot-selling" genres in Japan and the USA are very different, and

[23] However, in the market downturn following the financial crisis, Japanese firms did not suffer so much noticeable damage, while Western firms suffered significant losses. In this respect, the small market share of Japanese firms in overseas markets and their cautious attitude toward risk were positive factors.

Table 12.1 Sales of various firms before the financial crisis (2008)

Company	Total sales	Home console game software	Remarks
Nintendo	14,355	3743	Hardware company
Sony Computer Entertainment	10,209	Not announced	Hardware company
Namco Bandai	4605	846	61.1 billion yen for arcade
Square Enix	1475	415	Not including Taito
Sega Sammy	4590	1422	Including toys in home console game software 75.4 billion yen for arcade
Konami	2974	874	43.6 billion yen for arcade
Electronic Arts(US)	3091	2282	World's largest game software specialty
Activision(US)	1513	1402	Merger with Bizzard in December 2007
Take2(UK)	981	821	
Ubi(FR)	1058	963	

Japanese companies: 100 million yen, EA, Activision and Take2: million dollars, Ubi: million euros

Japanese companies are weak against US "hot-selling" games. There are three main differences between the Japanese and international rankings:

1. RPGs, a genre that ranks among the top 100 titles in Japan at least 20 titles each year, is weak in the USA.[24]
2. On the other hand, shooter,[25] a genre that ranks 10–20 titles out of the top 100 titles in the USA every year, is very weak in Japan.
3. Sports is quite strong in the USA, but the types of sports that sell well are basketball and American football, which are very different from those in Japan.[26]

The combination of cultural barriers such as differences in favorite game genres, geographical conditions that favor companies from that country to obtain the rights to use real names in sports games, and technical conditions such as weak technical capabilities and know-how to create Shooter, make it difficult for Japanese games to sell well overseas. On the other hand, Nintendo is the only company that can produce

[24]Furthermore, while turn-based combat is the norm in Japanese RPGs, most RPGs overseas are games in which the combat is also action oriented. Overseas, Japanese RPGs are called JRPGs, which are treated as a separate genre from the general RPGs.

[25]Shooters in Japan (called "shump" outside of Japan) and Shooters outside of Japan are completely different genres. The type in which the player's viewpoint is the same as that of the character being controlled (i.e., the main character is not on the game screen) is called FPS (First Person Shooter), and the type in which the player is looking at the back of the character (i.e., third person viewpoint) is called TPS (Third Person Shooter). The game genres are almost the same.

[26]Furthermore, even in soccer games, Konami's eFootBall (Winning Eleven) series is strong in Japan, while EA's FIFA series is strong overseas.

Table 12.2 Number of titles developed in Japan in top 100 titles in North America

	Nintendo	Other Japanese companies	Total
2005	14	16	30
2006	20	15	35
2007	25	9	34
2008	22	13	35
2009	25	10	35

Source: Prepared by the author from http://vgchartz.com

Table 12.3 Number of titles developed abroad in top 100 Japanese titles

	Overseas titles
2005	1
2006	0
2007	2
2008	1
2009	0

Source: Prepared by the author from http://vgchartz.com

hit titles overseas because it can create games for children and families, which appeal to a target audience that Western game companies are not good at (Table 12.2).

In addition, differences in artwork preferences, which had not been much of an issue in the past, now had a decisive impact: In the era of 2D graphics and the low polygonal expressiveness of the PlayStation era, characters were forced to be deformed, and as a result, there was no significant difference in their designs. As a result of the rise in the expressive power of game consoles, there is no longer any difference between the illustrator's settings and the in-game characters' drawings. As a result, the difference between the type of pictures favored in the West and the anime-style pictures found in Japanese games became clear, and the difference in taste for expression became obvious. This is particularly evident in the small number of foreign-made titles in the Japanese market (Table 12.3). Due in part to differences in user preferences, Japanese companies have struggled to sell games overseas, but the domestic market has not been eroded.

12.3.2 *The Increasing Scale of Game Development and Isolation from Global Markets*

As the performance of game consoles increased and the capacity of the media on which games were offered grew, game development became increasingly large-scale. The number of staff involved in development increased from single digits at the time of the Famicom to well over 100. The expansion of the scale of game development is confirmed by Dragon Quest, a major RPG with staff rolls written in real names from the first game released on the Famicom. Table 12.4 counts the

Table 12.4 Number of people appearing in Staff Roll of Chronological Dragon Quest

	DQ1	DQ2	DQ3	DQ4	DQ5	DQ6	DQ7	DQ8
Scenario Game Design	2	2	3	6	7	5	10	14
Graphics	4	2	2	3	7	10	24	61
Music & Sound	1	1	1	1	1	3	2	5
Programmer Engineer	3	6	6	10	19	10	23	13
Other development staff	3	3	5	9	34	0	0	15
Test Play QA	0	0	0	0	0	25	50	56
Sales promotion	1	2	2	5	3	9	17	49
Overlap	1	1	0	0	0	1	0	1
Total	13	15	19	34	71	61	126	212
Console	FC	FC	FC	FC	SFC	SFC	PS	PS2
Media	ROM	ROM	ROM	ROM	ROM	ROM	CD	DVD
Data size	512 K	1 M	2 M	4 M	12 M	32 M	2 disks	1 disk
Release	1986	1987	1988	1990	1992	1996	2000	2004

Data size: bit for ROM

number of people who appear in the staff rolls at the end of Dragon Quest games from the first to the eighth game, and categorizes them according to their work roles.[27] It clearly shows that development became larger and larger as the generation progressed from the Famicom to the PlayStation 2. The impact of the larger scale can be seen throughout, but the increase in the number of graphics-related departments is particularly significant among them. In addition, the interval between releases indicates that development on PS and PS2 requires not only more people but also more time.

Dragon Quest has not released a numbered title on PS3, but the scale of development on PS3 is generally even larger than on PS2. The 13th title (FF XIII) of Final Fantasy (FF), a major RPG that has been described alongside Dragon Quest, was

[27] In counting the number of people, Special Thanks are excluded. In the classification, heads of departments, such as graphic directors, were placed in their respective departments (in this case, the graphics department). Directors with no specific title were included in the "Other Staff" category, and producers were included in the "Sales Activities" category. As a result, some works have no staff at all. Dragon Quest did not add voices to the characters, but many games after the popularization of disc media added voices to the characters, so the names of voice actors are added to the staff roll at the end of the game. In addition to the number of people's names counted, DQ7 has four company names in the graphics system (TOSE, TAMTAM, TINY ART, and ARTE PIAZZA), and DQ8 has one company name in sound (TOSE). in DQ8, in addition to that, the end of the QA staff rolls "... and All QA Staff" at the end of the QA staff role in DQ8, suggesting that more people were actually involved in QA than in the table.

released on PS3 and had over 200 developers at its peak (180 artists, 30 programmers, and 36 game designers).[28] Final Fantasy XIII also struggled with communication within the huge development organization, leading to significant delays in development.[29]

The scale and cost of development vary greatly depending on what type of game is being developed and on what scale, but in the era of the PS3, the production cost of major titles (AAA titles) created with the maximum amount of resources and technology has surpassed that of the average Hollywood movie. For example, the development cost of Grand Theft Auto IV (Rockstar Games, 2008) is over $100 million, and other AAA titles across the board have development costs exceeding tens of millions of dollars. In order to recover the development cost of tens of millions of dollars, it is necessary to sell more than one million units, which cannot be recovered by selling only in Japan, with the exception of a few titles. However, in the Western market, which is several times the size of the domestic market, sales of Japanese games are not expected except for Nintendo and a few specific titles. As a result, it is very difficult to develop AAA titles in Japan, except for a few sequels that are popular overseas.

The lack of growth in global sales, despite soaring development costs, led the Japanese game industry to focus on a business model based on domestic recoupment. As a result of the different tastes in games and the lack of significant influx of foreign-made games, the Galapagosization of the Japanese market has developed.

12.3.3 Responding to Risks Associated with Large-Scale Game Development

Soaring development costs in a situation where overseas sales are not expected to be very high have led to a conservative approach to development. Specifically, there was an increase in the number of "titles that can be expected to generate solid sales," such as sequels to hit titles, ports (remakes) of old hit titles, and game titles using characters from animated films and existing hit titles. Consumers also supported sequel titles and remakes. Figure 12.3 shows the ratio of series sequels and ports to the top 100 selling titles in each year (series title ratio). Already from 1996, more than half of the titles were sequels, but in 2002–2003 and 2007, the ratio exceeded 80%. In general, new series titles tend to be created immediately after the

---

[28] Remarks made by Motomu Toriyama, Director of FF 13, in his speech at GDC Taipei in Taiwan in 2012.

[29] Game Developer's Magazine, a trade publication for game developers (now defunct), published a postmortem on Final Fantasy (an article in which the developers give a retrospective of the development process after development was completed), in which it is stated that in the early stages of development there was a "Lack Of A Shared Vision" in the early stages of development. http://www.gamasutra.com/view/news/121381/Exclusive_Behind_The_Scenes_Of_Square_Enixs_Final_Fantasy_XIII.php

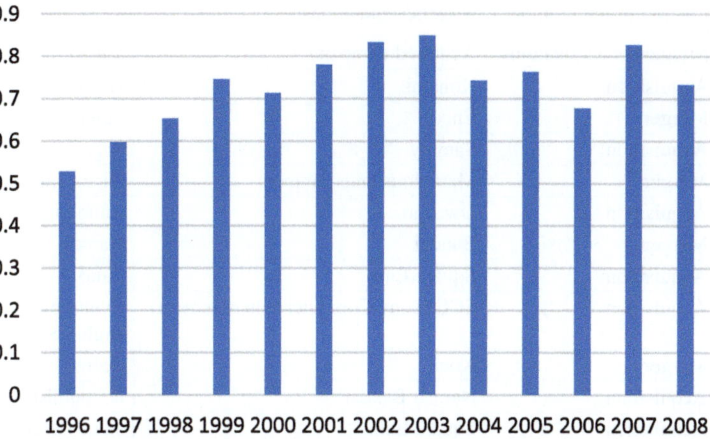

Fig. 12.3 Percentage of series titles among the top 100 titles sold during the year (In order to avoid counting the same title twice, the title that ranked in the top 100 for the second consecutive year counts only for the first appearance except for 1996. Therefore, the denominator other than 1996 is smaller than 100). Source: Created by the author from the annual editions of Famitsu Game White Paper

introduction of new hardware, and the series title ratio declined once from 2004 to 2006, when a number of new innovative games were released for the DS. However, sequels to DS hit titles and DS ports of past hit titles began to occupy the top positions, and the ratio of series titles returned to 70–80%.

The increasing importance of series titles in the game market has increased the importance of IP (Intellectual Property, which in the game industry refers to past good title assets) as a source of competitiveness for game companies. However, even for sequels to past excellent series, there are many series that sell fewer units than their predecessors as players become bored with the continued release of sequels. In addition, for series that were profitable when developed on a PS or PS2 budget but not profitable when developed on a large scale for PS3 or later, sequels were either not released or, if released, were released on portable game consoles such as the DS and PSP.

The series that were the last titles released for console and no sequels were Breath of Fire (the fifth title released for PS2 in 2002 was the last), Sakura Taisen (Sakura Wars) (the fifth title released for PS2 in 2005 was the last), Wild Arms (the fifth title released for PS2 in 2006 was the last), and Growlanser (the sixth title released for PS2 in 2007 was the last), and so on. Although ported versions of these games have been released for portable consoles, new titles are no longer being released. In the shump game genre, Gradius, which dominated the arcade game market, has not released a new title since Gradius V was released in 2004. Subsequently, for some titles, the PS4 generation, they were revived.

The shift to handheld devices has occurred regardless of genre, with Shin Megami Tensei and its derivative series Persona (RPG), Senjo no Valkyria (Valkyria

Table 12.5 Major intercompany mergers/acquisitions

	Mergers or acquisitions	Acquired company	Target of acquisition
2001	Acquisition	Konami	Hudson
2003	Merger	Enix	Square
2003	Acquisition	Sammy	Sega
2003	Merger	Marvelous entertainment	Victor Interactive
2005	Acquisition	Dwango	Chun Soft
2005	Merger	Bandai	Namco
2005	Acquisition	Square Enix	Taito
2007	Acquisition	SCE (Sony Computer Entertainment)	Evolution Studio (UK) Bigbig Studio (UK)
2009	Merger	Koei	Tecmo
2009	Acquisition	Namco Bandai	D3 publisher
2009	Acquisition	Square Enix	eidos (UK)

Chronicle) (SLG), Itadaki Street (Fortune Street) (board game), and Tokimeki Memorial (date simulation) also moving to handheld devices.

In addition, intercompany mergers and acquisitions continued as a response to risk. Table 12.5 shows the major mergers and acquisitions that occurred in the Japanese game industry from 2001 to 2009. Mergers and acquisitions were undertaken not only because they provide economies of scale, thereby increasing the risk of game development failure (i.e., the ability to withstand losses when huge titles fail to sell), but also because the powerful IP possessed by the company is an important management resource. In some cases, such as Square Enix and SCE, overseas game development companies (studios) have been acquired in order to gain the ability to develop leading content for overseas markets.

For small and medium-sized game companies left behind in the merger process, it has become very difficult to publish games on console game consoles. There were only three options left:

1. Concentrate on producing games for handheld game consoles.[30]
2. Enter the market after several years had passed since the launch of game consoles, when the price of development equipment had dropped and the environment for middleware and libraries had been improved.[31]
3. Launch graphic novel games that do not require technological sophistication.

[30] Since the launch of PS4, the situation is different again, as there are more cases of simultaneous development and release of the same title for both console and handheld devices.

[31] An example of a smaller video game company, and one that concentrated on handheld video game consoles, is Nihon Falcom. Another example of a company that counted after a long time after the launch of console games is Atlus, which released Catherine for PS3 and Xbox360 for the first time in 2011. However, Catherine is also a puzzle game rather than an RPG, which would have been not expensive to develop.

Table 12.6 Difference between estimated cost and suggested retail price at the time of release of each game console

Console	Release	Retail price	Estimated cost	Difference (rough estimate)
PlayStation 2	2000	39,800 yen $299.99 (US)	$440	−5000 yen
Xbox	2002 2001 (US)	34,800 yen $300(US)	$323	−2500 yen
Xbox360	2005	39795 yen $400 (US)	$525	−12,500 yen
PlayStation 3 (20G)	2006	49,980 yen $500 (US)	$805.85	−30,000 yen
Wii	2006	25,000 yen $250 (US)	Less than 15,000 yen	+10,000 yen

Data source: Nikkei Electronics each issues, iSuppli reports

12.4 Summary: End of the Era of "Game Consoles as a Technology Driver"

With the huge success of PlayStation, video game consoles became a place where new technologies were challenged. Cutting-edge technology was lavishly invested in CPUs and graphics chips, and hundreds of billions of yen were invested to build dedicated factories. This investment was intended to create a virtuous cycle that would increase the expressive power of games, attract new customers, and expand the market. However, the size of the domestic market in Japan stagnated, and portable video game consoles took over the leading role (see next chapter). Moreover, although the market size continued to rise when viewed on an international scale, the game industry found it impossible to bear the rising R&D and investment costs as each generation progressed.

Table 12.6 shows the estimated cost at launch and list price (suggested retail price) at the time of sale for each game console. Since the PlayStation 2, all game consoles except for Nintendo's Wii have not only had a reverse spread (cost > list price), but the reverse spread has been expanding.[32]

This is the result of holding down the selling price by placing the highest priority on the popularization of the hardware. The reverse spread is supposed to be recovered by increasing the hardware's popularity and the number of game software sold. However, in order for SCE to recover the 30,000 yen reverse spread for PlayStation 3, it would need to sell 30 games if it only received licensing fees from other companies, and 15 or more if it received revenue from its own game

[32] In reality, the reverse spread is even larger when shipping and other costs are taken into account, as well as the fact that hardware shipments to retailers are approximately 90% of the retail price.

development.[33] This is an amount that would be difficult to recover even during the entire product life cycle from the time consumers purchase the hardware until they stop using it. The Xbox360's reverse spread is lower than that of the PS3 at 12,500 yen, but even this is a level that requires several years to generate a profit from hardware purchasers.

Deficits due to the reverse spread would not be a problem if they had ended in a relatively short period of time and moved into a profitable position. However, in this generation of competition, it was the Wii that sold well at the time of its launch, while PS3 sales were sluggish. The huge backlog took a long time to clear, and the company continued to lose money throughout the period.[34] Finally, SCE became insolvent as of the March 2009 financial results.[35] SCE reinvested much of the profits earned from the PS into the PS2, which earned even greater profits. However, the struggles of PS3 (and PSP) drained all the accumulated profits.

Microsoft also invested $21 billion over the 5 years from 2002 to 2006 during the Xbox era, but hardware sales did not do well, and as of 2007, when the next hardware, the Xbox360, was launched, the game-related business segment reportedly had an accumulated loss of $5.4 billion. Although the company became profitable in 2008 after the launch of the Xbox360, the accumulated losses are not believed to have been eliminated as of fiscal year 2015.[36]

There are two reasons why the hardware backlog has become so huge and hardware sales have been sluggish:

1. As a game console, it was impossible to set a high price.
2. HD-compatible TVs (or even full HD-compatible TVs) that could take advantage of the high-definition screens of the PS3 and Xbox360 were not yet widely available in homes and were over-spec'd.

---

[33] Normally, the revenue received by a game company for each console game is about half the price of the package. In the case of a platform holder, this includes a license fee plus a package production fee. Since the package price is about 7000 yen, Sony earns less than 4000 yen per game developed in-house. Naturally, the remainder of the profit after development costs are recovered is the profit, which is 15 games at 2000 yen per game.

[34] According to some reports, the amount of the reverse spread itself has declined, but the reverse spread was still in place at the end of 2009.

[35] Sony renamed SCE as SNE Platform and separated the network business and game-related business. The network business was then merged into Sony Corporation, eliminating its debt, and the game division was transferred to a new company (company name: Sony Computer Entertainment). Therefore, strictly speaking, the current SEE (Sony Interactive Entertainment; changed its name from SCE in 2016) is a different company from the SCE of the PlayStation 1 and 2 days.

[36] Microsoft's gaming business is listed in the Entertainment and Device Division in the financial results. This Division once included the Zune music player and now the Surface tablet, so the details of the situation are unclear. However, total profit since 2008 have not exceeded $5 billion, and the accumulated losses in the gaming business do not appear to have been eliminated.

HD-compatible TVs became popular in Japan around 2010,[37] when terrestrial analog broadcasting stopped and it became necessary to purchase terrestrial digital TVs. The reverse spread had been eliminated by this time, and hardware unit sales improved as a result of the TV penetration push, resulting in improved earnings. However, the financial crisis of 2008 and the subsequent cooling down of the video game market overseas did not lead to a significant recovery.

Only Nintendo's Wii did not have a reverse spread, and hardware sales were favorable due in part to the new concept. However, the product life was short, probably due to lack of performance.

Thus, console video game consoles in Japan lost their attractiveness as a market due to the following three factors: (1) a shift in the market's center of gravity toward handheld consoles (discussed in detail in the next chapter), (2) soaring development costs due to the expansion of the scale of development, and (3) a major hardwares' reverse spread. The days when the game industry was the technology driver of the semiconductor industry due to the overwhelming number of units sold and high profitability are now a thing of the past. In the next generation, both the technology driver and the market center will shift to smartphones.

[37]More to the point, eco-points, which were given as part of the recovery from the Great East Japan Earthquake, helped popularize TVs.

Chapter 13
Console Games (4) Market Reversal by Handheld Game Consoles

Abstract This chapter provides an overview of portable video game consoles from the 1980s to the 2000s, which have not been previously discussed. The first successful handheld video game console was Nintendo's Game Boy, released in 1989, and its longevity was extended by the huge hit of Pokemon in 1996, and it remained the most popular video game console until the Game Boy Advance was released in 2000. In addition, the average age of game players has been aging, making it difficult for them to continue playing in front of the TV, and the rise in performance and development costs for portable game consoles has been slower than for home video game consoles connected to TVs.

Keywords GameBoy · Pokemon · GameBoy Advance · Nintendo DS · PSP · Aging Society · Market shift

In previous chapters, we have not discussed portable video game consoles. For a long time, handheld video game consoles played a supporting role in the home video game market, but the situation has been reversed since 2006. In this chapter, we will review the trend from Game Boy to Nintendo DS. Nintendo 3DS and PS VITA will be discussed in Chap. 15, along with smartphones.

13.1 Prehistory of Handheld Game Consoles: Game Pocket Computer

As already mentioned in Chap. 5, in the early 1980s, single-function game consoles called LSI games hit the toy market ahead of home video game consoles. Among these, Nintendo's Game & Watch was a big hit, leading to the Famicom, and in 1985, 2 years after the Famicom was launched, EPOCH released the Game Pokecom[1]

[1] Pokecom (Pocket computers) were portable computers widely used in the 1980s. It was more powerful than a functional calculator, but less than a desktop computer. It had a Qwerty-type keyboard and an LCD screen that could display a few lines of information, and it could run simple

Y. Koyama, *History of the Japanese Video Game Industry*, Translational Systems Sciences 35, https://doi.org/10.1007/978-981-99-1342-8_13

(Game Pocket Computer). The Game Pokecom was a game console with interchangeable cartridges which cost 12,000 yen. The Famicom, which was booming at the time, costs 14,800 yen. The Game Pokecom was not well received by consumers at a price that was only slightly lower than Famicom. As a result, only five games were released.

13.2 The First Generation of Handheld Video Game Consoles: Game Boy and Game Gear

Nintendo launched the Game Boy (abbreviated as GB in the chart) in 1989. The Game Boy was developed not by the Development Division 2, which developed the Famicom, but by the Development Division 1, which developed the Game & Watch. Like the Famicom, the Game Boy was developed as a toy (i.e., for children to play with), and was designed on the premise that it could be played with for enough time on dry batteries. For this reason, the screen display had four monochrome shades and a resolution of 160 × 144 pixels, which was smaller than that of the Famicom. The battery life was long, as it used a reflective LCD that did not need a backlight to conserve battery power and could be played for about 35 hours on four alkaline AA batteries.[2]

The four launch titles in April 1989 were Alleyway (a so-called Block-kuzushi game), Yakuman (a mahjong game), Baseball, and Super Mario Land, each of which was a hit due to its low price of 2500 yen.[3] Tetris,[4] which was released in June, led to the hardware's popularization. The Game Boy was equipped with a function that allowed users to play through communication by connecting two Game Boy consoles via a cable, and Tetris was the first title to make use of the communication function, becoming a big hit with 4.24 million copies sold (Table 13.1).

In 1990, the year after the Game Boy was released, Sega released the Game Gear (abbreviated as GG in the chart). The hardware performance was almost the same as

programs. The reason why Epoch released the product under the name Pokecom was because the Pokecom was positioned as an introductory device not only for engineers but also for junior and senior high school students.

[2] Source: Nintendo Web page Game Boy Specifications Comparison Chart for All Models http://www.nintendo.co.jp/n02/dmg/hardware/gbtaihi/

[3] The price of Game Boy titles varied greatly depending on the capacity of the ROM used, with titles in the later years of the hardware costing between 4 and 5000 yen.

[4] Tetris was a title developed by Soviet Union scientist Aleksei Pzhtonov and ported to various hardware in various countries. In Japan, the arcade version of Tetris (1988), created under license by Sega, was a big hit, and a Megadrive version porting it was scheduled for release, but the rights to sell the game on home consoles were licensed to Nintendo, so the Megadrive version was cancelled. In addition to arcades and home consoles, Tetris was also ported to various PCs in Japan.

Table 13.1 Pricing of the Past Game Boy

Released year	Name	Price
1989	Game Boy	12,000 yen
1994	Game Boy Bros	8000 yen
1996	Game Boy Pocket	6800 yen
1998	Game Boy light	6800
	Game Boy pocket (After price down)	5800 yen (Feb. 1998) 3800 yen (Nov. 1998)
	Game Boy Color	8900 yen

Table 13.2 Specifications of Game Boy and Game Gear

	Game Boy	Game Gear
Company	Nintendo	Sega
Released Year	1989	1990
Price	12,500 yen	19,800 yen
CPU	Customized Z80 (4 MHz)	Z80A (3.58 MHz)
Graphic Solution Colors	160*144 4 monochrome gradations	160*146 32 colors in 4096 colors
LCD	2.5 inch monochrome STN Reflection type (no backlight)	3.2inch color STN With Backlight
Power source	4 AA batteries	6 AA batteries
Operable time	35 h	3 h

that of the Mark III,[5] an 8-bit machine released by Sega, and it was by far more powerful than the Game Boy. It used a color LCD so that it could be played in color like a home video game console, but the hardware suffered from various side effects associated with the color LCD (Table 13.2).

The color LCD used by Game Gear had the following three problems:

1. The sales price did not allow the use of fast-responding TFT LCDs, and the Game Gear could only use slow-responding STN LCDs. STN LCDs left afterimages on the screen in action games with fast-moving characters and were not easy to play.
2. Color LCD components had not yet been made smaller and lighter, and the hardware was large and heavy.
3. The LCD backlight consumed a lot of electricity, and although it required six AA batteries to operate, the batteries lasted only about 3 h.

[5]By attaching a non-genuine adapter sold in Akihabara and other places, software for the Mark III/Master System can be run on the Game Gear without modification.

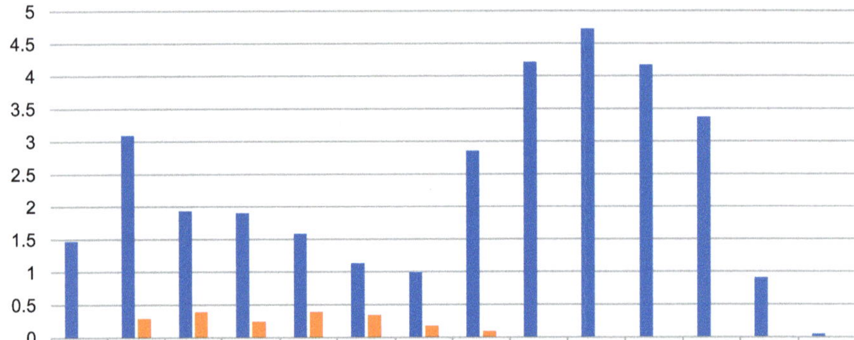

	1989	1990	1991	1992	1993	1994	1995	1996	1997	1998	1999	2000	2001	2002
GB	1.48	3.1	1.94	1.91	1.59	1.14	1	2.86	4.22	4.73	4.18	3.37	0.91	0.05
GG		0.3	0.4	0.25	0.4	0.35	0.18	0.1						

Fig. 13.1 Game Boy and Game Gear sales volume (millions). Source: *Information Media White Paper* 2003 edition

The Game Gear sold several hundred thousand units each year, eventually selling 1.78 million units in Japan, but the Game Boy was a failed hardware in Japan due to a significant sales gap.[6]

As shown in Fig. 13.1, Game Boy sales peaked for the first time in 1990 and then slowly declined from 1991 onward. In 1994, Nintendo tried to bounce back by selling the Game Boy Bros. at a reduced price (8000 yen), but by 1995, sales had dropped to 1 million units.

Six years after the hardware's release, the product's life cycle was nearing its end, but the market was revitalized in 1996 by the historic success of Pokémon (over 10 million units in total for Red, Green, and Blue). The Game Boy Pocket, with an even lower price and lighter weight, was released, and at its second peak from 1997 to 1999, the number of units sold was well over 4 million.

In 1998, during the Game Boy's second hit period, the Game Boy Color was released. It was an upward-compatible system with a color LCD, and was almost identical to the Game Boy, except that Game Boy Color-specific software and Game Boy/Color compatible software could play in 52 out of 32,268 colors. When it was first released, most of the software was compatible with both Game Boy and Game Boy Color, but after 2000, the last year of the hardware's life, most of the software was color-only software.

The Neo Geo Pocket was released in 1998 and the Wonder Swan in 1999, but they did not pose much of a threat, and the Game Boy eventually became a huge hit, selling 32.47 million units in Japan and 118.69 million units overseas combined. The

[6]The Game Gear lost the competition to the Game Boy overseas as well, but did better than in Japan. The total number of units sold in Japan and abroad exceeded 10 million, and more than 80% of the hardware was sold overseas.

Game Boy remained highly popular in an environment with virtually no competition, and passed the baton to the Game Boy Advance, which was released in 2001.

13.3 Second Generation of Handheld Video Game Consoles: Wonder Swan, Neo Geo Pocket, Game Boy Advance

The second generation of handheld video game consoles began with the Neo Geo Pocket (hereafter abbreviated as NGP in the chart), released by SNK in 1998. Reflecting technological advances, it used a 16-bit CPU (plus a Z80 for sound) but kept the LCD monochrome and could be played for 20 hours on two AAA batteries. It was the subject of an exciting TV commercial that made fun of the Game Boy, "I'm not BOY." However, sales were limited to about 20,000 units in the first week of sales,[7] as it had been announced that a color version would be released the following year. The color version released the following year also did not sell well, selling only 500,000 units as of December 2000.[8] Due to the poor sales of the Neo Geo Pocket, SNK began receiving support from Aruze in 2000, and in 2001, SNK was subjected to the Civil Rehabilitation Act.

In 1999, Bandai released the WonderSwan (abbreviated as WS in the chart). The Wonder Swan was a game console developed and planned by Gunpei Yokoi, who had retired from Nintendo. While following in the footsteps of the Game Boy with its monochrome LCD and long battery life (30 h of play time on a single AA battery), the WonderSwan also introduced new features, such as the ability to play either in portrait or landscape mode. The hardware price was kept quite low at 4800 yen.

At the time of the hardware launch, GUNPEY and other titles released at the same time were well received, and 1.55 million units were sold by the end of 2000.[9] At the end of 2000, WonderSwan Color was released with a color LCD. However, because of adopting the inexpensive FSTN LCD, it was not well received due to its difficult-to-read screen and high level of afterimages, and shipments during the 2 years were limited to 1.4 million units[10] (Fig. 13.2). When Nintendo released the Game Boy Advance (GBA) in 2001, it suffered from competition. In 2002, Swan Crystal with a TFT LCD was prepared, but competition had already been decided, and the

[7]http://www.geocities.co.jp/Playtown-Bingo/9553/np/uriage.html

[8]Nikkei Shimbun Newspaper, December 2, 2000.

[9]From the press release for the launch of WonderSwan Color, August 30, 2000. http://www.bandai.co.jp/releases/images/3/204.pdf#page=1

[10]Nikkei Shimbun, "Bandai's new handheld video game console with TFT LCD," May 9, 2002.

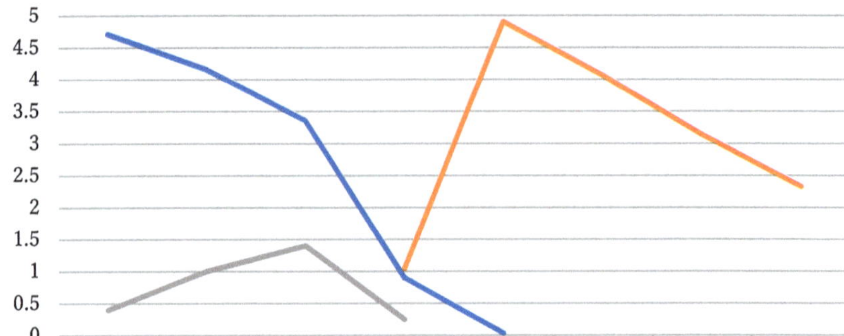

	1998	1999	2000	2001	2002	2003	2004	2005
GB	4.73	4.18	3.37	0.91	0.05			
GBA				1.06	4.92	4.08	3.15	2.34
WS	0.4	1	1.4	0.25				

Fig. 13.2 Game Boy, Game Boy Advance, WonderSwan sales volume (millions). Source: GB (until 2000) & WS: *Information Media White Paper* 2003 edition. GB (after 2000), GBA: Nintendo web page (Sales data published on the Nintendo Web page are based on the fiscal year. Therefore, FY 3/2001 refers to the year up to March 2001 (April 2000–March 2001). In the graph, it is displayed 1 year ahead of time to make it easy to see)

company withdrew from the handheld video game console market in 2003, producing only the units ordered by retailers.[11]

The Game Boy Advance (abbreviated as GBA in the chart below), released by Nintendo in 2001, was not only upwardly compatible with previous models and capable of running Game Boy software, but it was also the only one at the time with a 32-bit CPU and was released with a color LCD from the start. The Game Boy Advance was the first to enter the market, and it took full advantage of its latecomer and previous-generation advantages.

The Game Boy Advance quickly became popular in the market, partly due to replacement demand for the Game Boy (Fig. 13.2). The Game Boy used a reflective TFT LCD, which was the most common type of handheld video game console at the time, but the problem was that the screen was quite dark because of battery life considerations. Reflecting this, the Game Boy Advance SP, released in 2003, had a smaller body with a twofold structure and was equipped with a front light.[12] The Game Boy Advance SP also replaced the conventional dry cell batteries with rechargeable lithium-ion batteries, which became the standard for handheld video

[11] Bandai's representatives knew before the launch of WonderSwan that Nintendo was planning to release a successor to Game Boy with a color LCD. When Bandai explained this to then Nintendo President Yamauchi prior to the launch of WonderSwan, he urged Bandai to be cautious, saying, "Nintendo will soon release a color version of Game Boy, and black and white won't sell well. Bandai should avoid using black and white because it won't sell well" (Nikkei Business Daily, August 20, 2012).

[12] The Game Boy Advance SP's LCD remained reflective rather than backlit. Therefore, it was possible to play with the front light off in bright areas to improve visibility and reduce battery drain.

Table 13.3 NEOGEO Pocket, WonderSwan, Game Boy Advance Specification

	NEOGEO POCKET/Color	WonderSwan/Color	Game Boy Advance
Company	SNK	Bandai	Nintendo
Release	1998/1999	1999/2000	2001
Price	7800/ 8900 JPY	4800/8900 JPY	8800 JPY
CPU	TLCS-900H (6.144 MHz)	V30MZ[a]	ARM7 (Z80 is also installed for compatibility with Game Boy) (16.7 MHz)
RAM	16 KB	16 KB	384 KB
Graphic Solution Colors	160 * 152 8 monochrome gradations/ 146 in 4096 colors	224 * 144 8 monochrome gradations/ 241 in 4096 colors	240 * 160 512 in 32,768 colors
LCD	2.6inch TFT Reflection type (no backlight)	2.49inch/ 2.8 inch FSTN Reflection type (no backlight)	2.9inch TFT Reflection type (no backlight)
Power source	2 AAA batteries/2 AA batteries Lithium Button Battery (for backup)	1 AA battery	2 AA batteries
Operational time	20 h/40 h	30 h/20 h	15 h
Remarks	Connection with Dreamcast (NEOGEO POCKET had a function to connect the Dreamcast with dedicated cable and transfer game data to each other. There were only a handful of compatible software)	Release of Swan Crystal with TFT liquid crystal in 2002	Compatible with Game Boy/Color

[a]The V30MZ is the embedded core of the V30 CPU developed by NEC, and the Wonder Swan incorporates the V30MZ in the ASWAN, a one-chip LSI. ASWAN was developed by Koto Corporation (a company founded by Gunpei Yokoi, who retired from Nintendo)

game consoles in the future. In 2005, after the release of the Nintendo DS, a more compact Game Boy Micro was released.

Business was good for the Game Boy Advance, with final shipments totaling 8.151 million units in Japan and abroad. While the GameCube (2001) was sluggish in the console market, the Game Boy Advance was able to support the backbone of Nintendo's earnings. The old Game Boy hardware lasted for as long as 12 years, but SCE's decision to develop and launch a new handheld video game console led to the launch of the GBA's successor, the Nintendo DS, in 2004, 4 years after its launch (Table 13.3).

13.4 Portable Digital Pet Hits and Memory Cards

The digital pet Tamagotchi released by Bandai in 1996 became a huge boom, and its influence spread to the video game industry, resulting in the creation of a linkage with small video game consoles. The success of Tamagotchi led to the release of a myriad of digital pets, including a device that combined a pedometer with a digital pet and grew according to the number of steps taken. The Tekutekku Angel released by Hudson in 1997 and the Pocket Pikachu released by Nintendo in 1998 became hit products. The successor, Pocket Pikachu kin to gin to issho! (Pocket Pikachu Color with Gold and Silver!) not only had a color LCD, but also could communicate with the Game Boy Color via an infrared communication function, allowing users to exchange their walking achievements for items from the Game Boy Color gam Pokémon Gold and Silver.

Against this backdrop, SCE and Sega, both supplying home video game consoles at the time, entered this market in the form of handheld memory cards that were connected to the console and recorded game progress data, respectively.

Sega's Visual Memory, the standard memory card for the Dreamcast released in 1998, included a CPU, a monochrome LCD, a cross-key and two buttons, and a visual memory-to-memory communication function. Since few games were compatible with visual memory, and the games that could be played with visual memory were not very appealing, visual memory was not often played. In addition, many users used third-party products that only had a mere memory function, because the visual memory had less memory capacity to store vital save data due to the LCD screen and space for batteries.

In 1999, SCE launched the Pocket Station, a memory card with a CPU, LCD screen, and up, down, left, right, and decision buttons. The system was linked to the saved data of games played on the PlayStation, and the results of mini games could be reflected in the main unit's games. The Dokodemo Issho (everywhere with you) game released in 1999 was a huge hit, and the Pocket Station was in short supply for a while. Toro, the Dokodemo Issho character, became a mascot character that appeared in SCE advertisements for a long time, just like Nintendo's Mario and Sega's Sonic. However, other than Dokodemo Issho, there were no other hits, and the PlayStation 2 memory card released in 2000 reverted to a simple data storage function.

13.5 Handheld Video Game Consoles Third Generation: PSP and DS

Around 2001, when Nintendo launched the GBA, handheld video game consoles accounted for about 30% of all video game software sold in Japan. Much of this share was accounted for by Nintendo hardware, which was a major source of revenue for Nintendo, which was being pushed by home video game consoles.

With the PlayStation 2, which was released in 2000, also on track to become popular, SCE decided to enter the handheld video game console market as well.

On May 13, 2003, the day before E3,[13] SCE announced that it would release a handheld video game console simultaneously worldwide by the end of next year.[14] At that time, it was only announced that it would be equipped with a CPU almost equivalent to that of PlayStation and a high-definition LCD display, and that games would be supplied on optical disks. However, in response to SCE's announcement, Nintendo also took countermeasures, and the day before E3 2004, Sony and Nintendo unveiled their PSP and Nintendo DS consoles for the first time, respectively.

Nintendo had just launched the Game Boy Advance in 2001, and business was going very well. However, the Game Boy Advance was a high-performance 2D game console, and it was clear that it would be at a major disadvantage in terms of performance when competing with the 3D-enhanced game console released by SCE. Therefore, it was decided to launch the Nintendo DS as a new hardware that would be sold alongside the Game Boy Advance while maintaining compatibility with the Game Boy Advance.

The Nintendo DS (handheld, 2004) and Wii (console, 2006), which were launched one after the other, both feature completely new user interfaces. The background to this novel product design was clearly explained in the president's speech at the Foreign Correspondents' Club of Japan on December 7, 2006.[15] Satoru Iwata, then president of Nintendo in 2002, was greatly concerned that the domestic video game software market had been shrinking since its peak in 1997. He believed that people leave gaming and in 2003, he decided that the basic strategy was to expand the gaming population. To expand the gaming population, it was necessary to take bold measures, and the conclusion reached was to "reset the existing game grammar once and for all. The result was the Nintendo DS,[16] a game console with

---

[13]Every year in mid-May, the Electronic Entertainment Expo (commonly known as E3), the largest computer game-related trade show, is held in Los Angeles, and companies often make major announcements in conjunction with this event. SCE's announcement of its entry into the handheld video game console market was made the day before E3. The following year, SCE and Nintendo announced the PSP and DS, respectively, on the day before E3.

[14]Only Japan actually launched the following year, at the end of 2004, and the rest of the world did not launch until 2005.

[15]http://www.nintendo.co.jp/event/061207/index.html

[16]The following is a quote from the speech:

So, Nintendo set its basic strategy as the "Expansion of the Gaming Population" in 2003.

We were trying to reach this goal by introducing products that can be enjoyed by anyone regardless of age, gender, or gaming experience. Internally, we had been repeatedly using such keywords as "for 5 to 95 years old" or "Let people to enjoy from the same start line."

The first tangible game machine we offered was Nintendo DS.

We thought that we would need to renovate the user interface if we wanted everyone to start playing from the same start line, and DS ended up having very unique configuration with dual-screen, touch screen, and microphone command inputs.

two screens[17] and a touch panel,[18] a novelty never seen before. The Nintendo DS has two screens, upper and lower, with a touch panel on the lower screen only. The touch pen can be used with the included stylus, a finger, or the tip of a pen, and it is possible to write text by sliding the pen across the screen. A microphone is also included, making it possible to use voice input for games. Games could be played through a dedicated card slot, and a Game Boy Advance slot was provided for Game Boy Advance compatibility. It was also equipped with a wireless LAN, making it possible to play against other players on the Internet using Nintendo's Nintendo Wi-Fi Connection service. The DS Wireless Play and DS Download Play[19] functions also made it possible for friends to connect to a LAN and play together.

The PSP, on the other hand, was positioned as a "Walkman for the twenty-first century[20]"when it was first conceived and announced in 2003 and was designed to be a portable multimedia player with powerful video playback capabilities and high-quality sound speakers. The PSP's primary data media was a newly designed UMD (Universal Media Disc) with a maximum capacity of 1.8 GB, which was to provide video and music as well as games. Memory Stick, used in Sony digital cameras and other products, was used as the write/read media. Like the Nintendo DS, it also employed wireless LAN, allowing players to connect to each other and add new software features by updating the system's firmware[21] (Table 13.4).

Two game consoles of vastly different natures were launched one after the other on December 2 (DS) and 12 (PSP), 2004. Nintendo shipped 500,000 units toward the launch date and sold more than 1 million units by the end of the year. On the other hand, PSP could prepare only 200,000 units for the launch day on December 12, 2004, due to the inadequacy of the mass sales system, and only about

---

[17]The two screens were the task that former President Yamauchi, who led Nintendo from a toy manufacturer to a world-class corporation, entrusted to President Iwata, Senior Managing Director Miyamoto, and the rest of the executive committee when he retired. Inoue (2009), p. 223.

[18]The touch panel is pressure-sensitive, unlike those used in current smartphones, and only one point can be recognized. Therefore, pinch-in (the action of using two fingers to zoom in on a designated spot) is not possible.

[19]DS Wireless Play is played when everyone has the software, while DS Download Play is played by having the other player download the game when the other player does not have the software. Naturally, download play has more restrictions.

[20]Goto Hiroshige no Weekly Kaigai News: Kutaragi Ken shinokataru jisedai keitai ge-muki PSP no hontou no nerai. (Hiroshige Goto's Weekly Overseas News: Ken Kutaragi talks about the real aim of the next generation handheld video game console, the PSP.) http://pc.watch.impress.co.jp/docs/2003/0829/kaigai014.htm

From today's perspective, if one were to think of a "device that has become as popular with people as the Walkman was in the twentieth century," it would undoubtedly be Apple's iPod/iPhone. However, in 2003, the iPod was still just a music player, and the iPod Touch, which led to the current iPhone, was first released in 2007.

[21]Using the firmware update feature, the PS3 connectivity was added in 2006. Also in 2008, it became possible to connect to the PlayStation Store to purchase and play games directly. However, the ability to play illegal software (e.g., emulators of past game hardware) by installing illegally modified firmware also became a problem.

Table 13.4 DS and PSP specifications

	Nintendo DS	PlayStation Portable
Company	Nintendo	Sony Computer Entertainment
Year	2004	2004
Price	15,000JPY	Open (Official Internet shop Price:20,790JPY)
CPU	ARM946E-S 67 MHz	MIPS R4000 Custom 333 MHz
Memory	Main 4 MB + VRAM 656 KB	Main 32 MB+ DRAM 4 MB
Solution Colors	256*192*2 18bit colors (about 260 thousand colors)	480 × 272 32bit colors (about 1.67 million colors)
Display	3-inch TFT*2	4.3-inch ASV
Power	Lithium-ion battery AC adapter	Lithium-ion battery AC adapter
Playable time	6–10 h	4–6 h
Remarks	Compatible with GBA Touch panel on the bottom screen (single point touch)	

500,000 units were sold even during the month of December. In February of the following year, shipments exceeded 1 million units.

Although the competition appeared fierce immediately after its launch, the DS soon overwhelmed the competition in terms of sales volume. In 2006, Nintendo shifted the number of units sold to DS Lite with the release of its smaller de facto successor, DS Lite, and by 2006, annual sales exceeded 9 million units. Although sales declined from 2007 due to a lull in popularity and a shift away from the new concept (see below), it was still a haunted hardware that sold 4 million units per year. In 2010, with the announcement of the next-generation 3DS, sales plummeted to 2 million units, and the PSP overtook it in sales.

PSP, on the other hand, saw sluggish hardware sales, although the shortage of units shipped at launch was resolved. However, hardware demand increased from 2007 onward, and in 2010 and 2011, hardware sales exceeded those of the DS (Fig. 13.3).

In the hardware competition, it is very rare to see a case in which a hardware that has lagged far behind will turn around a few years later. There are reasons for this occurrence for both the DS and PSP.

Among the Nintendo DS titles that were released simultaneously with the console were a mix of games that were different from previous games, such as Daigasso! Band Brothers (Jam with the Band) and Chokkan Hitofude (Polarium), among the titles released simultaneously with the console. In the following year, 2005, Nintendo released a new type of game, touted as Touch! Generations, which became a hit. Among the blockbuster titles were the Nintendogs series, which allowed users to interact with and care for dogs, and Tohoku Daigaku Mirai Kagaku-gijutsu kyodo-kenkyu Center Kawashima Ryuta kyoju kansyu No wo kitaeru Otona no

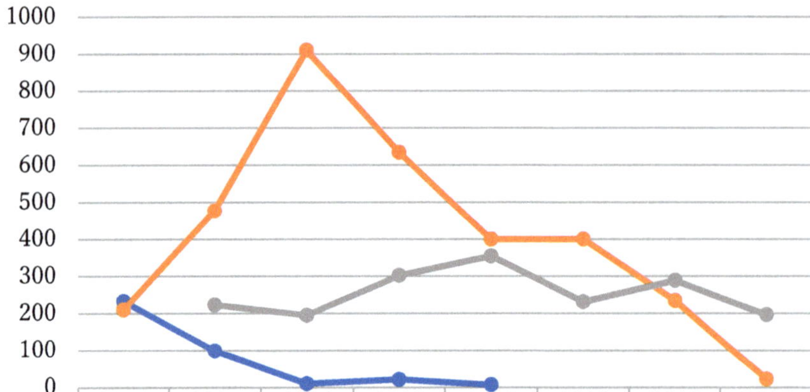

	2004	2005	2006	2007	2008	2009	2010	2011
GBA	234	100	11	22	8			
DS	212	478	912	636	401	401	235	23
PSP		223	195	302	354	231	289	196

Fig. 13.3 GBA, DS, and PSP unit sales. Source of data: PSP: Famitsu Game White Paper, each year edition (2004 figures are included in 2005), GBA and DS: Nintendo Web page (Figures published on Nintendo's Web page are in fiscal years, so "FY3/2001" refers to the one-year period ending March 2001 (April 2000 to March 2001). In the graph, the year is shifted by 1 year to make it easier to see)

DS training (Brain Age). The touch panel and two screens, an intuitive and easy-to-understand but unprecedented user interface, created a new and interesting user experience that led the game market. However, Touch! Generations did not produce a big hit until 2006.[22] Gradually, more and more existing types of games were released, and games that did not use the touch panel function at all, or if they did, they were only marginally better. Finally, it became a normal game console with a split vertical screen. Due to the large number of units in use, many titles were released until 2009 and 2010, the last year of the hardware's life, but only a few titles became hits, and it was highly characterized as hardware for light users.

On the other hand, the PSP did not have the novelty of the DS, and its hardware characteristics were geared toward game enthusiasts who wanted to play titles that were like those of existing game consoles. However, due in part to the poor response to the initial defect problem,[23] the hardware failed to sell to quality-sensitive enthusiasts, and the company got off to a sluggish start.

[22]The only exception is Rhythm Tengoku Gold (Rhtym Heaven), released in 2008. However, this was a sequel to a title released in 2006 for the Game Boy Advance, and it did not create anything new and interesting.

[23]Nikkei Business Online: "Sore ga PSP no shiyou da (That's the PSP Specification)," SCE President Kutaragi Kicks Off Game Console Trouble.

http://business.nikkeibp.co.jp/article/topics/20060308/100586/?rt=nocnt

The improvement in hardware sales since 2007 is directly attributable to the success of the Monster Hunter Portable series (Capcom). The first Monster Hunter game was released on the PS2 and was a hit for its cooperative play using an Internet connection. The port of this title, Monster Hunter Portable, made it easy for friends to gather in one place for cooperative play, allowing the full potential of the game to be utilized. The first Monster Hunter Portable game, released in December 2005, did not sell well at first because it was released before the hardware had become widely available, but it slowly spread by word of mouth.[24] The sequel, Monster Hunter Portable 2nd,[25] became a big hit, driving PSP hardware sales.

In addition, the launch of the PS3 in 2006 marked a generational shift in console hardware, and mid-level developers who developed games for enthusiasts shifted their main battlefield to handheld video game consoles due to the high development costs and difficulty of development. Many companies entered the PSP market, where the standard screen layout made it easy to port existing games, and the PSP became the hardware that attracted users who played games well.

13.6 Summary: Shift in the Leading Role... From a Complementary Role to the Center of the Market

The Nintendo DS and PSP have drastically changed the balance of power in the home video game market. Until then, handheld video game consoles had only played a complementary role in the console video game software market, but they have now reversed the market share.

Figures 13.4 and 13.5 show hardware sales and software sales for home consoles and handhelds from 2001 to 2010. From 2001 to 2004, home consoles and handheld video game consoles sold about the same amount of hardware, while software sales for home consoles dominated. As a result of the release of the PSP and DS at the end of 2004, from 2005 onward, handheld consoles overwhelmed home consoles in terms of hardware sales, and from 2006 onward, when hardware became popular to a certain extent, sales of software for handheld consoles also greatly exceeded those for home consoles.

The market structure has shifted significantly toward handheld devices for the following three reasons:

1. More than 20 years have passed since computer games first became popular, and the number of relatively older consumers has increased. They are not students or

[24]The low-priced version released in 2006 was also a hit, and continued to sell well after the release of Monster Hunter Portable 2nd in 2007, with final sales topping 1 million copies.

[25]Monster Hunter Portable 2nd was a huge hit, selling more than 1 million copies of the low-priced version, and its cumulative sales in Japan exceeded 4 million units. Monster Hunter has become one of the "national game series" along with Dragon Quest, Final Fantasy, and Pokémon.

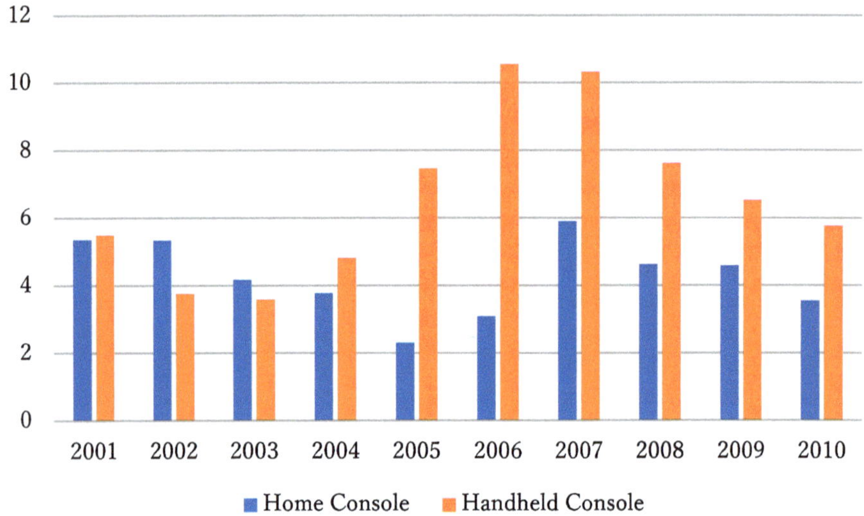

Fig. 13.4 Hardware sales volume of home console and handheld console (million units). Source: Game industry white paper DECADE

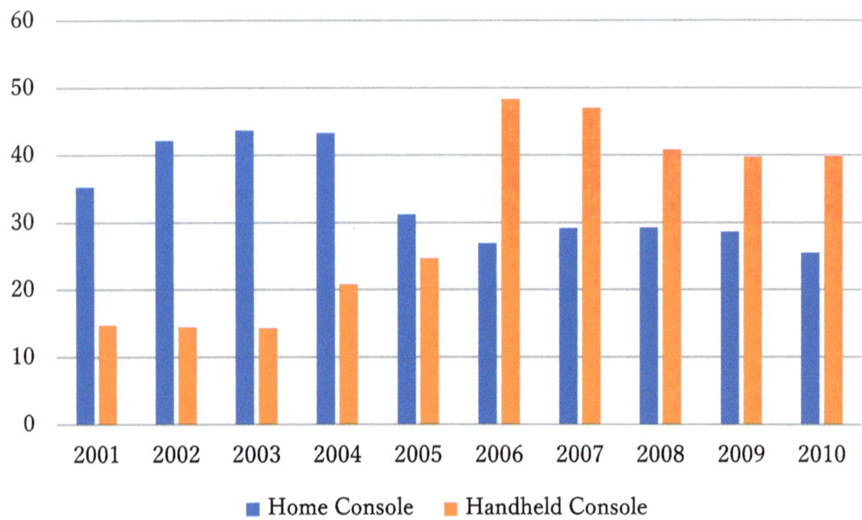

Fig. 13.5 Game software sales of home console and handheld console (million packages). Source: Game industry white paper DECADE

pupils who have plenty of time, but employed people who play in their limited leisure time. Therefore, it has become difficult for them to play in front of the TV at home, and they have shifted to portable consoles that allow them to play on the go.

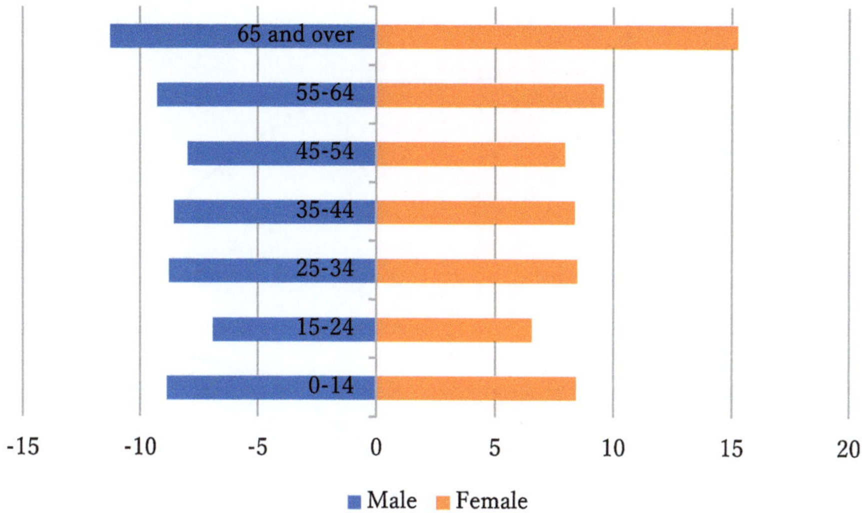

Fig. 13.6 Population pyramid in 2006 (Unit: million people). Source: Created by author from Japan e-stat population estimation data

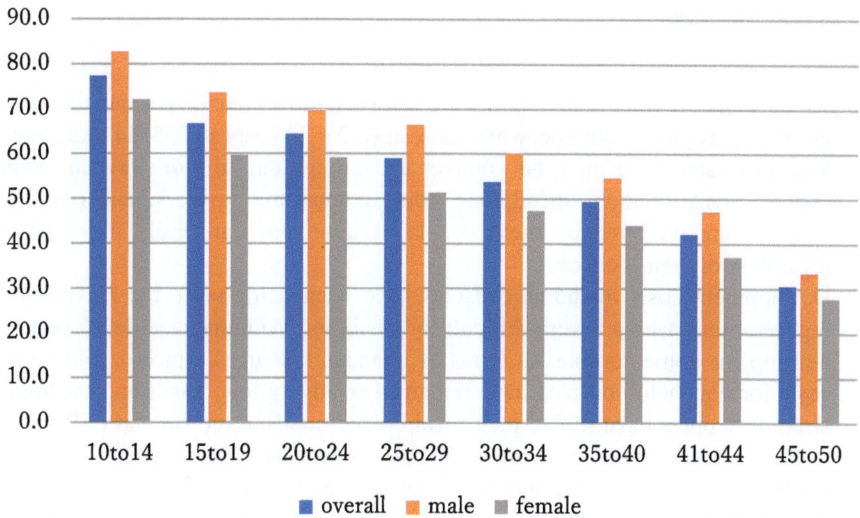

Fig. 13.7 Game consumption rate by age group (2010). Source: Survey on time use and leisure activities

Figure 13.6 shows the population pyramid as of 2006. It can be seen that there are fewer people aged 15–24 years and more people aged 25–34 years and 35–44 years. Figure 13.7 also shows game consumption rates for each age group, showing that the 25–34 age group is about the same as the 15–24 age group, and that even among the 35–44 age group, about 30% play games. Those aged

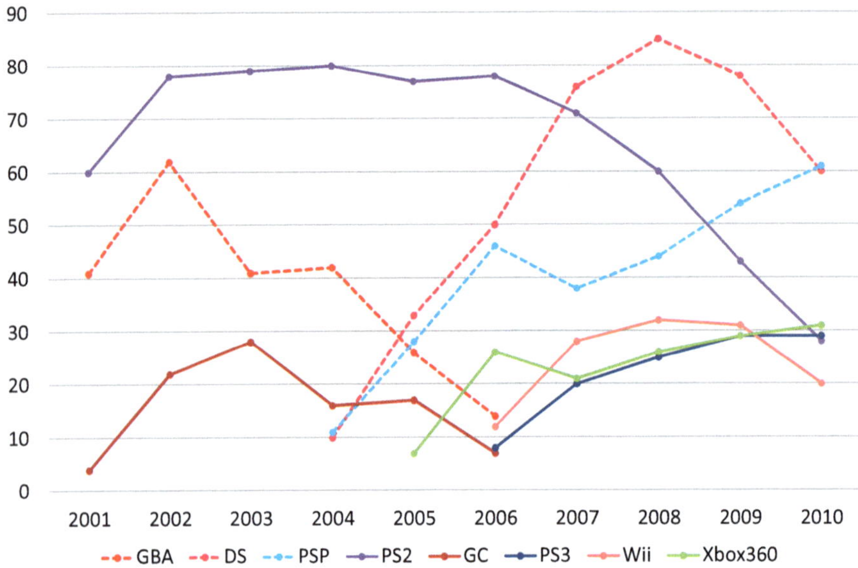

Fig. 13.8 Number of companies that released games on each hardware. Source: Game industry white paper DECADE

15–24 years, of whom the majority are students, have more disposable time and prefer to play games at home, while those aged 25–34 years and 35–44 years have less disposable time than the younger age groups due to work or household chores. Many of them spend long hours commuting to work, and portable consoles are preferred by these people because they can easily play games regardless of their location.

2. Development costs for home consoles have been rising since the PlayStation 3 generation, making it very difficult for small and medium-sized developers to develop for home consoles in terms of financial resources. Since development costs for handheld consoles have remained relatively low, small and medium-sized developers have shifted their main battlegrounds to the DS and PSP.

   Figure 13.8 shows the number of companies that released games on each hardware in that year. The number of companies launching games for the PS2 was about 80, but for the Wii, PS3, and Xbox360 generations, the number of companies launching games for each hardware was only about 30. On the other hand, the GBA had a maximum of about 60 companies, but the DS had a maximum of about 80 companies, and the PSP had 60 companies.

The reason for the small number of companies releasing games on the PS3 generation of home consoles is due to two factors: (1) the rising development costs have made it difficult for non-large companies to enter the market, and (2) users are increasingly turning away from home consoles. The development costs for home consoles ranged from several hundred million yen to several billion yen, and the number of personnel required for development reached several dozen to several hundred, making it quite difficult for small and medium-sized developers to bear the development costs. In such an environment, where most users shifted to portable consoles, small and medium-sized developers had no other choice but to sell their products on handheld consoles.

Although the center of the Japanese video game industry has shifted dramatically from home consoles to handheld video game consoles, the dominance of handheld video game consoles did not last long. With the rapid expansion of the market for cell phones and smartphones, the face of the market changed drastically.

Chapter 14
Mobile Phone Games: Prosperity of Social Games and Rapid Market Maturation

Abstract This chapter discusses the mobile phone game market. The Japanese mobile phone game market grew rapidly during the feature phone era with the spread of social games. The leading players in the market at that time were GREE and DeNA, which provided the software technology platform for social games. Social games expanded their market, but around 2010, high charging became a social problem. Guidance from the government led to self-regulation by industry associations. At the same time, smartphones began to spread, and the market transition was completed in just one or two years, thanks in part to the huge success of Puzzle & Dragons. The market continued to expand, even surpassing the home video game market to become the largest market for computer games.

Keywords Featurephone · Gacha · Smartphone · Pay to win · Free to play · Puzzle&Dragons · Kancolle

14.1 Mobile Phone Games Before Social Games

Like PC online games, mobile phone games are another area where the market was born with the advent of the Internet.

It was February 1999 when NTT DoCoMo announced i-mode, an Internet access service using mobile phones. i-mode made it possible to use Internet connection services, such as e-mail and web page browsing, that had previously been available via a PC, from a mobile phone in one's hand. Other mobile phone carriers also launched Internet access services, and Internet use on mobile phones became commonplace. This was the start of the mobile content business, which sold wallpaper, ringtones, and other content.

However, it took some time before mobile phones were used as gaming devices.

When i-mode first started, the performance of mobile phones (communication speed and CPU speed) was low, and the specifications of the mobile phone OS did not allow original programs to run. Therefore, the only games that could be played were web games, which were played by following links on web pages. It was not until 2001 that mobile phones were able to run applications on the Java Virtual Machine (JVM), which was supported by many companies. Although specifications

Y. Koyama, *History of the Japanese Video Game Industry*, Translational Systems Sciences 35, https://doi.org/10.1007/978-981-99-1342-8_14

differed slightly among carriers (and, more importantly, among devices), the memory size was only 20 KB–50 KB, and the screen size was only 120 × 130 pixels, so it was still difficult to run games for past home video game consoles such as the Famicom. It was not until 2003 that devices with performance and specifications that could withstand use in games finally appeared on the market. In 2003, an environment was finally developed in which applications could be run directly on the OS rather than on the Java Virtual Machine, which had strict memory limitations, and the use of LCDs with a screen resolution of QVGA (320 × 240 pixels) became common.

Mobile phone game services will become common around 2003. When existing game companies entered the mobile phone game market, there were two basic business models.

1. A game company's fan site service that allowed users to freely download small games[1] in addition to wallpaper, ringtones, etc. for a flat monthly fee of about 500 yen.
2. A "sell-out" service where small-scale titles are downloaded for 100 yen each, and large-scale titles are sold for 300–500 yen each.

As in the case of PC online games, SNS (social networking services) for mobile phones entered the market from a completely different place than existing game companies and established themselves in the market. SNS is a service where each user has his or her own page (My Page) where they can share their diaries with friends and exchange short messages. In order to promote interaction among users, SNSs provided a system where users could place their avatars (their alter egos) on their My Page and dress them up with paid or free items, or set up casual games for users to compete with each other in terms of play score. Among these sites, Mobagetown, established in 2006 as a game-oriented SNS for mobile phones, and GREE, established in 2004 and started as a SNS for PCs but became very successful with its service for mobile phones, emerged as the leading SNS site.

14.2 Market Expansion through Social Games

The mobile phone game market was growing steadily, but by 2007 the existing market of monthly services, sellouts, and avatar fees had matured to the point of almost no growth. In this environment, social games rapidly expanded their market size.

Although there is no clear definition of social games, the image people had of social games when they first appeared was "games in which competition, cooperation, and interaction with other players are central to the fun of the game". When they

[1]Most of the games offered by game companies for mobile phones were mobile phone ports of games developed in the past for arcades and home use, but some were originally developed.

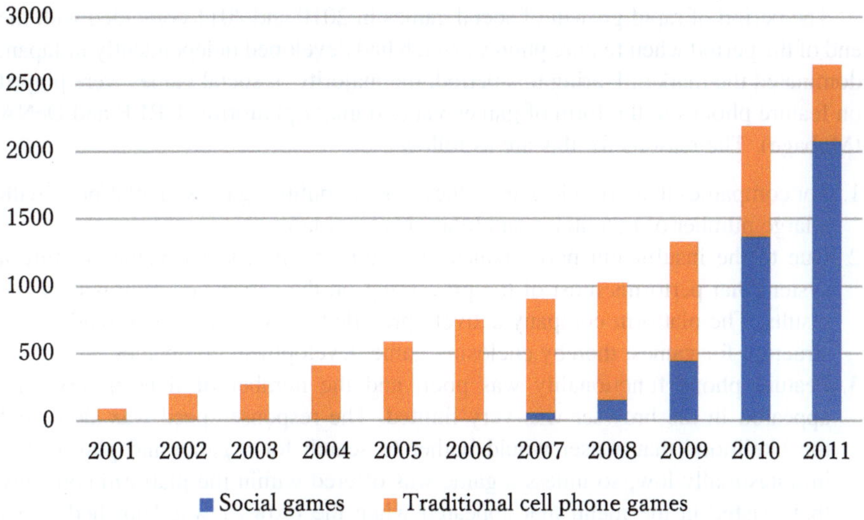

Fig. 14.1 Market size of existing mobile phone games (including avatars) and social games. Source: Information Media White Paper, each fiscal year

first appeared, many social games were offered as services on SNS. Due to the nature of SNS, games are often provided on a Web browser, with the internal processing of the game handled on the server side and the results displayed on a Web page on the handset (mobile phone) side.[2]

Outside of Japan, social games in their infancy grew mainly on PCs, spawning emerging powers such as Zynga Inc. In Japan, on the other hand, where Internet-capable mobile phones were already widely available, most of the social game market grew on mobile phones. Because the performance of mobile phones is limited compared to dedicated video game consoles and PCs, and because mobile phone users include young women and middle-aged men and women who do not play games very often, most games have simple game systems in which cooperation and competition with other players are a major part of the game play.

If we consider the period before 2010, when the market expanded rapidly and social attention was focused at once, to be the dawn of social games, games from the dawn of social games include Tsuri * Suta (Fishing Star) (GREE, service started in May 2007), Kaito Royale (Phantom Thief Royal) (DeNA, service started in October 2009), and Koishite Kyabajou (Lovely Hostess) (KLab, service started in December 2009). service launched in December 2009.

The expansion of the social game market has been tremendous, with rapid growth of more than 30 times from 6 billion yen to 207.8 billion yen in just 5 years from 2007 to 2011. (Fig. 14.1).

---

[2]Mobile phones were able to run Flash Lite, a functionally limited version of Adobe Flash. Therefore, games for mobile phones using Flash were being developed in the same way as browser games for PCs.

The period of rapid growth of social games in 2010 and 2011 coincided with the end of the period when feature phones, which had developed independently in Japan, dominated the market. During this period, the majority of social games were played on feature phones in the form of games via two major platforms, GREE and DeNA (Mobage). The reasons for this are as follows:

1. For companies that provide games, they want to publish games on platforms with a large number of potential users (platform externality).
2. Due to the insufficient performance of feature phones, social games require a system that performs most of the processing on the server and returns only the results. The platform company actively provided the system as a network infrastructure for games, thereby enclosing game development companies.
3. Feature phone functionality was poor, and the number of lines of text that appeared in the browser was very limited. The response speed was slow, and the likelihood that a user would bother to search for a game and play it was infinitesimally low, so unless a game was offered within the platform company that existed in the menu that appeared when the browser was launched, users would not even know it existed.

When a game development company provides a game through GREE or DeNA's game platform, it incurs a game platform usage fee. The usage fees are said to account for about 30% of sales, generating huge profits for both companies as the social game market expands.[3]

14.3 Social Game System Characteristics and Business Models

While the existing business model for mobile phone games was based on a fixed monthly fee service or download sales of individual titles, social games adopted the business model of free-to-play, paid item sales as a source of income, which had become the mainstream for online PC games.

Most free-to-play social games require players to have a certain amount of stamina, which they consume to play the game. Players cannot play games when their energy level is below the required level. If the player does not play, his/her stamina will gradually recover to the upper limit, but if the player wants to continue playing the game immediately, he/she needs to purchase a paid item that restores stamina. In addition to these paid items, the main source of revenue is the gacha.

Gacha refers to a paid lottery in which players win powerful items or game characters to advance in the game. The name "gacha" has become common because

[3]In addition to the platform usage fees to GREE and DeNA, the game developers also incurred platform usage fees to the mobile phone companies that collected the fees on their behalf. The game developers only kept about half of the apparent sales.

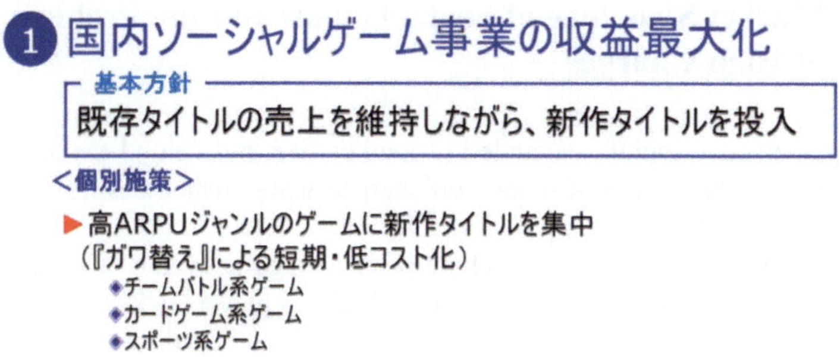

Fig. 14.2 One company's 2011 quarterly earnings report materials (partial)

of the "gacha-gacha" (a vending machine for capsule toys) style of game presentation that is often used in games. Players also purchase gachas by "spinning the gacha". The cost of a single gacha is generally between 100 yen and 500 yen, and the game is usually played 11 times for the cost of 10 times. The majority of the game systems are in the card battle format, which allows for easy expansion of the game by adding new characters and sales promotion through gachas.

The card battle format came to dominate the market partly because of the performance limitations of mobile phones at the time. The screen resolution of mobile phones was as small as QVGA (240 × 320), and the game had to be playable on this screen. Therefore, the layout on the screen was simple, with only two or three still images of deformed characters or a single large picture with detailed descriptions on the screen. Also, considering the processing performance of the device itself and the technical characteristics of running a game on a SNS, no more could be expected. The optimal solution in such an environment was a card battle nurturing game such as Kaito Royal.

This was not a bad situation for social game companies. This was because it was relatively easy to release a large number of titles as long as they had a base game engine. To put it another way, if they thought something would be popular in the market, they could easily profit by releasing a game with the same game engine but with a different surface called Gawa-Gae(skin change) as quickly as possible. Figure 14.2 is an excerpt from a company's financial results presentation for the fiscal year 2011. Note that the word Gawa-Gae is clearly written. Gawa-Gae enabled the company to keep development costs very low, around several million yen. This is about one-tenth of the cost of games for handheld video game consoles at the time.

The infrastructure to run the game is complete, and almost the same game system can be used. Moreover, the item-charging business model employed in social games can effectively use a price discrimination strategy (see Chap. 8), so as the number of potential users increases, sales will grow according to the amount each is willing to pay, from those who pay a small amount to those who pay a large amount. In this environment, social games have been able to achieve very high-profit margins and growth rates.

14.4 Market Structure of Social Games and the Problem of High Charges

Social games have rapidly expanded in market size, but behind the scenes, users spent quite a high amount of money on charged items, which has become a social problem (Photo 14.1).

The reasons that produced high charges were "regular events" and "gacha."

Table 14.1 shows the game charge rate of DeNA's players in 2010. About 80% of the players pay no money, but the rate increases with age. On the other hand, 0.6% of the respondents in their 10 s and 4.5% of those in their 40 s and 50 s answered that they charged ¥5000 or more.

見えないお金 下

我が子の小遣い新事情

見えないお金は電子マネーだけではない。インターネット上にはソーシャルゲームなど一見無料のようで、お金がかかるサービスがあふれている。子どもたちにはそれらの多くが魅力的に映る。突然の高額請求に驚く前に、親が知っておくべきことは多い。

ネットゲームで400万円

「限度額いっぱいでもう使えません」。昨年秋、高校2年の息子を持つある母親は、クレジットカードを使おうとした時、店員から思いもよらぬ宣告を受け驚いた。同じころ、夫にもカード会社から「一晩に何回も決済されているが大丈夫か」との警告の電話があったという。

不審に思い息子にただすと、親名義のカード5枚を無断で使い、携帯電話からネット上のソーシャルゲームをしていたと判明。2カ月間で使った料金は約400万円に達していた。

原因は「コンプリート(コンプ)ガチャ」。先月、消費者庁が景品表示法違反にあたると判断し、ソーシャルゲーム大手が廃止したアイテム商法にはまっていた。ゲームを有利に進める希少なアイテムを手に入れるため、「ガチャ」と呼ばれるくじを1回数百円で購入。アイテムをそろえようと何度も繰り返すので、高額の料金を費やす例が続出している。

□

国民生活センターの調べでは、無料をうたうオンラインゲームに関する相談は年々増えており、2011年度は840件。このうち未成年者が絡むものは286件、34%を占める。小学生が111件と最も多い。

今や小学生も2割が携帯電話を持ち(内閣府調べ)、ネットへの接触は常態化している。でもバーチャルな世界でかわされるお金は、全く見えない。「オンラインゲームは親のカードを使ったり、携帯電話料金に上乗せされたりして、お金を持たなくてもできる。子どもは現実のお金が使われていることを意識していない」と同センターの水越智子さんは解説する。

実際、コンプガチャが廃止されても、使い方に注意が必要な仕組みはなお残る。たとえば、ガチャには1回300円が11回3千円でお得、とうたう「11連続ガチャ」まである。「クリックして3千円をするのにわずか2秒。パチンコより早い。パチンコは財布からお金を出すが、ネットでは感覚がマヒするのだろう」。電子商取引に関する消費者相談を受けている社団法人ECネットワークの原田由里理事はこう批判する。

同理事は、ゲーム会社は今後もお金を払わせる新サービスを必ず出してくると指摘。それゆえ「親は子どもがそういう環境にあることを知って、関心を持ってほしい」と呼びかける。

本来、親がきちんと子どもにお金の管理法を教えていれば、トラブルは防げるはず。だが、厳しい見方もある。ベネッセ教育研究開発センターの樋口健主任研究員は「今の親たちは意識が弱い」と指摘する。

□

オンラインゲームに関する相談が増えている

件

900, 800, 700, 600, 500, 400, 300, 200, 100, 0

2009年度　10　11

成年

未成年: その他, 高校生, 中学生, 小学生

(注) 国民生活センターに寄せられたもの

親も直視し 金銭感覚養う

ジブラルタ生命が保育園児の親を対象に開催した「おこづかい教育出前教室」(千葉市花見川区)

同センターが昨年9月、小中学生の親に「現在の子育ての気がかり」を尋ねたところ「子どものお金の使い方」は15位。調査は1998年から4回目だが、傾向はずっと変わらない。

親の目は受験と就職に関することに向きがち。「でも、将来日本経済が伸びない中で、限られたお金を使うスキルを子どもが身につけることは、もっと大切。それを親が知恵を絞って考えないといけない時代だ」と樋口さんは強調する。

兆しはある。ジブラルタ生命が、社会貢献の一環として昨年9月から全国で開催している「おこづかい教育出前教室」。PTAや育児サークルなどの親を対象に、小遣いを使って子どもに金銭感覚を身につけさせるノウハウを伝授するもので、すでに4千～5千人が受講、盛況だ。

先月下旬に千葉市の保育園で開かれた教室に夫婦で来た中島紀明さん(32)は8月に生まれる子を思っての参加。「自分たちの子ども時代にはなかった、ゲームなどが今はあふれている。どう育てればいいのか、何事も準備しておきたかった」。別の教室参加者からは「自分の家計管理にも役立つ」という声も聞かれた。

横浜国大の西村隆男教授は「生活の基盤にはお金があり、それが暮らしを支えている。そのことを、ネット社会にどっぷりつかった子どもたちに、学校や家庭で口酸っぱく教える必要がある」と話している。

[illegible]が担当しました。

使い道は任せ、ウソを許さない

我が子にお金の使い方をどう学ばせればよいか。特定非営利活動法人(NPO法人)金融知力普及協会が監修する「おこづかい教育出前教室」で推奨している小遣いの与え方は、こんな方法だ。

お小遣い袋と貯金袋をつくり、毎月のお小遣いの3分の1は貯金袋に。残りを財布にいれて子どもに持たせ、使い道に口ははさまない。何かを買ったら必ずレシートをお小遣い袋に保管させる。レシートがないものは、その額をお小遣い袋の表面に記入する。

月末に親と一緒に「おこづ会議」を開き、収支があっていればほめ、小遣いの増額も。無駄遣いをしても決して叱らず、不正直・不公正なことをした時だけ怒る。前借りや借金は認めない。

これではしいものを手に入れるための計画的な貯金や、無駄なものは買わずに我慢することを覚え、買ったものは大切にする心が養われるという。

Photo 14.1 Article reporting on the high charge issue (Nikkei Shimbun Newspaper, June 22, 2012)

Table 14.1 DeNA game billing rates (2010 Survey)

	10's	20's	30's	40's	50's	Total
Do not pay	87.7%	75.6%	80.0%	78.2%	65.2%	78.5%
1–300 yen	3.2%	7.9%	4.3%	6.4%	9.0%	5.9%
301–500 yen	3.2%	2.4%	4.3%	4.5%	4.5%	3.7%
501–1000 yen	1.9%	10.2%	3.5%	2.7%	6.7%	4.9%
1001–2000 yen	1.3%	0.8%	2.6%	2.7%	5.6%	2.3%
2001–3000 yen	1.3%	0.0%	1.7%	0.9%	4.5%	1.5%
3001–5000 yen	0.6%	1.6%	0.0%	0.0%	0.0%	0.5%
5000 yen and more	0.6%	1.6%	3.5%	4.5%	4.5%	2.7%

Source: Moppy Labs, "Social Media Usage Trend Survey," 2010. http://pc.moppy.jp/lab/archives/271

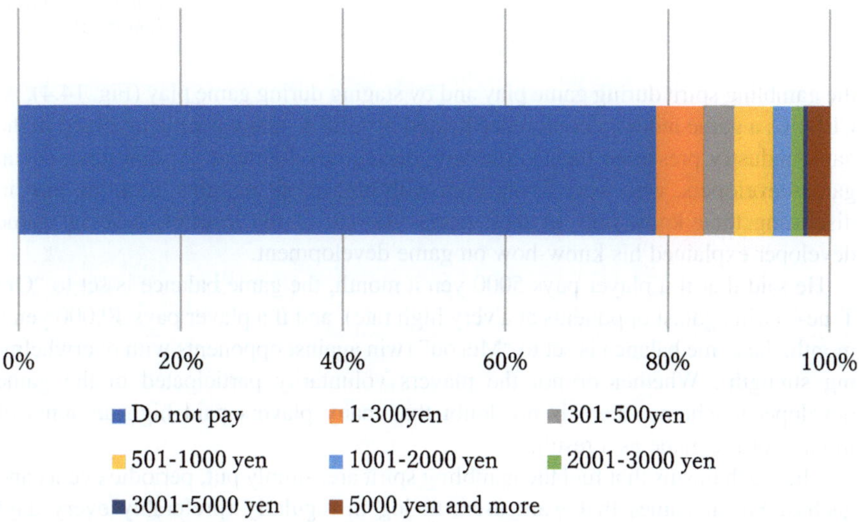

Fig. 14.3 Percentage of billing tiers

Figure 14.3 shows the percentage of respondents in each age group contributing to income from the "Overall" category in this table.[4] Almost half of the total revenue comes from players who pay more than 5000 yen, which accounts for only 2.7% of the total revenue. A large part of the revenue of social game companies depends on high payers.

If a large part of the sales of social games is dependent on high-paying users, it is highly likely that social games have been able to generate high-paying users more than just a price discrimination strategy by using various mechanisms to stimulate

[4]In creating the graphs, the median amount spent in each category (150 yen for 1–300 yen, 400 yen for 301–500 yen, and 5000 yen for more than 5000 yen) was used. Therefore, the percentage of income from higher-priced users is much higher.

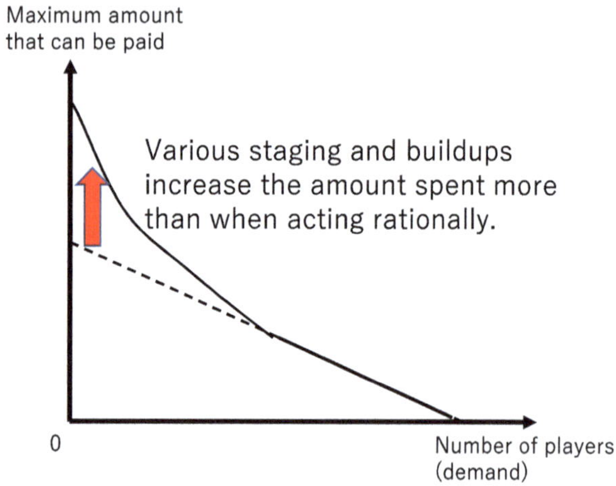

Fig. 14.4 Price discrimination strategies and staging raise maximum payments

the gambling spirit during game play and by staging during game play (Fig. 14.4). At CEDEC, a game industry conference hosted by CESA, many people involved in the game industry presented their know-how during development. At that time, social game developers, who were flying high with high-profit margins, took the lead in disclosing their know-how to their peers. At one of the lectures, a social game developer explained his know-how on game development.

He said that if a player pays 5000 yen a month, the game balance is set to "Ore Tsue-" (win against opponents at a very high rate), and if a player pays 30,000 yen a month, the game balance is set to "Musou" (win against opponents with overwhelming strength). Whether or not the players voluntarily participated in the game developer's scheme, there is no doubt that many players paid high amounts of money for the game as a result.

The mechanisms that fuel the gambling spirit are, simply put, periodic events and gachas. Social games that want users to log in regularly (preferably every day) always have some kind of event going on in the game. The contents of the events vary, but often there are gachas that increase the probability of certain rare characters that are powerful but have a very low probability of appearing in the game, or players who achieve high scores in competitions with other players receive limited items or limited characters that cannot be obtained through normal play or gachas as a prize. In order to get a high rank in an event, an avid player will continue to use stamina restoring items for a fee, and will also pay huge amounts of money for rare characters[5] that can only be obtained through gacha.

Stamina recovery items are capped at game play time for purchase, while gacha is more serious because it is not limited by play time. The problems with gacha can be summarized in the following three points:

[5]Characters in the game are classified into Rare, S-Rare, etc., according to their difficulty of acquisition (rarity), and the higher the rarity, the stronger the card.

1. The company does not sell the items that users want, but rather the "right to draw a lottery that may result in the acquisition of an item."
2. (Related to (1) above), the amount of money it costs the user to get the item he/she wants is unknown.
3. The amount of money spent per raffle is small and the time required per lottery is short.

User behavior can be easily interpreted from Prospect Theory, a basic theory of behavioral economics, and the reasons for the success and problems of the social game business model can be shown relatively easily.

1. Humans do not calculate gains and losses by the "total amount of loss (gain)" but by the "difference from a reference point." To cope with this problem, the reference point is shifted each time by collecting 300 yen each time .... Players spend one after another with the feeling that they "just paid 300 yen," which ultimately results in a high expenditure.
2. As the player moves away from the reference point, the growth rate of positive evaluation decreases gradually and the growth rate of negative evaluation increases gradually. Since a sense of avoidance increases when the per expenditure amount becomes high, keep it inexpensive (around 100 yen to 300 yen).
3. Humans tend to overestimate the probability of occurrence of phenomena with a small probability. In other words, people overreact to the fact that the probability is "not 100%" for phenomena that have "almost 100%" probability, and overreact to the fact that the probability is "not zero" for phenomena that have "a slight possibility" probability. Therefore, users are more likely to think that they may win a rare item than the actual probability.

Although the author does not believe that game developers were aware of Prospect Theory, it is likely that the social game format was one of the perfected forms that emerged as game developers pursued the know-how to enthuse people in game development. It is not difficult to imagine that these mechanisms produced a "pay to win" type of fierce competition over charges, which was even referred to as "beating each other with a wad of cash.[6]"

The Consumer Affairs Agency did not regulate gacha itself. However, on May 6, 2012, it was reported that the Consumer Affairs Agency plans to issue an opinion that a type of gacha known as "comp-gacha" violates the Act against Unjustifiable Premiums and Misleading Representations. According to the Consumer Affairs Agency's definition, "comp-gacha" refers to a system whereby players can obtain new items (or characters) that can be used in online games on the condition that they have all of a certain item (or character) through a gacha. This was considered to be a "picture matching" under the Law for Preventing Unjustifiable Premiums and

[6] As a story that illustrates the intensity of the charging process, the names for money charged are used by the high paying players in a self-deprecating manner. According to them, "no charge" means "a charge that has no impact on one's life," "a small charge" means "a small impact on one's life," and "light charge" means "a charge that is enough to buy a light car.

Misleading Representations.[7] The day after the report, the stock prices of both DeNA and GREE were halted and the market urged the industry to clean up its act.

In March 2012, the six major social game companies established the "Liaison Council on Improvement of Social Game Usage Environments, etc." in consideration of the social impact, and were studying self-regulation proposals (monthly fee of 10,000 yen or less for youth users). This movement accelerated after the comp-gacha report, and the Japan Social Game Association (JASGA[8]) was established in November 2012.

However, social games were forced to undergo major changes regardless of such self-cleansing efforts (Photo 14.2).

14.5 Drastic Changes in the Market Environment Due to the Spread of Smartphones

The prosperity of social games was built on feature phones, which had limited performance. The situation changed drastically when the center of the market shifted to smartphones (Fig. 14.5).

Smartphones have greatly improved CPU and screen resolution. In addition, programs that run on smartphones, called native applications, can be freely downloaded from the App Store (iPhone) or Google Play (Android). Due to limitations in terms of device performance and interface, social games had to be developed as browser games under the GREE or DeNA platform, but that restriction has completely disappeared. In addition, existing social games that run on feature phones are (1) not screen friendly on smartphones in terms of screen resolution, (2) smartphones do not support Flash, and (3) smartphones are almost exclusively touch panel operated. Therefore, it was necessary to develop a smartphone version of the native application for each game.

The main battleground for mobile phone games has shifted rapidly to smartphones. Figure 14.6 shows the ratio of social game sales platforms based on a social game developer's quarterly financial results. It can be seen that the ratio of feature phones has drastically decreased from 60% to one-third. Browser games played via the Web (smartphone versions of existing social games) have remained flat, and native applications have grown to make up for the sharp decline in the feature phone market.

[7]The Consumer Affairs Agency [Public Comment on the Publication of the Premiums and Representation Law's (Premiums Regulation) Approach to "Card Matching" and Amendments to the Operational Standards of the Premiums and Representation Law] (Card Awase ni Kansuru Keihin Hyouji Hou(Keihin Kisei) jouno Kangaekata no Kouhyou Oyobi Keihin Hyoujihou no Un-you Kijun no Kaisei ni Kansuru Public Comment ni tsuite)
http://www.caa.go.jp/representation/pdf/120518premiums_1.pdf

[8]JASGA merged with the Computer Entertainment Supplier's Association (CESA), a home video game-centric industry organization, on December 2, 2014, after only 2 years of activity.

「コンプガチャ」違法の観測

グリー、DeNAの株価急落

交流サイト（SNS）経由でゲームを提供するソーシャルゲーム各社が収益モデルの見直しを迫られる可能性が出てきた。利用者が特定のカードをそろえると希少性の高い仮想アイテムを入手できる「コンプリートガチャ（コンプガチャ）」について、消費者庁が近く景品表示法に抵触するとの見解を示す見通しになったためだ。コンプガチャが禁止されれば業績に悪影響が出るとの観測から、株式市場ではグリーなど関連各社の株価が大幅に下落している。

ソーシャルゲームは無料で利用できる。ただ、顧客はゲームを有利に進める目的でアイテムを購入することが多い。アイテムへの課金収入は大手のグリー、ディー・エヌ・エー（DeNA）の収益源だ。

ソーシャルゲーム大手2社の株価の動き
(2011年12月30日終値を100として指数化)
消費者庁による規制観測が浮上
SNS各社が利用健全化のため協議会を設置
DeNA
グリー
仮想アイテムの現金取引が問題に
「コンプガチャ」への規制観測が強まる
120
110
100
90
80
70
60
2012/1
2
3
4
5

収益モデルの見直しも

問題のコンプガチャは、特定のアイテムをそろえるとさらにゲームを有利に戦えると顧客に示し、利用を促す。1カ月に10万円近くを投じる利用者もいるとみられる。

景表法は射幸心を過剰にあおるなどとして、複数の異なる絵柄などを集める見返りに懸賞を与える行為を禁じている。消費者庁は「詳細は検討中だが、コンプガチャは景表法に抵触しているとの見解を示す方向で準備している」（片桐一幸・表示対策課長）という。見解に従わない場合は行政処分の対象になるため、各社は今後、対応を迫られることになる。

各社はコンプガチャの収益規模を開示していないが、市場では「売上高の1～3割を占めるのではないか」（国内証券）との見方もある。サービスを停止すれば業績への悪影響は避けられない。

ソーシャルゲームを巡っては年初から行政が規制をかけるとの観測があった。だが収益モデルの根幹に関わる問題が浮上したのは今回が初めて。

7日の東京株式市場ではグリー、DeNAの株価がいずれも制限値幅の下限（ストップ安）まで下落した。SNSにゲームを供給するKLab、ドリコムも一時ストップ安まで売られた。SNS大手6社は3月に協議会を設置、自主規制による利用の健全化に乗り出している。社会と折り合いを付けながら成長を持続できるかが問われている。

▼コンプガチャ　コンプリートガチャの略語。ソーシャルゲームを有利に進めるためのアイテムは、「ガチャ」と呼ばれる有料の電子くじで入手できる。コンプガチャは2つ以上の特定のアイテムをそろえることで、希少性のより高いアイテムを入手できる仕組み。該当するアイテムが当たるまで利用者が繰り返しガチャを使うことになり、射幸心を過剰にあおるとの指摘が出ていた。

Photo 14.2 Newspaper article on the illegalization of comp-gacha (May 8, 2012, Nikkei Newspaper)

With this expansion of native app market share, the platform providers, GREE and DeNA, lost the commission income they had earned from games developed by other companies that were offered through their platforms. In the feature phone era, both companies provided social game developers with various infrastructure functions, from game server operations to billing agency services, and earned commission income. Users looked for the next game to play from the games offered within both platforms, so the two companies effectively had most users. Therefore, social

Fig. 14.5 Ratio of smartphones among total mobile phones sold (%). Source: JEITA (http://www.jeita.or.jp/)

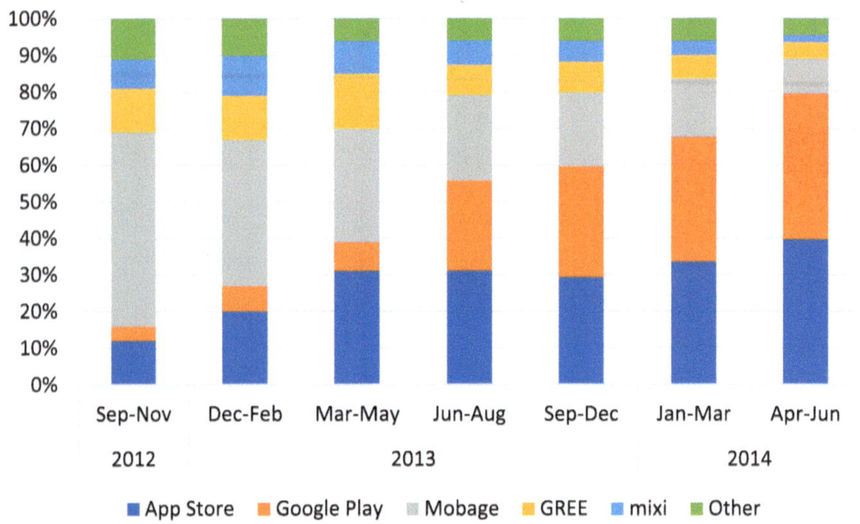

Fig. 14.6 Percentage of one company's social game sales to smartphones (December 2011–February 2013)

game developers had no choice but to do business on top of the infrastructure provided by both companies.

In the smartphone era, users search for games through App Store and Google Play, so there is no user enclosure by the two companies. In addition, App Store and Google Play provide the billing infrastructure, which is the minimum requirement

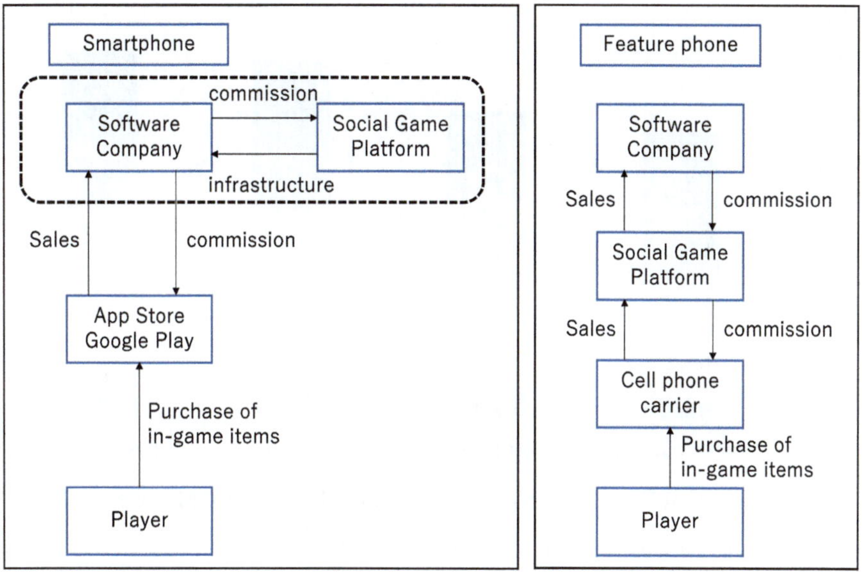

Fig. 14.7 Difference between Galapagos and Smartphone Business Models. Dotted lines indicate only some social games

for operating social games and is difficult to build on one's own in terms of security issues and commission rates. Therefore, game companies with the technical skills to operate their own game servers can operate all of their own servers, eliminating the need to pay platform usage fees to Gree and DeNA.

Figure 14.7 shows the differences in business models in each era. In the feature phone era, software companies released games via social game platforms DeNA and GREE, and all sales were collected through both companies. However, when developing native apps for smartphones, there is no need to go through both companies, and thus no fees are incurred.

In the case of browser-based social games, where the game system is similar to that of the feature phone era and the accumulation of infrastructure assets provided by both companies is substantial, the platforms of the two companies are used to optimize development and operation costs. Even in such cases, as indicated by the dotted line, they are not in an essential position in the supply chain, but are only used as partners, and when the software company has the technical and financial strength to build and utilize its own infrastructure, it will change to its own operations. In fact, proprietary games with a high degree of novelty tend to be developed as native applications.

The shift to native apps for social games opened growth possibilities for other companies besides DeNA and GREE, creating two big players: GungHo for Puzzle & Dragons and mixi for Monster Strike. However, most other existing social game companies struggled to adapt to smartphones.

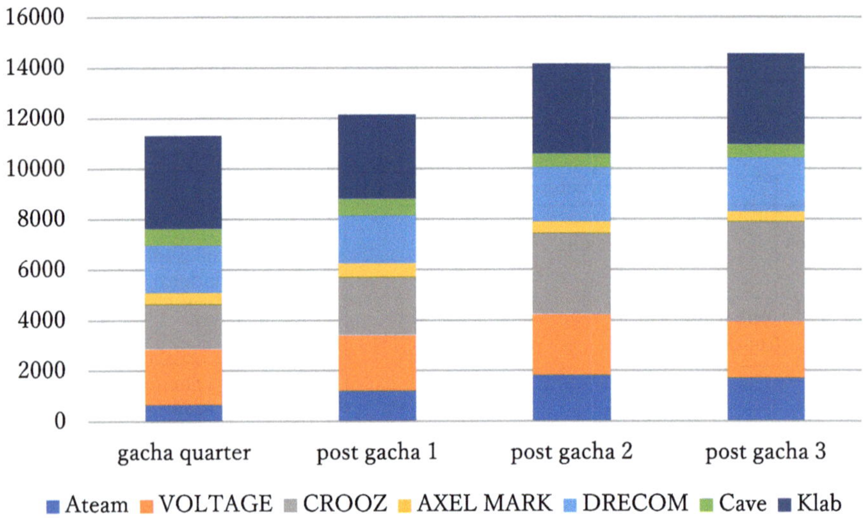

Fig. 14.8 Social game development companies' sales (million yen)

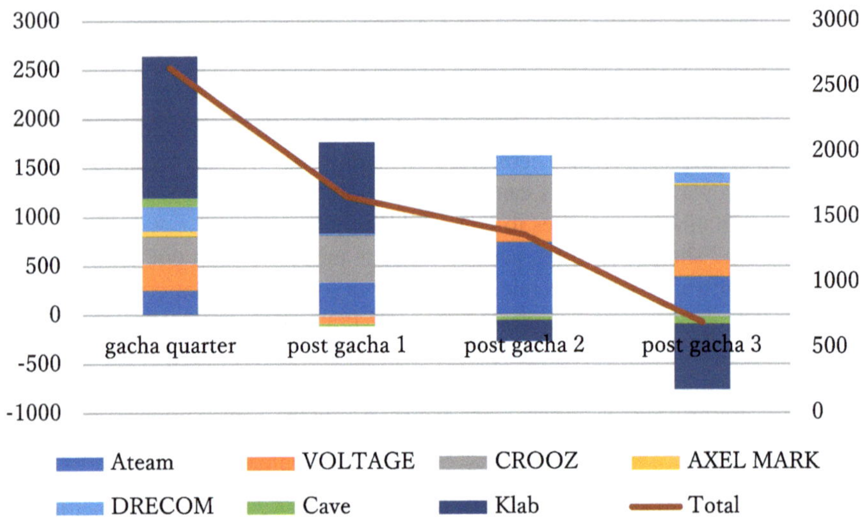

Fig. 14.9 Sales and operating profit of social game development companies (million yen)

Figs. 14.8 and 14.9 show sales and operating profit trends for the seven listed companies that develop social games for the year since the comp-gacha scandal. Although each company has a different fiscal year and quarter, the quarter that includes the comp-gacha scandal (May 2012) (denoted as "gacha quarter") and the three subsequent quarters are denoted as post-gacha 1-3.

*Calculated only for segments related to social games; for Klab and Cave, the period before the riots was March–May, and the period after the riots was

June–September. For other companies, the period before the disturbance was April–June, and the period after the disturbance was July–September. Note that Cave changed its business segment to a single segment for all companies after the end of May.

**Ateam is unable to calculate the most recent quarter before the disturbance due to the timing of its listing. Therefore, the column for the period before the uproar is the cumulative total up to the third quarter divided by three as a reference.

***Ateam's sales and operating profit before the turmoil used one-third of the cumulative total up to Q3.

Few companies lost sales after the comp-gacha, but operating profits fell for many, with three companies losing money in the first post-gacha quarter. The combined operating profits of the seven companies have plummeted, with the sum of the seven companies' operating profits in the three post-gacha quarters being only about a quarter of what it was in the gacha quarter. If the disruption was caused by the response to the comp-gacha, both sales and profits should have declined, and profits should not have continued to fall over three quarters. The market structure has changed (i.e., the market has matured).

The significance of the continued decline in profits is serious, despite the fact that sales did not decline after the comps-gacha. Although the companies' annual reports do not specify the reasons for the increase in sales and profits, the two reasons for the increase in sales and profits are as follows:

1. Development costs are rising due to the creation of richer content in line with the increasing performance of smartphones.
2. Increasing losses due to the declining success rate of newly launched games (intensifying competition for survival in the market).

The basic performance of smartphones also surpasses that of home portable game consoles such as the Nintendo 3DS and PlayStation VITA.

In addition, screen resolution is on par with HDTVs, which is a big difference when viewed from a mobile phone. In other words, social games have rapidly evolved from a level of primitive expressive power that was below that of the Famicom era—"press number 5 button and watch the reaction to see how the screen changes"—to a level that is not much different from current mobile games, or even better.

As a result, to put it simply, in the era of mobile phones, it was fine to "make dozens of games for a few million yen each, and if one of them hit, the business was profitable," but in the smartphone era, "each game costs tens of millions of yen, so it is necessary to carefully promote each title and nurture it into a hit."

In fact, the development cost of a game like GungHo's Puzzle & Dragons, the first big hit title by a native smartphone app, is said to be around 45 million yen (*ASCII Cloud*, No. 2, 2013), which is not much different compared to games for the PSP. Furthermore, since then, the recording of movie scenes and character voices has become standard, and it is not unusual for production costs to run into hundreds of millions of yen. Social games have followed the same path as the home video game industry: more advanced performance → higher development costs → lower profitability.

14.6 Change in Game Design and Business Model: From "Pay to Win" to "Free to Play

14.6.1 Impact of Puzzle & Dragons

While standard social games on feature phones are becoming increasingly specialized in "pay to win" type game design with "competition with other players" and "payment involved," Puzzle & Dragons (GungHo, 2012; also known as Pazudora) was the first native application hit in the smartphone era and became a blockbuster hit on a par with Space Invaders in the history of the game industry.

The differences between Pazudora and the standard social games of the time are as follows:

1. Interesting enough as a single-player (stand-alone) game.

   The production cost of native applications for smartphones is considerably higher than that of social games for feature phones. Pazudora's development costs are at a level that sets it apart from other mobile phone and browser-based social games, and the game has been well designed for that reason.

   Unlike social games on mobile phones, which tend to be more like "work" than a game, Pazudora is new in that it is (1) a puzzle game that requires constant thinking, and (2) it uses a user interface that assumes a touch panel. Moreover, the puzzles are interesting enough to be played in spare time.
2. Can be played quite well without paying for it.

   The items charged in Pazudora are unified into one item called magic gems, which can be used to recover energy (i.e., continue the game without waiting), continue when the HP of all characters in the game reaches zero, and pay for rare gacha. In Pazudora, players can play several times (about 30 min) until their in-game stamina runs out without having to pay to purchase magic gems. The game can be played for free to pass the time on the train on the way to work (or school) and on the way home, as the energy is recovered in a few hours. Compared to existing social games, the portion of the game that can be played without paying is longer, so even if you play without paying, you will not feel too much stress.

However, just as in existing social games, the enemies in Pazudora become much stronger after a certain level of progress in the game, and there are situations in which a certain amount of money is required. Even at that time, it is not necessary to immediately draw strong characters from the gacha. The game differs from existing social games in that it is possible to use magic gems to continue the game and somehow defeat the enemy, which is like a continuation in arcade games.

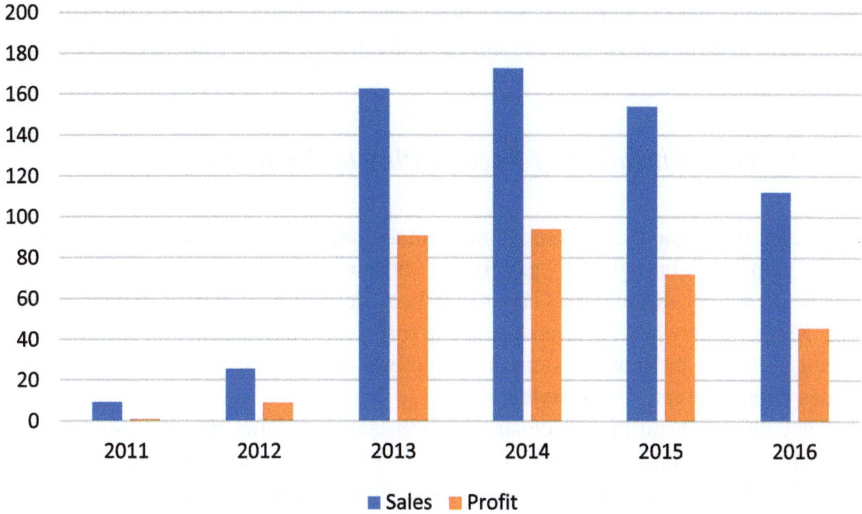

Fig. 14.10 GungHo's net sales and operating income (Billion Yen). Source: Prepared by the author from Gung Ho IR materials

However, as the game progresses further, it becomes extremely difficult to progress without repeatedly spinning gacha to obtain strong characters or continuing over and over again with boss enemies (Ishi-Jab[9]). Although the number of high payers may be smaller than in existing social games, as long as gacha is explicitly left as the final system, the number of users who succumb to the temptation is large, and Pazudora is not very different from existing social games in that this leads to revenue.

The tremendous impact of Pazudora can be clearly seen in GungHo's sales and operating profit trends (Fig. 14.10). In 2011, before the launch of Pazudora, sales were less than 10 billion yen, but in 2012, the year Pazudora was released, sales more than doubled and profits more than seven times. In 2013, sales reached 163 billion yen and operating profit 91.2 billion yen. In 2014, the company's popularity continued to grow, and both sales and operating income remained high. More than 90% of sales were related to Pazudora.[10]

If more than 90% of the 163 billion yen is Pazudora-related sales, that means that more than 10 billion yen per month goes into Gungho as Pazudora-related sales. If the approximate amount of money that goes to a game developer for the sale of one packaged game for home video game consoles is 3000 yen, this is equivalent to more

[9]Defeat the enemy by using a lot of magic gems (=continuing over and over again).

[10]In its annual securities report, GungHo explicitly shows Pazudora-related sales in its net sales: 91.1% in 2013 and 91.5% in 2014. Note that the securities report shows Pazudora-related sales, which include arcade and home video game versions, character goods, etc., but most of the sales are definitely for the smartphone game.

than 3 million packaged games being sold every month for Pazudora. This tremendous sales volume has completely changed the history of the video game industry.

14.6.2 Generalization of Free to Play by Kancolle

In the end, it was the PC browser game Kantai Collection (Kancolle), not the mobile phone game, that brought the "pay to win" business model to a complete end.

The developer, Kadokawa Games, has been developing home video games, and with Kancolle they have entered the online (browser) game market for the first time. Because of this, the game system is distinctly different from existing online/social games with their card battle style.

Kancolle has been in service since it was launched, after the development of a standard home video game or more.[11] The game is a "fleet-building simulation game," and it has a unique system that divides a single battle into six phases: search-and-destroy, opening bombing, opening torpedo attack, bombardment (one or two rounds), torpedo battle, night battle, and so on. The complexity of the system allows for a wide range of acceptable play styles, and players are encouraged to create their own unique styles, making the game more interesting than social games.

To prevent players from engaging in pay-to-win behavior, Kancolle is further advancing the "interesting enough to play as a stand-alone game" direction shown by Pazudora. Specifically, (1) there are no elements that can only be obtained for a fee or are limited to top players,[12] and (2) it is very difficult to play in a "gacha" way.[13]

Kancolle, like Pazudora, has no cooperative or competitive elements with other players. The only elements in Kancolle are ranking in the same server, which is

[11] At the time of service, there were more than 100 characters (ship daughters) available, and all of them had detailed characterizations based on historical facts, as well as voices. The amount of data prepared (pictures, text, and voice) makes it impossible to imagine that the development cost was less than the cost of Pazudora. Therefore, it is certain that the development cost is equivalent to the cost of a single home video game.

[12] In Kancolle, there is no lottery named "XX Gacha" directly. However, ship construction and equipment development consume resources, and ships and equipment appear with a probability, so these are functionally the same as gacha. The important point is that the system does not make users think that they can purchase a large amount of resources with a credit card and use them to repeatedly build and develop ships in a gacha-like manner.

[13] However, there is still an element of periodic events, which is common in social games. Some players purchase a large amount of resources, which are consumables in the game, for a fee. However, events are held every 3 months, which is longer than in social games, and the purpose of the events is to defeat the boss at the deepest level of the special map by each player. There is no element of competition among players. The management clearly states that the items obtained as a reward for clearing the event are only "pre-installed" and will be available at a later date through normal play. There is no sense of intimidation that players will never be able to obtain them again unless they are forced to pay for them.

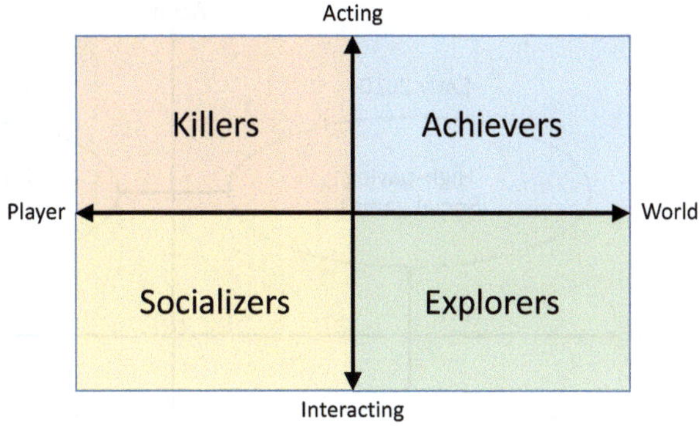

Fig. 14.11 Bartle's four classifications

reflected in the reward at the end of the month, and the daily training (virtual competition) with 10 other players. There are no elements typical of social games, such as defeating other players as enemies, outperforming them in competition, or trading resources and items. In addition, there is no interaction with fellow players.[14] Kancolle is going down the "pay to win" route, which was half a step forward with Pazudora, and is designed to prevent players from paying high amounts of money as much as possible.

14.7 Changing Trends in Game Design

The gaming frontier, which has been shifting toward online and social games since 2000, has come full circle with Pazudora and Kancolle.

Bartle's Four Classifications is a classification of player preferences in online games. This classification divides player preferences along two axes: Player (other players)-World (game world) and Acting (players who value acting on their own) -Interacting (players who value acting together with other players). The types of players in each quadrant are named as follows (Fig. 14.11):

- Achiever (Acting & World): A player who aims to achieve something by himself. This is like the motivation of players of traditional RPGs and adventure games in non-online games.

[14] A phenomenon that has existed in PC online games for a long time, the so-called "Gachi-zei" (people who take the game seriously) are allowed to act in such a way that they select the strength of their friends who join their party to defeat powerful enemies, and some unscrupulous players cheat other players in trade. When room is made for them to do so, it deteriorates the atmosphere of the game. Therefore, it is quite difficult to include elements of interaction with other players; in Kancolle, trade was supposed to be implemented in the original development plan, but as the development scale became huge, the priority of implementation dropped, and as a result, it seems that it was never implemented (*Febri*, Vol. 19, October 2013).

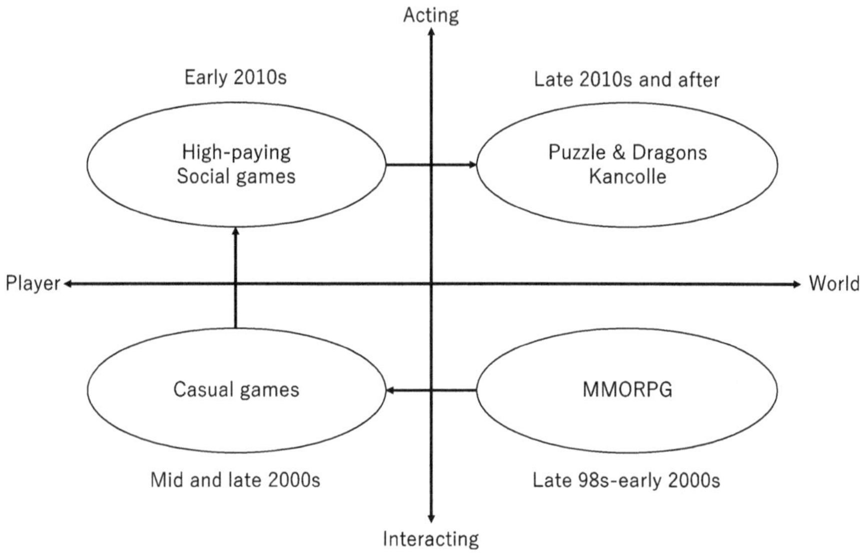

Fig. 14.12 Trend evolution of online and social games

- Killer (Acting & Player): A player who aims to defeat other players. In existing games, it is like the motivation of players of fighting games.
- Socializer (Interacting & Player): A player who places importance on interaction with other players. This is an area that has not existed in existing games.
- Explorer (Interacting & World): A player who values accomplishing something with other players.

Overlaying these four quadrants with the trends in online and social games since the late 1990s, they have come full circle over time (Fig. 14.12).

1. The age of Explorer = the age of MMORPGs: This corresponds to the start-up period of online games in the late 1990s and early 2000s. The first online games that became popular were small MORPGs such as Diablo and Phantasy Star Online and large-scale MMORPGs such as Ultima Online. Leading-edge players at the time were attracted by the fun of being able to adventure with friends over a network.
2. The age of Socializer = the age of casual games: After 2000, broadband connections spread rapidly to households as the price of ADSL dropped. The constant Internet connection attracted light users who had not played many games before, and casual game portal sites expanded their influence as a place where light users could casually play games and have fun on message boards.
3. The age of Killer = the age of social games: In the 2010s, the social game market exploded in size. Social games actively promoted competition among players by offering battles against other players and ranking functions, and increased sales by offering in-game items that give players an advantage over the competition and gachas that allow them to draw strong characters.

4. The age of Achiever = the age of Pazudora and Kancolle: The rapid success of Pazudora in 2012 led to a gradual shift to games that are basically played stand-alone, have very weak comparison and cooperation elements with other players, and can be enjoyed even with almost zero payment.

This first quadrant (Achiever) is where most packaged games for home video game consoles played alone belong. Even in home video games, games that are played for a long time, such as Monster Hunter, have become a hit. With the popularity of games such as Pazudora and Kancolle, it can be said that the return of users to Achiever was an inevitability of the times.

14.8 Summary of Mobile Phone Games: From an Auxiliary to a Leading Role

The mobile phone game market, which emerged in the 2000s, changed dramatically before and after the emergence of social games. Furthermore, even after the advent of social games, the market changed drastically before and after the advent of smartphones.

Before the advent of social games, the mobile phone game market was dominated by the development and sale of small-scale games, and was a "pocket money-making" market for existing game companies. This changed drastically in the era of social games, when in-game item charges became mainstream. The user base became more varied, and the size of the market skyrocketed. Social games on feature phones had low development costs and very high-profit margins. However, the "pay-to-win" game design and business model that encouraged users to pay for social games became a social problem.

Pazudora appeared while cell phones were shifting from feature phones to smartphones, and the shift from an excessive "pay to win" business model to a "free to play" business model was underway. The emergence of Kancolle as a PC online game in this environment confirmed the shift in the business model.

In the home video game market, the market shifted from console to handheld devices with the introduction of the Nintendo DS. Furthermore, the appearance of smartphones, which surpassed portable game consoles in terms of performance, advanced cell phones to the center of the game industry.

Chapter 15
Present

Abstract This chapter outlines the current game industry as a whole from the perspective of inter-market competition, rather than individual markets as in the previous chapters. With the rise in computer performance, the performance gap between platforms has disappeared, and now PCs and game consoles, as well as cell phones and handheld game consoles, are competing for players. At the same time, the current inter-market competition is also a competition between business models: package sales and service sales. Currently, the service-type business model and the smartphone platform are expanding in scale, far ahead of the others, but package-type and home video game consoles will not disappear anytime soon, partly due to differences in gaming characteristics.

Keywords Inter-market competition · Business model competition · Package-type games · Service-type games

The history of the Japanese video game industry spans only about 50 years, but after 14 chapters, we have finally reached the final chapter. Until the 1990s, the history of the Japanese video game industry consisted of three distinct areas: arcade, PC, and home video games, which developed independently while interacting with each other. Since the end of the twentieth century, two new markets have emerged. Online games appeared on PCs, and non-online games on PCs became almost exclusively adult. In addition, the improved performance of cell phones has created a new market for games for mobile phones.

In the current computer game market, the influence of each market is becoming stronger. The market is no longer a relaxed relationship of mutual influence in terms of content, but rather an intense competition for customers under a declining population and slowing market growth. There are two main battlegrounds. The first is handheld game consoles and smartphones. Both are handheld devices that can be held in one hand and compete with each other as a way to pass the time. The other is console-type game machines and PCs, which compete as terminals for playing games in front of a monitor installed in the living room (or one's own room) at home.

Y. Koyama, *History of the Japanese Video Game Industry*, Translational Systems Sciences 35, https://doi.org/10.1007/978-981-99-1342-8_15

Table 15.1 DS and 3DS unit sales in Japan (million units)

	Release year	2nd year	3rd year	4th year	5th year	6th year	7th year
DS	2.12	4.78	9.12	6.36	4.01	4.01	2.35
3DS	1.06	4.79	5.69	4.35	3.07	2.36	1.99

Source: Nintendo Web page
The DS was released in November and the 3DS in February. Since Nintendo's fiscal year ends in March, the period after the release date is completely different for the year of release

The competition between these two markets is not mere platform competition. It is also a competition of business models. Specifically, the competition is between (1) the business model of selling packaged games, which has been used for home video game consoles for more than 30 years, and (2) the business model of providing games as a service, which started in game arcades and is currently used mainly on PCs and smartphones.

The final chapter focuses on competition among markets and business models, rather than on individual markets.

15.1 Inter-market Competition (1): Handheld Game Console Vs. Smartphone

15.1.1 Struggles of Handheld Game Consoles

In February 2011, Nintendo released the Nintendo 3DS (3DS), and in December 2011, Sony released the PlayStation Vita (Vita).

The 3DS retains the basic design of the Nintendo DS, with two screens and a touch panel only on the bottom, but the main screen, the upper screen, supports naked-eye stereoscopic viewing and has a larger screen size and resolution than the lower screen. A 2GB SD card was installed for storing various data, and like the Wii, a Virtual Console service was implemented to allow users to play games from past hardware titles. When it was first released, the price was 25,000 yen, the highest price for any Nintendo game hardware in the past. As a result, more than 1 million units were sold in the first month, but the sales slumped to 210,000 units in the next quarter. Nintendo suddenly announced a price change to 15,000 yen on August 11, 2011, less than 6 months after its launch.[1] As a result, the number of units sold rose, but it was only 60–70% of the number of DS units sold (Table 15.1).

Vita supports both wireless LAN (Wi-Fi) and 3G lines for network connectivity, and models with both 3G and Wi-Fi lines as well as Wi-Fi only models were

[1]For those who purchased before the price change, the Nintendo 3DS Ambassador Program offered 20 free titles (10 Famicom and 10 Game Boy Advance titles) to those who purchased by August 10, 2011. See Nintendo 3DS Ambassador Program (http://www.nintendo.co.jp/3ds/ambassador/index.html).

Table 15.2 Specifications of 3DS and PS Vita

	Nintendo 3DS	PlayStation Vita
Company	Nintendo	Sony Computer Entertainment
Year	2011	2011
Price	25,000 yen (Reduced to 15,000 yen in the same year)	24,980 yen (Wi-Fi model) 29,980 yen (3G/Wi-Fi model)
CPU	Nintendo 1048 OH ARM (Operation speed undisclosed)	Cortex-A9 (Operation speed undisclosed)
GPU	Pica2000	SGX543MP4+
RAM	128 MB	Main 512 MB + VRAM 128 MB
Resolution Colors	800*240 (upper screen) 320*240 (lower screen) 32-bit colors	960*544 32-bit colors
Display	3.53-inch TFT (upper screen) 3.02-inch TFT (lower screen)	5-inch OLED
Power source	Lithium-ion battery, AC adapter	Lithium-ion battery, AC adapter
Playable time	3-5 h	3-5 h
Remarks	Cameras on the front and back. The horizontal resolution of the upper screen is high for stereoscopic viewing. The resolution without stereoscopic viewing is 400*240.	Cameras on the front and back

released. The OLED display is a Sony device with excellent color reproduction, as is typical of Sony's emphasis on audio/visual functions. The retail price was set at 24980 yen for the Wi-Fi model and 29,980 yen for the 3G/Wi-Fi model, but the actual price exceeded 30,000 yen because a memory card to store saved data and downloaded games was required to actually play games. Like the 3DS, PS Vita's sales were slower than those of its predecessor, the PSP, at the time of its launch. Sales finally recovered in 2013 when the price of both models was reduced to 19,980 yen and the successor, which was lighter, was released. The domestic shipments ended on March 1, 2019, without a turnaround like the PSP (Table 15.2).

Although they differ in scale, the common reason for the sluggish hardware sales of both 3DS and Vita is the high price of the console. Compared to the price of the previous hardware at the time of launch, the price of the 3DS was 10,000 yen higher than that of the DS, and the price of the Vita was 5000 yen higher than that of the PSP. This is the cost of the higher total cost of components due to the large increase in the performance of the game consoles. However, both companies could have easily predicted that increasing the price of the console would have resulted in sluggish sales. Nevertheless, the reason for prioritizing higher performance over higher prices is probably due to the rising performance of mobile phones, especially smartphones, which are rapidly becoming popular around the world.

Prior to smartphones, mobile phones had a variety of uses other than games, such as voice calls, e-mail, and Web browsing, and could be used at a reasonably practical level. On the other hand, handheld video game consoles have been equipped with web browsers since the DS and PSP, and of course the 3DS and Vita as well, but they are far inferior to phones in terms of operability and comfort of operation for uses other than playing games. The performance of handheld video game consoles continues to rise, and at this rate, except for avid game users, those who exceed the minimum performance level of handheld video game consoles will be OK with only a phone that can do everything on one device. Both companies feared that potential users would lose the incentive to carry a handheld video game console.

The traditional cell phone, the feature phone, did not exceed the minimum performance required of a handheld video game console for most people, both in terms of performance as a computer and in terms of the interface for playing games. Before social games, the mobile phone game market was stagnant from 2007 to 2009. Social games began to attract attention in 2010, but they were completely different from handheld video game console games, both in terms of the beauty of the screen and the content of the games.

The smartphone surpassed this "minimum line for a game console with its overwhelmingly high basic computer performance and easy-to-understand touch interface."[2] Moreover, It was Puzzle & Dragons that was interesting enough to be used as a game for home video game consoles (see Chap. 14).

15.1.2 Smartphone Breakthrough

The first iPhone was launched by Apple in 2007. It did not sell well, selling only 6.2 million units, but the iPhone 3G, released the following year in 2008, became very popular, and sales increased with each new model released every year thereafter. In 2010, the year before the release of the 3DS and Vita, the spread of smartphones accelerated dramatically, with Apple selling approximately 40 million iPhones worldwide, far exceeding the 31.18 million sold in 2008, the year of the Nintendo DS's best-selling year. iPhone sales exceeded 72 million units in 2011 and 100 million units in 2012. Along with the iPhone, Android-based devices, whose operating system is developed by Google, are competing fiercely for a share in the smartphone market on a global level. iPhone alone has a huge difference in production volume from video game consoles, but when Android devices are added to the mix, the

[2]The touch panels of the Nintendo DS and 3DS are pressure-sensitive and can recognize only one touched location. On the other hand, most smartphone panels are capacitive, allowing multi-touch operation. Therefore, a smartphone's touch panel can be used for a variety of operations. For example, only smartphones can perform the so-called "wipe" operation (i.e., expanding the area to be touched).

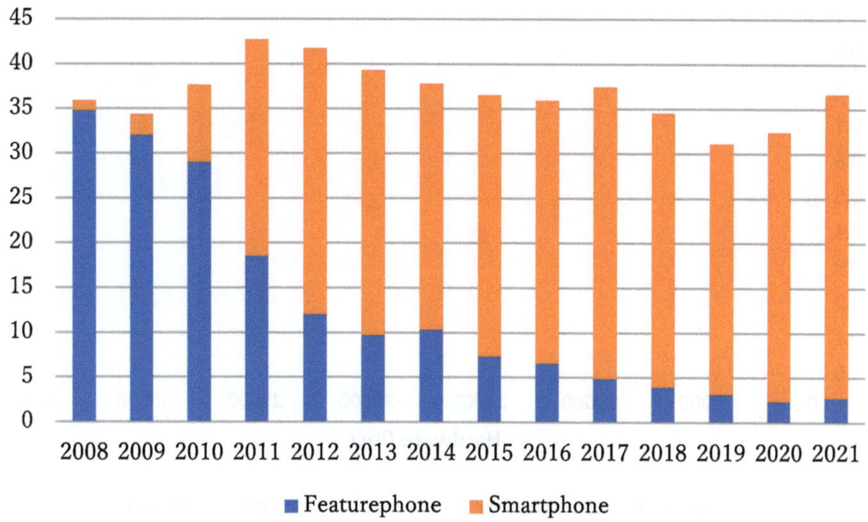

Fig. 15.1 Mobile phone shipments (million units). Source: MM Research Institute, "Overview of Mobile Phone Shipment in Japan," each year

difference in production volume between handheld video game consoles and smartphones is staggering.

Figure 15.1 shows the actual number of smartphones shipped in Japan. The year 2011 marked a major turning point, with an overwhelming increase in the number of smartphones shipped. Since shipments of 3DS peaked at 5.69 million units in the third year, the number of smartphones shipped in Japan is more than five times that of handheld video game consoles. Of course, not all smartphone users play games, but there is no doubt that the number of people playing games on smartphones exceeds the number of users of handheld video game consoles.

Originally, the business of game consoles was based on economies of scale to reduce component purchase prices and increase the number of units sold with overwhelming cost performance. It was the overwhelmingly low price and high performance that enabled the popularization of DVD for PlayStation 2 and Blu-ray for PlayStation 3. The fact that smartphones have surpassed game consoles in terms of unit sales means that they are losing out to smartphones in terms of cost performance, which is the greatest competitive advantage of game consoles. In addition, unlike handheld video game consoles, which can be priced as low as 25,000 yen–30,000 yen, smartphones can be priced much higher. In the case of the iPhone 4S, released in 2011, the same year as the 3DS and Vita, even the smallest model with 16GB capacity costs more than 50,000 yen. The high price of the device itself means that it is possible to produce a high-performance product. In this respect, smartphones have an overwhelming advantage over handheld video game consoles.

Handheld video game consoles have many disadvantages besides performance. Smartphones do not require a large amount of cash at the time of purchase, and there is little hesitation to purchase them. Not only smartphones but older cell phones can

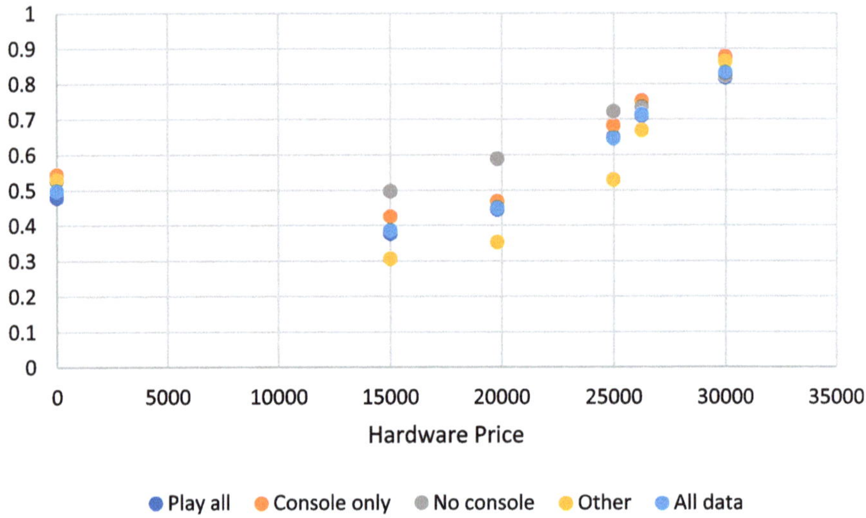

Fig. 15.2 Percentage of those who think game hardware is "expensive" (2012 Koyama Lab. survey)

often be purchased at a substantial discount or for virtually zero yen by offsetting the cost with various services.[3] Even the latest models are often sold in the form of installment payments with the device price added to the monthly cell phone bill. These contractual systems were in place before smartphones were available, but they have undoubtedly facilitated the spread of smartphones as a result.

Figure 15.2 shows the percentages of respondents who "feel that each game hardware is expensive" based on a survey of 2060 computer game players conducted by the author in 2011.[4] The respondents were asked whether they play household videogames, PC online games, or mobile phone games (both non-social and social). Of these, respondents were divided into three groups: "only home video games" (Console only in graph), "never play home video games" (No console in graph), and "others" (e.g., both home video games and social games). The prices of game

[3] Selling mobile phone handsets at reduced prices means that mobile carriers are passing on the cost of handsets to users who do not replace them frequently, and moreover, there is room to lower calling rates to cover the cost of the handsets. In June 2019, the Ministry of Internal Affairs and Communications announced a policy to virtually eradicate discounts on cell phone handsets within 2 years. Considering the fact that several relatively inexpensive handsets in the 30,000-yen range rank high among SIM-free handsets, which users purchase at their own expense, the situation may change again after handset price discount sales by cell phone carriers' end.

[4] This survey was conducted from December 21 to 27, 2012, in cooperation with Macromill, Inc. As the first step, screening survey questions were sent to a pool of about 30,000 respondents, and at least one or more of the following four items were called for in the following survey to investigate in detail: Home video games, Online games, Mobile games (non-social cell phone games), and social games (including smartphone games). The survey data consisted of 206 samples of men and women in their teens to 50 s, for a total of 2060 samples.

hardware as of the time of the survey (December 2012) were clearly indicated, and respondents were asked to answer whether they thought this game console was expensive or not. For the iPhone 4S, a smartphone sold at the time of the survey, respondents were asked to answer whether they thought the purchase was expensive without specifying the price, since the price was unstable due to preferential treatment by mobile phone carriers.

As can be seen immediately at first glance, the percentage of respondents who feel that the hardware is expensive increases as the hardware price increases, regardless of the price-performance ratio of the hardware. Among the respondents, the ratio of those who do not play household video games who feel that the price is high is particularly high. In addition, the percentage of respondents who feel that the price is high for the iPhone, regardless of the game playing style, is concentrated at around 50%. The percentage of respondents who feel that the price is high is one indicator of whether the price exceeds 50% or not, but even for the 3DS, which is the least expensive console, the percentage of respondents who do not play household games who feel the price is high is 50%. Although handheld video game consoles are cheaper in terms of both price and production cost, the percentage of respondents who think they are more expensive than the iPhone smartphone is high. This indicates that it is very difficult for handheld video game consoles to compete with smartphones.

Furthermore, the core of smartphone games is free to play, as typified by Puzzle & Dragons, which can be downloaded online and played free of charge in principle. Users who are interested in a game can download it and try it for free. There is no need to pay a large sum of money to buy a game at a store. The difficulty level is lower than that of handheld video game consoles at every stage, from purchasing the hardware, to acquiring the game, to starting to play. Handheld video game consoles are in an overwhelmingly difficult situation compared to smartphones. Currently, there are only two major groups of people who go out of their way to play games on handheld video game consoles rather than smartphones. One is elementary and junior high school students. Parents of elementary and junior high school students often avoid giving them item-priced games or even smartphones for educational reasons. The influence of smartphones is still weak among this group, and handheld video game consoles continue to be the most familiar information terminal for them.

In addition to the *Pokémon* series, which is the most popular title for elementary and junior high school students, Yokai Watch (2013), released by Level-5 for 3DS, became a huge hit and a social phenomenon. The other is the avid gamer of conventional games who is not satisfied with games for smartphones, which are mainly free to play and item priced. This trend is particularly high for Vita, which has a high screen resolution and performance, and has released many mid-hit titles that have sold around 100,000 copies and have been well received by enthusiasts, such as Persona 4 the Golden (Atlus, 2012) and Ys: Folitage Ocean of Celceta (Nihon Falcom, 2012). After the PlayStation 3 generation of home consoles, games for handheld video game consoles, which have lower development costs than home consoles, such as RPG series that were released on home consoles in the past, have been on the rise, and this trend has been further reinforced as a result.

Table 15.3 Mobile shift in game consumption

	Handheld console	Featurephone	Smartphone
2004	Launch of DS and PSP		
2006	Market structure change Handheld > Home console		
2007		Non-Social game market is almost saturated	
2008		Social games become common	iPhone sales start in Japan
2011	3DS launched and struggling Price reduction during the same year	Social games market become peak and social problem	Share of smartphone sales in Japan exceeds 50% of total mobile phone sales
2012		Regulation of comp-gacha	Puzzle & Dragons
2016	Launch of Switch		Pokémon GO
2017			Kouya Koudou (Knives Out)
2019	Launch of Switch Lite		

Table 15.3 shows a chronological list of events occurring on handheld video game consoles, feature phones, and smartphones. In 2004, the Nintendo DS and PSP were launched, and in 2006, handheld video game console games surpassed home console games in terms of market size. In the same year, the market size of games for mobile phones reached 74.8 billion yen, but the growth of the non-social game market for mobile phones slowed down, reaching 84.8 billion yen the following year, after which it hardly grew at all. The item-paying social game market began to take off in 2007 and grew rapidly from 2009 to 2011. In the meantime, SoftBank started selling the iPhone in 2008. In 2012, the Consumer Affairs Agency (CAA) issued an opinion that comp-gacha, a type of gacha, violates the Act against Unjustifiable Premiums and Misleading Representations, leading social game companies to self-regulate by setting a monthly limit on the amount of money charged. In 2012, users left social games for feature phones due to the comp-gacha scandal, but what seems to have had an even greater impact was the release of Puzzle & Dragons on smartphones. The number of smartphones in use has been rapidly increasing since 2011, and paid applications for smartphones have been considered a strong possibility. In this context, Puzzle & Dragons was born as an example of a game for smartphones with a set business model.

Although smartphone games have caught the market trend with Pazudora, as seen in the previous chapter, development costs are skyrocketing.[5] As a result, the gap between winning titles that can continue to generate profits that far exceed their development costs over the long term and losing titles that end their services without generating much profit despite the high development costs has widened.

To increase the number of new players in smartphone games, they need to be constantly exposed to people's eyes, and it is important to be (and continue to be) at the top of the application ranking. In addition, commercials on TV are frequently conducted to increase people's awareness.[6] In 2014, colopl aired game commercials for Quiz RPG: The World of Mystic Wiz and Shironeko Project 7042 times, and Gungho aired commercials for Puzzle & Dragons 6071 times. The cost of TV commercials alone is estimated to be in the hundreds of millions of yen, indicating the stiff competition and high profits to be gained when smartphone games are successful.

Smartphone game users are spreading to middle-aged and older adults. Pokémon GO, which began service in 2016, is played by many middle-aged and older users. In 2018, Kouya Koudou (Knives Out), a battle royale game developed by China's Netease Games, also ranked in the list. Although the gameplay of Kouya Koudou is very different from existing Japanese games, it is very popular among young people in their teens and twenties, and is actively being played on the Internet. For a long time, the Japanese game market has been protected from foreign games due to differences in graphics and game genre preferences, but the success of Kouya Koudou is symbolic of the changing tastes of Japanese consumers, especially among the younger generation.

---

[5]The trend toward higher development costs is accelerating, with some games now costing several hundred million yen, and even more than one billion yen. The following news site reported the following statement from a representative of Sega's network division.

"Another notable trend is the soaring development costs. If marketing and operational development costs, as well as the initial development costs, are added up, I think it will be 1.5 billion yen in the first year in Japan alone, and possibly more than 2 billion yen if TV commercials are used. And it is becoming clear which companies are ready to invest and which are not."

[New Year's Eve Special: Low-cost and rapid overseas expansion", Sega Games, which produced several hit titles last year, is next looking to create "world-class titles.] (Nenshi Kikaku: "Tei Cost Katsu Jinsoku na Kaigai Tenkai wo"... Sakunen Hukusuu no Hit Saku wo Umidashita Sega Games ga tsugi ni Misueru noha "Sekai ni Tsuyou suru Title" no Soushutsu)

http://gamebiz.jp/?p=154751

[6]The reason why there are so many commercials for smartphone games is partly because of their financial power, but also because it is difficult for games to spread by word of mouth. In the survey conducted by the Koyama Laboratory, the percentage of respondents who recommended a game they liked to others was lower for social games than for home video games. In many cases, both social games and smartphone games offer items for inviting friends to play the game, and there is a possibility that people may think that introducing a game is not purely for fun, but for profit. This may be the reason why it is difficult to introduce games by word of mouth and why they rely on TV commercials.

15.2 Market Competition (2): Home Consoles Versus PCs

15.2.1 Home Consoles Are Becoming Inexpensive High-End PCs

The PlayStation 3 and Xbox360, released at the height of the home video game console market, were launched at prices far below their production costs, with huge development costs being used as a technology driver. As already mentioned, this resulted in huge losses that threatened the sustainability of the business. Both PlayStation 4 (PS4 in the graphs below) and Xbox One adopted the same x86-64 architecture as PCs for their CPUs, which greatly reduced the cost of technology development. In addition, both PS4 and Xbox One use AMD's APU (Accelerated Processing Unit: a chip that integrates the CPU and GPU) to reduce the number of components and manufacturing costs. As a result, the manufacturing cost of PS4 is $381 ($399 in the USA) and that of Xbox One is $471 ($499 in the USA), which is slightly lower than the main unit price. Although the company probably incurred a loss in terms of shipping prices, the loss was small and at a level that would allow it to maintain continuity as a business.

The previous two models (PS2 and PS3) were more powerful than the best PC at the time of their release, but less expensive. However, because of keeping manufacturing costs low, PS4 has a performance level comparable to the current high-performance (but not the highest performance) PCs, but at a lower price. Of course, the hardware design, including the OS and data transfer bus width, is tuned for games, so it is far more powerful than playing games on a PC with a similar CPU and GPU, but it no longer has an overwhelming performance advantage over the PC.

In addition, due to significant architectural changes, PS4 is no longer compatible with previous hardware (PS1 ~ 3 in the case of PS4). SCE has made PS3 titles playable via PlayStation Now,[7] a cloud-based streaming gaming service, but the number of supported games is limited and there is a separate service fee. On the other hand, Xbox One is compatible with Xbox 360 titles, and titles that have been purchased and are available on the console can be played for free. However, as with the original Xbox 360 titles, software processing is required on the console side, and not all titles are supported.

On the other hand, Nintendo's WiiU did not participate in the performance race, but only converted the Wii, which did not support the HD quality display that has become the current standard for TVs, to HD and adopted the WiiU Gamepad, a controller with a 6.2-inch LCD screen. The WiiU Gamepad can display the actual game screen and can also be used as a sub-screen for games, enabling a variety of

[7] PlayStation Now began closed beta testing in North America in 2014 and officially launched in 2015. In Japan, the service was launched after a closed beta test in 2015.PlayStation Now also offered the service on Sony and Samsung Smart TVs, Blu-Ray disc players, and PS Vita, but ended in 2017. The service was later extended to Windows PCs and PlayStation 5. The service is now integrated into the PlayStation Plus service.

Table 15.4 Release date of each hardware

	Release date	
	Japan	North America
Wii	December 2nd, 2006	November 19th, 2006
PlayStation 3	November 11th, 2006	November 17th, 2006
Xbox 360	December 10th, 2005	November 22nd, 2005
WiiU	December 8th, 2012	November 18th, 2012
PlayStation 4	February 22nd, 2014	November 15th, 2013
Xbox One	September 4th, 2014	November 22nd, 2013

expressions through the developer's ingenuity. As a computer, it is superior to the previous generation's high-end consoles PS3 and Xbox360, but is the lowest among the PS4 and Xbox One consoles of the same generation. This is partly due to the fact that it was released in 2012, 1 year earlier than the other two, but it is also the result of the pursuit of compactness and low power consumption, as was the case with the previous generation Wii. As for backward compatibility, the WiiU can play games from the previous model, the Wii, but it is not compatible with the GameCube.

Table 15.4 lists the release dates for each hardware. The world's fastest release date for any hardware is not in Japan. Even in the previous generation of hardware, when the relative position of the Japanese game industry was declining, Wii and Xbox360 were released after the North American market, but the lag between their release dates was less than 1 month. In this generation, except for the Wii U, the gap between release dates in North America has widened, with the PS4 releasing 3 months later and the Xbox One, which is unlikely to succeed in Japan, 10 months later than its predecessors. The attractiveness and priority of the Japanese market, where home consoles are in even greater decline than overseas, is declining even more than the market share.

PS4 and Xbox One have also introduced upward-compatible devices that support 4 K resolution (2160p: progressive rendering of 3840*2160 pixels). The PlayStation4 Pro (PS4 Pro[8]) from Sony, which supports 2160p output, were launched in 2016, and the Xbox One S from Microsoft, which supports 4 K video and Ultra HD Blu-Ray (Blu-ray with 2160p support) (games are not supported), were launched in 2016. The Xbox One X, which also supports games in 4 K resolution, was released in 2017. This is a strategy designed for heavy gamers who want to play games with higher image quality and frame rates. Although these hardware consoles are 0.5 generation advanced as game consoles, they are PS4 (or Xbox One) consoles with a more powerful CPU and graphics chip to support high resolution, and no exclusive titles will be prepared for them. In this respect, it differs from the past 0.5 generation evolution of Nintendo's handheld video game consoles (GB to GB Color, DS to DSi, 3DS to New 3DS).

[8]PS4 Pro supports 2160p screen output, but internal processing upscales after rendering at resolutions smaller than 2160p (e.g., 2560*1440 or 2840*1600). In addition, it did not support Ultra HD Blu-Ray, which was supported by Microsoft.

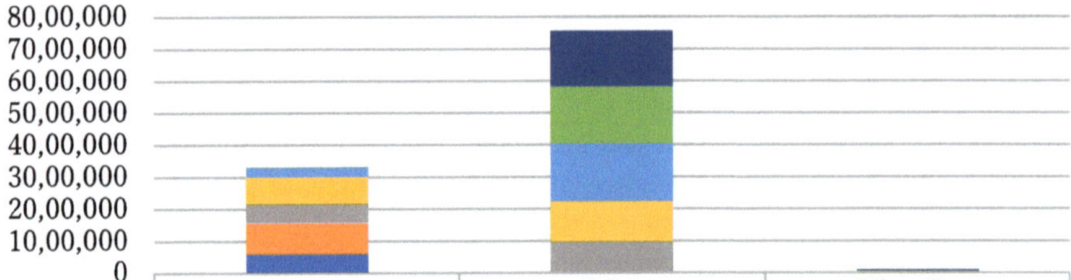

	WiiU	PS4	XboxOne
2018		1726251	16272
2017	16327	1785153	13430
2016	289001	1808499	11209
2015	848556	1268967	18897
2014	591947	992112	45636
2013	9,64,047		
2012	6,33,377		

Fig. 15.3 Sales of the three hardware titles in Japan Source: VGChart.com. PS4 and Xbox One include successor upward-compatible devices

Figure 15.3 shows the number of units sold for each hardware from 2012, when the WiiU was launched, to 2018. The WiiU has been sluggish in terms of sales. In particular, in 2013, the second year when it was expected to gain momentum, sales did not reach 1 million units (960,000 units), less than one-third of the Wii's second year (3.6 million units according to Famitsu.com data[9]). In 2014, the number of units sold declined from 2013, which is the same as the sales pattern of the second- and third-largest hardware brands in terms of sales volume alone. PlayStation 4 sold just under 1 million units in 2014, and sales continued to grow steadily in 2015. In addition, PlayStation 4 had the fastest global penetration pace ever, with a large increase in the number of countries in South America and Asia where the console was launched.

The PlayStation 5 (PS5) and Xbox Series X|S, successors to the PS4 and Xbox One, were both released in November 2020. Due to the sluggish market, Japan did not have the fastest release date for new consoles in recent years, but this generation of consoles was released on the same date as the rest of the world. Microsoft's Xbox Series X|S was released 2 days earlier, on November 10, while Sony's PS5 was released on November 12.

Microsoft launched two successor models to the Xbox One: the Xbox Series X with 4 K/120fps rendering performance and the Xbox Series S, a lower-priced model with WQHD/120fps rendering performance and no disk drive. Although there is no difference in performance, Sony also released two models: the PS5 Console with a

[9]The results differ between the Famitsu Game White Paper (January–December) and Nintendo's official data (April–March) due to the different counting periods.

disk drive and the PS5 Digital Edition without a disk drive. Both the Xbox Series X and PS5 have a rendering performance of 4 K/120fps, which is comparable in performance to the high-performance gaming PCs released in the same year. There is little difference in hardware architecture or the games that can be played, and the only differences between home consoles and PCs are price and a simpler user interface.

From launch to November 2022, the Xbox Series X|S sold a combined total of about 400,000 units in Japan, while the PS5 sold about 2.22 million units.[10] The Xbox Series X|S has sold better than its predecessor, the Xbox One, but never in sufficient numbers; PS5 sales are comparable to the first 2 years of PS4 sales, but there was a lack of PS5 distribution in Japan, with some mass retailers selling the PS5 by lottery. The lack of distribution has also led to problems with resale by users at high prices.

Competition in packaged games was easily settled at an early stage in Japan. In Japan, the PC-9801 dominated the PC market for a long time without improving its basic performance, and the market shrank rapidly after the launch of PlayStation and Saturn in 1994, which marked a generational shift in home video game consoles.

On the other hand, PCs are the main source of online games. In the early days of online gaming, home video game consoles led the market, but the PC has taken over the central position. In 2014, PCs accounted for 85.9 billion yen, while home video game consoles accounted for 5.2 billion yen, including online games for handheld video game consoles. The proportion of games for home video game consoles increased as a result of an increase in the number of games for home video game consoles that charged for items, but in 2018, PCs accounted for 75% of the 77.3 billion yen market size for online game management services for PCs and home video game consoles combined.

The reasons for the mainstream use of PCs in online games are as follows:

1. New ways of playing games, such as browser games, have emerged. Browser games are often played in the spare time of people who normally run a PC, and there is little room for home video game consoles to enter the market.
2. For games that have been in service for a long time (especially MMORPGs), the performance of home video game consoles has become a thing of the past, and they are a bottleneck for updating. Especially in the case of MMORPGs that have been in service for more than 5 years, the performance of home video game consoles, which was equal to or better than that of PCs at the beginning of the service, is now outdated.

Taking MMORPGs as an example, Final Fantasy XI, which had a tremendous impact on the launch of the online game market, shifted its weight from PlayStation 2 to PC as its service life exceeded 10 years. Final Fantasy XIV, the second Final

[10] According to Famitsu's estimates (https://www.famitsu.com/news/202212/08285768.html).
To be exact, there are 171,827 units for Xbox Series X, 223,025 units for Xbox Series S, 1,919,558 units for PS5 Console, and 299,694 units for PS5 Digital Edition.

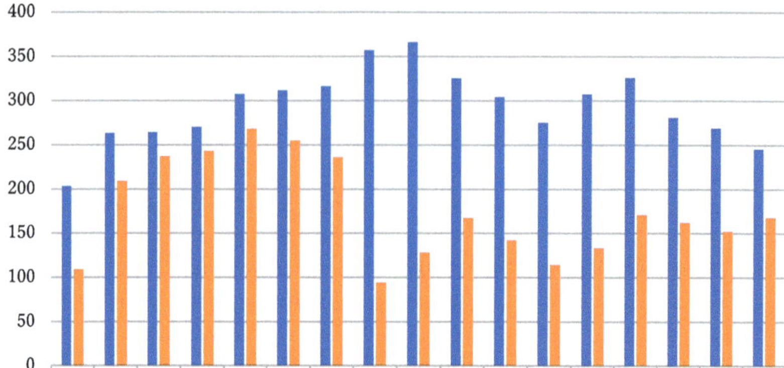

	2005	2006	2007	2008	2009	2010	2011	2012	2013	2014	2015	2016	2017	2018	2019	2020	2021
PC	204	264	265	271	308	312	317	358	367	326	305	276	308	327	282	270	246
Home Console	110	210	238	244	269	256	237	95	129	168	143	115	134	172	163	153	169

Fig. 15.4 Number of online game service titles for PC and home console. Source: JOGA Online Game Market Research Report 2022

Fantasy MMORPG, was launched in 2010 for Windows prior to the home console version. The PlayStation 3 version was not only launched at the same time as a major update of the PC version in 2013,[11] but also has the limitation that the playable resolution is 720p (1280 × 720 pixels), which is rougher than the highest resolution of the PC version (1920 × 1080 pixels). Unlike PCs, which run Windows except for a very small number of users, the number of home video game consoles in widespread use is important. If the popularity of home video game consoles is sluggish, it is inevitable that the business will be dominated by PC versions. In the case of Dragon Quest X, the initial plan was to release the game on the Wii and gradually migrate to the WiiU after the WiiU became popular, but due to the sluggish sales of the WiiU, a Windows version was released, and the Windows version is now the core of the business.

Figure 15.4 shows the number of game titles offered online on PC and home video game consoles. The online service for home video games includes PC titles such as MMORPGs, as well as "online-enabled" games that implement the network battle function in both handheld console games[12] and packaged games released for home video game consoles.

[11] At the time of service launch, FINAL FANTASY XIV had numerous bugs, shortcomings in specifications, and inadequacies in progress management, such as the large number of Chinese language terms that remained in the game, and users had numerous complaints. Therefore, the service was terminated after 2 years and restarted as "FINAL FANTASY XIV: A Realm Reborn" with significant changes that were virtually like new development. At the beginning of the service, it was planned to release a package for PlayStation 3 with the old version, but the release was cancelled and the new version was released in time for the start of the new version.

[12] The majority of online games for handheld video game consoles are ports of games for smartphones. In other words, this is a market for secondary use of content. Many users are

In the case of home video game consoles, there is a major problem of generational change in game consoles. Basically, when a next-generation console is released and passes the period of popularization, games for the previous generation of consoles are no longer released. As a result, the number of people playing games on these consoles decreases, leading to the cessation of services. The exception to this is games such as Final Fantasy XI on the PlayStation 2, which gained many users, but in this case, the question was always when to terminate the service after the release of the next-generation consoles, PlayStation 3 and even the next-generation console, PlayStation 4.[13]

15.2.2 *Nintendo Switch*

Nintendo's Switch was developed as a gaming console that would integrate the two markets of handheld video game consoles and home consoles. On March 17, 2016, Nintendo announced at a press conference that it was developing a new dedicated game console under the development code name NX, which was launched as Nintendo Switch (Switch) on March 3, 2017.

The Switch is a game console that explores new ways of playing games that are typical of Nintendo. There are three types of play modes: TV mode, in which the Switch is connected to a TV; tabletop mode, in which the Switch's display image is shared; and handheld mode, in which the controllers are combined on either side of the Switch.

In TV mode, the Switch is connected to a docking station called the Switch dock, which is no different from a regular home console. When playing in handheld mode, the main unit is disconnected from the docking station. The Switch is equipped with a 6.2-inch LCD and a battery, and becomes a handheld video game console by combining the left stick and right button of the controller (Joy-Con) used when playing in front of the TV with the right and left sides of the console, respectively. The Joy-Con also contains a battery and can be separated from the main unit and played as a tabletop mode in which the Joy-Con is used as a wireless controller. In the tabletop mode, two players can play against each other, with each player using one Joy-Con.

When Nintendo announced the release of the Switch, the first PV showed the Switch being taken outdoors and played by several people in tabletop mode. This is in line with Nintendo's policy since the Wii in that it is not for enthusiasts, but for party use where everyone can play together.

---

elementary and junior high school students who do not have smartphones (or whose parents do not allow them to have smartphones). Although the market size is much smaller than that of smartphones, it is a market that cannot be ignored if it is to lead users to their own content in the future.

[13]Finally, the PS2 version of FF11 ended on March 25, 2016, and the Xbox 360 version on March 31, 2016.

While the gimmicks of the Switch are very elaborate, the user interface (UI) is very orthodox. The Joy-Con has a stick +4 buttons + L (or R) button, not much different from past consoles. The LCD is capacitive and multi-tap compatible, not much different from smartphones and tablet PCs. This means that smartphone games can be ported directly to the Switch if necessary. In addition to the standard interface, the Switch is equipped with an acceleration sensor, gyro sensor, and brightness sensor on the main unit. The left Joy-Con has an acceleration sensor and gyro sensor, while the right Joy-Con has an acceleration sensor, gyro sensor, and motion IR camera. These interfaces are suitable for party games played by moving the body, as has been the case since the Wii, but like the Wii, they have not been effectively utilized since the release of a few titles immediately after the hardware's launch. In addition, a device (Alps Alpine's Haptic Reactor) that enables realistic tactile feedback was installed, and depending on the ingenuity of game designers, this device could also be applied to VR (virtual reality), but this has not been fully utilized.

The Switch attracted worldwide attention from the moment it was announced in the news. From March 3, 2017, when it was launched, to the end of March, it became a hit with shipments of 600,000 units in Japan and 2.74 million units worldwide. Sales have continued to grow since then, with 8.23 million units sold in Japan and 34.74 million units sold worldwide as of the end of March 2019, 2 years after its release.[14]

Although the Switch is a latecomer as a home console, it is inferior to rival consoles such as the PlayStation 4 and Xbox One in terms of performance. As with the Wii and Wii U, this is a strategy aimed at becoming the second or later console for consumers. While Sony and Microsoft are releasing upward-compatible PlayStation4 Pro and Xbox One X home consoles, Nintendo released Switch Lite on September 20, 2019. It is a lightweight device (275 grams; the Switch weighs 398 grams) by eliminating the gimmick, reducing the screen size to 5.5 inches, and omitting various sensors. This was ahead of the launch of a new Pokémon game for Switch (Pokémon Sword and Pokémon Shield: November 15, 2019).

Although Pokémon can be played by individuals, the game design is based on the premise that players gather together with their game consoles and battle Pokémon that they have raised themselves. Therefore, the business model of Pokémon differs from that of home consoles, in which one console is purchased per household, to that of handheld video game consoles, in which each player purchases a console and the same number of games are purchased. The Switch was positioned as the successor to both the WiiU and the 3DS, but it is now more of a successor to the 3DS.

[14]The sales volume of the WiiU was not disclosed by Nintendo until the end of March 2017. At that point, the WiiU sold 3.34 million units in Japan and 13.56 million units worldwide. The Switch sold 17.79 million units worldwide as of the end of March 2018, surpassing the WiiU's sales volume a little over a year after its launch.

15.2.3 Expansion of Internet Services and Widespread Download Sales

One of the major recent trends common to both home video game consoles and PCs is the spread of download sales. At first glance, the expansion of downloadable games seems natural, as the number of Internet users, especially home broadband Internet users, is increasing, making it possible to purchase and play games without having to go to a store. In addition, downloadable games have the advantage of not incurring the cost of packaging, which lowers the price of the product, and of not incurring warehousing costs and taxes on inventory. There are many other advantages for game companies, such as no opportunity loss due to no selling out, the possibility of distributing trial versions in advance, and the ability to know the demographics and trends of purchasers based on the account information of users who have purchased the game. However, the game companies have been selling their games in packaged form at retail outlets, and download sales, which do not earn money for the retailers, could cause a backlash from the retailers.

Download sales of home console video games began much later, with the PlayStation 3, Wii, and Xbox 360, the seventh generation of video game consoles. The STBs for TVs and Internet-capable TVs, which were pioneers in this field, failed in terms of business. The strategy by companies to install hardware in the living room and use the TV as a monitor to connect to the Internet continued to fail. The Internet connection rate for this generation of home video game consoles was also low and did not spread widely. In addition, home console games were very large in size, making it difficult to sell packaged games in stores as downloads.

Game companies started their business by selling relatively small-size download-only games and older generation consoles in the CD-ROM era, but it would take time for full-fledged download sales to spread. Download sales of packaged games on the Xbox360 began in 2009, and download sales of packaged games on the PlayStation 3 began in 2011. Nintendo did not start selling packaged games by downloading for the Wii, starting with the WiiU.

In the handheld video game console market, SCE began offering downloadable titles of the original PlayStation titles for the PSP in 2006. However, at the beginning of the service, games were downloaded to PC or PlayStation 3, and then transferred to the PSP system, which was not easy to use. It was not until 2008 that packaged games could be downloaded directly from the PSP system. In 2009, SCE released the PSP go, a model exclusively for download sales without a UMD drive, but sales were sluggish and the model was discontinued in 2011 while the regular PSP was still on sale. Nintendo did not sell downloadable games for the Nintendo DS. Instead, Nintendo released the Nintendo DSi,[15] a higher-end version of the

[15]The DSi sold 17.79 million units worldwide, surpassing WiiU sales in a little over a year after its release. In addition, it was effectively 0.5 generation ahead of its predecessor, with some DSi exclusive titles that did not run on the DS. Although only one title was sold in Japan, multiple titles were released outside of Japan. Nintendo also adopted the strategy of "advancing the handheld

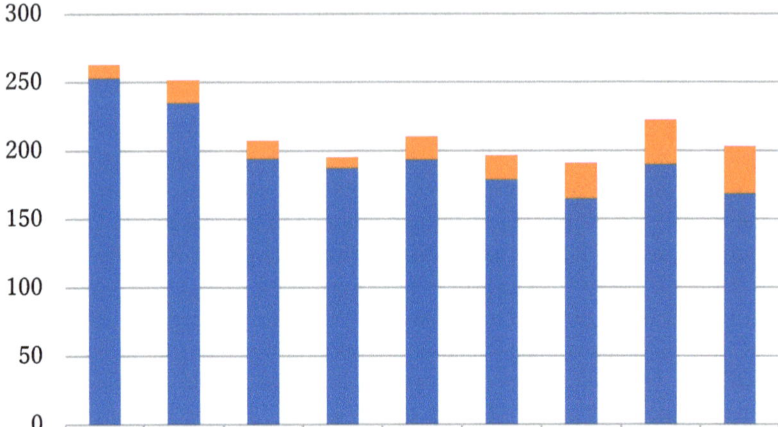

	2013	2014	2015	2016	2017	2018	2019	2020	2021
Download	10.3	16.5	13.1	7.9	16.8	17.4	25.9	32.2	34.6
Package	253.7	235.6	194.9	188	194.2	179.6	165.7	190.6	169.1

Fig. 15.5 Trends in the size of the home video game software market. (billion yen) Source: CESA White Paper on Games, various annual editions

DS, in 2008, and started selling DSiWare, a title exclusively for the DSi, for downloading. Download sales of packaged games for the console began with the Nintendo 3DS.

The market size of downloadable games for home video game consoles has been included in the CESA Game White Paper since the 2014 White Paper (2013 for statistics). Figure 15.5 shows the market size of home video game software since 2013. The market size of home video game software declined sharply in 2015, partly due to the replacement of hardware, and sales of packaged software fell below 200 billion yen. The market size of download sales has increased in recent years to exceed 20% of packaged sales. Markets where the same content is available in both physical media and electronic data include books and music, but the proportion of digital sales in 2021 were higher than in games.[16] Due to data size issues, download sales of home video games have not spread very far.

video game console by 0.5 generation 'and' preparing exclusive games for the console" in the Game Boy era (Game Boy to Game Boy Color) and Nintendo 3DS (Nintendo 3DS to Nintendo new3DS).

[16]Of the publishing market in 2021, paper publications (books and magazines combined) will amount to ¥1208 billion and electronic publishing to ¥466.2 billion (Japan Association of National Publishers and Publishing Science Institute, January 25, 2022). Of the music market in 2021, the size of the music software market, which includes audio records (\128 billion) and music videos (\65.6 billion), is \193.6 billion, and the music distribution market, which includes downloading and streaming, is \89.5 billion *(Recording Industry in Japan 2022*, Recording Industry Association of Japan).

On the other hand, PCs have always had a culture of freeware and shareware,[17] and downloading and installing software was natural. In addition, in the 2000s, when Internet use became widespread, most of the packaged games sold in the market were already adult games, and free distribution of software for installation was common in online games (especially MMORPG). Online download sales were mainly for adult games, and sales of packaged games for the general public (non-18) were effectively downloaded sales of older titles. Although sales channels were supposed to have been expanded through download sales, no new companies appeared to develop and sell packaged games for the PC. Porting from home video game consoles has not led to a revival of the declining PC game market, with only historical simulation games from Koei Tecmo and RPGs from Nihon Falcom being released.

Looking outside of Japan, download sales were widespread at an earlier stage than in Japan, partly due to the difficulty of establishing a nationwide distribution network in foreign countries (especially in the USA) because of the country's geographical location. In the case of Electronic Arts (EA), the largest US company, digital sales (full game downloads, additional content, and others) for home video game consoles reached $1.068 billion in FY2015. This represents 35.5% of total sales for home consoles ($3.011 billion). For PCs, only the combined figures for download sales and browser games[18] have been released, but digital sales here amounted to $638 million, or 72.7% of total PC/browser game sales.

Unlike Japan, the PC game market in the USA has continued the cycle of various innovative games being created and ported to home video game consoles throughout the MS-DOS and Windows eras. Even today, many games are released for both PC and home consoles. In such an environment, innovative games were first released on PCs, and high-end PCs have a higher screen resolution and FPS (Frames per second), and have maintained a reasonable market size, especially among high-end users. As the gap between PCs and home consoles has narrowed due to generational changes in game consoles, the importance of the PC game market has declined, but the PC market has been maintained to some extent. Figure 15.6 shows the size of the US video game market. In the graph, "PC" and "Home" refer to physical package sales until 2009, and do not include download sales. The "Other Delivery Formats" section from 2010 onward includes mobile phones and other devices.[19] Therefore, it is not possible to make a strict argument, but it can be confirmed that the physical package market for PC games was about 40% of the home video game market in 2000, at 1.78 billion dollars, but the market size has been declining year by year, and by 2014, it had dropped to a negligible size. In addition, the physical package market

[17] Of the software that can be downloaded, freeware is the one that is completely free, and shareware is the one that can be tried out and paid for if liked.

[18] However, the figures are almost exclusively for packaged games for the PC, as EA's browser game business is very small.

[19] Other delivery formats include subscription-based billing, downloadable games, add-on content, mobile phone applications, SNS games, and other physical delivery.

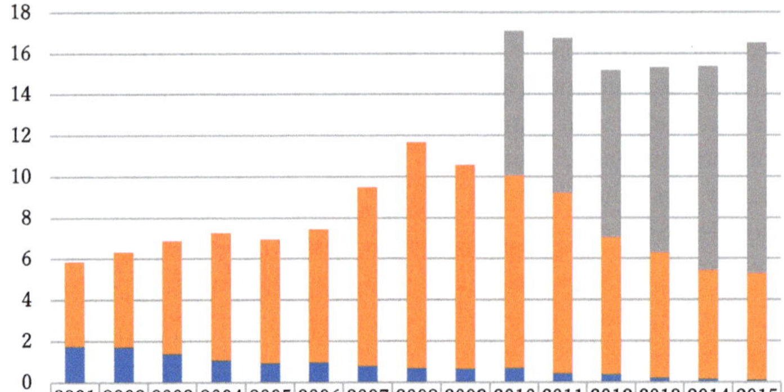

	2001	2002	2003	2004	2005	2006	2007	2008	2009	2010	2011	2012	2013	2014	2015
Other Dilivery Formats										7	7.5	8.1	9	9.9	11.2
Console	4.1	4.6	5.5	6.2	6	6.5	8.7	11	9.9	9.4	8.8	6.7	6.1	5.3	5.2
PC	1.78	1.75	1.4	1.1	0.96	0.98	0.82	0.7	0.68	0.7	0.45	0.38	0.22	0.17	0.11

Fig. 15.6 US game market size ($ billion). Source: ESA *Essential Facts*, annual editions (The data format has changed since 2016 (Essential Facts 2017) and is not shown in the graph. After 2016, the total market size and the ratio between physical format and digital format are shown, going back to 2010. According to this, the share of digital formats in 2010 was 31%, but by 2018 it had risen to 83%)

is less than half the size of the home video game market compared to its peak in 2008. The download sales have made up for the decline in the physical package market.

15.2.4 STEAM and the Expansion of Indie Games

Steam, a platform operated by the game company Valve, is playing a role in the worldwide expansion of download sales. By purchasing a game online or registering the rights to use a packaged game on Steam, the game can be installed and played on any PC with an Internet connection. Game updates are also performed automatically. DRM (Digital Rights Management) is an important issue in download sales, but Steam is characterized by its DRM management, which is very user-friendly.

Valve is a privately held company, so official information is not publicly available, but by 2020, Steam will have 120 million active accounts (the number of accounts that actually purchase and play games) worldwide, with more than 9000 games offered in a year, and will have reached the level of a global infrastructure. The number of active Steam accounts (the number of accounts that actually purchase and play games) is 120 million worldwide, and more than 9000 games are offered in a year. The total sales of games on Steam in 2022 are estimated to be $6.6 billion.[20]

[20] See the following two articles:

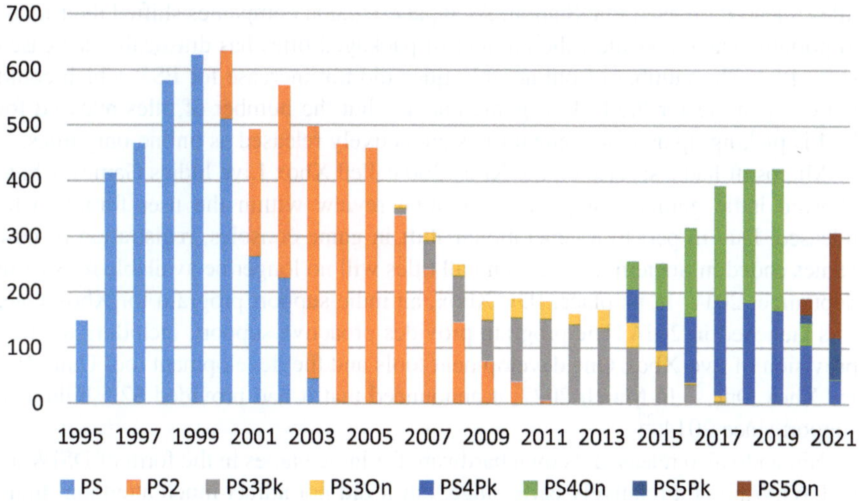

Fig. 15.7 Number of each PlayStation sales titles (released in Japan). Pk refers to packaged titles, Onl refers to online-only titles. Titles released in 1994 are included in 1995 Source: Prepared by the author from data from Famitsu.com

This huge market is not only created by download sales of existing packaged games, but also includes many works by independent companies (or individuals/creative groups) called "indies," which provide a valuable infrastructure for them to access the global market. In Japan, games produced by individuals or circles have long been distributed as "doujin games" at doujinshi sales events such as Comic Market, or sold on consignment at doujinshi consignment stores such as Torano Ana and Melon Books. Although many titles were of a high standard, sales were limited to Japan only due to the lack of language (especially English) support and sales channels. Around 2010, when Steam became famous as a global market, some Japanese doujin circles began to release localized games in collaboration with overseas localization companies, for example, by translating in-game messages into English.

Indie games are also attracting attention from the home video game console side. This is not only because competition with PCs and smartphones is fierce, but also because the number of titles released has decreased due to the huge scale and development costs of regular packaged games. Another reason is that the soaring development costs have made game development more conservative, and the number of sequels and related titles to existing titles has increased, making it difficult to come up with new and innovative game designs. Figure 15.7 shows the number of

"96 Steam Statistics You Must Know: 2023 Market Share Analysis & Data," https://financesonline.com/steam-statistics/

"Steam games market size will decline in 2022 after reaching $6.6bn in 2021,"

https://www.gamedeveloper.com/blogs/steam-games-market-size-will-decline-in-2022-after-reaching-6-6bn-in-2021

titles released on each PlayStation. As Japanese game companies shifted their focus to portable game consoles, the number of packaged titles has drastically decreased since PS3. The number of online-only titles did not increase for PS3, which could not compensate for the lack of game lineups, but the number of titles released for PS4 is picking up as independent titles are actively released as online-only titles.

Microsoft had a service on the Xbox 360 called Xbox Live Indies Games, which allowed indie games that passed a mutual review within the user forum to be released. Due in part to a generational shift in game consoles, registration of new games ended in September 2015, and all titles will no longer be available for sale in September 2017. In its place, ID@Xbox, an indie support program for Xbox One, was launched in 2014. The program provides proactive support, including the free provision of two Xbox One development tools and the development tool Unity Pro for Xbox One.[21] In March 2022, it announced that it had provided $2.5 billion in support since 2014.[22]

Nintendo also released its own hardware for indie games in the form of DSiWare and WiiWare at a relatively early stage, but it did not attract much attention. Indie games are also available for download on the 3DS and WiiU, but the response has not been as strong as that of the other two companies, possibly due to the different user bases. It was not until the launch of the Switch that indie game releases became more active.

In the past, indie games were actively developed and released on smartphones. In the early days of the smartphone game market, from around 2009 to 2010, there were big hits such as Angry Birds (Rovio Entertainment) developed by a Finnish venture company. However, as more and more companies entered the market, the number of games became large, and the price of a single game dropped to a few dollars, making the market less attractive. In addition, the trend in smartphone games has shifted from sell-only downloads to free distribution and item charges, and development costs have skyrocketed as games have grown in size, and the momentum of indie games has waned.

Existing packaged games, whose development has become large scale and the number of sales required to recover costs has increased, often drift toward safe content that can be accepted by a large number of people. On the other hand, indie games are developed by a small number of people with a low budget and require a small number of units to recover costs, so they can stay in business as long as they have strong support from a few people. Therefore, it is easy to be original in content. Indie games meet the demands of enthusiasts who are not satisfied with existing packaged games. For example, a large percentage of indie games use 2D graphics and pixel characters that were used in home video game consoles in the days of

[21] In addition, Microsoft is building a system that enables the development of multi-platform applications that run not only on Xbox, but also on regular PCs running Windows and smartphones (iOS and Android).

[22] Celebrating Nine Years of ID@Xbox
https://news.xbox.com/en-us/2022/03/24/celebrating-nine-years-of-idxbox/

16- and 8-bit CPUs. This is a type of game that is not released because it is not profitable under the existing packaged game business model, and also because it is difficult to develop a game with 3D graphics on a low budget.

There are also some "sharp" indie games that have a high level of artistry and a message to society that are not possible with regular packaged games. The growth of indie games around the world is based on a certain movement of people who are dissatisfied with existing games and want to create their own games that they really want to play.

15.2.5 Resurgence and Expansion of Subscription Services

The increase in the number of game consoles with permanent Internet access has led to a resurgence of subscription services in the game console business. Subscription services are a type of business model in which the right to use a service for a fixed period of time, such as 1 month or 1 year, is sold. In the game industry, subscription services were pioneered in the early days of mobile phone games, when companies provided wallpaper and game services for a fixed monthly fee, but this business model was discontinued with the spread of smartphones.

Online services offered by various companies provide free-of-charge news distribution of new title releases and game download sales. However, services that require the provision of server resources, such as online backup of saved data and network matches with other players, are fee-based services. As an incentive for users to subscribe to the service, paid services often include services that allow users to purchase certain titles at a discount or to play (download) past games for free. The fee is several hundred yen (a few dollars) per month for each company, and a large discount is offered if the user pays for 6 months or a year at a time.

The earliest subscription service for game consoles was Microsoft's Xbox Live. Launched in 2002 in the USA and 2003 in Japan, Xbox Live offered account management, news hosting, network services for games that could be played online, and voice chat support. When the Xbox Live service started in 2003, customers purchased a starter kit for 6800 yen to get started, and a 1-year basic service fee was included in the cost of the starter kit.[23] The service fee announced the following year was 680 yen per month or 4980 yen per year (both excluding tax). Since the Xbox360 was released in 2005, services such as account management and message exchanges between players have been free of charge, as high-speed Internet connections have become completely commonplace. Online game matching and other services were handled through a paid gold membership service.

[23]However, some games required a separate premium service fee. Phantasy Star Online 1 & 2 released by SEGA were the first games that required a separate monthly fee of 600 yen.

https://web.archive.org/web/20031004073023/http://www.xbox.com/ja-JP/live/service/fee_structure.htm

Sony launched the network service PLAYSTATION Network[24] on November 11, 2006, to coincide with the launch of PlayStation 3, and started network services such as online game matching and video content distribution, in addition to community functions such as account management, friend registration, and message exchange.[25] In addition, on June 29, 2010, the company launched PlayStation Plus, a subscription-based service that allows users to download and play several past games for free and offers discounts on specific titles.[26] The number of downloadable and discounted game titles changes monthly, giving users an incentive to continue the service.

Nintendo was the latest of the three companies to launch a subscription service, with its service for the Nintendo Switch being the first. It is one generation later than other companies in terms of game consoles. Online play services, such as competitive and cooperative play, had been offered free of charge since the Switch's launch. At the time of the Switch's launch, it was announced that the subscription service would begin in the fall of 2017, but Nintendo Switch Online ultimately launched on September 19, 2018. At the official start of the Switch Online service, subscribers were offered "Family Computer Nintendo Switch Online," a service that allowed them to play Famicom games for free. Twenty titles were available at the time of the service launch on September 19, with titles being added on an irregular basis. In addition, "Super Famicom Switch Online," a service in which Super Famicom games can be played for free, was launched on September 6, 2019.

The number of game titles released and the number of games sold have been growing as the market for console video games itself has become more difficult due to the influence of smartphones. In this context, subscription services have become an important source of revenue for game hardware companies, as they provide a stable revenue stream.

15.3 Summary of the Current Situation: Drastic Changes in the Environment, Fierce Inter-Market Competition, Shift from Packages to Services

At no other time in the history of the video game industry has market competition been as intense as it is today. As computer performance has improved, the performance barrier between home video game consoles and other platforms has completely disappeared. Home consoles are as powerful as a moderately powerful PC, while handheld video game consoles are no more powerful than a smartphone. There is no significant difference in the types of games that can be played.

[24] PLAYSTATION Network renamed PlayStation Network in 2008, then PSN, and now PlayStation Network.

[25] https://www.jp.playstation.com/info/release/nr_20061026_psn.html

[26] https://www.jp.playstation.com/info/release/nr_20100616_ps_plus.html

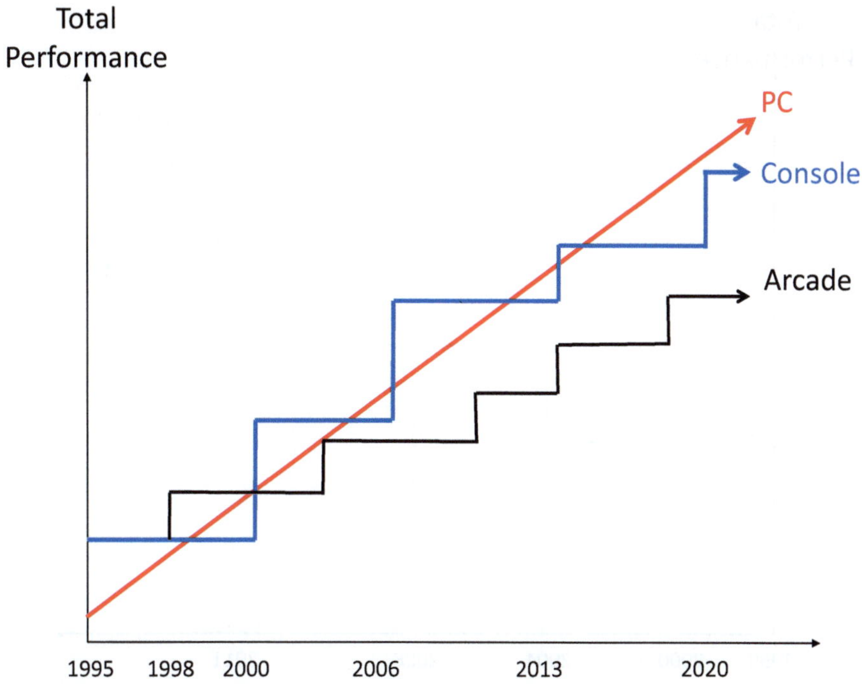

Fig. 15.8 Image of performance increase in 3D period (stationary console)

Figure 15.8 shows a conceptual diagram of the performance increase of PCs, home video games (console type), and arcade games after the 3D era. The late 1990s, when the PC standard shifted from PC-9801 to Windows, coincided with a period of accelerated performance growth of CPUs and graphics boards. New CPUs and graphics chips were released one after another, and their performance increased continuously, which is shown as a straight line in the figure. The performance of home video game consoles increases significantly in the year when a new model is released, but there is no change in other years, resulting in a staircase-like graph. PS2 (2000) and PS3 (2006) were launched with performance far exceeding that of PCs at the time, and exceeded the performance increase line for PCs, while PS4 (2013) and PS5 (2020) did not show much performance increase. Since arcades are now only compatible with home consoles and PCs, and new arcade platforms are being released less frequently, the performance of arcades has been rising in a staircase-like manner below the performance of both consoles.

Figure 15.9 shows a conceptual diagram of the performance increase of handheld video game consoles and mobile phones/smartphones since around 2000. As with home consoles, the graph shows a staircase-shaped performance increase for GBA (2000), DS/PSP (2004), and 3DS/VITA (2011). On the other hand, the graph for mobile phones is a straight line, as new models are introduced one after another, but performance jumped up and the pace of performance increase increased after the first

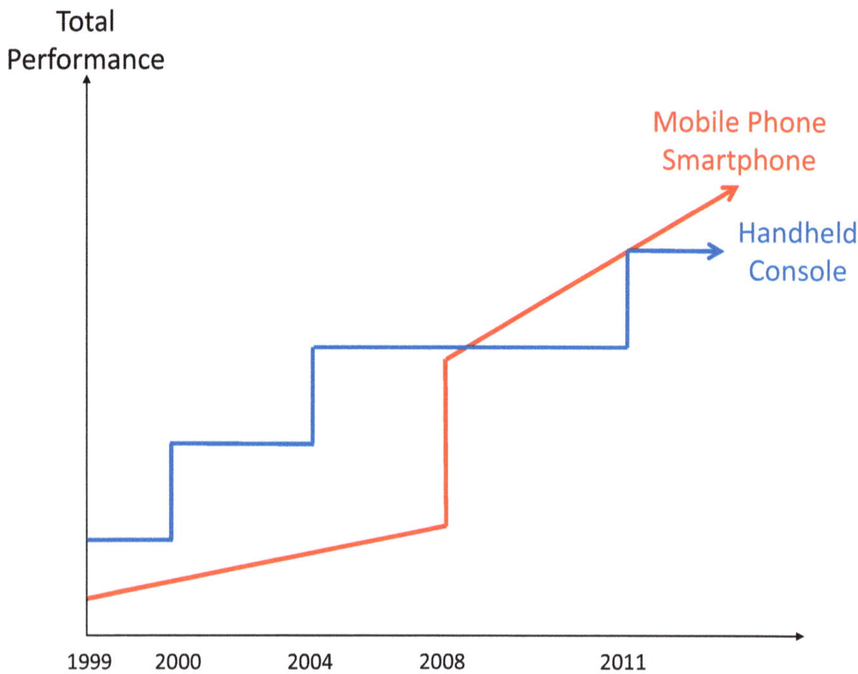

Fig. 15.9 Image of performance increase in 3D period (handheld console)

iPhone was released in Japan in 2008. The performance of the iPhone 3G became almost equal to that of handheld video game consoles, and with each new model released, the performance of the iPhone 3G increased significantly, surpassing that of handheld video game consoles. In 2011, the Nintendo 3DS and PS VITA were released, but their performance was not much different from that of the smartphones available at the time, and today the performance of smartphones dominates handheld video game consoles.

The strengths of home video game consoles are about the following points:

1. Easier to handle than PCs and smartphones.
2. They can be safely given to children.
3. The user interface (UI) of the controller and physical buttons makes some games easier to play than those using a keyboard and mouse (PC) or touch panel (smartphone).

There is no strong appeal to high school students and older who have their own mobile phones and PCs and who want to play games as a casual pastime.

However, there is also a group of enthusiasts who mainly play games for home video game consoles or only play games for home video game consoles. This group also includes those who play games on downloadable platforms such as Steam. This is because there is a big difference between packaged games for these platforms and games played on smartphones and PCs online.

The role of home video games as the driving force of the Japanese video game industry has come to an end. In the future, home video game consoles will mainly target elementary and junior high school students who do not yet have handheld video game consoles, enthusiasts who are not satisfied with smartphone games, and niche markets such as family and party markets (which is the direction that the Wii has taken). The mainstay of the game industry has been replaced by smartphones.

The change in the game industry, which started with online games on PCs and reached completion with the spread of smartphones, can be called a shift from goods (packages) to services. The packaged games referred to here are games that are sold as so-called sell-out-type games, including home video games and downloadable games on Steam.[27] In a business model that aims for one-time sales through packaged game sales, even if a game is a big hit, the number of copies sold may range from several million to 10 million, and profits are capped at a few billion yen. However, in the business model where games are sold as a service and in-game items are sold, it is no longer a dream that a blockbuster hit can generate a total profit of 100 billion yen or more over several years (or even more than 10 years).

On the other hand, platform providers that sell home video game consoles have also begun to generate stable revenues by offering subscription services that combine services that allow users to play past packaged game properties and connect to online games. Revenue from subscription services more than makes up for the decline in licensing revenue due to the decrease in the number of packaged games sold, and supports the financial results.

Of course, the fact that service-type games have become mainstream does not mean that packaged games will disappear completely. Packaged games have a certain interest as a finished product that service-type games do not have, and there are still many enthusiastic users. In addition, many of the indie games that are active around the world are downloadable, sell-out games. It remains to be seen how much of the packaged games market share will ultimately be able to survive, and depending on that share, the dedicated game consoles may not be able to survive, but the packaged games market is not likely to disappear.

[27] Steam may seem like an outdated platform, but Steam is not only a download sales platform, but also a PC online game community, and sales of in-game items are quite large. This means that Steam has adapted to the service-oriented nature of the game industry.

15.4 Looking Back on the History of the Japanese Game Industry

So far, in a total of 15 chapters, the history of the game industry has been discussed from the dawn of the industry to the present. Throughout this history, there have been issues that have appeared over and over again, even though the target markets and game genres have changed. Specifically, there are these three issues.

1. "Social harm" issue
2. "Intellectual property rights" issue
3. "Home server" and "personal server" issues (limited to home game consoles)

The first is the "social harm" problem, which is based on social ill-impression of games, such as "games are for delinquents" or "games make you stupid. In this report, we discussed the following:

- Game arcades and juvenile delinquency.
- Game arcades and gambling.
- Famicom and elementary school students.
- Adult software.
- The problem of high charges for social games.

The gaming industry is an open industry, and the revenues that can be earned from success are large, so entrants from a variety of fields continue to enter the industry. Competition within the industry is intense, and the leading companies change frequently. Although it sounds like a young and vibrant industry, it also means that the industry (or industry) does not accumulate lessons learned from past social problems because companies that do not know the history of problems with games are entering the industry one after another. There is a possibility that problems will continue to occur in the future.

Games are not useful goods (functional goods) in a clearly identifiable way, nor are they goods that add value to usefulness, such as fashion. They are pure entertainment. Furthermore, they have a strong image of being "amusements for children to play," regardless of how they are actually played. Among entertainment, novels, music, paintings, movies, etc., which have a long history and are associated with the image of being enjoyed by mature adults, have established a social status, while games, which have a short history, have been forced to prove that they "can exist in society" and "are healthy entertainment played by many ordinary people," and this will continue to be the case.

intellectual property rights, the following points were discussed:

- A series of lawsuits on arcade games (F1, Pac-Man)
- Piracy of games on the Famicom
- Fake rentals in PC games

In addition, there are other serious problems that were not mentioned in this document, such as the problem of magic consoles in the Nintendo DS and illegal emulators and illegal ROM images of home video game consoles circulating on the Internet. Games are completely digital information goods, and their quality does not deteriorate when copied. Therefore, this problem will never disappear completely, but it should be noted that rampant copying in a sluggish market like the PC games of the 1980s and early 1990s will hasten the decline of the market.

Regarding the third point, "home server" and "personal server," the following points were discussed:

- Famicom disk system and online trading.
- PSX, a PS2-compatible DVD player.
- The spread of smartphones.

There has always been a movement to use the huge installed base of game consoles for other purposes. Conversely, there has always been a movement for other devices to incorporate game functions. Nintendo's Wii has become a home server by providing a weather forecast and news channel, but it has not been used very much. Sony failed with the PSX, but its PS3 recording unit, TORNE, was a huge success, showing that the high-performance CPU and easy-to-use UI of a game console can be used with existing home appliances. PCs, home video game consoles, and smart TVs will continue to compete for the position of home server that sits in the living room, but home video game consoles will continue to be the leading option, and various combinations and combinations will continue to be born.

In addition, handheld video game consoles and other devices such as music players, digital cameras, and PDAs (electronic organizers) were in competition with each other as the competition among handy electronic devices that are usually carried around. The first Game Boy peripheral, the Pocket Camera (Nintendo, 1998), and the electronic organizer software NANONOTE (Konami, 1992) were also released. On the other hand, "XEVIOUS" and "PAC-MAN" were released for ZAURUS (MI series, a color ZAURUS), an electronic organizer from Sharp. The PSP was advertised as "the Walkman of the twenty-first century" before its release. The smartphone, which has swallowed up everything from electronic organizers to cameras, handheld video game consoles, and more, can be traced back to Apple's creation of the iPod Touch, a music player with a multi-touch LCD, wireless LAN connectivity, and a built-in operating system. The iPod Touch was the first of its kind in the world. As for handy electronic devices, the music player has swallowed up all handheld video game consoles and mobile phones, a path that was unimaginable 10 years ago, but perhaps electronic organizers and handheld video game consoles could have taken over the mobile phone functionality. These three problems are not problems within the game industry, but problems that arise at the interface with society (or the economy). The game industry will continue to face these three problems again and again in the future, although the forms will change little by little.

Bibliography

(1) Japanese-language Document

Aida, H., & Otsubo, A. (1997). *[The new electronic nation video games: The battle for giant wealth] (Shin Denshi rikkoku video game Kyohu no Koubou)*. NHK Press.

Akagi, M. (2005). *[It Started with "PONG"—The origins of Arcade TV Games] (Sore ha "PONG" kara Hajimatta: Arcade TV Game no Naritachi)*. Amusement Press.

Akagi, M. (2006). *[Arcade TV game list] (Arcade TV Game List)*. Amusement Press.

Asakura, R. (1998). *[Sony's Revolutionaries] (Sony no Kakumeiji Tachi)*. IGD communications.

Asano, K. (2001). *[Game industry crisis!] (Game gyokai Kiki Ippatsu!!)*. Shoeisha.

ASCII Shoseki Henshubu. (ed.) (2006). [The revival of the PC-8801] (Yomigaeru PC-8801 Densetsu Eikyu Hozonban), Ascii

Computer Entertainment Supplier's Association, [CESA game whitepaper (each year edition)] (*CESA Game Hakusho (Kaku Nendo ban)*), 1997–2021.

Deguchi, H., Tanaka, H., & Koyama, Y. (ed.) (2006). [Content industry theory: The Japanese model as intermixture and propagation] (*Contents Sangyouron: Konkou to Denpa no Nihon gata Model*). The University of Tokyo Press.

Digital Content Association of Japan (2010). [Research and study on the application of advanced technology in digital content production] (Digital Contents Seisaku no Sentan Gijutu Ouyou ni Kansuru Chousa Kenkyu), http://www.dcaj.or.jp/project/report/pdf/2009/dc_09_03.pdf

Endo, M., Iwatani, T., Nishikado, T., and Ishimura, S. (Speech) and Koyama, Y. (encapsulation) (2011). [Keynote Speech at the 2010 Annual Conference of the Japan Society for Digital Game Studies: "The Dawn of Video Games in Japan" (Part 1)], (Nihon Digital Game Gakkai 2010nenji Taikai Kityou Koen, "Nihon Video Game no Reimei (Zenpen)"), Journal of digital games research, Vol.5, No.2, p13-30.

Endo, M., Iwatani, T., Nishikado, T., and Ishimura, S. (Speech) and Koyama, Y. (encapsulation) (2012). [Keynote Speech at the 2010 Annual Conference of the Japan Society for Digital Game Studies: "The Dawn of Video Games in Japan" (Part 2)], (Nihon Digital Game Gakkai 2010nenji Taikai Kityou Koen, "Nihon Video Game no Reimei (Kouhen)"), Journal of digital games research, Vol.6, No.1, p43–56.

Famitsu DC Editorial Office (2002). [Sega arcade history] (*Sega Arcade History*). Enterbrain.

Famitsu DC Editorial Office (2002). [Sega Consumer History] (*Sega Consumer History*), Enterbrain.

Fujihara, M. (2013). *[Work attitudes and career development issues of game developers] (Game Kaihatsu-sha no Syuro Ishiki to Career Keisei no Shomondai), in [Research report on the*

Y. Koyama, *History of the Japanese Video Game Industry*, Translational Systems Sciences 35, https://doi.org/10.1007/978-981-99-1342-8

application of advanced technologies in digital content creation] (Digital Contents Seisaku no Sentan Gijutsu Oyou ni Kansuru Chosa Houkokusho). Digital Content Association of Japan.

Fujii, T. (2004). [The birth of "Final Fantasy"—A case study of home video game software development by Square Inc.] ("Final Fantasy" no Tanjou—Kabushiki Kaisya Square ni yoru Kateiyou Game Soft Kaihatsu no Jirei). *Okayama Economic Review, 36*(1), P41-62.

Fujikawa, Y. (1999). [Sources of dynamism driving software development: Competition between Nintendo and Sony business models] (Soft Kaihatsu wo Suishin suru Dynamism no Gensen – Nintendo to Sony no Business Model kan Kyousou). In M. Shimaguchi, T. T. H. Katahira, & J. Ishi (Eds.), *[The age of marketing innovation, Volume 2—Product development innovation] (Marketing Kakushin no Jidai Dai 2 kan – Seihin Gijutsu Kakushin)* (pp. 363–387). Yuhikaku.

Fujimoto, T. (2003). *Capacity building competition - why is japan's automotive industry so strong?* [Nouryoku Kouchiku Kyousou-Nihon no Jidousha Sangyou ha Naze Tsuyoinoka]. Chuo-Kouron Shinsha.

Fujita, N. (1998). [The formation and rapid collapse of the video game industry in the U.S.—The formation process of the modern video game industry (1)] (Beikoku ni okeru Video Game Sangyo no Keisei to Kyugeki na Houkai—Gendai Video Game Sangyou no Keisei Katei (1)). *Keizai-ronsō : The Economic Review, 162*(5&6), 54–71.

Fujita, N. (1999a). [The Japanese video game industry before the Famicom—The formation process of the modern video game industry (2)] ("Famcom" Toujou Mae no Nihon Video Game Sangyou—Gendai Video Game Sangyou no Keisei Katei (2)). *Keizai-ronsō : The Economic Review, 163*(3), 59–76.

Fujita, N. (1999b). [A comprehensive study of the development of the "Famicom" and the formation process of the video game industry—The formation process of the modern video game industry (3)] ("Famcom" Kaihatsu to Video Game Sangyou Keisei katei no Sogoteki Kousatsu—Gendai Video Game Sangyou no Keisei Katei (3)). *Keizai-ronsō : The Economic Review, 163*(5&6), 69–86.

Fujita, Y., Fujimoto, E., and Ogura, H. (1998). [Copyright and used software issues] (*Tyosakuken to Tyuko Soft Mondai*), Systemfive.

Fukaya, M. and Fukaya, K. (1989). [Famicom syndrome] (*Famicom Syndrome*) Dohosha Printing.

Henmi, K., Ohnishi, K. (1997). [Nintendo and Sega: Breakthrough and great competition in the entertainment industry (Big Business in Japan)] (*Nintendo to Sega—Entertainment Sangyou no Yakushin to Daikyousou (Nihon no Big Business)*), Otsuki Shoten.

Hichibe, N., Hirabayashi, H. and Akao, K. (1996). [The University of Games] (*Game no Daigaku*). Mediafactory.

Hosokawa, A. (1994). [Future Famicom shop management] (*Korekara no Famicom Shop Keiei*), Manegement Information Publisher.

Information Processing Society of Japan Special Committee on History (ed.) (2010). *[Computer history in Japan].* Ohm Sha.

Inoue, O. (2009). *[Nintendo—Equation for creating "Surprises"] (Nintendo: "Odoroki" wo umu Houteisiki).* Nihon Keizai Shimbun Publishing.

Japan Productivity Center (1993). [White Paper on the Leisure Industry] (Leisure Hakusho)

Kaminogo, T. (1986). *[The secret of Nintendo] (Nintendo no himitsu).* Gendai Shuppan.

Kindaichi, W. (2011). [Includes a searchable CD-ROM database of all cases Chozetsu Daikagirin, Fall 2011, Complete All Hardware Edition] (Zenken Kensakukanou CD-ROM database tsuki Chozetsu Daigirin 2011nen Aki Kanzenn Zenkishuban), Tokuma Shoten.

Kobashi, R. (1998). [Software innovation—Nintendo's de facto standard formation and software development] (Soft no Innovation- Nitendo no de facto Standard keisei to Soft kaihatsu), Hiroyuki Itami, Matao Miyamoto and Seiichiro Yonekura (ed.) [Casebook: Management Behavior of Japanese Companies 3—Innovation and Technology Accumulation](Casebook Nihon Kigyou no Keiei Kodo 3- Innovation to Gijutsu Chikuseki), p334-360 Yuhukaku.

Koyama, Y. (2006). [Survey of software release postponement rates in the Japanese home video game industry] (Nihon no Kateiyou Game Sangyo ni okeru Soft Hatubai Enkiritsu Chousa). *Simulation and Gaming, 16*(2), 93–102.

Koyama, Y. (2006). [Co-evolutionary structure of the Japanese game industry: Shift in innovation leadership] (Nihon Game Sangyo no Kyoushinka Kouzou—Innovation Leader no Koutai). *Game Amusement Society Journal, 1*(1), 63–68.

Koyama, Y. (2008). [Launch postponement rate trends in the Japanese home video game industry—Complexity of game development and adaptation as an industry] (Nihon no Kateiyou Game Sangyo deno Hatubai Enkiritsu Suii- Game Kaihatsu no Hukuzatsuka to Sangyo to siteno Tekiou). *Journal of Digital Games Research, 2*(1), 76–84.

Koyama, Y. (2009). [Co-evolutionary structure of the Japanese game industry: Increasing modularity and disruptive innovation] (Nihon Game Sangyo no Kyoshinka Kouzou—Module ka no Shinten to Hakaiteki Innovation). *Keizai-ronsō : The Economic Review, 183*(3), 47–58.

Koyama, Y., Hichibe, N., & Nakamura, J. (2015). Industry structure of PC novel games in Japan. In E. Kabashima (Ed.), *[Communication research for media and content industry] (Media contents Sangyo no communication Kenkyu)*. Minerva Shobo.

Koyama, Y., Miyake, Y., & Takahashi, T. (2009). [Exploration of game history: The Famicom Boom as seen through the eyes of TAKAHASHI Meijin] (Game shi Tanpou Takahashi Meijin no me kara Mita Famicom Boom). *Journal of Digital Games Research, 3*(2), 205–219.

Maeda, H. (2015). [International game & computer guidebook] (*Kaigai no Game & Pasocom Guidebook*), Oakla Publishing.

Matsumoto, A. (2012). *[The amazing mechanism of social games] (Social Game no Sugoi Shikumi)*. ASCII Mediaworks.

Miyazawa, A., Takeda, M., & Yanagihara, T. (1999). [Computer game technology] (*Computer Game no Technology*). Iwanami Shoten.

Mizukami, K. (2012). *New game development and entry in the Famicm Era* [Famicom jidai no Shinki Kaihatsu to San-nyu]. The proceedings of The Content Culture History Society of Japan.

Mobile & Game Studio (2012). [Masanobu Endo's game design lecture live broadcast] (*Endo Masanobu no Game Design Kougi Jikkyo Chukei*), Softbank Creative.

Nakafuji, Y. (1997). [The establishment and development of the amusement industry in Japan—From Eaves-throwing business to game centers and urban amusement parks] (Wagakuni ni okeru Amusement Sangyo no Seiritsu to Hatten—Nokisaki Shoubai kara Game Center soshite Toshi no Naka No Yuenchi he). *Bulletin of Shinshu Junior College, 1*(9), 66–76.

Nakamura, I. (2009). [The transition and future of game images: An introduction to game design in racing games] (Game Eizo no Hensen to Mirtai—Race Game ni Miru Game Design Joron). *Journal of Digital Games Research, 3*(1), 81–92.

National Police Agency (1981). [White Paper on Police] (Keisatsu Hakusho Showa 56 nen), https://www.npa.go.jp/publications/whitepaper/index_keisatsu.html

National Police Agency (1984). [White Paper on Police] (Keisatsu Hakusho Showa 59 nen), https://www.npa.go.jp/publications/whitepaper/index_keisatsu.html

National Police Agency (1985). [White Paper on Police] (Keisatsu Hakusho Showa 60 nen), https://www.npa.go.jp/publications/whitepaper/index_keisatsu.html

Nichigai Associates (2005). [The Bestseller 1985-2004] (*The Bestseller 1985-2004*). Nichigai Associates.

Nikkei, BP (1998). [New generation game business] (*Shin Sedai Game Business*). Nikkei Business Publication.

Nishida, M. (2008). [Aesthetics vs. Pragmatics—The 15-year history of "Team Kutaragi" versus Nintendo's all-out war] (*Bigaku vs Jitsuri —"Team Kutaragi" tai Nintendo no Souryokusen 15 nen shi*), Kodansha.

Oaeda, H. (2014). [The rise and fall of the home video game consoles] (*Kateiyou Game ki Kouboushi*). Oakla Publishing.

Oaeda, H. (2014). [The rise and fall of the hobby personal computers] (*Hobby Pasokom Kouboushi*). Oakla Publishing.

Oiwa, S. (2013). *[Overview of the software development engineer fee survey and future directions] (Software Kaihatsu Gijutusha Ryoukin Chousa no Gaiyou to Kongo no Houkousei ni tuite)*, Keizai Chousa Kenkyu Review, Vol.12, p62–p69.

Oshita, H. (1993). *[Sega game kingdom] (Sega Game no Oukoku)*. Kodansha.

Oshita, H. (2001). [The flight of Enix—A true story of the warring states period in the game industry] (Enix no Hishou Jitsuroku Game Gyokai Sengokushi), Shoin.

Sakamoto, A. (2004). *[Video games and children's minds] (TV game to Kodomo no Kokoro)*. Memotaru Shuppan.

Sano, M. (2013). [Historical turning structure of product innovation] (Seihin Innovation no Rekishiteki Tenkai Kouzou). *The Ritsumeikan Business Review, 52*(2&3), P71-90.

Sasaki, J. (2013). *80's microcomputer encyclopedia* [80 nendai Maikon Dai-Hyakka]. Ema Publishing.

Sayawaka (2012). [Our game history] (*Bokutachi no Game shi*). Kodansha.

Sekiguchi, W. (2000). [Standard-bearers of the PC revolution] (*Pasocom Kakumei no Kishu tachi*), Nihon Keizai Shimbun Publishing.

Shibao, H. and Kasai, O. (1994). [Intorduction to game designer] (*Game Design Nyumon*). Shogakukan.

Shigihara, M. (2007). [Game craftsman vol. 1] (*Game Shokunin Dai 1 shu*). Micro Magazine.

Shimizu, K.-i. (1995). [Fujitsu's multimedia business] (*Fujitsu no Multimedia Business*). OS Shuppansha.

Shin, K. (2002). [Game development frontline: This is how "Samurai" was created—660 Days of War by ACQUIRE Production Section 2] (*Game Kaihatsu Saizensen "Samurai" ha Koushite Tsukurareta- Acquire Seisaku 2ka no 600 nichi Sensou*). Shinkigensha.

Shintaku, J., Tanaka, T., Yanagawa, H. (2003). [Economic analysis of the game industry: Structure and strategy of content industry development] (*Game Sanyo no Keizaibunseki: Contents Sangyou Hatten no Kouzou to Senryaku*). TOYO KEIZAI.

Shiratori, R. (ed.) (2003). [Research on social acceptance of games—Ratings in practice in countries around the world] (*Game no Shakaiteki Juyou no Kenkyu—Sekai Kakkoku ni Okeru Rating no Jissai*). Tokai University Press.

Sunagawa, K. (1998). [Succession of entrepreneurial activities and technological strategies in the Japanese Game Industry: Formation of Software Development Organizations in Sega and Namco] (Nihon Game Sangyo ni miru Kigyosha Katudou no Keiki to Gijutu Senryaku – Sega to Namco ni okeru Software Kaihatu Soshiki no Keisei). *Japan Business History Review, 32*, 4.

Tadano, Y. (ed.) (1994). Yuji Hayami, Yoshikuni Nobuoka ando Atushi Hosokawa (Author), [Future Game Center Management] (*Korekara no Game Center Keiei*). Keiei Joho Shuppansha.

Takahashi, K. (1991). [Super Famicom: Nintendo conspiracy] (*Super Famicom Nintendo no Inbou*). Kappa Books.

Takahashi, K. (1993). [Collapse of the "Dragon Quest" and "Nobunaga's Ambition" software industries] (*"Dorakue" "Nobunaga" Soft Sangyo no Houkai*), Kappa Books.

Takahashi, S. (1996). [Game front super abnormal] (*Game Sensen Chou Ijou*), Life Sha.

Takeda, G. (1998). [System LSI in the N64 video game console] (Video Game ki "N64" ni okeru System LSI). *The Journal of Institute of Electronics, Information and Communication Engineers, 81*(11), 1174–1177.

Takeda, T. (1996). [Sold fights, bought fights. Nintendo's blueprint for victory] (*Urareta Kenka, Katte imasu. Nintendo Shouri he no Aoshasin*). KK Bestsellers.

Takeda, T. (1999). [The secret of Nintendo] (*Nintendo no Himitsu*). Zest.

Takeda, T. (2000). [It's The Nintendo] (t's The Nintendo イッツ・ザ・ニンテンドウ). T2 Shuppan.

Takita, S. (2000). [Japan, a game powerhouse: Rise and fall of the Gods] (*Game Taikoku Nippon Kamigami no Koubou*). Seishun Publishing.

Tamada, Y., Ishida, J.-I., Yamakata, R., Yokota, T. and Uno, T. (2009). [Platform competition and vertical restrictions—Focusing on the Sony Computer Case] (*Platform Kyousou to Suichokuseigen—Sony Computer Jiken wo Chushin ni*). Japan Fair Trade Commission FY2007 Joint Research Report.

Tane, K. (2007). [Why did the PlayStation 3 fail?] (*Puresute 3 ha Naze Shippai shitanoka?*). Shoyusha.

Tane, K. (2011). [Game history as a cultivation] (*Kyouyou to shiteno Game shi*). Chikuma Shobo.

Tateishi, Y. I. S., Nagai, J.-I., Yao, C. and Abe, J. (2017). [Contemporary media events: From public viewing to live video games] (Gendai Media Event ron: Public viewing kara Game Jikkyo made), Keiso Shobo.

TeD factory (1999). [Wander Swan official guidebook] (*Wander Swan Official Guidebook*), Exfire Magazine Janan.

Tokuoka, M. (2011). [Social game industry update] (*Social Game Gyoukai Saishin Jojou*), Softbank Creative.

Tokuoka, M. (ed & a) (2015). [Gaming today: 18 keywords to look through the game industry] (*Game no Ima: Game Gyoukai wo Mitoosu 18 no Keyword*). Softbank Creative.

Tokyo Photographic Art Museum (2003). [Family computer 1983–1994] (*Family Computer 1983-1994*), Ohta Books.

Tomatsu Industry gourp (ed.) (2007). [Business model analysis of content companies as revealed by disclosure information] (Kaiji Jouhou kara Wakaru Contents Kigyou no Business Model Bunseki), Chuokeizai-Sha.

Ueda, S. (1995). *[SEGA, a comprehensive amusement company] (Sogo Amusement Company "Sega")*. Meta Brain.

Uemura, M. (1990). [Famicom Media: The technical background] (Famicom Media Sono Gijutsuteki Haikei ni tsuite). *Journal of the Society of Instrument and Control Engineers, 29*(6), 53–58.

Uemura, M., Hosoi, K., & Nakamura, A. (2013). *[The Famicom and its era] (Famicom to Sono jidai)*. NTT Publishing.

Wada, T. (2003). [Distribution of home video game software—Risk-return structure and market impact] (Kateiyou Game Soft no Ryutsu—Risk to return no Kouzou to Shijou heno Eikyou). *Akamon Manegement Review, 2*(11), 563–580.

Xingyuan, W. (2006). *[Korean online game business research] (Kankoku no Online Game Business Kenkyu)*. TOYO KEIZAI.

Yamana, I. (1994). [Battle of king of games] (*King of Game no Battle*). Nippon Jitsugyo Publishing.

Yamana, I. (1997). [Three kingdoms of the game industry] (*Game Gyokai Sangokushi*). Diamond inc.

Yamashita, A. (1998). [The truth about the PlayStation hit] (*PlayStation Dai Hit no Shinjitsu*). JMA Management Center.

Yamazaki, I. (2013). [Complete guide to portable video game console] (*Keitaigata Game ki Complete Guide*). Shuhunotomosha.

Yamazaki, I. (2014a). [Complete guide to video game console] (*Kateiyou Game ki Complete Guide*). Shuhunotomosha.

Yamazaki, I. (2014b). [Nintendo complete guide—Toys] (*Nintendo Complete Guide Gangu hen*), Shuhunotomosha.

Yanagawa, H. (2022). [How the gaming industry succeeded—The role of architectural competition] (Game Sangyo ha ikanishite Seikou shitaka- Architecture Kyousou no Yakuwari). In M. Aoki & H. Ando (Eds.), *[Modularity: The nature of new industrial architectures] (Module ka Atarashii Sangyo Architecture no Honshitsu)* (pp. 145–168). Toyo Keizai.

Yanagawa, H., & Kuwayama, N. (1999). [Analysis of the home video game industry—A new model of intercompany relations] (Kateiyou Game Sangyo no Bunseki—Atarashii Kigyou kan Kankei no Model). *Tsusan Journal, issue*, 40–44.

Yata, M. (1996). *[The future of the game nation: All about the world's leading content business] (Game Rikkoku no Miraizo – Sekai wo Lead suru Contents Business no Subete)*. Nikkei Business Publisher.

Yumoto, H., Nishimura, S.-i., Ohtani, K., Hayashi, N. and Maeda, H. (2004). [Applke] [1976–1986], *(Apple)[1976-1986]*. Mainichi Communications.

(2) English Document

Baer, R. H. (2005). *Videogames: In the beginning*. Rolenta Press.
Barton, M. (2008). *Dungeons and desktops: The history of computer role-playing games*. A K Peters/CRC Press.
Campbell-Kelly, M. (2004). *From airline reservation to sonic the Hedgehog: A history of the software industry*. MIT Press.
Cohen, S. (1984). *ZAP! The rise and fall of Atari*. Arthur Pine Associates.
Dillon, R. (2011). *The golden age of video games*. CRC Press.
Entertainment Software Association, *Essential facts about the computer and video game industry*, 2005-2015.
Ernkvist, M. (2008). "Down many times, but still playing the game: Creative destruction and industry crashes in the early video game industry 1971–1986", *History of Insolvency and Bankruptcy*, 161–191.
Forster, W. (2005). *The encyclopedia of Game Machines: Consoles, handhelds & home computers 1972-2005*. Gameplan.
Jankowski, N. W., & Hanssen, L. (Eds.). (1996). *The contours of multimedia: Recent technological, theoretical and empirical developments*. University of Luton Press.
Kent, S. L. (2001). *The ultimate history of video games: The story behind the craze that touched our lives and changed the world*. Three Rivers Press.
King, B., & Borland, J. (2003). *Dungeons & dreamers: The rise of computer game culture from geek to chic*. McGraw-Hill.
Laramee, F. D. (Ed.). (2005). *Secrets of the game business* (2nd ed.). Jenifer NIles.
Levy, S. (1984). *Hackers: Heroes of the computer revolution*. O'Reilly.
Takahashi, D. (2002). *Opening the Xbox: Inside Microsoft's plan to unleash an entertainment revolution*. Prima Lifestyles.
Weiss, B. (2007). *Classic home video games 1972-1984: A complete reference guide*. McFarland.
Wolf, M. J. P. (Ed.). (2008). *The video game explosion: A history from pong to playstation and beyond*. Greenwood Press.
Wolf, M. J. P. (Ed.). (2012). *Before the crash: Early video game history*. Wayne State University Press.
Wolf, M. J. P. (Ed.). (2012). *Encyclopedia of video games: The culture, technology and art of gaming*. Greenwood.
Zackariasson, P., & Wilson, T. L. (Eds.). (2012). *The video game industry: Formation, present sate, and future*. Routledge.

(3) Web

Classic Video Game Station Odyssey (1998), [Interview with Masayuki Horie, Epoch Inc] (Epoch Sha Horie Masayuki shi Interview) http://www.ne.jp/asahi/cvs/odyssey/hyperlink/setframe_creators_horie1.html
Derek Strickland Report: Valve rakes in $1.5 billion revenue from Steam sales in 2014, http://www.tweaktown.com/news/46666/report-valve-rakes-1-5-billion-revenue-steam-sales-2014/index.html, (2014)
ESA (2019). "Strongly disagrees" with UK DCMS loot box report, https://www.gamesindustry.biz/articles/2019-09-12-esa-strongly-disagrees-with-uk-dcms-loot-box-report
Funatsu, M. (1998) [Special Interview with Windows CE Developer for Dreamcast] (Dreamcast you Windows CE Kaihatsusha Tokubetsu Inverview), http://pc.watch.impress.co.jp/docs/article/980624/e3_4.htm
GIMINI (1978). TV GAME CIRCUITS. http://www.pong-story.com/GIMINI1978.pdf

American Psychiatry Association (2023). Internet Gaming https://www.psychiatry.org/patients-families/internet-gaming

Newzoo Global Esports Market Report 2019 | Light Version, https://newzoo.com/insights/trend-reports/newzoo-global-esports-market-report-2019-light-version/

Nikkei Xtrend (2008), [This is how Nintendo's Famicom was born] (Nintendo Famicom ha Koushite Umareta), http://trendy.nikkeibp.co.jp/article/special/20080922/1018969/ (Viewed January 5, 2016, link currently broken)

PONG (1996). In A Chip. http://www.pong-story.com/gi.htm

Renesas Technology (2010). [SuperH Development Story], (SuperH Kaihatsu Story), http://japan.renesas.com/products/mpumcu/superh/related_sh/theme/index.jsp, (Viewed January 5, 2016, link currently broken)

Virtual Reality Society (2017). The Unreleased Sega VR Headset ? So much effort squandered, https://www.vrs.org.uk/unreleased-sega-vr-headset-much-effort-squandered/

Wiltz, C. (2019), The story of Sega VR: Sega's failed virtual reality headset, https://www.designnews.com/electronics-test/story-sega-vr-segas-failed-virtual-reality-headset/74451237860349

MIX
Papier aus verantwortungsvollen Quellen
Paper from responsible sources
FSC® C105338

If you have any concerns about our products,
you can contact us on
ProductSafety@springernature.com

In case Publisher is established outside the EU,
the EU authorized representative is:
Springer Nature Customer Service Center GmbH
Europaplatz 3, 69115 Heidelberg, Germany

Printed by Libri Plureos GmbH
in Hamburg, Germany